W9-AEJ-931

www.wadsworth.com

www.wadsworth.com is the World Wide Web site for
Thomson Wadsworth and is your direct source to dozens
of online resources.

At *www.wadsworth.com* you can find out about supple-
ments, demonstration software, and student resources.
You can also send email to many of our authors and pre-
view new publications and exciting new technologies.

www.wadsworth.com
Changing the way the world learns®

Rhetorical Theory

An Introduction

TIMOTHY A. BORCHERS
Minnesota State University, Moorhead

THOMSON
WADSWORTH

Australia • Canada • Mexico • Singapore • Spain
United Kingdom • United States

THOMSON
—★—
WADSWORTH

Executive Editor: Holly J. Allen
Acquisitions Editor: Annie Mitchell
Assistant Editor: Aarti Jayaraman
Editorial Assistant: Trina Enriquez
Technology Project Manager:
 Jeanette Wiseman
Marketing Manager: Kimberly Russell
Marketing Assistant: Andrew Keay
Marketing Communications Manager:
 Shemika Britt
Project Manager, Editorial Production:
 Rita Jaramillo

Art Director: Maria Epes
Print Buyer: Lisa Claudeanòs
Permissions Editor: Stephanie Lee
Production Service: Matrix Productions Inc.
Photo Researcher: Connie Gardner
Copy Editor: Lauren Root
Cover Designer: Ross Carron
Cover Printer: Webcom Limited
Compositor: International Typesetting
 and Composition
Printer: Webcom Limited

Printed in Canada
1 2 3 4 5 6 7 08 07 06 05 04

For more information about our products, contact us at:
**Thomson Learning Academic
Resource Center
1-800-423-0563**

For permission to use material from this text or product, submit a request online at
http://www.thomsonrights.com.

Any additional questions about permissions can be submitted by email to
thomsonrights@thomson.com.

Library of Congress Control Number:
2004118285

ISBN 0-534-63918-6

**Thomson Higher Education
10 Davis Drive
Belmont, CA 94002-3098
USA**

Asia (including India)
Thomson Learning
5 Shenton Way
#01-01 UIC Building
Singapore 068808

Australia/New Zealand
Thomson Learning Australia
102 Dodds Street
Southbank, Victoria 3006
Australia

Canada
Thomson Nelson
1120 Birchmount Road
Toronto, Ontario M1K 5G4
Canada

UK/Europe/Middle East/Africa
Thomson Learning
High Holborn House
50-51 Bedford Road
London WC1R 4LR
United Kingdom

Latin America
Thomson Learning
Seneca, 53
Colonia Polanco
11560 Mexico
D.F. Mexico

Spain (including Portugal)
Thomson Paraninfo
Calle Magallanes, 25
28015 Madrid, Spain

To Susanne and Oliver

Contents

III LINGUISTIC REFLEXIVITY   111

5 RHETORIC AND MEANING   113

Preface

Each of us has the need to make sense of our world, make decisions, and learn who we are. Rhetorical theorists have provided a comprehensive account of how individuals fulfill each of these needs. *Rhetorical Theory: An Introduction* brings their theoretical insights to undergraduate readers.

Goals

Rhetorical Theory: An Introduction provides a succinct, accessible account of rhetorical theory for advanced undergraduate students. Current in its theory and practical in its approach, the book encourages students to make sense of their personal, professional, and civic worlds. The book is organized around the key topics of rhetorical theory and includes a variety of perspectives about rhetoric. Students will learn how to become more effective communicators, but they will also be able to evaluate the effectiveness and implication of the rhetoric that surrounds them.

Topical Rather than Chronological Organization

The theories of rhetoric are often presented in chronological format. That is, students usually follow the history of rhetoric from its beginnings in ancient Greece to its contemporary practice in Europe and the United States. When rhetorical theory is presented this way, the similarities and differences between different ways of thinking about rhetoric are not readily apparent.

This book takes a topical, rather than chronological, approach to rhetorical theory. Similar theories are grouped together in chapters that focus on related concepts and topics. Although subsequent chapters may cover the same time period, theorists are grouped according to their central purpose or argument. The result is that students are better able to track the central ideas in rhetorical theory instead of being overwhelmed by a series of theorists that have nothing in common but the time period in which they wrote. This approach will enable students to more easily grasp important issues and concepts.

Focus on Undergraduate Students

The study of rhetoric has become so specialized that an entire course can be devoted to particular areas of study, such as classical rhetoric, feminist rhetoric, or cultural studies. The typical undergraduate student today does not need the depth of these specializations. Instead, undergraduate students need a broad exposure to rhetorical theory without being overwhelmed by names, dates, and technical language. Students today also need to see how theory relates to their daily existence.

Rhetorical Theory: An Introduction is designed to meet the needs of undergraduate students. It covers the history and essential topics of rhetorical theory, including examination of the most complex theories. Most important, the text provides sufficient context so that the student understands why theories have been created and how they relate to the real world and other ideas.

Additionally, this book uses the voice that I use in the classroom. The writing style engages the students without becoming overly technical. Examples have been carefully chosen to provide a wide variety of meaningful demonstrations of rhetorical analysis that are closely related to the text's discussion. Overall, the coverage is succinct, conceptual, practical, and aimed at upper-division undergraduate students.

Variety of Perspectives

This book integrates non–Western approaches to rhetoric with what have been the most dominant approaches. The book surveys feminist and gendered rhetorical theories as well as those from African, Chinese, and Native American cultures. In addition, the work of Stuart Hall—a black theorist from Great Britain—is prominently featured in the chapter on cultural studies. Susanne Langer, Cheris Kramarae, and Kathleen Hall Jamieson are prominently featured at key points in the discussion as well.

Engaging Pedagogy

Textbooks on rhetorical theory too often lack the pedagogical and editorial features that students and instructors have come to expect. In this book, pictures serve to reinforce the text's content. Discussion questions, glossary terms, and chapter summaries help students learn the material. Additionally, each chapter provides the following items: a Biography of a Theorist, which portrays one of theorists discussed in the chapter; a Critical Insights feature, which applies theory to practice; and an Internet Exercise to help students extend their learning to new contexts.

Instructor and Student Supplements

An Instructor's Manual is available for this book that includes test questions (multiple choice, true/false, and essay), activity suggestions, a sample syllabus, chapters outlines, and potential video materials. Students have access to a website containing links, activities, and practice quizzes.

Acknowledgments

I am indebted to my colleagues, students, mentors, friends, and family for their support, encouragement, and insight.

My colleagues and students at Minnesota State University Moorhead have been supportive and helpful throughout the writing process. In particular, Theresa Hest, Denise Gorsline, and David Tschida have answered innumerable questions and have been a constant reality check for me about what undergraduates need to know in a course on rhetoric.

I am indebted to the staff at the MSUM library. In particular, Dianne Schmidt was especially helpful in filling interlibrary loan requests.

My students—too numerous to name—have been a constant source of ideas and inspiration.

The individuals at Wadsworth-Thomson have been most helpful in guiding this project to its completion. Deirdre Anderson had the confidence in this project when it was a reading packet for my students. Annie Mitchell has since guided this project to completion, providing helpful advice, encouragement, and deadline extensions.

A great deal of credit goes to the reviewers of the text, including Bernardo Attias, California State University, Northridge; James A. Aune, Texas A&M University; Stephen H. Browne, Pennsylvania State University; Beth M. Waggenspack, Virginia Polytechnic Institute and State University; and David E. Williams, Texas Tech University. Their praise encouraged me, and their criticism sharpened the analysis and coverage of the book. I thank them for their perceptive and thorough comments. In particular, I am indebted to Rita Rahoi-Gilchrest, Winona State University and Matthew Sobnosky, Hofstra University for their detailed critique.

Finally, I wish to acknowledge the support of my wife, Susanne Williams. She was, and is, a constant source of support, encouragement, and inspiration to me. Our young son Oliver was and will always be an inspiration to me as well.

PART I

The Nature of Rhetoric

1

Defining Rhetoric and Rhetorical Theory

Learning Objectives

After reading this chapter, you should be able to:

1. Define rhetoric, rhetorical theory, and rhetorical criticism.
2. Identify the key characteristics of rhetoric and rhetorical theory.
3. Choose how to limit the study of rhetoric.
4. Explain the influences of culture and technology on rhetoric.
5. Describe the major developments in the study of rhetorical theory.

When my son, Oliver, was a little more than a year old, he would slowly creep to the electrical outlets in our living room. Although they were covered, my wife and I would give him a firm "no" every time he neared the outlets. One day, Oliver was again creeping toward an outlet when I said "no" to him. Unlike our previous encounters, Oliver looked me in the eye, turned toward the outlet, and kept crawling. From that moment, I believe, Oliver learned what it meant to be a rhetorical being. He knew the meaning of "no" and he knew that he could make choices relative to that word. He also knew there were consequences to the rhetorical choices he made. We'll come back to the word "no" in Chapter 6. You'll see that it is one of the most significant words in all of rhetoric.

In fact rhetoric influences our lives at every level. Consider the difficult decision the world faced in February 2003. On one side, the leaders of the United States and Great Britain sought to convince the world's people that Iraq's president Saddam Hussein, having failed to disarm as called for in various United Nations resolutions, was a menace to the world community. On the other side, the leaders of France, Germany, and Russia, along

© Tom and Dee Ann McCarthy/CORBIS

FIGURE 1.1   The homecoming football game is a rhetorical opportunity for your school to showcase itself to prospective students, build spirit among current students, and encourage donations from past students.

with millions of worldwide protestors, argued that war should be avoided. No one knew if Hussein possessed weapons of mass destruction and no one could tell if he was planning to use them against the United States or other world nations. As you decided whether to support the war or not, you watched and read rhetorical debates and you used rhetoric when you discussed the possible war with others.

Think of the ways your school uses rhetoric. Whether it is to convince prospective students to attend it, encourage current students to work their hardest, or persuade alums to donate, your school is vitally interested in effectively using rhetoric. Through the school's website, promotional materials, and frequent e-mail communication, the faculty and administrators use rhetoric to influence how you feel about your school and yourself. Likewise, homecoming is probably a popular event on your campus. The name of this event reveals that alums are welcomed back to campus. But on most campuses, homecoming is also a way of boosting school spirit and showcasing the campus to the community, through parades, events, and football games (see Figure 1.1). As you go about your daily activities on campus, think of how you are influenced by the school's rhetoric.

From the moment you began to understand the meaning of words or symbols, you have used—and been used by—rhetoric. Our perceptions of who we are, those around us, and the social structure in which we operate are based on rhetoric. Sociologist Joseph Gusfield (1989) puts it bluntly: "We cannot avoid rhetoric.

When we speak, act, dress, eat, and generally conduct our lives we communicate and, in doing so, persuade others, including ourselves" (p. 17). This book will introduce you more formally to rhetorical theory and its function in our world today.

This opening chapter defines rhetoric from a variety of perspectives. We'll examine some of the basic characteristics of rhetoric upon which many theorists agree and see where theorists disagree about defining rhetoric. We'll also survey a brief history of rhetorical theory. Finally, we'll glance at the structure and contents of this book.

DEFINING RHETORIC

Before we go further, it is important to define what is meant by **rhetoric.** You may have heard the term used in a sense that means flowery or showy speech that doesn't really accomplish anything. For instance, you may have heard that a politician "used a lot of rhetoric but didn't really say anything," or you may have heard someone say that a plan contained "a lot of rhetoric, but no action." Rhetoric has a far deeper meaning that often escapes popular uses of the term.

Basically, rhetoric includes words, images, and gestures presented to an audience for some kind of purpose. Rhetoric is usually thought to include the content of those words, images, and gestures as well as the style or form in which they are presented. As we continue our discussion, you might find it useful to come back to this definition because a great number of the theorists we are going to discuss have quite different views. For now, though, consider rhetoric to be a type of communication. Rhetorical theory is, essentially, explanations for how rhetoric works and what it does. As we begin our discussion, you'll note that much rhetorical theory is aimed at clarifying what is effective rhetoric. As we continue, though, you'll notice that rhetorical theory emphasizes the implications of how rhetoric is used.

Communication scholars Lucaites, Condit, and Caudell (1999) summarized the various approaches to rhetoric: "In some instances, the definitions attributed to rhetoric have made it so narrow as to include little more than style and delivery within its purview; in other instances its meaning has been so broad as to colonize and include all other forms of discourse, ranging from logic to poetics" (p. 19). In this section, we'll study selected definitions for rhetoric to give you a sense of the range of perspectives theorists have taken toward this topic.

Definitions of Rhetoric

The ancient philosopher Aristotle was one of the first theorists to define rhetoric, and his definition is one of the most influential yet today (Lucaites, Condit, & Caudell, 1999). Rhetoric, said Aristotle, is "the ability, in each particular case, to see the available means of persuasion" (p. 36). His definition focused on persuasion, an association that is still quite common today among theorists and critics. Aristotle observed that persuaders could make use of a variety of rhetorical tools, such as style, arrangement of ideas, delivery, and proof of arguments. Rhetoric, in Aristotle's day, was usually seen as intentional, strategic, and oral in nature. Rhetorical theorists of ancient times were interested in how speakers used rhetoric to achieve purposive ends, such as passing laws or making judicial decisions. Rhetoric was not seen as occurring in the normal, everyday communication of individuals. Instead, rhetoric took place in formal settings for particular purposes. Without the aid of technology, rhetoric was primarily oral. Speakers used words delivered in their own voice to audiences that were immediately present. We'll discuss in more detail in this chapter and throughout the book how the practice of rhetoric has changed since ancient Greece and how theory has adapted to these changes. We should also point out that not all ancient Greek theorists agreed upon a definition or function for rhetoric. Aristotle's definition, though, is useful to help us understand the scope and nature of rhetoric.

An anonymous book, the *Rhetorica ad Herennium,* written in ancient Rome during the first century B.C.E. provides us with an operational definition of rhetoric. This book identifies the five canons of classical rhetoric: invention, arrangement, style, memory, and delivery. Rhetoric is created as a result of these five processes. Invention refers to the discovery of ideas about which someone speaks. Thinking of a topic, focusing your thoughts, and deciding how to prove your ideas are all elements of invention. Arrangement refers to the order, or structure, of ideas presented by the speaker. Style includes the words and manner of speaking used. Memory refers to how the speaker remembers what will be said. (In ancient times, writing and printing technologies were not widely available , so speakers had to create other ways of remembering their ideas.) Finally, delivery includes the speaker's vocal characteristics and physical mannerisms. At this point you have no doubt recalled your instruction in a public-speaking class, which was probably based on the five canons.

Another illustrative definition is that offered by the Renaissance philosopher Peter Ramus (1515–1572), who separated rhetoric from other processes. In essence, Ramus believed that rhetoric comprised *only* style and delivery. The remaining canons of rhetoric, as defined by ancient theorists, belonged to other disciplines, such as philosophy.

Later, Francis Bacon developed a theory of the human mind that afforded rhetoric a far more significant role than Ramus assigned. We'll study Bacon's theory of rhetoric in a later chapter. For now, let's briefly identify his definition of rhetoric: "The duty and office of rhetoric is to apply reason to imagination for the better moving of the will." Bacon's view of rhetoric also marked a significant departure from Aristotle's theory of rhetoric. Whereas Aristotle approached rhetoric from the perspective of the speaker, Bacon sought to understand the mind of the audience. That is, he took a predominantly psychological approach to rhetoric. However, Bacon was again concerned with the persuasive aspect of rhetoric, and his theory provides a rich account of how speakers can create rhetorical messages.

The twentieth century saw new ways of looking at rhetoric. In the mid-1900s, rhetorical theorists began to focus more on the implications of rhetoric within particular cultures and less on how communicators could use rhetoric to create effective messages. Thus, theorists began to emphasize the social, cultural, and ethical dimensions of rhetoric. Illustrative of this thinking is communication scholar Marie Hochmuth Nichols, who defined rhetoric in 1969 as "the theory and practice of the verbal mode of presenting judgment and choice, knowledge and feeling" (p. 7). Rhetoric, then, was linked to making choices and passing judgment, which implies the use of ethical standards. She was also concerned with the type of knowledge produced by rhetoric. It should be noted that many ancient theorists were also concerned with the relationship between rhetoric, knowledge, ethics, and judgment, but these aspects of rhetoric have received far greater attention in recent years. Nichols limited her definition of rhetoric to language. We'll discuss the important function of language in rhetoric, but we'll also broaden our study of rhetoric to include nonverbal symbols as well.

Rhetorical theorist Kenneth Burke used the word *identification* as a synonym for communication. In 1969, he defined rhetoric as "the use of language as a symbolic means of inducing cooperation in beings that by nature respond to symbols" (Burke, 1969b, p. 43). Cooperation is achieved when a speaker and audience identify with each other. There is some give and take by both the speaker and audience for cooperation, or identification, to be achieved. Thus, Burke is interested in receivers, or audience members, and their perception of rhetoric. Burke's focus on symbolic communication and cooperation marked a departure from previous ways of viewing rhetoric. For Burke, symbols are the essential element of rhetoric; he downplayed other aspects in order to understand the full power of symbols on how we relate to others.

The definitions offered so far have viewed rhetoric from the perspective of powerful speakers who used rhetoric for specific goals: to gain political or legal power or to communicate scientific findings. Not all theorists we study will approach rhetoric from this perspective. In Chapters 8 and 9, for instance, we'll examine how women and people from non-Western cultures define and study rhetoric. For example, Foss and Griffin (1995) present us with a definition of rhetoric that focuses on the relationship between the person producing rhetoric and his or her audience. They define rhetoric as *invitational rhetoric,* which is "an invitation to understanding as a means to create a relationship rooted in equality, immanent value, and self-determination" (p. 5). As we continue, keep in mind that rhetoric is practiced by a variety of people who have very different orientations to the world. Consequently, the ways we study rhetoric will vary from culture to culture and theorist to theorist.

Communication scholar Thomas Farrell (1976) highlights several important elements of rhetoric in the following definition: "a collaborative manner of engaging others through discourse so that contingencies may be resolved, judgments rendered, action produced" (p. 83). Farrell broadened his definition by using the word "discourse," which presumably includes nonverbal forms of communication as well. Farrell's definition is also useful for us because it focuses on the collaborative nature of rhetoric and its uses. In other words, Farrell was interested in rhetoric as a social act that is shared between two or more people to accomplish something.

Rhetoric, then, involves symbols—verbal and/or nonverbal—and it is concerned with coordinating action between individuals. Rhetoric helps us make choices, and it is created in the interaction between unique individuals. Most important, a culture's conception of rhetoric is unique to that culture. As cultures change, so too do conceptions of rhetoric. We'll see the interconnection between rhetoric and culture throughout this book.

Finally, Rosteck (1999) defined rhetoric as the use of language and other symbolic systems to make sense of our experiences, construct our personal and collective identities, produce meaning, and prompt action in the world. This inclusive definition will be useful for us as we focus on the implications of rhetoric. Rosteck saw rhetoric as the way we communicate a wide range of information to others and and the way we understand our own identity. Rosteck's definition views rhetoric both as strategic—in that it can accomplish some kind of action—but also as constitutive of our experiences, culture, and identities.

In the next section of this chapter, we'll unpack his definition to explore more closely some of the key characteristics of rhetoric. For now, let's clarify some basic terms that we have been using and will continue to use.

Basic Terms

The word *rhetoric* often refers both to the symbols that are used in communication as well as to the theory about those symbols. You might read that "President Bush's rhetoric toward Iraq was tough," for instance. In this case, the writer is referring to the words and other symbols used by Bush as he spoke about Iraq. You might also read that "Aristotle's rhetoric focused on persuasion." In this case, the writer is referring to Aristotle's theory about rhetoric. If you think about it, it makes some sense to use the same word to refer to both product and theory. After all, when theory is communicated, it functions rhetorically, to persuade others to accept its validity. Some theorists, such as Nichols, combine rhetoric and rhetorical theory in their definition of the subject.

To clarify what is meant by rhetoric, however, we'll use the term to designate the symbols used by people to communicate. We might also refer to this sort of communication as *rhetorical practice* on occasion. We'll call the person doing the communicating the **rhetor.** The term **rhetorical theory** will be reserved for theories that describe rhetorical practice. **Rhetorical theorist** will be used for a person who created a particular rhetorical theory.

Rhetorical Criticism

We must define one last set of terms before we can proceed to study rhetorical theory. **Rhetorical criticism** is the process of using rhetorical theory in order to understand and evaluate rhetorical practice and generate future rhetorical theory. Rhetorical criticism is the method used by rhetorical researchers, whereas social scientific researchers use surveys, experiments, or ethnography. *Rhetorical critics* are people who practice rhetorical criticism. An essential relationship exists between all of these terms. Rhetorical theory is useless without the practice of rhetoric and application of theoretical principles. In essence, rhetoric invites theorizing

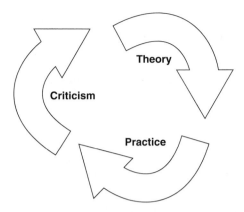

FIGURE 1.2   A circle of arrows can represent the relationship between rhetorical theory, practice, and criticism. Each influences the other, and without one aspect of this relationship, the others would be less informed.

about its principles, strategies, and effects. Accordingly, rhetorical theory is used to critique rhetoric so that rhetors have a better understanding of its impact. Consequently, new rhetorical theory is developed or existing theory is modified through the critical application of rhetorical principles. This relationship is illustrated in Figure 1.2. Rhetorical criticism is explored in closer detail in Box 1.1. Additionally, current rhetorical theory blurs the distinction between theory and criticism. We'll take up this point in later chapters of the book. In short, although we focus here on rhetorical theory, we can't ignore the other aspects of rhetoric: its actual practice and critical component.

CHARACTERISTICS OF RHETORIC

The various definitions of rhetoric identify several essential characteristics, or issues. Although rhetorical theorists take somewhat different stances toward them, we'll discuss those that predominate in their work. Specifically, we'll discuss the following characteristics:

1. Rhetoric is symbolic.
2. Rhetoric involves an audience.
3. Rhetoric establishes what is probably true.
4. Rhetorical theory is inventive and analytic.

Rhetoric Is Symbolic

First of all, rhetoric is inherently symbolic. **Symbols** are letters, images, or gestures that represent, or stand for, something else. The word "cat" is a symbol, for

---

BOX 1.1   Critical Insights: The Nature of Rhetorical Criticism

We have just defined rhetorical criticism as the application of rhetorical theory to rhetorical practice in order to understand and/or evaluate rhetoric. In each chapter of this book, we'll study an example of rhetorical criticism that draws on one of the theories discussed in the chapter. Doing so will allow you to better understand and appreciate the practical nature of rhetorical theory.

In this first chapter, we'll describe in a bit more detail the process of rhetorical criticism. The critic—the person who conducts the rhetorical criticism—begins by identifying some kind of rhetorical artifact to study. An artifact provides data for the study (Foss, 1996). It may be a speech, film, advertisement, or any other rhetorical event, act, or process. Or, the critic may generate a meaningful and significant question about rhetoric and then find an artifact to examine to answer the question. In any case, generally the critic must develop some kind of research question about an artifact of rhetoric.

The next step of rhetorical criticism is to identify a rhetorical method, which is an aspect of rhetorical theory that will help the critic answer his or her question. We'll discuss a great deal of theory in this book, much of which has

been used as a rhetorical method. For instance, in the next chapter we'll discuss the types of proof rhetors may use to persuade an audience. The critic may use what is discussed in that chapter to analyze and evaluate the proof used by a speaker, such as President Bush.

The next step is to use the method to analyze the rhetorical artifact. At this point, the critic illuminates the techniques of rhetoric used by the rhetor. The goal of rhetorical analysis is to generate insight about the artifact that would not be readily apparent without the criticism.

Finally, the critic evaluates the rhetoric based on his or her analysis. The critic may assess the effectiveness of the rhetorical artifact, its accuracy, or some other aspect. The critic should also be sure to answer the research question—which may ask for an evaluation. Finally, the critic should suggest ways that rhetorical theory can be modified in light of the analysis. We have discussed how rhetorical theory, practice, and criticism are related. By commenting on rhetorical theory, the critic is able to complete the circle identified previously.

As you read this book, we'll look at some examples of rhetorical criticism so you can better understand the dynamic relationships between theory, practice, and criticism.

---

instance, that stands for a fluffy animal with a long tail. We understand that the nonverbal symbol of a wave is often seen as a greeting to someone. When we communicate, we rely on symbols to explain, express, or persuade. The symbolic nature of communication makes it complex in several ways.

First, symbols are, by nature, *arbitrary and subjective.* That is, words, images, and gestures do not necessarily have meanings that we all share. If I say the words, "affirmative action," for example, several ideas may come to your mind. You might think about a law that effectively guarantees equal rights for all, or you might think about an unfair way of using quotas in employment and education. There is not necessarily a direct relationship between the word and what it means for each individual audience member. That is, the association between a sign and what it represents is not natural. Although we might share some ideas about what words mean, we also have a variety of perspectives on the meaning of symbols. We can also make up words and give them meaning. At my university, classrooms are filled with metal chairs that have writing surfaces attached to them. I encourage my students to call these pieces of furniture "chesks" to illustrate the dynamic and arbitrary nature of symbols.

Second, symbols include a *variety of signs,* such as letters and words, pictures, and nonverbal gestures. Although a great deal of rhetorical theory we study will focus on spoken words, technology has increased the types of symbols humans use when they communicate and blurred convenient distinctions between spoken, written, and mediated symbols. Even silence can be a symbol when it is used to communicate a message to someone. If you've ever given someone "the silent treatment," you know how powerful the symbolism of silence can be.

Rhetoric Involves an Audience

Of central importance to rhetorical theory is the relationship between rhetor and audience. Rhetoric takes place in the interaction between people. When you try to convince your friends to go to a particular movie over another, you are using rhetoric. When the president of the United States persuades the public to support a particular law, he has used rhetoric. Barilli (1989) pointed out that rhetorical audiences are ordinary people, "subject to feeling tired, bored, or bewildered, if arguments are too hard to follow" (p. ix).

The audience for a rhetor includes those individuals who have the ability to determine the meaning of the symbols exchanged in an interaction. We might think of rhetors and audiences as belonging to the same "rhetorical community." That is, a rhetorical community exists to make certain decisions or decide on moral action. Depending on the topic of discussion, the rhetorical community will be larger or smaller. When you and your friends decide where to eat or what movie to see, the rhetorical community consists only of you and your friends involved in the decision. When the president proposes a federal tax cut proposal, the rhetorical community consists of all Americans. Given that many nations, and their citizens, around the world had the ability to influence the debate over the recent Iraq war, we could say that the rhetorical community for that debate included many of the world's citizens.

As a result, rhetoric is practical, suggesting that it is used to accomplish something or achieve some end. Rhetoric, when it is effective, is able to bring people together to make a decision that is popularly accepted. In some ways, democracy is dependent on rhetoric. We assume in this society that people are free and able to discuss important issues and that after hearing arguments from others, we make our decisions and act accordingly. Of course, we're not always on the winning end of these arguments, and at times it seems that our decisionmakers do not always listen to the rhetoric of all the citizens. Yet despite these limitations, our culture's government system is based on the principles inherent in rhetoric.

So far, we have discussed audiences that are relatively easy to define and limited in scope. Our study of rhetoric will also address the rhetoric that exists in popular culture, such as television programs, clothing, music, or magazines. When you watch a television show, for instance, you are being subtly influenced in many ways. However, you aren't asked to necessarily vote on any kind of decision. You do, however, participate in a discussion about the kinds of values and beliefs our culture celebrates. In this way, we form our individual and collective identities by sharing in rhetorical situations with other individuals. In a sense, the

rhetorical community for this type of exchange consists of all members of the culture in which the rhetoric occurs. We are all, potentially, influenced by the rhetoric of television, film, and advertising. Keep in mind that the audience for a particular rhetor may be quite large and not easily identified.

Some theorists further complicate the idea of the speaker audience relationship by suggesting that such a distinction obscures the relationship between rhetor and audience. Communication scholar Michael Calvin McGee (1990) has made the point that in contemporary culture the audience member often does the job of assembling rhetorical messages. The sources of rhetoric are often unkown to us; instead, we are surrounded by fragments of their messages that we combine to create a meaningful, whole message. Consider channel surfing, or using your remote control to choose from among the television channels available to you. If you like to channel-surf, you frequently watch several programs at once, or at least you interrupt your favorite programs with other shows during commercial breaks. You, the audience member, are assembling the fragments of rhetorical messages to create a new rhetorical text. In essence, argues McGee, you, the audience member, have become the creator of the rhetorical messages. We'll take up this controversial point later in the book.

No matter how large or small the rhetorical community, a democratic society such as ours demands that individuals play an active role in determining policies and values. As you consider all the ways you use rhetoric, consider the influence you have within various rhetorical communities. Lucaites and Condit (1999b) noted that "the ability to contribute to public discourse was taken by classical teachers of rhetoric as an essential attribute of the educated citizen and thus very highly valued" (p. 3). The same is true of educated citizens today in a society such as ours.

Rhetoric Establishes What is Probably True

As our opening example about the Iraq war indicated, we are often asked to make decisions or take action when we don't know all the facts—when we aren't certain about a future course of action. Rhetoric is used in these situations to help us determine what is probably true. You might think about knowledge as existing on a continuum. At one end are certain truths, such as the theory of gravity. The scientific theory of gravity is true in all situations on earth. On the other end of the continuum are issues we accept only on faith, such as the love of a significant other. In the middle of this continuum are beliefs we form that are based on "informed opinion" (Bryant, 1953, p. 20). The creation of informed opinions is based on rhetoric. Lucaites and Condit (1999a) explained that people seldom wait for "certain truths to be delivered to them by the priests of truth and knowledge" but instead, they "act on their shared and compromised visions of the most probable course of action, based on what they believe they know, here and now" (pp. 610–611).

Throughout history, rhetoric has played a more or less significant role in how people form their opinions. In ancient Greece, male landowners were privileged to debate political and legal issues, hearing the ideas of other individuals and then basing their opinions on what they heard. In this type of culture, rhetoric was seen as very important. In the Middle Ages, church leaders or monarchs communicated their will to the people, and the people had little means or desire to challenge the opinions of their leaders. Thus, rhetoric played a less significant role in forming opinions. Later, scientists would communicate to the public what was found to be true using scientific methods. However , people did not necessarily use rhetoric to challenge the findings of science. Today, technology makes it possible for individuals to challenge the ideas of their political or religious leaders and the scientific community. In addition, the increasing degree of diversity in our society has introduced new and disparate voices to our conversations. Consequently, rhetoric is experiencing a "revived interest" among scholars from a variety of disciplines (Rosteck, 1999, p. 2).

One reason for this revived interest is the view that rhetoric is "epistemic" (Scott, 1968). Rhetoric, according to communication scholar Robert L. Scott, generates truth and knowledge. Rhetoric is not seen as a "conduit," or a pipe, for an objective, independent truth (Lucaites & Condit, 1999b, p. 3). Instead of thinking that rhetoric obscures truth, rhetorical theorists believe that rhetoric creates what is thought to be true in a particular situation. A central concern of rhetorical theorists has been the universality of the truth established through rhetoric. Scott (1968) has argued that we should not consider truth "as something fixed and final but as something to be created moment by moment in the circumstances" in which we find ourselves. Barilli (1989) has explained that "the final right to assess the degree of closeness to the true belongs to the demos, that is, the people, a community, an assembly of politicians, judges, the participants in a discussion, in a debate, and so on" (p. ix).

Some theorists question the usefulness of truth that is only based on what is probably true in a particular situation. Plato, for instance, was concerned that the people would not always make the best decisions about what is right and wrong. He believed that flowery rhetoric could easily sway opinions and ideas of truth. The theorists we discuss will each enter this discussion in some way. Communication scholar Donald C. Bryant (1953) put it simply: "Rhetoric exists, however, because a world of certainty is not the world of human affairs. It exists because the world of human affairs is a world where there must be an alternative to certain knowledge on the one hand and pure chance or whimsy on the other" (p. 20).

Rhetorical Theory is Inventive and Analytic

Rhetorical theory suggests ways of producing effective communication, and it provides a way to analyze communication. Bryant (1953) explained that rhetoric provides "assistance to the speaker in discovering what questions to ask and how to go about answering them" (p. 31). The clearest example of this idea may be Aristotle's theory, which classified the types of arguments people made and identified specific strategies that could be used to make the rhetoric effective. You may have taken an introductory speech class prior to taking this class. Perhaps you took a public-speaking class. If so, you have already been exposed to rhetorical theory. Many public-speaking classes rely, at least in part, on rhetorical theory. You may have given an informative speech and/or persuasive speech to demonstrate the types of speeches the ancient theorist Aristotle observed. Or, you may have been told to use Aristotle's ideas about appeals to emotion, credibility, and logic in your speech. This class continues your study of effective communication. Our focus, though, extends far beyond the medium of face-to-face oral communication. In Chapter 10, for instance, we'll study Kathleen Hall Jamieson's theory of electronic eloquence, which explained how rhetors can be effective when communicating via television.

As you read this text, however, you'll see that not all theorists suggest ways to create effective speeches or other forms of communication. Instead, some rhetorical theorists are more interested in how rhetoric creates our world, our experiences within that world, and our conception of ourselves. Many theorists we'll encounter, particularly those of the twentieth century, are primarily interested in the kinds of worlds we construct through rhetoric. Less interested in creating effective rhetoric, instead they are concerned with critiquing how rhetoric affects our relationships with others, our views of truth, and our value systems. Lucaites and Condit (1999b) noted that rhetoric should be seen as a "substantial dimension of many facets of the human social experience" (p. 10).

To expand the concept of rhetoric as method even further, we can study what happens when rhetorical theory critiques itself. We have previously discussed the relationship between rhetorical theory, criticism, and practice. Underscoring this relationship is the idea that theory constantly revises itself. Rhetoric in this sense is self-reflexive. The questions rhetoric asks of other subjects, can also be asked of itself. We use rhetoric to question whether a particular type of proof may be the most effective for a given situation, for instance. In essence, we constantly revise rhetorical theory in light of how rhetoric is used within a culture.

LIMITS OF RHETORIC

Although rhetorical theorists generally agree on the ideas in our previous discussion, there is a great deal of disagreement when it comes to determining the limits of rhetoric. We'll discuss some of the points of controversy here. For each issue, you might think of a continuum, a line with two divergent ideas upon which there are many intermediary points. Some theorists hold extreme views on these issues, but other theorists fit somewhere in the middle of the continuum. To facilitate your introduction to rhetorical theory, we'll take a fairly inclusive approach to rhetoric in this book, choosing to discuss the following points of controversy regarding rhetoric's limit:

1. Is rhetoric limited to persuasion?
2. Is rhetoric intentional?
3. Is rhetoric comprised only of words?
4. Is rhetoric limited to public address?
5. Is rhetoric concerned with propositions or style or both?

Rhetoric and Persuasion

In its earliest form, rhetoric was concerned with communication that was persuasive in nature. This focus should be apparent from the various definitions of rhetoric that we discussed previously. Theorists today continue to associate rhetoric with persuasion. However, there is often a fine line between informative, persuasive, or expressive communication. In fact, some theorists are not concerned about trying to distinguish informative and expressive communication from persuasive communication. Donald C. Bryant (1974) asserted that such divisions are "fictions" and that "most artifacts of discourse exhibit various dimensions" (p. 239). As you read this book, think about how each theorist views the relationship between persuasion and rhetoric. Some theorists will equate these two terms, while others broaden rhetoric's definition beyond that of persuasion. In particular, read the summary section for each chapter that surveys the various ways of defining rhetoric presented in the chapter.

Rhetoric and Intention

What is important to Bryant and other theorists is that rhetorical communication is instrumental. That is, rhetoric is designed to achieve some kind of goal, or outcome. Yawning in class simply because you are tired would not be considered rhetoric from this perspective, since you didn't intend to send a message with your yawn. It is important to point out, though, that many of a rhetor's consequences are unintended. When a celebrity wears her hair in a particular way, she may not be trying to influence how others wear their hair. But still, her fans may be influenced to wear their hair like the celebrity. Some theorists are not concerned about the rhetor's intent, but rather about the outcome of the rhetoric, whether it was intended or not. Likewise, an image may have persuasive effects that are not explicitly stated. The audience member has to "read into" the image in order to determine the message. If we view communication from a rhetorical perspective, then the rhetor's intent is not necessarily that important, nor is the nature of the rhetoric. What is most important, from a rhetorical perspective, is the influence that rhetoric has on an audience. In any case, intentional persuasion that results from the use of symbols will be the subject of our discussion in this book.

Rhetoric and Discourse

Discourse usually refers to words, whether spoken or written. The earliest rhetoric, of course, consisted of spoken words. As you'll read in a few pages, the earliest study of contemporary rhetoric also began with oral speech as the focus. The study of gestures and other nonverbal symbols was also considered the domain of rhetoric. As the media of rhetorical messages changed, however, rhetors began using images, sometimes at the complete expense of words. Consider commercial logos. Without using words, Nike, for example, is able to wield considerable influence with its logo. Some theorists today focus exclusively on words and gestures, while others are developing a rhetorical theory of visual images to help them understand persuasion and influence. Throughout the early part of the book, we'll focus on rhetoric as words and gestures. In Chapter 10, though, we'll spend time understanding the visual nature of rhetoric. The visual nature of rhetoric will be important in Chapters 11 and 12 as well.

Rhetoric and Public Address

In a similar vein, some theorists contend that rhetoric is concerned with public address, and others use a rhetorical perspective to effectively study film, television, interpersonal communication, and other forms of communication. In its earliest conception, of course, public address was the form of rhetoric most widely used, studied, and taught. But as orators began having their messages transmitted via radio, television, and the Internet, the nature of the public address "event" changed. Today, it is almost impossible, and perhaps ineffective, to study the specific speaking event exclusively. Critics must also consider the medium's influence and the large audience exposed to the speech. Doing so, however, blurs the line between public address and other forms of communication. Although it's easy to see how the president's State of the Union speech is rhetoric, it is problematic to say that a photo opportunity on an aircraft carrier is not. From there, it is not that much of a stretch to also claim that television, film, and advertising are rhetorical as well. In fact, much of our discussion in Chapters 7, 10, 11, and 12 will look at rhetoric that takes place in these different types of media.

Rhetoric's Substance

Finally, rhetorical theorists have, since the beginning of time, questioned the nature of rhetoric's substance. Some theorists contend that because rhetoric is interested in advancing arguments in support of truth, it is similar to philosophy. Others reject this idea and assert that rhetoric is simply the style and ornamentation attached to something we already know to be true or that rhetoric in fact hinders our search for truth because of its ornamental qualities. Most theorists today reject such totalizing statements, believing that rhetoric combines propositions with poetics, or arguments with style. For example, Barilli (1989) stated that "Rhetoric is a comprehensive, total way of using discourse. This means that the physical aspects of speech are not sacrificed to the intellectual dimension" (p. vii). You'll see this controversy play out in Chapters 2-4. In the end, most theorists generally accept that rhetoric includes both style and content.

INFLUENCES ON RHETORIC

Rhetorical practice is constantly changing and as it does, rhetorical theory constantly changes as well. For example, a speech by Cicero to the Roman Senate in 55 B.C.E. was very different from a televised presidential address given today to a worldwide audience. Cicero, for instance, could see his entire audience and probably knew many of its members. President Bush, on the other hand, does not have physical contact with his audience, nor does he personally know even a fraction of the total audience. The changing nature of rhetorical practice and rhetorical theory is due to several factors that we'll briefly discuss here. We'll talk about each of these factors in later chapters. Specifically, we'll examine two developments that have had significant impacts on rhetorical theory: culture and communication technologies.

Culture

Perhaps the most significant influence on rhetoric is that of culture. The setting in which a specific group of people communicate plays a great role in how they communicate and in how that communication, in turn, affects their situation. Let's examine how political structures and expectations about equality influence rhetoric.

The political system of a culture plays a significant role in the type of rhetoric used by that culture. In democratic societies, such as ancient Greece or contemporary United States, rhetoric is used to make all kinds of political and legal decisions. Candidates are elected to office after using campaign rhetoric and securing the majority of the public's vote. When elected, officials use rhetoric to debate the merits of proposed policies and choose action they believe is in the community's best interest. Our country's legal system is built on the principle of "innocent until proven guilty." The phrase itself is an example of rhetoric, and rhetoric is used to prove the guilt or innocence of those accused of crimes. In totalitarian cultures of ancient and modern times, rhetoric's function as a deliberative tool is limited. It is widely believed that the famous rhetor Cicero had his hands and head displayed in the Roman Senate after his death as a warning to those who would use rhetoric to question the government. You'll read more about Cicero in the next chapter.

A culture's expectations of equality are linked, in some ways, to the culture's political system. In the United States, for instance, freedom of speech (which is really the freedom to use rhetoric) is codified in the constitution so that all can enjoy that freedom. Our rhetoric, then, reflects this idea. At the same time, there are those in U.S. culture and other cultures that construct rhetorical theory in a way that identifies and counteracts the unequal exercise of power in that culture. Feminist theorists, for instance, highlight the ways that traditional rhetorical theories reinforce inequality and are creating theories that aid in the liberation of those who are oppressed. A feminist theory might suggest ways that magazine advertisements demean women and suggest ways to resist what is advertised. The practice and potential of equality in a culture will be a major influence in the contemporary theories we discuss.

Communication Technologies

The first instances of rhetorical practice featured a speaker and audience who were united in time and place. Without amplification technology, the audience had to be within earshot of the speaker. Today, of course, rhetoric can be broadcast instantaneously to the entire world via satellite or the Internet. As the media of communication change, so too do the expectations for the communication and the impact of the communication on the audience.

Without going into too much detail at this point, let's consider how a politician would have constructed a message in ancient Greece and compare that with how it may be done today. In ancient Greece, the rhetors would have had to communicate about topics with which everyone in the audience had experience. Additionally, the speaker would have had to communicate in a way that was easy

---

BOX 1.2   Internet Activity: Rhetorical Influences

We have just discussed the influence of culture and technology on rhetorical practice and its theory. Using what you know, read a speech published in the Online Speech Bank located at http://www.americanrhetoric.com/speechbank.htm and consider how it was influenced by culture and technology. Read a speech on a topic that interests you and then answer these questions: How does the speech reflect the culture's political system? How does the speech reflect the culture's ideas about equality? How does the medium of the speech influence the speaker's choices? Was the speech effective? Why or why not? Would the speech have been as effective in a different culture? Why or why not?

---

for the audience to remember, since they didn't take notes or record the speech. Finally, the speaker would have had to project his voice to be heard by distant audience members.

Today, on the other hand, communicators can call on a range of cultural knowledge, since we are exposed—by media—to a range of issues and experiences. The speaker would have to compose the message so it would be attractive to audience members accustomed to visual images. For instance, images and graphics would probably be used to enhance the message. Finally, the speaker would have to choose which media—television, print, or Internet—would be most effective at delivering the message to a mass audience. It's easy to see from these examples that technology influences how rhetoric is created and analyzed. We'll explore this influence in greater detail in later chapters. As you consider the ways that culture and technology influence rhetorical practice, complete the Internet Activity, Rhetorical Influences, in Box 1.2.

A BRIEF HISTORY
OF RHETORICAL THEORY

We have just discussed two influences on rhetoric: culture and communication technologies. In this section, we'll focus on the impact these influences have had on rhetorical theory and practice. As we proceed in our study of rhetorical theory, it will be easy to lose track of the "big picture" by focusing too intently on the specific theorists. We can, to some degree, lump theorists from particular time periods together because they have common ways of seeing the world and rhetoric's role in that world. Of course, any such categorization is problematic, because not all theorists during a given time period have similar views. However, Scott (1975) attempted to create groupings of theorists by addressing the social forces that have led to particular ideas about rhetoric.

Scott's focus is on how messages result from the "interacting of speakers, listeners, and the world in which they live" (Scott, 1975, p. 440). Scott contended

Table 1.1 Time Periods in Rhetorical History

Dates	Period Names	Pattern of Emphasis (in order of importance)
200 B.C.E–95 C.E.	Pragmatic-dominant	1. Speaker 2. World 3. Listener
1400s–1500s	Aesthetic	1. Speaker 2. Listener 3. World
1700s–1800s	Pragmatic-subordinate	1. World 2. Speaker 3. Listener
1900s–present	Social	1. Listener 2. Speaker 3. World

SOURCE: Adapted from Scott, Robert L. (1975). A synoptic view of systems of Western rhetoric. *Quarterly Journal of Speech, 61,* 439–447.

that at different points in time, theorists will emphasize one of the three elements—speaker, listener, or world—more than the others. A speaker-oriented theory addresses the choices made by speakers in creating rhetoric. Thus, a focus on how speakers can use evidence or emotional appeals is considered speaker focused. A worldly view of rhetoric assigns to the speaker the role of messenger. That is, the speaker simply uses rhetoric to convey some kind of external, objective truth. A listener perspective on rhetoric means that audience members are active agents in the creation of rhetorical messages. Messages are viewed as "mosaics" in which audience members combine the ideas of several speakers to form beliefs about what is true or false. Scott's categorization scheme featuring these terms is presented in Table 1.1. Let's study the implications of how Scott has viewed the history of rhetorical theory.

Pragmatic-Dominant Rhetorical Theory

Scott's first category, pragmatic-dominant, included ancient theorists from Greece and Rome who asked and answered very pragmatic questions about rhetoric and who saw the speaker as influencing the events of the world through rhetoric. Thus, rhetoric played a dominant role in world events. Specifically, theorists during this period—also called the classical period—asked questions concerning what may be said on behalf of a cause and how it might best be said (Ehninger, 1967). Communication scholar Douglas Ehninger has called this time period the "grammatical" period because theorists of that time were first developing the terminology for rhetoric that would guide its study in future years. This terminology focused on the choices available to the speaker. Thus, the speaker was seen as the primary focus; events of the world were seen as secondary, because they resulted from the speaker's statements. The audience was not given much consideration during this era. Principle theorists reflective of this thinking were Isocrates and Cicero.

Aesthetic Rhetorical Theory

You'll notice that there is a considerable gap between Scott's first and second time periods. This period of time is often known as the Middle Ages, or medieval period, and lasted from the end of the Roman Empire (approximately 400) to the beginning of the Renaissance (approximately 1400). Powerful forces, such as the church and various monarchies, diminished rhetoric's role in determining truth and elevated the stylistic aspects of rhetoric. That is, rhetoric usually consisted of sermons, letterwriting, or poetry, forms that emphasize the stylistic elements of rhetoric.

More attention, however, has been focused on the late Middle Ages and early Renaissance periods, from the 1400s to 1700s. Scott has called this time the aesthetic period of rhetoric. Rhetoric was used during this period to embellish the truth or ingratiate the rhetor to a very small audience. That is, attention was paid to the aesthetic qualities of rhetoric, which is a way of referring to rhetoric's style. Rhetoric during this period consisted of sermonmaking and the art of letterwriting. Rhetors wrote beautiful letters in order to show that they were worthy of positive judgment (Scott, 1975, p. 444).

Pragmatic-Subordinate Rhetorical Theory

As we have just seen, rhetoric was focused on style during the Middle Ages and the Renaissance. At the same time, humans explored their world using new scientific techniques and tools, and they developed new ideas about the nature of human emotion and intellect. Scientific discoveries would shape the role of rhetoric in the time period Scott discusses next, the pragmatic-subordinate. Rhetoric would come to play a pragmatic role in the 1700s–1800s, but it would be subordinate to science. That is, rhetoric would be used to communicate what science had found. The world, as discovered through science, would be the dominant element and the speaker would receive secondary emphasis during this time. Representative theorists from the pragmatic-subordinate period are George Campbell and Richard Whateley. We'll discuss their ideas in Chapter 4.

Social Rhetorical Theory

The final time period in Scott's conceptualization is called social (1900 to the present), because it reflects a new emphasis on the audience. Scott sees the listener as receiving the primary emphasis during this period, with the speaker receiving secondary emphasis. As we explore contemporary rhetorical theory, you'll see how an increasing effort is made to understand the interaction of speaker and audience. Whereas the meaning of words was mostly taken for granted during the earlier periods, we'll spend a great deal of time as we study contemporary rhetoric discussing understanding, misunderstanding, and how audiences perceive a speaker's message. Rhetorical theory during this period also attempts to reduce human conflict, although Scott did not see this as the defining characteristic of contemporary theory.

What's Next?

Scott's categorization of rhetorical theory ended with the social period. However, he was writing in 1975 and the world has changed much since then. We have the Internet now, for example, which has significantly changed how humans interact and create rhetorical messages. As you continue your study of rhetoric, consider whether you would add a new period to Scott's four, or whether you believe we are still in the social period that he described. Perhaps we are moving from a listener-speaker-world order of emphasis to a listener-world-speaker order. Consider again the outbreak of the war in Iraq. In some ways, it didn't matter which news source you viewed or read about the war. Although you could find reporting that differed from the mainstream, much of the reporting was similar. Audiences may have synthesized the glut of information they received and formed their beliefs about the world from it. Consequently the speaker, or source, of the message was less important than the listener and the world the messages reflected. We'll come back to some of these ideas later in the book, but in the meantime continue to reflect on Scott's classification as you read. As you try to keep track of the various theorists we discuss, their time periods, and significant events that occurred in history, it may also be helpful for you to consult Appendix A, which presents a timeline of rhetorical theory.

THE ACADEMIC STUDY
OF RHETORIC IN THE UNITED STATES

From our previous discussions, you can see that the study of rhetoric has been around since the earliest recorded history. The discipline enjoys a long tradition in the universities and colleges of the United States. We'll briefly survey that history here so you can gain a better understanding of the study on which you are embarking.

The first university in the United States was Harvard, founded in 1636. Based on the European model, the university taught a basic curriculum, including rhetoric. The prevailing view of rhetoric during the later part of the twentieth century was *elocutionism*—learning the correct pronunciation for words and the proper gestures to use when speaking. Since many of Harvard's early students were training to be preachers, rhetoric—knowing how to properly give speeches—played an important role in their training. Rhetoric was soon taught in departments of English as well. In fact, many English departments today continue to teach rhetoric. Although their teaching is usually concerned with composition, there is a great deal of similarity between rhetoric as studied in English departments and that studied in departments of speech or communication. (This book is most compatible with the view of rhetoric presented in the field of communication.)

In 1914, seventeen English instructors withdrew from their departments of English, distanced themselves from the elocutionist view of rhetoric, and formed an organization called the Academic Teachers of Public Speaking. The group wanted to "redevelop in Academia Americana the principles, teaching, practice, and theory of oral discourse, especially public address" (Bryant, 1974, p. 233). A journal, the *Quarterly Journal of Public Speaking,* was used to disseminate the ideas of the speech teachers. The group of seventeen grew to include teachers of argumentation from English departments, debate coaches, theater instructors, and speech pathologists. Their organization, later called the National Association of Teachers of Speech, published the *Quarterly Journal of Speech Education.* The new discipline revived the works of Aristotle, Plato, Cicero, Quintilian, and other classical and British rhetorical theorists. The focus was public address: its practice and analysis.

During the fifties and sixties, the social scientific tradition of communication scholarship emerged as a viable alternative to rhetoric as a way of studying communication. Since then, study of communication has embraced both perspectives: the rhetorical and social scientific. Rhetoric is today taught in departments of communication, speech, speech communication, theater (or speech and theater), and English. Where once teachers of rhetoric joined with teachers of theater and speech pathology, they now teach separately at many colleges and universities. The organization originally founded in 1914, the Academic Teachers of Public Speaking, came to be known as the Speech Communication Association (SCA) and is now called the National Communication Association (NCA). Although many communication journals publish articles that develop or apply rhetorical theory, the *Quarterly Journal of Speech* continues to be the premier publication for rhetorical scholarship. To learn more about the NCA, check out its web page at http://www.natcom.org.

OUTLINE OF THE BOOK

This chapter has provided you with a general introduction to rhetoric—its scope, some of the controversial issues involved in its study, and a broad view of how it has been studied throughout history and, recently, in the United States. With this introduction in mind, we can embark on a more detailed exploration.

In the first set of chapters, we'll explore some of the traditional functions of rhetoric. Chapter 2 addresses rhetoric as persuasion, the primary function for rhetoric that we have discussed in this chapter. Chapters 3 and 4 extend the early discussion of rhetoric by discussing its relationship to religion, science, and argument. Chapter 3 looks at rhetoric's use in religion and the belletristic movement, which was concerned with taste and style. Chapter 4 examines rhetoric's role in the study of science and rhetoric as argumentation. Essentially, the next three chapters move the study of rhetoric from ancient Greece and Rome to Great Britain and the United States, laying the groundwork for a discussion of rhetoric in contemporary society.

Chapters 5 and 6 discuss a contemporary view of rhetoric that centers on meaning. Chapter 5 gives a basic overview to contemporary rhetoric and what is called the "linguistic turn" in rhetorical theory. Chapter 6 examines dramatism, one of the primary theories of rhetoric that is based on the view that rhetorical meanings create powerful frameworks for organizing our experiences.

Chapters 7-9 explore how rhetoric maintains and promotes ideology and how rhetoric is positioned in relation to economics and mediated cultural values. Chapter 7 exlores how rhetoric maintains and promotes ideology; Chapter 8 looks at feminist theories; and Chapter 9 surveys non-Western rhetorical theory, such as that from Africa, China, and Native American cultures. Together, these chapters describe a view of the world that is very different from that of classical, Enlightenment, or modern times and challenge some of the fundamental assumptions about rhetoric as presented by the classical theorists. These perspectives also provide foundation for discussion in future chapters.

The final three chapters address the newest developments in rhetorical theory and extend earlier discussions of meaning and power. Chapter 10 focuses on the influence of media and visual images. Chapter 11 looks at the impact of postmodernism. Chapter 12 examines the related discipline of cultural studies.

SUMMARIZING RHETORICAL THEORY

At the end each chapter, we'll come back to the issues described in these first pages to get a sense of the similarities, differences, and relationships between various theories of rhetoric.

Defining Rhetoric

As you have already seen in this chapter, theorists differ on how they define the characteristics and limits of rhetoric. Although there will be similarities in how theorists from a given time period define rhetoric, there will be wide differences as well. Each chapter will end with a summary of the definitions of rhetoric by the primary theorists it has discussed.

Rhetoric and Knowledge

We have suggested that rhetoric is concerned with what is probably true in a given culture at a given time. This statement refers to **epistemology,** the study of knowledge or ways of knowing. Although theorists more or less agree that rhetoric creates what is accepted as knowledge, or truth, some theorists see rhetoric as playing a greater role in the creation of knowledge than others. Particularly, rhetorical theorists are interested in the certainty of knowledge, the relationship between knowledge and experience, and the process by which knowledge arises (Littlejohn, 1996). At the end of each chapter, we'll summarize how the theorists we have discussed view the relationship between rhetoric and truth.

Rhetoric and Identity

Ontology concerns the nature of human existence or, you might say, how humans create identities for themselves. For a rhetorical theorist, the nature of identity is key to understanding the nature of rhetoric and its impact on how individuals think, feel, and act in their social environments. We'll be particularly interested in whether human experiences are individualized or social, how humans choose to act, and whether human experience can be explained generally or specifically (Littlejohn, 1996). Again, we'll summarize our findings, showing how the theorists discussed in the chapter view the relationship between rhetoric and identity.

Rhetoric and Judgment

Since the earliest study of rhetoric, theorists have tried to understand the relationship between rhetoric and **ethics,** which is the reasoned study of what is right and wrong. Theorists have been interested in whether and how rhetoric can be used to pursue justice, equality, and higher levels of understanding. Some theorists see rhetoric as playing a significant role in questions of ethics and judgment, whereas others see rhetoric and ethics as separate issues. We'll summarize at the end of each chapter how theorists we've studied deal with the interplay of rhetoric and ethics.

DISCUSSION QUESTIONS

1. Which definition of rhetoric discussed in this chapter makes the most sense to you? Why?

2. When have you been a rhetorical critic? What are some other examples of rhetorical criticism from popular culture?

3. Choose several current, popular television shows or movies. What are the social truths that emerge from these shows? How widely accepted are their messages?

4. Where do you limit rhetoric? Where do you place yourself on each of the continuums we have discussed in this chapter? Are there any additional ways of limiting rhetoric not discussed in the book?

5. In what ways do you think contemporary culture influences the practice of rhetoric? How do current forms of communication technology influence rhetoric?

6. Are we still in a social period of rhetorical theory or have we moved on to something else? Provide examples to illustrate your ideas.

7. Consider the department in which you are taking this course. How is communication studied? Does the rhetorical or social scientific tradition dominate the courses offered and interests of the faculty? Are the two traditions taught equally? If you can, investigate the history of your department. What other disciplines, if any, are taught in the department? How is your department's history similar to other departments we have discussed? How is it different?

GLOSSARY TERMS

rhetoric   The use of language and other symbolic systems to make sense of our experiences, construct our personal and collective identities, produce meaning, and prompt action in the world.

rhetor   A person who creates and/or performs rhetoric.

rhetorical theory   A set of theories that explain rhetoric.

rhetorical criticism   The process of using rhetorical theory to understand and evaluate rhetorical practice and generate future rhetorical theory.

symbol   A letter, image, or gesture that represents something else.

epistemology   The study of knowledge and what is considered to be true or false.

ontology   The study of the nature of human existence and how humans perceive themselves to be.

ethics   The study of how people make and justify decisions about what is right and wrong.

PART II

Important Rhetorical Functions

2

Rhetoric as Persuasion

Learning Objectives

After reading this chapter, you should be able to:

1. Describe the characteristics of classical rhetoric and the influence of ancient culture on how rhetoric was practiced.
2. Identify the major theorists of the classical period.
3. Understand how rhetoric was defined, how it was taught, how it was seen to be different from dialectic, and its purposes.
4. Describe the five canons of rhetoric and apply them to rhetorical practice.

Christopher Reeve, the actor best known for his movie portrayals of Superman, was paralyzed in a horse riding accident in 1995. Following his injury, Reeve spoke often and passionately about the need for research into spinal cord injuries. Late in his life, Reeve took up the controversial position that the federal government should fund stem cell research, which he, and others, believed would prompt a cure for spinal cord injuries and diseases such as Alzheimer's and Parkinson's. One of the most famous speeches Reeve made was at the 1996 Democratic National Convention in Chicago (see Figure 2.1).

On this occasion, Reeve stirred his audience with a combination of rhetorical techniques. Emotionally, he called on the audience—including the convention delegates and others watching on television—to take care of our country's neediest citizens. With compelling delivery, Reeve asserted that "America does not let

FIGURE 2.1   Christopher Reeve speaking at the 1996
Democratic National Convention.

its needy citizens fend for themselves." He also used the example of a young man
shot innocently by a bullet in New Jersey. Reeve argued that "We have a moral
and an economic responsibility to ease his suffering." By citing statistics, Reeve
was able to support his claim that spending more money on research would reduce
the amount the nation spends on health care each year. In the years between his
accident and death, Reeve used his celebrity status to gain credibility with audiences and convince them that more research was necessary.

Each of the techniques used by Reeve—credibility, emotional appeals, and
evidence—were originally identified by the ancient rhetorical theorists we'll
study in this chapter. Western rhetoric traces its history to ancient Greece, but
keep in mind that not all rhetorical traditions we'll discuss in this book stem from
that of ancient Greece and Rome. However, the dominant way of thinking about
rhetoric in our culture and other Western cultures stems from the ideas of Aristotle,
Plato, and the other theorists we'll discuss here. The rhetorical theory of the

period lasting from approximately 400 B.C.E. to 100 C.E. is often called **classical rhetoric.** The primary purpose of rhetoric during this time was persuasion.

The Greeks had developed a democratic form of government in which citizens passed laws and made legal decisions. The tool they used to carry out these tasks was rhetoric. In particular, ancient citizens fought legal battles over land and its ownership. It was important, then, that they could use rhetoric to defend themselves and sue others. Many of the theorists we'll study taught others to defend themselves and gained great popularity as teachers. The ancient Greeks and Romans were also interested in learning all they could about the world, from biology to physics to ethics to rhetoric. Thus, they observed, recorded, and passed on what they learned about these disciplines.

This chapter lays the foundation for our future study of rhetoric by focusing on one of rhetoric's earliest uses, to persuade others. We'll begin by identifying several characteristics of classical rhetoric. Then we'll briefly identify some of the major theorists of this period and their view of rhetorical theory. We'll then discuss the major ideas of classical rhetoric before identifying how they viewed knowledge, identity, and judgement.

CHARACTERISTICS
OF CLASSICAL RHETORIC

During the time period we'll discuss this in this chapter—400 B.C.E. to 100 C.E.—the civilizations of Greece and Rome used a democratic form of government in which citizens cast votes to determine local law and legal matters. Prior to their use of democracy, tyrants ruled Greece using a more totalitarian governing style. As the tyrants fell from power, Greek citizens sought to reclaim land that was taken from them. To do so, they used rhetoric to win their case in the courts. The use of rhetoric to influence the affairs of the state spread throughout the land and soon democracy was practiced locally, in the 200–300 autonomous city-states, that made up Greece. The largest city-state was Athens, the modern capital, which had a population of approximately 200,000. Greek culture celebrated human perfection through athletics, science, dramatics, and rhetoric. The ancient Greeks were so proficient in their endeavors that you can still walk on brick streets they built and view the great temples at which they worshipped. The Greeks were polytheistic, worshipping many gods, including Zeus and Apollo.

War was a constant part of the life of ancient Greece as the city-states fought off foreign invaders in a series of wars. Although they sometimes joined forces to fend off invaders, such as the Persians, the Greek city-states did not formally or political unite with each other. In fact, Greek city-states often fought each other. The Peloponesian War, between Athens and Sparta, lasted from 431 to 404 B.C.E. The Greeks eventually fell to the Romans in 168 B.C.E.

By the first century C.E. Rome controlled a great portion of the world, from Great Britain to Egypt and from Spain to Mesopotamia. The Romans borrowed extensively from the Greek culture they subsumed. However, they also adapted this culture to serve their own ends. The Romans developed their own culture of art, literature, and rhetoric. A primary difference between the two great civilizations was that Rome used a central governing authority over their empire, whereas the Greeks maintained distinct city-states united by a common culture, religion, and democratic form of government. The Roman government used its military to maintain control over its empire, and much effort was put into establishing a strong military presence in occupied lands. Politically, the Roman Senate used rhetoric to make laws and legal decisions. An intricate political structure determined how elections would be run, who could serve on the Senate and for how long members would serve. The Roman Republic was marked by a series of class struggles, between the slaves and working poor on one side and the ruling class on the other.

In the end, personal and political struggles between war heroes and political officials led to the fall of the Roman Republic and the birth of the Roman Empire. Through political arrangement, Julius Caesar was appointed dictator for life by the Roman Senate in 46 B.C.E. He would rule only two years, however, before being assassinated in 44 B.C.E. by Gaius Cassius Longinus and Marcus Junius Brutus. A series of emperors ruled a democracy that existed in name only. Elections were rigged so that powerful leaders could maintain or gain power. The Roman Empire began to dissolve because of disorganization and conflict. By 476 C.E.—at the start of the medieval period—Roman power had shifted to Europe and Byzantium. The Middle Ages would be marked by religious rule and feudal warlords who maintained local political control. We'll examine the rhetoric of the Middle Ages in Chapter 3.

This short history of ancient Greece and Rome serves to highlight the important role rhetoric played in their cultures as well as suggest some of the significant influences they exerted on the formation of rhetorical theory. Primarily, ancient citizens used rhetoric to make laws and legal decisions. They spoke in front of other citizens, attempting to win support for the rightness of their positions. The Greek teacher and rhetor Demosthenes (Figure 2.2) is a good example. He was famous for his orations, many of which have been recorded as samples of effective rhetoric. Consider the example of Demosthenes as we discuss the characteristics of classical rhetoric. Specifically, we will explore how classical rhetoric was oral, persuasive, and public.

Oral Aspect

Imagine a world without text messaging, the Internet, or even loudspeakers. The ancient rhetors inhabited such a world and consequently relied primarily on oral, face-to-face communication. Kennedy (1963) noted that although many ancient Greeks could read, writing on the stone, bronze, clay, wood, wax, or papyrus media that were available was "difficult and unnatural" (p. 3). Ancient rhetors used their voice to speak face-to-face to audiences. The oral nature of classical rhetoric had several implications for how it was practiced and taught.

Without widespread use of writing media, it was necessary to remember a great deal of information to be an effective speaker. Since they had no books to study or notes to guide their speeches, rhetors needed to have command of information as well as the many rhetorical devices that we'll study later in the chapter.

© Bettmann/CORBIS

FIGURE 2.2 Demosthenes Delivering His Oration Against Philip of Macedonia.

Imagine having to give an effective persuasive speech based only on the information you already know and without the aid of notes, and you can get an idea of the conditions facing ancient speakers. As a result, they developed numerous memory devices. You may have used these devices to learn the order of the planets or the order of musical notes. For instance, the sentence "My Very Eager Mother Just Served Us Nine Pizzas" can help you remember the order of the planets. The first letters of each word in this sentence are also the first letters of the planets, starting from the nearest to the sun: Mercury, Venus, Earth, Mars, Jupiter, Saturn, Uranus, Neptune, and Pluto. Ancient people relied on devices like this to remember facts and stories.

Fundamentally, ancient cultures, which relied on oral communication, were essentially different from contemporary Western culture, which relies primarily on electronic communication. Walter Ong, a theorist we'll study in a later chapter, explained that cultures based on oral communication lacked abstract thought and centered on the communicators' immediate experiences. Oral speakers were not able to conduct research, for instance, and they did not talk in vague, theoretical language. Instead, their language was direct, specific, and immediate. We'll study more of Ong's theory in Chapter 10. As we continue our exploration of classical rhetoric in this chapter, keep in mind the face-to-face setting in which it was originally experienced.

Persuasive Aspect

As we have already discussed, the primary goal of classical rhetoric was persuasion. In particular, orators addressed political and legal issues. **Judicial rhetoric** was performed in the courts and usually argued for or against the guilt of someone accused of wrongdoing. **Deliberative rhetoric** was conducted in the legislature and was designed to speak for or against a proposed policy, such as going to war.

Another recognized type of rhetoric was **demonstrative rhetoric,** which praises or blames some individual on a special occasion, such as a funeral eulogy. These types of speeches were persuasive in nature because they tried to persuade the audience to accept or reject particular values or actions displayed by the individual being commemorated. Perhaps the most famous of the ancient epideictic, or demonstrative, speeches is Pericles' Funeral Oration in 431 B.C.E. for the Athenian soldiers who died in the Peloponnesian War with Sparta. In the speech, Pericles praises the values of Athens and its citizens. His speech was very idealistic and encouraged Athenian citizens to see their city from his perspective.

When rhetoric is viewed as persuasion, there is an implicit assumption that truth is relative. Many of the ancient theorists agreed with this view of truth, believing that vigorous discussion of the issue at hand would result in the audience following the more correct course of action. Not all ancient theorists agreed with this view. Some, such as Plato, believed that rhetoric obscured truth. He saw rhetoric as playing a dangerous role in the political and legal affairs of the state. We'll discuss his line of reasoning in a few pages.

Public Aspect

If rhetoric was persuasive, then it required an audience to act on the rhetor's words. Classical rhetoric took place in front of an audience that would eventually take action on the topic discussed. Because rhetoric was viewed as a public event, private conversations between individuals—even if they were persuasive in nature—were not considered to be rhetoric. Likewise, the famous Greek plays—which were often persuasive—were not viewed as rhetoric. Barry Brummett (1994) argues, "The Greek rhetorical legacy encourages people to assume that only the texts of public speaking had rhetorical functions" (p. 39), and he outlines four characteristics of those texts.

First, rhetorical texts were essentially *verbal*—they used words to communicate. We discussed this point earlier when we said that Greek rhetoric was oral. Second, Greek rhetoric was *expositional,* which means it included a series of claims and backing for those claims. You might think of Greek rhetoric as consisting of a series of arguments. Third, Greek rhetoric was *discrete;* it was confined by specific boundaries. A speech is a good example of this idea. When the speaker started speaking, the rhetoric began; when he finished, the rhetoric ended. Finally, Brummett explains that Greek rhetoric was *hierarchical,* creating expectations about the roles of speaker and audience member. The speaker had a privileged position of power.

Additionally, the public nature of oratory in the classical period caused rhetorical theorists to study the relationship between rhetor and audience member.

Plato spoke of knowing the audience's soul and Aristotle wrote of understanding the audience's emotions. Ideas about arrangement and evidence were also predicated on the need to persuade audience members. The relationship between rhetor and audience continues to be an important aspect of rhetoric that continues to influence rhetorical theory today.

THE MAJOR THEORISTS

Before we discuss how rhetoric was defined and studied in the classical period, it is important to learn a bit about the lives of several major theorists from this period. The life experiences, training, and political views of these theorists played a significant role in what they saw as being the goals of rhetoric and the appropriate ways it should be practiced. In this section, we'll examine the formative influences on the Sophists, Plato, Aristotle, Isocrates, Cicero, and Quintilian.

The Sophists

A number of teachers traveled throughout fifth century B.C.E. Greece teaching citizens to be effective rhetors so they could win cases in the courts and be effective politicians. They also taught a variety of other subjects including politics, grammar, and mathematics. These teachers are often referred to as the **Sophists,** although they were not united in any kind of formal sense.

The Sophists were effective teachers, explained Jarratt (1991), because they had experienced other cultures through their travels. As a result, "they believed and taught that notions of 'truth' had to be adjusted to fit the ways of a particular audience in a certain time and with a certain set of beliefs and laws" (p. xv).

The Sophists saw truth as relative, which explains, in part, their success in sparking a rhetorical revolution in ancient Greece. As Barilli (1989) explains, "rhetoric finds fertile ground only in a situation in which one doubts that truth may exist as a given outside the interaction of human beings, their exchange and comparison of opinions that necessarily occur through language" (p. 4). The epistemological relativism of the Sophists provided such a fertile ground for rhetoric.

Jarratt (1991) notes that the portrayal of the Sophists by Plato and Aristotle has been influential in historical views of classical rhetoric. In particular, she notes that "the Sophists' rejection of transcendent truths and eternal values, their ability to move a popular audience with a range of rhetoric techniques, {and] their interest in social exigencies" all made them subject to the scorn of Plato and Aristotle. Additionally, the Sophists accepted pay for their teaching, which was contrary to Plato's idea that teachers had a public obligation to teach their students (Jarratt, 1991, p. 2).

Some of the most popular Sophists included Protagoras, Gorgias, and Hippias. Protagoras is famous for saying that humans are the measure of all things. Humans used rhetoric to determine what was probably true in a given situation. Jarratt (1991) explains that Protagoras "found it both impossible and unnecessary to determine any single Truth about appearances; more important is negotiating useful courses of action for groups of people given their varying perceptions about the world" (p. 50).

Gorgias, who became the object of Plato's scorn, would take up any argument instantly, using an array of metaphors, flowery speech, and confusing arguments to persuade the audience. He is known for saying that nothing exists, or if anything does exist then it cannot be known, or if it is known, then it can't be communicated (Jarratt, 1991, p. 53). However, closer inspection of Gorgias's view of rhetoric reveals a foreshadowing of what contemporary theorists would recognize: that there is a gap between words and what they mean (Jarratt, 1991, p. 54). In a time when such ambiguity was seen by teachers such as Plato and Aristotle as dangerous, Gorgias recognized both the limits and potential of language's arbitrariness.

Hippias would teach students various mnemonic devices so they could quickly memorize bits of information. The students could, in turn, recite the information in a convincing manner, but they lacked knowledge about the meaning of what they had memorized.

Plato

One of the most influential of the earliest theorists was Plato, who vigorously opposed the teaching and views of the Sophists. Even today, Plato's writings about philosophy, politics, and rhetoric are highly regarded and are often cited in several disciplines. Plato was born into a wealthy and politically active family in Athens in approximately 428 B.C.E. Plato was an early student of Socrates, who was condemned to death by the Athens courts and later killed himself. Following Socrates' death, Plato traveled to Italy and Sicily for a period of time, facing persecution from the leaders of these governments in each case. He returned to Athens and started a school known as the Academy. Aristotle, whom we will study later, was Plato's most famous student. Plato died in approximately 348 B.C.E. and is believed to be buried on the site of his former school.

Socrates' death would fuel Plato's skepticism of democracy and rhetoric. Plato believed that truth was absolute and feared that the Greek citizens would use rhetoric to mislead and deceive. Consequently, Plato had a generally negative view of oratory. We'll examine his definition of rhetoric in the next section and his views of rhetoric's relationship to truth and morality later in this chapter. Plato's writings are in the form of dialogues between characters. His most critical thoughts on rhetoric are contained in *Gorgias,* a dialogue in which the Sophist of the same name is a main character. Plato generally softens his view toward rhetoric in *Phaedrus.* You can access online versions of these dialogues. *Gorgias* is available at http://classics.mit.edu/Plato/gorgias.html, and *Phaedrus* can be located at http://classics.mit.edu/Plato/phaedrus.html.

Aristotle

Aristotle (384–322 B.C.E.) was born in the northern part of Greece, the son of a physician. Aristotle received early training in biology from his father, who intended to pass down his medical knowledge to his son. However, both of his parents died when he was young, so Aristotle was raised by an uncle who taught him the

Greek language, rhetoric, and poetry, to complement his early biology training. When he was seventeen, Aristotle went to Athens to study at Plato's Academy. Aristotle was an instructor at Plato's school for twenty years; the subject of his teaching is not known, but it probably included rhetoric and dialectic. Scholars cite a number of reasons why Aristotle may have left the Academy following Plato's death. Although Aristotle was greatly influenced by Plato, he did not agree with his teacher on many topics. For one, Plato believed that we could not know reality except in an ideal, abstract sense; Aristotle believed that by observation we could come to know the reality of experiences.

In any case, Aristotle left Athens for the island of Assos, where he married Pythias and recorded his observations about the world. The early scientific training of his father influenced how he observed and classified the natural world. In fact, many disciplines trace their early history to Aristotle. Besides writing about science, Aristotle wrote about politics, ethics, logic, and rhetoric. In 335 B.C.E., he started his own school, the Lyceum, at Athens. The curriculum of the Lyceum included a broad range of subjects, such as logic, rhetoric, philosophy, physics, and biology.

Aristotle is said to have written more than 150 books. Many of these writings are compilations of his lecture notes, and some may even be the work of other teachers at the Lyceum. *On Rhetoric,* Aristotle's foremost book on rhetoric, is thought to have been written in 350 B.C.E. This book lays out Aristotle's classification scheme concerning rhetoric, showing its principle components and techniques. You can read it online at http://classics.mit.edu/Aristotle/rhetoric.html.

Isocrates

Isocrates was another of the great teachers of ancient Greece. Unlike Plato, Isocrates was more practical about rhetoric and less idealistic. Isocrates was born in 436 B.C.E. to a wealthy family in Athens. He was a student of Socrates and Gorgias and was described by Plato as having great promise. Isocrates fled Athens during a period of political turmoil and opened a school on the island of Chios. He later returned to Athens and opened what is considered to be the first permanent institution of higher liberal arts education. He focused on politics and, specifically, on the morality of politics. For fifty years, he was a famous teacher, training young Athenian men in the ways of politics. Isocrates died of self-inflicted starvation in 338 B.C.E.

Isocrates was a poor speaker and compensated by having a rhetorical style lacking in much of the ornamentation that characterized his contemporaries. In fact, it is often noted that Isocrates created a literary form of rhetoric that was meant to be published and read rather than spoken and heard. His training also focused on specific rhetorical situations. Isocrates rejected ideas of absolute truth espoused by Plato and believed that general theories of rhetoric had only limited applicability. Many of Isocrates' ideas about rhetoric come from two books: *Against the Sophists* and *Antidosis.* These books do not develop a handbook of rhetorical theory, as we have seen with Aristotle, but instead support the argument that rhetoric was necessary for Greek democracy to flourish. You can read a variety of

Isocrates' speeches and writings by accessing the list online at http://classics.mit.edu/Browse/browse-Isocrates.html.

Cicero

Marcus Tullius Cicero was a Roman orator during the era of the Republic. He was largely responsible for bringing Greek philosophy and rhetoric to Rome and reinterpreting the great works of Greeks such as those of Aristotle. He was born in 106 B.C.E. Although aristocratic, Cicero's family did not have wealth or political status. Cicero was ambitious and chose a career in law. He trained for his profession by studying rhetoric, law, and philosophy. As an attorney, Cicero gained a great deal of experience as an orator and formed a solid network of supporters. Managing to transfer his success in law to politics, he was elected to many high Roman offices, including the Roman Senate.

Cicero is remembered for exposing corruption and treason. In 60 B.C.E. Julius Caesar took power and invited Cicero to join the government. Cicero resisted, believing in the Republic and its democratic style of government, which Caesar threatened. Cicero was forced from Rome in 58 B.C.E. and had his property seized because of an earlier political action he had taken. He later returned and regained his property. Although he could not participate in politics, he practiced law and wrote several books for the next four years. When Caesar was murdered in 44 B.C.E., Cicero was able to return to politics. He made his mark in a series of speeches in the Senate outlining a course for the Roman government. However, Cicero made enemies with his position and was ordered murdered by the government leadership in 43 B.C.E. In fact, Cicero's hands and head were cut off and later nailed to the speaker's podium in the Senate as a warning to future orators. Cicero's demise parallels the demise of democracy in Rome, as we have outlined in the previous section of this chapter.

In his writings about rhetoric, including *On Invention, On the Orator,* and *The Orator,* Cicero pursues a practical use for rhetoric in much the same way that Isocrates did. In fact, much of Cicero's work revitalized the Greek classics, including those of Aristotle, Plato, and Isocrates. He believed that Roman orators should be trained in liberal education as well as the art of rhetoric. Contemporary scholars have studied not only Cicero's books, but also his political speeches and personal letters to learn about his theory of rhetoric. You can read some of Cicero's most famous speeches by accessing the list online at http://classics.mit.edu/Browse/browse-Cicero.html.

Quintilian

Quintilian was a successful orator in Spain and Rome and is perhaps best known for his ideas about the training of rhetors. Quintilian was born in Spain in 35 C.E. His father was a well-known Roman orator who sent Quintilian to Rome to study rhetoric. Becoming an effective rhetorician, Quintilian returned to Spain, where he set up a public school and received a state salary. Several important students attended Quintilian's school.

Quintilian wrote several books, including *Insitutio Oritoria,* which concerns the education of a rhetor. In many ways, the book covers much of the same information as the theoretical works of Aristotle and Cicero, such as arrangement, style, and invention. Quintilian is perhaps best known for teaching that a true rhetorician is "a good man skilled at speaking." In Quintilian, we see much of Isocrates and Cicero but also glimpses of Plato's idealistic view of rhetoric.

CONCEPTIONS OF RHETORIC

The five orators/teachers we have just discussed, along with the Sophists, were the most influential rhetorical theorists during the classical period. As we begin to explore their contributions to rhetorical theory, we'll first examine how they defined rhetoric, what they saw as rhetoric's purpose, and how they distinguished rhetoric from other disciplines, such as philosophy.

Defining Rhetoric

During the classical period, there was much discussion about the definition and purpose of rhetoric. Prior to 462 B.C.E., most important legal decisions in ancient Greece were made by a single judge or a small panel of judges (Kennedy, 1963). Then democracy began to spread in the Greek legal and political system. For instance, juries of six thousand Greek citizens were soon used to decide legal cases. As a result, the period of time between 400 and 300 B.C.E. is often called the golden age of rhetoric because the Greeks recognized the role of rhetoric in persuading jurors and began systematically to study the subject. Keep in mind, too, that at this time, early theorists and teachers were just beginning to distinguish academic topics from each other. That is, the divisions between disciplines that we so readily accept today weren't as apparent then. Therefore, it was important that the early theorists define the subjects of their studies so as to isolate their defining characteristics.

Aristotle suggested one of the most widely used definitions of rhetoric: "an ability in each [particular] case to see the available means of persuasion" (*On Rhetoric,* p. 37). That is, the purpose of rhetoric is to teach about the various tools of persuasion. This definition is similar to what we have called rhetorical theory in the first chapter. Aristotle's definition was practical and reflected his goal of classifying the tools of persuasion used by the ancient orators.

Plato was more idealistic in his definition of rhetoric. Plato feared that rhetoric was a tool used to deceive the public. Plato refused to call rhetoric an art; instead, he called it a knack. Plato wrote in his dialogue *Gorgias* that the knacks may become confused with the arts: "Yet because they are closely related and deal with the same matters, Sophists and rhetoricians become confused and do not know either what to make of themselves nor do others know what to make of them" (465, 26). However, later in the dialogue, Plato hints that rhetoric may be used for the pursuit of the good when it makes just the unjust. The Sophists in Plato's *Gorgias* struggled to establish rhetoric as a distinct art, whereas while Plato argued that rhetoric was not a true art, rather a false art aimed at pleasure. Plato revised his position to say, in *Phaedrus,* that rhetoric was an art, but one that closely followed a prescription.

An ancient book entitled *Rhetorica ad Herennium,* provides a comprehensive account of rhetorical theory. The book was written in approximately 100 B.C.E. by an unknown Roman author. Because it was similar to Cicero's book *De Oratore,* it was once widely believed that Cicero was the author of *Rhetorica ad Herennium.* Now, however, the book is, by most accounts, anonymous. Based largely on Greek rhetorical theory, it was influential from the days of the Roman Empire until the Renaissance period of the 1500s. The book outlined the task of the public speaker: "to discuss capably those matters which law and custom have fixed for the uses of citizenship, and to secure as far as possible the agreement of his hearers" (Book 1, line 2). We might consider this to be the role of rhetoric as well.

Echoing the idealism of Plato's definition, Quintilian sought to include a quality component in his definition of rhetoric. He wrote, "Some think that even bad men may be called orators, while others, of whom I am one, restrict the name of orator and the art itself to those who are good" (*Intitutio Oratoria,* p. 301). His definition of rhetoric was "the science of speaking well" (p. 315). This definition includes the quality component and requires that the rhetoric be effective and that it be performed by an individual of good quality.

Rhetoric's Functions

Aristotle, and the theorists that would follow him, identified three species of rhetoric: demonstrative, judicial, and deliberative. Each type of speech has a different audience. Aristotle wrote that an audience member is either "a spectator or a judge, and [in the latter case] a judge of either past or future happenings" (*On Rhetoric,* p. 47). *Demonstrative* speeches, sometimes called epideictic speeches, either praise or blame some individual or group. In doing so, this type of speech persuades the audience to accept the values that are espoused in the speech. *Judicial* speeches either accuse or defend and are presented in the courtroom. *Deliberative* speeches are presented to members of a legislative assembly. Their purpose is to persuade the assembly to pass or reject a new policy. Additionally, Aristotle observed that each type of speech addresses a particular time frame. The demonstrative speaker addresses the present, the judicial speaker the past, and the deliberative speaker the future. Each speech is geared to a different end, as well. Demonstrative speakers have shame or honor as their purpose, judicial speakers aim at the just or the unjust, and deliberative speeches have as their focus the advantageous or the harmful (p. 49). (See Table 2.1.)

Many of the major theorists accepted Aristotle's distinction between types of rhetoric. In addition, Quintilian identifies the orator's aims to instruct, move, and charm (p. 397) no matter the overall purpose of the speech. Barilli (1989) explains that rhetors must teach on an intellectual level, touch the feelings of the audience, and keep their interest alive so they do not become bored. Quintilian believed that rhetors must achieve these three goals whether they are performing demonstrative, deliberative, or judicial rhetoric.

Table 2.1 Types of Rhetoric

Type	Time Context	End	Example
Judicial	Past	Just/Unjust	Closing argument in a legal trial
Epideictic	Present	Honor/Dishonor	Funeral eulogy
Deliberative	Future	Advantageous/Harmful	Speech to Congress

Rhetoric and Dialectic

The ancient theorists struggled to differentiate rhetoric from **dialectic,** which is a rigorous interaction between ideas to determine truth. You might think of dialectic as a method of philosophy whereby a series of questions are asked and answered about a subject until the true nature of the topic being discussed is apparent.

Plato believed that anyone could use dialect to discover the good and true but that only those who already possess truth could use rhetoric (Brownstein, 1965). Rhetoric, Plato thought, was inferior to dialect and had no connection to truth or morality. Aristotle, on the other hand, repeatedly says that rhetoric is "like" dialectic (*On Rhetoric,* p. 35). In fact, Aristotle says that rhetoric is the counterpart to dialectic. He wrote that "people, in some way, share in both; for all, to some extent, try both to test and maintain an argument [as in dialectic] and to defend themselves and attack [others, as in rhetoric]" (pp. 28–29). Rhetoric is the presentation of argument, whereas dialectic is the testing of argument, according Aristotle.

Cicero believed that philosophy, which is the aim of the dialectic method, is not necessary in the training of an orator. Instead, he thought that orators should experience their world and gain knowledge from their experiences. Plato, wrote Cicero, "depicted in his pages an unknown sort of republic, so completely in contrast with everyday life and the customs of human communities were his considered statements concerning justice" (*De Oratore,* 224, p. 159). On the other hand, Quintilian believed that the subjects of philosophy—courage, justice, self-control, for instance—also played a role in rhetoric. His teaching united the study of these values with that of rhetoric. In any case, the ancient theorists disagreed about the necessity for orators to have philosophical training and for the use of the philosophical method in rhetorical practice.

Rhetorical Education

Since the earliest rhetorical theorists were also teachers, it is not a coincidence that they spent a great deal of time considering the proper method of instruction for future rhetors. In fact, the Greek and Roman cultures depended on their citizens' ability to carry out government functions, and rhetoric was necessary to those functions. As we have just discussed, Plato initially seems to believe that rhetoric could not be taught; instead, it was a knack. Of course, Plato's major complaint with rhetorical instruction was what he considered to be the unprincipled teaching of the Sophists. However, a closer look at his writings reveals that with careful instruction, rhetoric could be learned so that it would preserve justice. Writing in *Phaedrus,* Plato argued that rhetoric was not just a knack, but that it was a scientific "art" learnable by most people.

Plato favored a "scientific" approach to rhetoric. The student of rhetoric must first know the truth about every single subject, he or she must know the soul of the audience, and the rhetoric should be arranged and adorned with style. Additionally, rhetors should receive instruction in justice as well as speech making. Plato believed that "A true rhetorician must first be a just man" (*Gorgias,* 508, p. 84). Plato summed up his view of rhetorical training with this statement:

> If a man composes his work with the full knowledge of the truth and can come to the aid of what he has written when he is challenged and has the power to demonstrate from his own mouth the poverty of his writings, he ought not to be designated by a name drawn from them, but by one that indicates his serious pursuits." (278, p. 74)

Cicero, echoing Plato, claimed that orators must have knowledge about which they speak. He wrote, "For it is from knowledge that oratory must derive its beauty and fullness, and unless there is such knowledge, well-grasped and comprehended by the speaker, there must be something empty and almost childish in the utterance" (*De Oratore,* 20–21, p. 17). Cicero, however, also recognizes the importance of innate ability: "but there are some men either so tongue-tied, or so discordant in tone, or so wild and boorish in feature and gesture, that, even though sound in talent and in art, they yet cannot enter the ranks of the orators" (115, p. 81). Finally, Cicero acknowledged that training was also an important aspect of being an orator.

Quintilian was very interested in the training of orators. In fact, the aim for his famous work on rhetoric was "the education of the perfect orator" (*Institutio Oratoria,* 8, 9). An orator must first be a good person, according to Quintilian, possessing an excellent character. A good orator must also have knowledge of the subject matter. In fact, Quintilian outlined a course of education for a young orator, starting at birth. Finally, the orator should "be a thorough master of the science and the art of speaking" (18, p. 15). Despite such training, Quintilian admitted, natural talent is also important for an orator. He wrote, "The student who is devoid of talent will derive no more profit from this work than barren soil from a treatise on agriculture" (26, p. 19).

The Rhetorica ad Herennium outlined the manner of acquiring rhetorical skill: theory, imitation, and practice. Theory, the book explains, "is a set of rules that provide a definite method and system of speaking" (p. 9). If you recall your training in public speaking, you can probably remember learning such rules as what should be included in an introduction and conclusion, and ways of organizing the main points of your speech. The same would have been true of the way some ancient teachers taught their students. Imitation refers to reciting effective speeches to learn what qualities made the speech effective. Practice, according to the *Rhetorica ad Herennium,* consists of applying the concepts of theory and gaining experience using them.

Table 2.2 Five Canons of Rhetoric

Canon	Definition
Invention	Determination of topics and supporting material
Arrangement	Structure of the speech
Style	Use of language to create a desired effect on the audience
Delivery	Presentation of the speech, involving verbal (vocal) and nonverbal aspects
Memory	Remembering what to say in a speech

THE FIVE CANONS OF RHETORIC

Rhetorica ad Herenium outlined for the fist time what has come to be known as the **five canons of rhetoric.** Although the Greeks discussed each of the canons, it was not until later that they were codified in a systematic way. The five canons of rhetoric are invention, arrangement, style, delivery, and memory (see Table 2.2).

Invention concerns identifying the issues involved, creating arguments in support of the rhetor's position, and finding proof to support this position. Arrangement is the ordering of the rhetoric, which usually includes an introduction, statement of claim, proof, and conclusion. Style concerns the artistic elements of the speech, such as using a metaphor. Delivery is the verbal and nonverbal characteristics of the rhetor's presentation. Memory refers to recalling the speech when presenting it and the recall of information used in the speech

The five canons are an excellent example of rhetoric being inventive and analytic, as discussed in Chapter 1. As you read about the five canons on the next few pages, you'll probably remember instruction you have received in public speaking. The ideas we'll discuss here have been used for centuries by orators as a method of creating rhetoric. In addtion, rhetorical critics have used the five canons as a method for critical analysis. Read the Critical Insights box for this chapter (Box 2.1) to see how one such critic used classical rhetoric.

It is beyond the scope of this chapter to recount each theorist's instruction for each of the five canons. Consequently, we'll survey the most significant, comprehensive, or important instruction of the theorists we have discussed as it relates to each of the five canons.

Invention

The canon of **invention** involves finding and developing the subject of the rhetoric. Generally, theorists have divided invention into three areas: stasis, the search for issues; proof, the support for the claims; and topoi, or common arguments the rhetor can summon in different situations.

BOX 2.1   Critical Insights: Classical Rhetoric and Criticism

Classical rhetoric was the primary influence on rhetorical critics during the 1950s and 1960s. Although rhetorical critics today often rely, at least in part, on the theories from classical rhetoric, they have largely turned to more contemporary theory for critical insights. However, we can learn much about the history of public address by looking to some effective rhetorical criticisms that used the theories from the classical period.

Doris Yoakam Twichell (1955) provided an account of Susan B. Anthony's rhetoric using the classical approach. Twichell spends a great deal of time describing the time in which Anthony lived, her personality and history, and the cause for which she struggled: the right to vote for women. It is not uncommon in classical rhetorical criticism to discuss the speaker and his or her time, in addition to the particular rhetorical strategies used by the speaker.

Twichell (1955) outlined some of the basic rhetorical techniques used by Anthony and exemplified how these techniques were used. Anthony's use of evidence was noteworthy. Twichell wrote, "Her recorded speeches are crowded with statistics and direct quotations from authorities, law, and history" (p. 115). Also, "Susan B. Anthony excelled in argument. She

stated issues and defended them, making frequent use of the rhetorical question, sarcasm, and 'withering invective'" (p. 115). Twichell noted that Anthony masterfully used the Aristotelian "enthymeme " (see later discussion): "She put her basic premises succinctly, pointed to generally entrenched beliefs, and emphasized the new ideas that must necessarily be accepted" (p. 115–116). As a good critic should, Twichell quoted extensively from Anthony's speeches to support her arguments.

Twichell further analyzed Anthony's speeches for their style and delivery. Her speeches were "filled with words and phrases that had emotional meaning for the people of her time" (p. 114). In terms of delivery, Twichell noted, "Her utterance was rapid, and she made few pauses, but so good was her articulation that the attentive listener did not lose a word" (p. 123). In the end, Twichell (1955) concluded that "Susan B. Anthony was an effective public speaker, but probably not a great one" (p. 130). Reading Twichell's rhetorical criticism of Anthony's speech provides an interesting, and illuminating, account of how classical rhetorical theory can inform our understanding of rhetorical practice.

Stasis It was necessary to first understand the issues involved in the situation under critique, and for this, the ancient theorists developed the idea of stasis. The word **stasis** means stopping point, or the place where two rhetors may disagree about a particular issue. The idea of stasis is most developed in Cicero's work. He claimed that stasis was useful for "all of the issues disputed among" people, including legal disputes or discussions of policy. In *Rhetorica ad Herennium,* the topic of stasis is discussed in a chapter on legal speaking, indicating that it may be most useful for this genre of rhetoric. In fact, contemporary theorists have developed an alternate set of issues for deliberative rhetoric: the stock issues.

The first issue is that of *disputed facts;* the rhetors may argue about what happened or will happen in a given situation. In a legal trial, for instance, the prosecution accuses the suspect of committing some illegal act while the suspect denies that the action took place. The second issue concerns the *nature* of what happened. In a legal trial, for instance, the accused may not deny that an action took place but may argue that the action was justified for some reason or other. The third issue of stasis is *definition* of terms. In a legal trial, once again, the crime that was allegedly committed must fit some definition. For instance, second-degree murder often requires premeditation. Thus, for the definition of second-degree murder to be upheld, the prosecution must show that a particular action took place. In essence, the judicial speaker using stasis must show that the facts of the case fit the definition of the crime about which he was arguing and that there were no extenuating circumstances that would warrant a different decision. Those accused of a crime could dispute the facts of the case, argue that the facts did not fit the definition of the crime at hand, or contend that there were extenuating circumstances that explain the accused's actions.

Proof Rhetoric examines persuasion, and persuasion must convince its listeners. Thus persuasion must use demonstrations, or proof: "For we most believe when we suppose something to have been demonstrated" (Aristotle, *On Rhetoric,* p. 33). Aristotle recognized the fact that teachers of his day did not understand the importance of proof: "They concern only with how they may put the judge in a certain frame of mind, while they explain nothing about artistic proofs, and that is the question of how one may become enthymematic" (p. 32). Aristotle seems to be saying that those interested in persuasion must make it a part of their lifestyle, or be "enthymematic," constantly examining proof and enthymemes, a word we will define later.

Aristotle divides proof into two categories, artistic and inartistic:

> Of these *pisteis,* some are atechnic ["inartistic"], some entechnic ["embodied in art, artistic"]. I call atechnic those that are not provided by "us" [i.e., the potential speaker] but are preexisting: for example, witnesses, testimony of slaves taken under torture, contracts, and such like; and artistic whatever can be prepared by method and by "us"; thus one must use the former and invent the latter. (37)

In other words, inartistic proof is given by the situation and can only be used by the rhetor. The rhetor cannot make up inartistic proof.

The rhetor can generate three additional kinds of proof, though. Aristotle called these artistic forms of proof. He explained that "for some are in character [*ethos*] of the speaker, and some in disposing the listener in some way [*pathos*], and some in the argument [*logos*] itself, by showing or seeming to show something" (37). Let's discuss each of these forms of proof in more detail.

Aristotle devotes much of Book 2 of *On Rhetoric* to the study of the character of the speaker (*ethos*) and emotions (*pathos*). The study of **ethos** is very important because audiences judge not only the argument presented, but the speaker as well. He says, "It is necessary not only to look to the argument, that it may be demonstrative and persuasive but also [for the speaker] to construct a view of himself as a certain kind of person" (p. 120). Three qualities are necessary: "practical wisdom [*phronesis*], virtue [*arete*], and good will [*eunoia*]" (p. 121). These traits are powerful. Aristotle argued, "Therefore, a person seeming to have all these qualities is necessarily persuasive to the hearers" (p. 121). Christopher Reeve was generally thought to have these characteristics. He was knowledgeable about stem cell research, he was a respected spokesperson for the cause, and he appeared to have the best interests of his audiences in mind.

Aristotle also believed the speaker should know about his or her audience so as to use effectively **pathos,** or an appeal to emotion. Instead of knowing an abstract idea, such as the "soul," Aristotle believed effective speakers understood the audience's "emotions." Aristotle argued that three questions regarding the emotions of audience members must be answered: "[W]hat is their state of mind?," "[A]gainst whom" are the emotions directed?, and For "what sort of reasons" do people feel the way they do? (*On Rhetoric,* p. 121) Without knowing the answers to all three questions, Aristotle argued, it would be impossible to connect emotionally with the audience. In Book 2 of *On Rhetoric,* he uses these questions to examine a variety of emotions: anger, calmness, friendliness, enmity, fear, confidence, shame and shamelessness, kindliness, pity, indignation, envy, and emulation. Aristotle argued that a speaker must understand each of these emotions to persuade his or her audience. Reeve's speech to the Democratic National Convention illustrates how Reeve used emotional proof. Reeve knew that his audience was fearful of the future, yet hopeful that a cure for debilitating diseases could be found.

The third artistic proof is **logos,** or reasoning. There are two types of reasoning: induction and deduction. One form of induction is reasoning from examples, or reasoning from particular cases to a general conclusion. For example:

Aristotle was from Greece and he was smart.

Plato was from Greece and he was smart.

Isocrates was from Greece and he was smart.

Conclusion: All people from Greece are smart.

Obviously the conclusion to this argument cannot possibly be valid, based on the information that is provided. All we know for certain is that these three men were smart and from Greece. Induction, as a method of proof, is only probable in its conclusions. It cannot prove a claim with perfect certainty. We have to make a leap to the conclusion, that all people from Greece are smart. (By the way, this claim is suspect, since we have examined only a few examples of Greeks who were abnormally smart.)

Deduction relies not on example, but on enthymemes. There is considerable discussion about what Aristotle meant by *enthymeme.* Let's first discuss a syllogism, before clarifying this term. A syllogism is a series of three statements. The first is a generalization that has been proven true. The second statement applies a particular case to see if it is included or excluded from the generalization. The third statement is the conclusion, which flows logically from the first two. For example:

All people are mortal. (Generalization)

Socrates is a person. (Particular case that is included in the generalization.)

Socrates is mortal. (Conclusion)

"The enthymeme," Aristotle argued, "is a sort of syllogism [or reasoning]" (p. 33). Unlike the logically valid syllogism, the premises of an enthymeme, or "rhetorical syllogism" (*On Rhetoric,* p. 186) are not always true. Instead, they are based on a more informal expression of argument. Kennedy (1963), in a footnote, sums up the difference between the syllogism and enthymeme, "The Aristotelian distinction between a syllogism and an enthymeme thus seems largely one of context—tightly reasoned philosophical discourse in the case of the syllogism versus popular speech or writing with resulting informality in the expression of the argument in an enthymeme" (33n). Bitzer (1959) goes further to suggest that an enthymeme is a type of syllogism produced in the interaction between speaker and audience. The audience supplies, through its own base of information, statements that help form a speaker's syllogism. In other words, when people use rhetoric, they don't speak in tightly argued syllogisms. Instead, they rely on the audience to provide some of the proof for what the speaker is saying. Let's consider an example from President Bush's 2004 campaign rhetoric:

Political liberals raise taxes. (Unstated generalization)

"Much as he tried to obscure it, on issue after issue, my opponent showed why he earned the ranking of the most liberal member of the United States Senate." (Particular statement to show that Kerry is included in the category of liberals, from a speech given by President Bush in Minnesota on Oct. 12, 2004.)

John Kerry will raise taxes. (Unstated conclusion)

Using what his audience knew of liberals, Bush was able to make the case that because John Kerry was a liberal, he would raise taxes. Bush was able to avoid a complicated discussion about political ideology by drawing on his audience's own knowledge of and feeling toward various political positions.

Topoi The subjects of all argument are topics, or *topoi*. Kennedy defines a *topos* as "place" or "space where a speaker can look for 'available means of persuasion'" (45n). We are forced to turn to Kennedy, because Aristotle did not define *topos*, believing the word would be "easily understood" (45n). Chapter 23 of Book 2, presents twenty-eight of these commonplaces, or lines of argument, that may be used. Speakers may employ any of these strategies to win the argument. Topoi provide arguments that can be used from situation to situation. Table 2.3 provides several topoi, their definitions, and an example of each.

Arrangement

The second of the five canons of rhetoric is **arrangement,** which concerns the order or structure of the speech. If you think back to a public-speaking class you may have taken, you'll probably remember that structure was an important component in communicating effectively. Highlighting the importance of proof, which we have just discussed, Aristotle claimed there were really only two necessary parts to a speech: "state the subject and [then] to demonstrate it" (p. 258). Logically, he claimed, only this order made sense. Listeners would not believe what is not demonstrated and it is "ineffective" (p. 258) to demonstrate something without stating it first. "The first is the statement [prothesis], the other the proof

Table 2.3 Topoi

Topoi	Definition	Example
More and less	If the lesser of two things is true, the greater is as well.	"If my opponent raised taxes on the poor, he will surely raise taxes on the middle and upper classes as well."
Turning what has been said against oneself upon the one who said it.	Using an opponent's words against him or her.	"My opponent said last year that health care reform was not possible. Now, she is arguing in favor of reforming health care."
Previous judgment	Assumes that reasonable people make similar judgments about similar issues.	"My position has been consistent: I have always supported military action when it has multinational support."
Consequence	Looking to the consequences of an action to determine if it is desirable.	"Investing in higher education will result in an economic return equal to six times the original investment."

[pistis]" (p. 258). Although Aristotle later claimed there could be four parts to a speech, including the introduction and conclusion, other theorists provide a more comprehensive account of a speech's arrangement.

Parts of a Speech Cicero, who believed that arrangement was one of the most important aspects of rhetoric, identified seven parts to a speech:

1. The entrance, to introduce the subject and assure the audience of the speaker's right intentions

2. The narration, which provides background information about the topic at hand

3. The proposition, or the speaker's thesis

4. Division, which outlines the main concepts, or points, of the speech

5. Confirmation, or the support for the claims made in the speech

6. Rebuttal, which is an attempt to overcome potential disagreements

7. Conclusion, or the synopsis of evidence and final appeal to the audience's emotions

Introduction and Conclusion Let's look a bit more closely now at the introduction and conclusion to a speech. Aristotle claimed that the introduction "should imply that the speech is concerned with "the audience, marvels, and pleasures (p. 263). The prooemium, or introduction, makes clear "what is the 'end' [*telos*] for which the speech [is being given]" (p. 262). He also mentioned that the speaker may gain the goodwill of the audience with the prooemium. *Rhetorica ad*

Herennium explains that the goal of the introduction is to make the hearer attentive, receptive, and well-disposed toward the speaker and the topic. Depending on the nature of the speech, the speaker may use a direct approach or subtle approach in the introduction.

The *epilogos,* or conclusion, starts with the speaker claiming to have performed "what he promised" (281). Finally, "Asyndeton is appropriate for the end of the discourse" (282). The speaker should somehow part with his or her audience. Typically, Aristotle explained, speakers would ask the audience to carefully evaluate what was said and make a decision about which course of action to pursue.

Style

In addition to proof and arrangement, the **style** of the speech was important. Aristotle summarized his views on style, the third of the five canons, with the definition "to be clear" (p. 221). If the speech is not clear, it has not served its function. Later authors would expand on Aristotle's ideas. Most notably, Cicero and the *Rhetorica ad Herennium* provide instruction in how rhetors can stylize their remarks.

Levels of Style Both Cicero and *Rhetorica ad Herennium* acknowledge three types of style used by rhetors: grand, middle, and simple. The grand style uses ornate words and features a smooth arrangement of the words. It is marked by various rhetorical devices that we will discuss later. Grand style also includes figures of thought and figures of diction that we'll discuss later in this section. As we compare the three types of style, we'll refer to recent statements from President Bush. In his 2003 State of the Union speech, Bush used grand style in this passage: "Many challenges, abroad and at home, have arrived in a single season. In two years, America has gone from a sense of invulnerability to an awareness of peril; from bitter division in small matters to calm unity in great causes. And we go forward with confidence, because this call of history has come to the right country." Two features from this passage are indicative of the grand style. Bush used the figure of speech known as *antithesis*—combining opposing ideas in the same sentence—when he said "from a sense of invulnerability to an awareness of peril; from bitter division in small matters to calm unity." He also used *alliteration*—using the same consonant sound at the beginning of words located near each other—when he said, "And we go forward with *confidence,* because the *call* of history has *come* to the right *country*." The italicized words indicate his use of alliteration.

Although the grand style makes use of rhetorical figures and elegant language, the middle style uses words that are more common in meaning but that are not everyday speech. President Bush, in a radio address of August 9, 2003 used the middle style to praise U.S. efforts in Iraq:

> Our country and the nations of the Middle East are now safer. We're keeping our word to the Iraqi people by helping them to make their country an example of democracy and prosperity throughout the region. This long-term undertaking is vital to peace in that region and to the security of the United States. Our coalition and the people of Iraq have made remarkable progress in a short time, and we will complete the great work we have begun.

BOX 2.2   Analyzing Reeve's Speech

Text of Christopher Reeve's speech at the 1996 Democratic National Convention, August 26, 1996. (Condensed, but in its original structure.)

Thank you very, very much. Well, I just have to start with a challenge to the president. I've seen your train go by. And I think I can beat it. I'll even give you a head start.

If America really is a family, then we have to recognize that many members of our family are hurting. *And just to take one aspect of it, one in five of us have some kind of disability. You may have Parkinson's Disease or a neighbor with a spinal cord injury or a brother with AIDS.*

And if we're really committed to this idea of family, we've got to do something about it.

Now, first of all, our nation cannot tolerate discrimination of any kind. And that's why the Americans with Disabilities Act is so important. It is a civil rights law that is tearing down barriers both in architecture and in attitude. Its purpose is to give the disabled access not only to buildings but to every opportunity in society.

Now, of course, we have to balance the budget. And we will. We have to be extremely careful with every dollar we spend. But we've also got to take care of our family. And not slash programs that people need. *Now, one of the smartest things we could do about disability is to invest in research that will protect us from diseases, and will lead to cures.*

Right now, for example, about a quarter million Americans have a spinal cord injury, and our government spends about $8.7 billion a year just maintaining these members of our family. But we only spend $40 million a year on research that would actually improve the quality of their lives and get them off public assistance or even cure them. We've got to be smarter and do better.

The money we invest in research today is going to determine the quality of life for members of our family tomorrow. *Now, during my rehabilitation I met a young man named Gregory Patterson. He was innocently driving through Newark, New Jersey, and a stray bullet from a gang shooting went through a car window right into his neck and severed his spinal cord. Five years ago he might have died. Today because of research, he's alive.*

Now, America has a tradition that many nations probably envy. We frequently achieve the impossible. But that's part of our national character. That's what got us from one coast to another. That's what got us the largest economy in the world. That's what got us to the moon. Now, in my room while I was in rehab, there was a picture of the space shuttle blasting off. It was autographed by every astronaut down at NASA. On the top of that picture it says, "We found nothing is impossible."

Now, that should be our motto. *It's not a Democratic motto, not a Republican motto. It's an American motto.* It's not something one party can do alone. It's something we as a nation have to do together.

Illustrative passages are italicized.

Arrangement: Introduction—gets the audience's attention and established good will

Proof: Pathos

Arrangement: Central idea of the speech

Arrangement: First Main Point

Arrangement: Second Main Point

Proof: Claim to be proven in the next paragraph.

Proof: Reasoning that proves previous claim. Reeve is saying that if the government spent more on research, it could save money on health care.

Proof: Pathos

Arrangement: Third main point

Ethos: Reeve attempts to show good will to all Americans, no matter their political party.

BOX 2.2   Continued

So many of our dreams, so many dreams at first seem impossible, and then they seem improbable. And then when we summon the will, they soon become inevitable.

So if we can conquer outer space, we should be able to conquer inner space, too. And that's the frontier of the brain, the central nervous system and all the afflictions of the body that destroys so many lives and rob our country of so many potential.

Now, 56 years ago, FDR dedicated new buildings for the National Institutes of Health. *He said that "The defense this nation seeks involves a great deal more than building airplanes, ships, guns and bombs. We cannot be a strong nation unless we are a healthy nation."* He could have said that today. President Roosevelt showed us that a man who could barely lift himself out of a wheelchair could still lift this nation out of despair.

America is stronger when all of us take care of all of us. Giving new life to that ideal is the challenge before us tonight. Thank you very much.

Topoi: If we can conquer outer space, we should be able to conquer our personal limitations as well.

Enthymeme: We cannot be a strong nation unless we are a healthy nation. (Generalization) We are not yet a healthy nation. (Specific case—unstated) We are not yet a strong nation. (Claim—unstated)

Arrangement: Conclusion

From the speech made by Christopher Reeve at the 1996 Democratic National Convention. Reprinted with permission.

You'll note that Bush's style is clear, conversational, and direct; it lacks the ornamentation of the grand style.

The simple style sounds like everyday speech. It lacks ornamentation and smoothness. President Bush used the simple style on July 2, 2003 in a press conference when he sought to express support for U.S. troops in Iraq who were facing daily attacks by Iraqis loyal to Saddam Hussein. Bush said, "There are some who feel like that, you know, the conditions are such that they can attack us there. *My answer is, bring them on.* We got the force necessary to deal with the security situation." The key part of this passage—which is italicized—reflects a style of speaking that we don't typically associate with the presidency. Bush was antagonizing U.S. enemies by issuing them a challenge often used by in popular culture. In fact, the directness of this passage raised the ire of Bush's political opponents, who saw it as an invitation to attack U.S. troops. The *Rhetorica ad Herennium* cautions that each type of style can be taken too far. In this case, Bush may have pushed the limits of the simple style.

Qualities of Style   Each type of style must have certain qualities if it is to be appropriate and suitable to the speaker's purpose. The *Rhetorica ad Herennium* identifies three qualities of style: taste, artistic composition, and distinction. Taste refers to the correctness and clarity of the words that are used, and artistic composition to the "arrangement of words that gives uniform finish to the discourse in every part" (p. 271).

The *Rhetorica ad Herennium* pays most attention to distinction, or the effect of making the speech ornate and varied. Two primary techniques can be used to accomplish distinction: figures of diction and figures of thought. A figure of diction (or speech) derives adornment from the choice of words, and a figure of thought from the sorts of ideas involved. There are hundreds of rhetorical figures. You can find a comprehensive list provided by Dr. Gideon Burton of Brigham Young University at the website: http://rhetoric.byu.edu/.

Some typical figures of diction include:

- *Alliteration:* Repeating the same letter or sound within nearby words; usually occurs with the initial consonants. President Bush, in his 2005 inaugural address, provides this example (as indicated by boldface): "At this second gathering, our **duties** are **defined** not by the words I use, but by the history we have seen together.

- *Repetition:* Repetition of the same word or phrase at the beginning of successive clauses, sentences, or lines. John Kerry's acceptance speech at the 2004 Democratic National Convention contained this example of repetition (as indicated by boldface): "A great American novelist wrote that you can't go home again. He could not have imagined this evening. Tonight, I am home. **Home where** my public life began and those who made it possible live. **Home where** our nation's history was written in blod, idealism, and hope. **Home where** my parents showed me the values of family, faith, and country."

- *Tricolon:* Three parallel sentences or phrases of the same length occurring together in succession. For example, "I came; I saw; I conquered."

Some of the more common figures of thought include:

- *Antithesis:* The juxtaposition of contrasting words or ideas, usually in parallel structure. President John F. Kennedy said, "Ask not what your country can do for you, ask what you can do for your country."

- *Paradox:* A statement that on its face is self-contradictory, yet upon closer inspection makes a seemingly true statement. For example, "Whosoever loses their life, shall find it."

- *Oxymoron:* Placing two ordinarily opposing terms adjacent to one another. For example, "deafening silence" or "friendly fire."

Delivery

The *Rhetorica ad Herennium* provides one of the most comprehensive treatments of the fourth of the five canons, **delivery,** of any of the ancient theorists. It divided delivery into two components: voice quality and physical movement. Voice quality has three aspects: volume, stability, and flexibility. Volume refers to the loudness or softness of the speaker's voice and is primarily a gift of nature, according to the *Rhetorica ad Herennium.* Stability, which refers to the health of the voice, can be conserved by following several guidelines, such as not exerting the voice until it is warmed by speaking. The book notes, "For the windpipe is injured if filled with a violent outburst of sound before it has been soothed by soft intonations" (p. 193). This advice differs from the practice of some ancient speakers, who spoke loudly and in a shrill manner. In fact, the *Rhetorica ad Herennium* notes that "How often we must be duly thankful to nature, as here! Indeed what we declare to be beneficial

---

BOX 2.3 Internet Activity: Presidential Rhetoric

We have said that the five canons can be used by rhetors to create rhetorical messages and also by critics to analyze rhetoric. Access the president's website at http://www.whitehouse.gov. Choose a recent speech by the president and use the five canons to analyze and evaluate the speech. Use the questions provided here to guide your analysis. What type of proof does the president use? How is the speech arranged? Describe the stylistic elements of the speech, such as use of metaphor or rhetorical figures. If you can watch the speech, describe the president's delivery. How might memory have been an important part of the creating and delivering the speech? Finally, was the speech effective? Why or why not?

---

for conserving the voice applies also to agreeableness of delivery, and, as a result, what benefits our voice likewise finds favour in the hearer's taste" (p. 195). In other words, a pleasant, smooth delivery is not only good for the voice but it is pleasing to the audience as well.

The final aspect of vocal delivery is flexibility—the ability to vary the intonations of the voice. Like stability, this aspect of speaking can be cultivated by theory and practice. There are three forms, or tones, of vocal flexibility: conversational tone, tone of debate, and tone of amplification. A conversational tone is closest to natural conversation. It can be used to narrate a series of events or elicit a laugh from the audience. The tone of debate is used to present and refute arguments. It can be quick and full-voiced or punctuated with frequent pauses. Finally, the tone of amplification is used to rouse the hearer to wrath or move the audience member to pity. Each type of tone is useful for a particular type of speech, as outlined by the *Rhetorica ad Herennium.*

Physical movement, the second component of delivery according to the *Rhetorica ad Herennium,* includes gesture and facial expression. Gestures should not be conspicuous, the treatise claims, and facial expressions lend credibility to what is said. Additionally, gestures should match the tone of the speaker. For instance, to enhance conversational tone of the narrative, the speaker should lightly move the right hand and use facial expressions that correspond with the tone of the speech.

Memory

The fifth and final canon is **memory.** Although Aristotle does not discuss memory, the *Rhetorica ad Herennium* calls it the "guardian of all parts of rhetoric" (p. 205). Without access to libraries of research, ancient rhetors could only rely on their memory of past experiences to construct speeches. The great teachers of rhetoric included instruction in how to memorize large amounts of information. Usually, the student was encouraged to create mental pictures of the objects, ideas, or items to remember.

Memory's status as an important canon of rhetoric has waxed and waned, depending on how rhetoric has been used in particular cultures. Using your knowledge of the five canons, analyze and evaluate a recent speech by the United States president by completing the Internet Exercise, Presidential Rhetoric (see Box 2.3).

SUMMARIZING CLASSICAL RHETORIC

In the previous chapter, we discussed some of the important ideas that rhetorical theory addresses. We'll summarize the rhetorical theory of the classical period here in general terms.

Defining Rhetoric

Classical theorists, though slightly different in their approach, generally equated rhetoric with the study of persuasion and influence. There was also general agreement among classical theorists that students could be taught the art of rhetoric through instruction, imitation, and practice. Some theorists saw natural ability as being important, but most believed that training in rhetoric could improve even the poorest of rhetors. Plato and Quintilian add an ethical element we'll discuss later in this section. In short, they believed that rhetoric had be effective and performed by someone with high moral values.

Rhetoric and Knowledge

You'll recall from the first chapter that epistemology is the study of knowledge. We have seen that there were three ways of looking at the relationship between rhetoric and knowledge in the classical ages. We have discussed that Plato, in his dialogue *Gorgias,* believed that rhetoric was a tool to deceive audiences and that it could not be used to establish the truth. Truth, he believed, was known separate from rhetoric and that, in fact, rhetoric hindered the search for truth. Instead, individuals should use the dialectic method to determine truth.

The Sophists, on the other hand, thought that rhetoric could be used to find what was probably true in a given situation. Remember that the Sophists traveled throughout Greece and were exposed to a variety of ways of thinking. This background conditioned them to think that various audiences had various ways of arriving at truth. In short, the Sophists were most concerned with using rhetoric to determine relative truth.

The other key figure in the ancient debate over epistemology was Aristotle. He argued that in some situations, truth, or knowledge, was certain and in other situations it was probable. Rhetoric, he wrote, was used in the realm of probable truth and could be used to promote what was probably true. He differs from Plato, who believed in absolute truth in all situations. You'll see that these three schools of thought regarding rhetoric and truth—rhetoric obscures truth, rhetoric establishes relative truth, and rhetoric conveys what is probably true—will continue to be present in rhetoric theory even to contemporary times.

Rhetoric and Identity

The three views of the relationship between rhetoric and knowledge mirror those of the relationship between rhetoric and identity. Plato believed that only our souls could know reality and that very few individuals have the ability to know truth. Plato believed that every human has the potential to know truth, since "a soul which has never seen the truth cannot pass into this human form of ours" (*Gorgias,* 249, p. 32). Different people see different levels of truth and thus are destined, at birth, to have a given occupation, with future seekers of wisdom and beauty, lovers, and Muses hierarchically superior. To the Sophists, reality was a product of social interaction and was always changing. Reality was , in other words, relative to the situation.

Rhetoric and Judgment

Plato, of course, had the most to say about rhetoric's relationship to ethics. "Rhetoric, like every other practice, is always to be used to serve the ends of justice, and for that alone" (*Gorgias,* 527, p. 107). Plato initially argued that rhetoric was a knack— a form of flattery aimed at pleasure. Yet he refined this position to include the fact that the pleasurable sound of rhetoric may be used to eradicate injustice. In this case, rhetoric, as an art of pleasure, aims at the good, at justice. So although rhetoric is a false art, when practiced by "moral artists," rhetoric can achieve the good. Not surprisingly, Quintilian shared many of Plato's ideas about rhetoric and morality. Quintilian argued that a rhetor must have good character and have sound goals in mind.

As we have seen, the Sophists had a view of truth that was relative. This view extended to their view of ethics. Jarratt (1991) explains that "questions of value must be referred to subjective perception and to the historical and geographical specificity of local custom" (p. 96). Ultimately, the Sophists' view of epistemology, ontology, and ethics are all linked by a common belief in relativism. That people were the measure of all things extended throughout each of these philosophical orientations. Despite the relativist position adopted by the Sophists, morality and ethics were a concern for them. As Jarratt notes, "Though there is no philosophic 'good' grounding the sophistic project, questions of ethics permeate their work" (1991, p. 96).

Aristotle represents the middle ground between Plato and the Sophists. Rhetoric was a way to promote justice, he believed, but he also recognized that probability played a key role. That is, rhetors could only discuss what was probably true. Like Plato, and Isocrates, Cicero, and Quintilian, Aristotle firmly believed that a student of rhetoric should be a student of many subjects and possess a wide range of knowledge in order to be effective.

DISCUSSION QUESTIONS

1. Does the distinction between deliberative, judicial, and demonstrative speaking hold true today? Cite an example of each from contemporary culture. To what degree do these speeches reflect the four qualities of public rhetorical texts outlined by Brummett—verbal, expositional, discrete, hierarchical?

2. Can you name a contemporary equivalent to the Sophists? Who? How is this group similar to the Sophists? How is it different?

3. How are contemporary educational systems similar to those of ancient Greece and Rome? How are they different?

4. To what extent are the five canons an effective tool for evaluating and creating rhetoric today?

5. Which of the five canons do you think is most important? Which do you think is the least important?

6. Choose an advertisement from a recent magazine. How does the ad appeal to the reader's emotions? How is logical reasoning used? How does the ad develop the credibility of the brand or product advertised?

7. For each of the issues that are summarized at the end of the chapter—epistemology, ontology, and ethics—which view of rhetoric most closely reflects your thinking on the topic?

GLOSSARY TERMS

classical rhetoric   The rhetorical theory of the period lasting from approximately 400 B.C.E. to 100 C.E.

judicial rhetoric   Rhetoric used to prove the justice or injustice of a past act.

deliberative rhetoric   Rhetoric used to argue that a future action would be advantageous or harmful.

demonstrative rhetoric   Rhetoric used to praise or blame an individual or group that encourages the audience to accept or reject particular values. Often called epideictic rhetoric.

Sophists   A group of teachers in ancient Greece whose subject matter included rhetoric. The Sophists believed that truth and morality were relative.

dialectic   A philosophic method of determining truth through a series of interactions.

five canons of rhetoric   The five main components for a rhetorical text, including invention, arrangement, style, delivery, and memory.

invention   The first canon of rhetoric, which concerns developing the substance of the speech.

stasis   A theoretical framework for identifying the points in a rhetorical dispute.

ethos   Proof based on the rhetor's credibility.

pathos   Proof based on an appeal to the audience's emotions.

logos   Proof based on logical reasoning.

arrangement   The second canon of rhetoric, which concerns the ordering of a rhetorical text.

style   The third canon of rhetoric, which concerns the verbal ornamentation of a speech, using such techniques as rhetorical figures.

delivery   The fourth canon of rhetoric, which concerns the vocal qualities and physical movements used by a rhetor.

memory   The fifth canon of rhetoric, used to recall information for a speech.

3

Style, Delivery, and
Rhetorical Theory

Learning Objectives

After reading this chapter, you should have a better understanding of the stylistic aspects of rhetorical theory. Specifically, you should be able to:

1. Describe what is meant by sublimity and identify examples of sublimity in contemporary rhetoric.
2. Discuss the impact of the Roman Empire and Christianity on the practice of rhetoric in the third, fourth, and fifth centuries and in the Middle Ages.
3. Evaluate Peter Ramus's argument concerning the distinction between rhetoric and logic.
4. Characterize the belletristic and elocutionary movements, identifying their chief proponents and principles.

No doubt you have heard the word *rhetoric* used to refer to the flowery or ornate use of language. This use of the term usually takes a negative perspective, indicating that pleasing words are somehow misleading or that they substitute for genuine action. Consider the following examples:

- The leaders of Pakistan recently urged Indian leaders to practice a "*rhetorical* restraint regime" to avoid jeopardizing peace talks between the two countries.
- The Telegraph of London recently ran the headline "Iran is important, but don't mistake its noisy *rhetoric* for reality."

Table 3.1 Major Events in Rhetorical Theory: Middle Ages to Twentieth Century

Time Period	Chapter 3 *(Focus on style and delivery)*	Chapter 4 *(Focus on logic, science, and argumentation)*
Roman Empire	200: Longinus *(On the Sublime)*	
	396: St. Augustine *(On Christian Doctrine)*	
Middle Ages	1135: *Rationes dictandi*	
	1200: Various preaching texts	
Renaissance	1544: Talaeus *(Institutiones Oratorie)*	
	1555: Ramus *(Dialectique)*	
		1605: Francis Bacon ("Advancement of Learning")
Enlightenment		1690: John Locke *(Essay of Human Understanding)*
	1762: Thomas Sheridan *(Lectures on Elocution)*	1776: George Campbell *(Philosophy of Rhetoric)*
	1783: Hugh Blair *(Lectures on Rhetoric and Belles Lettres)*	
		1828: Richard Whately *(Elements of Rhetoric)*
		1958: Stephen Toulmin *(Uses of Argument)*
		1958: Chaim Perelman *(The New Rhetoric)*

■ The online edition of the *Oil and Gas Journal* proclaimed that "US political *rhetoric* over energy prices expected to heat up this summer."

Perhaps you have heard *rhetoric* used like this in other situations.

After reading the first two chapters of this book, though, you should realize by now that rhetoric is a term that has far wider meaning and that its everyday use largely ignores the theoretical principles that inform it. Following the fall of the Roman Republic and up to the beginning of the twentieth century, a great number of influential theorists focused their attention on the stylistic and presentational qualities of rhetoric. One theorist we'll study in this chapter, Peter Ramus, even taught that rhetoric should only concern style and delivery and that matters of proof, invention, and arrangement belonged to the discipline of philosophy.

We will cover about seventeen hundred years of history in this chapter, from 100 B.C.E. to 1800. The previous chapter addressed each of the five canons; the ideas we discuss in this chapter will be linked by a common focus on style and delivery. Part of this chapter will examine Robert Scott's ideas about the aesthetic period that we discussed in the first chapter. Chronologically, this chapter overlaps in some ways with Chapter 4. Table 3.1 displays the relationship between these

two chapters and will help you keep in mind the larger picture regarding the theories of rhetoric we'll be discussing there. Specifically, we'll address six key topics
here: the Second Sophistic, the Christianization of rhetoric, rhetoric in the Middle
Ages, humanistic education and rhetoric, the belletristic movement, and the
elocutionary movement.

THE SECOND SOPHISTIC

When we finished Chapter 2, the time was 100 C.E., and the Roman Republic—the democratic government of ancient Rome—had been replaced by the
Roman Empire—a period of time marked by the rule of totalitarian Caesars.
Rome would control Western Europe, Spain, and parts of northern Africa for the
next three hundred years, until about 400 C.E. During this time span, however,
the Roman Empire would be split between East and West. In large part, the empire
was pagan, although the seeds of Christianity were being sown throughout the
region. In fact, the Catholic Church would become a significant political and cultural force throughout much of Europe. We will look more closely at the relationship between the church and rhetoric in the next section of this chapter.

The time period between the Roman Republic and Middle Ages (roughly
50 to 400) is often known as the **Second Sophistic** in the history of rhetoric. As
in the ancient Greek culture some 400 years earlier, traveling teachers of rhetoric
became popular. Enos (1995) explained that the Roman sophists revived much of
the rhetorical theory from the Greeks, quoting works by Aristotle and others.
However, the purpose of rhetoric was much different in the Second Sophistic
than in the First Sophistic. Instead of seeing rhetoric as a tool for political action,
teachers of the Second Sophistic focused more on stylistic matters. Rhetoric was
used for ceremonial or epideictic forms (Enos, 1995). The Second Sophistic, noted
Enos, "stressed artistic features and literary refinement" (1995, p. 68). During this
period, rhetoric was taught in the educational system of Rome, and students
learned rhetoric in much the same was as the Greeks. Yet, again, the purpose for
which rhetoric was practiced was significantly different, because of the lack of a
democratic government in Rome.

Perhaps the most illustrative text of the Second Sophistic and its approach to
rhetoric is *On the Sublime*. The book was most likely written by a Roman teacher
named Cassius Longinus in 200 A.D. The text focuses on how to achieve style in
rhetoric. In this section, we'll explore this ancient but significant work by defining what Longinus meant by the sublime and then by showing how he taught
rhetors to achieve subliminity. You can read the entire book online at http://
classicpersuasion.org/pw/longinus/.

What is the Sublime?

The **sublime,** according to Longinus, is the use of language to momentarily lift
the audience members outside of themselves. He defined the sublime as "The
process by which we may raise our natural powers to a required advance in scale"

(*On the Sublime,* section I). The sublime was not an appeal to logic, or even emotion, but an appeal to the stylistic and aesthetic faculties of the audience. Longinus traced the sublime to the speaker's use of language: "Subliminity is always an eminence and excellence in language" (section I).

The sublime has a powerful impact on audience. In fact, Longinus placed the sublime ahead of logical, pathetic, or ethical appeals. He argued,

> For it is not to persuasion but to ecstasy that passages of extraordinary genius carry the hearer: now the marvelous, with its power to amaze, is always and necessarily stronger than that which seeks to persuade and to please: to be persuaded rests usually with ourselves, genius brings force sovereign and irresistible to bear upon every hearer, and takes its stand high above him. (section I)
>
> For it is a fact of Nature that the soul is raised by true subliminity, it gains a proud step upwards, it is filled with joy and exultation, as though itself had produced what it hears. (section VI)

According to Longinus, subliminity is remembered, it is impossible to resist, and it promotes reflection on the part of the listener.

Subliminity is more than the manipulation of language, though. To Longinus, subliminity can only be achieved by excellent speakers who possess a "genius" for style. The speaker must know more than how to use the canons of invention and arrangement. Rather, a single passage may reveal the speaker's eloquence and "genius." Longinus states, "Sublimity, we know, brought out at the happy moment, parts all the matter this way and that, and like a lightening flash, reveals, at a stroke and in its entirety, the power of the orator" (section I). After defining the sublime, Longinus explains the dangers of trying to create the sublime without having the natural and artistic ability to do so.

Sources of the Sublime

Longinus saw the sublime as a product of both nature and art. A speaker had to have natural abilities to achieve the sublime, but there were also ways of learning how to create sublimity in a speech. Longinus stressed that natural ability was a primary factor and that artistic elements were secondary. In all, five qualities are necessary for the sublime. Two qualities are natural—passion and great thoughts—and three are the result of artistry—use of figures, diction, and composition. Let's explore the various elements of the sublime.

Natural Qualities   Two qualities of the sublime cannot be taught; a speaker must be born with passion and great thoughts. Longinus did not discuss passion at length, but he did notice that some speakers could be sublime without passion, although they are limited in their eloquence. Additionally, the presence of passion does not necessarily make a speaker sublime. Longinus cites examples of Roman orators who were passionate but not sublime. In sum, he explains the role of passion in creating the sublime thus: "I should feel confidence in maintaining that nothing reaches great eloquence so surely as genuine passion in the right place" (section VIII). Likewise, the sublime comes from speakers who have a great mind. Longinus explains,

> The true Orator must have no low ungenerous spirit, for it is not possible that they who think small thoughts, fit for slaves, and practice them in all their daily life, should put out anything to deserve wonder and immortality. Great words issue, and it cannot be otherwise, from those whose thoughts are weighty. So it is on the lips of men of the highest spirit that words of rare greatness are found. (section IX)

Longinus suggested three particular methods of communicating great thoughts: silence, amplification, and appeals to imagination. In some situations, the speaker doesn't have to say anything to communicate a profound thought. Silence, then, is a form of sublimity that speakers with a great mind have mastered. Additionally, amplification—the arrangement of thoughts in ascending order—can be used to create the sublime if it is not done mechanically. That is, amplification must be accompanied by great thoughts and used by a great speaker in order to achieve the sublime. Finally, the ability to use imagination, or to "see the things of which you speak, and place them under the eyes of your hearers" (section X) is the sign of a great mind, according to Longinus.

Artistic Qualities In treating the artistic methods of creating sublimity, Longinus begins with a discussion of the proper use of figures of speech and thought. You'll recall that we briefly discussed rhetorical figures in the previous chapter. Longinus notes that a speaker must handle them properly in order to achieve greatness. There are hundreds of figures of speech and thought that a speaker may use to achieve sublimity. In *On the Sublime* Longinus highlights a few of them.

Asyndeton is achieved by dropping connecting words—such as "and"—from a series of words or statements. Longinus quotes Xenophon for an example: "Locking their shields, they pushed, fought, slew, died." You'll note that the word "and" is not included before the last word in the series, "died." The effect of this rhetorical figure, according to Longinus, is to "carry the impression of a struggle, where the meaning is at once checked and hurried on" (section XIX).

Hyperbaton is a disturbance of the proper sequence of phrases or thoughts. Longinus explains this figure in vivid detail, saying that a speaker may "put forward one set of ideas, then spring aside to another, thrusting in a parenthesis out of all logic, then wheel round to the first, and in their [the audience's] excitement, like a ship before an unsteady gale, drag phrases and thoughts sharply across, now this way, now that" (section XXII). The effect is that the words don't seem to be prepared but that they emerge naturally from the speaker. Longinus cites an example from Dionysius of Phocace, who extolled his audience, "Our fortunes rest on the edge of a razor, O Ionians, whether we are to be free or slaves" (section XXII). Longinus notes that natural order would have been to start with the recognition of the audience—"O Ionians." Then, the speaker would have presented the choice—to be free or slaves—before telling them of the consequence of their choice. By rearranging the natural order, the speaker was more eloquent and more able to achieve the sublime.

Longinus also discusses *periphrasis,* which is the use of plain words to mean something far more elegant. This figure must be handled carefully and is one of the more difficult to use, according to Longinus. Plato, for instance, referred to death as an "appointed journey" and the funeral rites as "a public escort" given by the deceased friends and relatives. Longinus explained that plain speech used in this way creates harmony with the thoughts and eloquent words that surround the plain speech.

The second artistic method of achieving sublimity is diction, or choosing the right words and grand words. Beautiful words, said Longinus, are "the light of thought" (section XXX), but they must be chosen and used carefully. Using grand words in places where they do not fit would be similar to fastening "a large tragic mask upon a little child" (section XXX). Particular care should be taken when employing metaphors. Longinus explained that two or three, at the most, are appropriate for a subject. As with all elements of sublimity, proportion is key. A speech that takes on too many ornamental elements does not achieve greatness, or sublimity.

Finally, Longinus addressed the issue of composition, which is the arrangement of words. The correct ordering of words creates rhythm, melody, and beauty: "Composition, I say, must by all these means at once soothe us as we hear and also dispose to stateliness, and high mood, and sublimity" (section XXXIX). Among the elements of composition that detract from sublimity are broken rhythm, excessive conciseness of expression, and words that sound poorly when placed together.

Conclusion

Longinus's *On the Sublime* was reportedly written in 200 C.E. The book details a specific way of using rhetoric to achieve style, eloquence, and sublimity. For nearly a thousand years after the book was written, rhetorical scholars were influenced by his treatment of style and considered style as one of the most important canons of rhetoric. For a contemporary example of Longinus's view of sublime rhetoric, read the Critical Insight box for this chapter (see Box 3.1). As we continue our discussion below, you'll continue to see how style dominated the study of rhetoric.

CHRISTIANIZATION OF RHETORIC

The rhetoric of the Second Sophistic was largely thought to be a pagan practice incompatible with the goals of Christianity, which was beginning to make its way across the Roman Empire. Church leaders were at first critical of rhetoric, but were forced to use rhetoric themselves. Initially, noted Barilli (1989) church leaders used rhetoric to defend Christianity against charges brought by the pagans. Yet tension would exist in church thinking about rhetoric. Church leaders were fearful that effective eloquence would outweigh the true facts upon which the Christian faith rested. St. Augustine, the once revered teacher of rhetoric who renounced rhetoric for Christianity (see Figure 3.1), would provide the church with a way to

---

BOX 3.1   Critical Insights: Ronald Reagan's Sublime Rhetorical Style

Former President Ronald Reagan was, by most accounts, an exceptional speaker. His mastery of sublimity can easily be seen in a speech he gave on January 28, 1986 following the explosion of the space shuttle Challenger. Let's examine the sublime features of two of the speech's passages.

First, let's discuss the following passage: *"Your loved ones were daring and brave, and they had that special grace, that special spirit that says, 'Give me a challenge and I'll meet it with joy.' They had a hunger to explore the universe and discover its truths. They wished to serve, and they did. They served all of us."* You'll notice here several sublime features:

- The use of the figure of speech alliteration with the words "special grace, that special spirit that says . . ."
- Reagan used plain words—"they served"—to mean something far more grand. The astronauts who perished in the explosion, in fact, gave their lives in service to the nation.
- Reagan's choice of the word "joy" when referring to how the astronauts met challenges is interesting as well. Usually we don't think of meeting challenges with joy, but rather with determination or hard work. His use of the word "joy" creates an element of interest and surprise that lends to the speech's style.

Now, consider the final passage from the speech: *"The crew of the space shuttle Challenger honored us by the manner in which they lived their lives. We will never forget them, nor the last time we saw them, this morning, as they prepared for their journey and waved good-bye and 'slipped the surly bonds of earth' to 'touch the face of God.' "* Here, Reagan again touches on the elegant:

- If you have heard Reagan deliver this speech—or any of his speeches—you can hear the naturalness in his voice. According to Longinus, the speaker's ability to be natural is a key element of achieving the sublime. In this passage, Reagan's smooth natural delivery comes through almost without effort.
- Reagan's use of the statement—"slipped the surly bonds of earth"—also creates the sublime. Longinus wrote that the sublime consisted of great ideas and places. Surely there can be no greater expanse, nothing more sublime, than space.

Read Reagan's complete speech at http://www.reaganfoundation.org/reagan/speeches/challenger.asp and look for more examples of the sublime.

---

use rhetoric to make the truth effective for an audience. Enos (1995) noted that St. Augustine "recognized and promoted the study of rhetoric as a tool for strengthening Christianity. It was St. Augustine who baptized rhetoric into Christianity" (p. 101). You can read more about St. Augustine in Box 3.2, Biography of a Theorist.

Although we are discussing St. Augustine in this chapter—within a stylistic framework—keep in mind that St. Augustine offered a comprehensive theory of rhetoric. He focused on each of the five canons of rhetoric that we studied in the previous chapter. In fact, much of his primary work, *On Christian Doctrine*, provided guidance in how pastors could invent topics for discussion and prove them for their audiences. However, the overall purpose for St. Augustine's rhetorical theory—as a sermonic art form—fits more closely with later discussion in this chapter than it does with that in our previous chapter, where we saw rhetoric viewed as a political and legal tool.

On Christian Doctrine provided St. Augustine's most complete view of how Christian clergy could use rhetoric. Augustine believed that there were "two

FIGURE 3.1   Artist's Painting of St. Augustine.

things necessary to the treatment of the scripture: a way of discovering those things which are to be understood, and a way of teaching what we have learned" (p. 117).* *On Christian Doctrine* is divided into four books, or chapters. The first three books are devoted to a study of how priests could learn the truth from the scriptures. The fourth book focuses on how these truths could be effectively presented by the clergy member. Let's take a closer look at Augustine's ideas about how rhetoric could be used effectively by Christian clergy.

Discovering the Truth in Scripture

St. Augustine, like Cicero, taught that the goals of rhetoric were to educate, delight, and persuade. The content, though, for St. Augustine is not the search for truth, but rather to make the truth of the scriptures effective for the audience. The first three books of *On Christian Doctrine* focus on learning what is truthful from the

---

*All quotations from St. Augustine, *On Christian Doctrine,* trans. by D. W. Robertson, Jr.
© 1958. Reprinted by permission of Pearson Education, Inc. Upper Saddle River, NJ.

BOX 3.2 Biography of a Theorist: St. Augustine

St. Augustine was born on November 13, 354 in Algeria, which is in northern Africa. His mother was a devout Christian, his father converted on his deathbed. Young Augustine grew up following the pagan ways of his father and the Romans. Augustine was greatly influenced by Cicero, whom we studied in the previous chapter. Augustine taught for a while in his hometown of Carthage, before going to Rome. There he gained one of the most prominent academic positions in Milan, the chair of rhetoric, which held the promise of a successful political career. In 387, Augustine was baptized on the night before Easter. He rejected the study of rhetoric, at which he had previously excelled. He soon became a priest and by 395 was Bishop of Hippo, which was in Africa. Augustine died in 430, as the German barbarians, the Vandals, took over his city. Augustine's life parallels, in many ways, the fall of the pagan Roman Empire and the rise of the Christian Middle Ages.

Augustine's chief work concerning rhetoric is *On Christian Doctrine*, which is often thought of as a training manual for clergy members. Enos (1999) noted that this book "excluded the paganism of the Second Sophistic, incorporated the precepts of rhetorical doctrine into Christian education and emerged with a new era of Christian rhetoric" (p. 101).

---

scriptures. Here St. Augustine tells his readers that they must understand the nature of language, symbols, and meaning but also that they must rely on their faith and prayer to learn the truth of the scriptures.

Initially, Augustine focused on some of the linguistic difficulties present in the scripture and how clergy could make sense of these difficulties. Augustine begins Book I with a study of signs and meanings. He distinguishes between signs and the things that they represent. Augustine spends the rest of the time in Book I discussing faith and a person's relationship to God.

In Book II, Augustine explains that signs are either natural or conventional. Natural signs, like smoke billowing from a fire or animal tracks in the snow, are not the subject of Augustine's study. Instead, he focuses on conventional signs, which are created by people to convey ideas to others. Augustine addresses two central issues relative to signs and meaning. First, he focuses on reasoning and truth; second, he addresses issues of ambiguity in meaning. In both cases, Augustine recounts much of his classical training in rhetoric and how it may be useful for religious pursuits.

Augustine thought that the study of reasoning, for instance, can be of value when determining the meaning of scripture: "The science of disputation is of great value for understanding and solving all sorts of questions that appear in sacred literature" (p. 67). In fact, he believed that reasoning was created by God. However, humans can reason incorrectly, especially if they start with faulty propositions about what is true or false. The "truth of propositions," Augustine explains, "is a matter to be discovered in the sacred books of the Church" (p. 68). When faced with a choice between following a true proposition or a faulty inference, Augustine is clear:

> There are those who boast when they have learned the rules of valid
> inference as if they had learned the truth of propositions. And on the other

hand, there are some who know many true propositions but think ill of themselves because they do not know the rules of inference. But he who knows that there is a resurrection of the dead is better than another who knows that it follows from the proposition that there is no resurrection of the dead that 'then Christ is not risen,' (p. 70)

Augustine also acknowledges the difficulty in distinguishing between the literal and figurative meanings of words and offers advice for clergy on how to read the scripture because of this difficulty. He explains, "When, however, from a single passage in the Scripture not one but two or more meanings are elicited, even if what he who wrote the passage intended remains hidden, there is no danger if any of the meanings may be seen to be congruous with the truth taught in other passages of the Holy Scriptures" (p. 102). Thus, by turning to Scripture, one can learn to choose from a range of possible meanings.

It is important to note that knowing the truth of propositions is often a matter of faith and is found in the Bible. Augustine offers this lengthy view of the role of faith in learning the meaning of the scriptures:

> Students of the Holy Scriptures are not only to be admonished that they know the kinds of expression that are used there, and that they observe vigilantly and hold by memory the manner in which things are customarily said there, but also, and this is the most important, that they pray for understanding. For in these books concerning which they are studious they read that 'the Lord giveth wisdom: and of his mouth cometh prudence and knowledge.' (*On Christian Doctrine,* p. 117)

Yet the Christians could still learn from the pagan rhetorical theories, according to Augustine. In Books II and III, Augustine provided an account of rhetoric that is reminiscent of Cicero or Aristotle. James J. Murphy, a rhetorical scholar who has studied Augustine noted, "It is plain throughout that he intends the student of this subject to master the ordinary things taught in the schools" (Murphy, 1960, p. 407). Additionally, Murphy summarized Augustine's view of how knowledge of rhetoric was important to the Christian clergy: "Throughout the three books he is concerned with the uses of words, and points out that the preacher needs a knowledge of language to equip himself with the tools of understanding" (p. 407).

Preaching

Book IV is where St. Augustine changed his focus to that of preaching, demonstrating how clergy can use rhetoric effectively. He opens Book IV by defending the teaching of rhetoric to Christian ministers and asks whether the pagans, those advocating falsehood should "speak briefly, clearly, and plausibly while the defenders of truth speak so that they tire their listeners, make themselves difficult to understand and what they have to say dubious?" (p. 118). He then asks, "While the faculty of eloquence, which is of greater value in urging either evil or justice, is in itself indifferent, why should it not be obtained for the uses of the good in the service of truth if the evil usurp it for the winning of perverse and vain causes in defense of iniquity and error?" (pp. 118–119). Thus, Augustine sees rhetoric as a neutral art form, but one that should be taught to those seeking to understand and communicate the truth—the Christians. Murphy (1960) observed that "Augustine appreciates the role of God's grace in preaching, but he warns that the preacher must do his work well too" (p. 410).

Augustine's focus was clearly on the canons of style and delivery when he instructs about rhetoric. He defines oratory, or eloquence, as "a most skillful use of vocabulary and plentiful verbal ornaments" (p. 119). Several key ideas emerge from Book IV of *On Christian Doctrine*.

First, Augustine is concerned that speakers are understandable. Some things, noted Augustine, are not understood or poorly understood and eloquent speech may further hinder the audience's ability to understand the topic. Clarity in presenting these ideas was of foremost importance for Augustine. In particular, the preacher must take care to monitor his audience during the sermon. As soon as the audience understands, the speaker should move on to a new topic. Thus, Augustine argued against using a prepared delivery style in favor of an extemporaneous style.

Christian preachers should also seek to use all three aims of speaking: to teach, please, and persuade. No matter how clearly stated is the instruction and how eloquent is the presentation, the preacher must move the audience to take action. He explained, "It is necessary therefore for the ecclesiastical orator, when he urges that something be done, not only to teach that he may instruct and to please that he may hold attention, but also to persuade that he may be victorious" (p. 138).

Despite the fact that the preacher must be eloquent and that his talent influenced his effectiveness, Augustine believed that that preacher was a mouthpiece for the true words of God. Thus, it was important that the speaker also be a good person, who lives up to the virtuous rhetoric he practiced. Augustine puts it succinctly: "However, the life of the speaker has greater weight in determining whether he is obediently heard than any grandness of eloquence" (p. 164).

Echoing Cicero, Augustine discussed the three levels of style: plain, middle, and grand. Each style has a different end, but Augustine noted that the speaker must manage all three simultaneously. He explained, "But no one should think that it is contrary to theory to mix these three manners: rather, speech should be varied with all types of style in so far as this may be done appropriately" (p. 158). If the speaker would maintain one style for too long, he would lose the listener. Throughout his discussion of style, Augustine was very conscious of speaking in a way that matches the audience's expectations. His theory of rhetoric was very audience centered, particularly in terms of educating clergy about the style they should employ. Overall, he urged the speaker to be sensitive to the audience and have the ability to adapt if necessary.

Conclusion

In all, Augustine demonstrated how Christians could use rhetoric in ways that were consonant with their faith, not in ways opposed to it. Enos noted, "Modifying, rather than opposing, rhetoric gave Christians a system of expression that rivaled the pagan-oriented Second Sophistic" (1999, p. 101), and "Sophists taught rhetoric with an eye toward success in the city of man; St. Augustine offered a rhetoric that instructed with a perspective directed toward success in the city of God" (p. 102). By learning the truth from scripture and then making that truth effective for audience, Augustine also provided a bridge from the Greek and Roman study of rhetoric to the study and practice of rhetoric by the Christians in the Middle Ages. Enos makes this conclusion about St. Augustine's role in the history of rhetoric: "St. Augustine's treatise illustrates how rhetoric not only survived Christianity but became assimilated into it" (Enos, 1999, p. 102). In sum, through Augustine we have seen how the pagan practice of rhetoric was adapted to fulfill the needs of the church. Although St. Augustine provided a comprehensive theory of rhetoric, his focus shifted from the political and legal ends that characterized rhetoric in the classical period. As we proceed, you'll see a continued emphasis on nonpolitical forms of rhetoric as well as a shift toward viewing rhetoric as being concerned mainly with style and delivery.

RHETORIC IN THE MIDDLE AGES

The period of time following the collapse of the Roman Empire, in about the fifth century, until the Renaissance, or the fifteenth century, is known as the Middle Ages, or medieval period. This period of time was marked by the spreading influence of the church and the presence of feudal kingdoms, which were essentially local forms of government. In this section, we'll survey a brief history of the Middle Ages and two dominant rhetorical arts of this period.

History

The Romans were constantly threatened by outside invaders from the north and from the east. The Roman Empire would split into "three distinct cultures: Byzantium, Islam and the Frankish kingdoms of the West" (Enos, 1999, p. 103). The center of Byzantium, to the east, was Constantinople, located in what is now Turkey. The Catholic Church, as we saw in the previous section, had gained political and legal power in both the Western and Eastern parts of the Roman Empire. Church leaders were influential in many aspects of society in the Middle Ages, including determining how rhetoric would be taught and used. In Byzantium, church leaders tolerated rhetoric to a greater degree than in the West. Enos noted, "As a rule, Byzantine emperors also supported rhetoric—with the stipulation that it be compatible with Christian doctrine" (p. 103). In fact, many of the ancient Greek and Roman rhetorical texts—written by pagans such as Aristotle and Cicero—were taught in Byzantine schools, but by Christian teachers. Greek and Roman culture, and their significant texts, were well preserved in Byzantine libraries and its educational system. Likewise, in the Muslim culture, Latin and Greek texts, in particular, were translated and preserved. Enos noted that in both the Byzantine and Muslim cultures, rhetoric survived, was assimilated into the new cultures, and faced no direct threat.

In the Western part of the now defunct Roman Empire, Christianity significantly changed the practice of rhetoric and little effort was made to preserve the Greek and Roman texts. For nearly a thousand years—from approximately 400 to 1400—locally powerful political and military leaders, or lords, would govern small kingdoms in what is now Western Europe. People lived in small villages, or manors, that surrounded the lord's castle. Members of the lord's village would fight against invaders, but mostly lived in isolation. We often refer to this form of government as feudalism. There was no central form of government in Europe during the Middle Ages. During this period, however, Europeans were united by their faith.

Some of the feudal lords sought to keep the Latin culture alive by studying and teaching its literature, art, and rhetoric. Among the famous teachers was the English poet Alcuin of the eighth century. Yet it should be stated that a great deal of Greek and Latin culture was lost among the new societies of the West. The remainder of this chapter will primarily focus on rhetoric as it was practiced in Europe, particularly France, Germany, and Great Britain.

Medieval Arts

Throughout the Middle Ages, rhetoric took a very different form than it had in the Roman Empire. Public deliberation by government officials was replaced by more bureaucratic decisionmaking. In addition, written, rather than oral, communication would become widespread. We'll discuss here two significant forms of rhetoric during the Middle Ages: the art of letter writing and the art of preaching.

The art of letter writing, known as *artes dictaminis,* became an important medium through which government and church officials conducted business. Given the decentralized nature of government and the growing amount of land that government controlled, letters became the only practical means through which business could be carried out. Importantly, the theory and practice of letter writing reflected, for the first time, a focus on written forms of rhetoric, rather than oral.

Initially, the art of letter writing followed stock formulae (Conley, 1990, p. 94). In other words, people followed specific models based on the type of letter they were writing. Later, theorists developed textbooks that developed ways of creating effective letters. One such book, anonymously written, was *Rationes dictandi,* which first appeared in 1135. This book was heavily influenced by the Roman theorist Cicero, notes Conley. *Rationes dictandi* outlined the five key parts of a letter:

1. *Salutatio,* which was the salutation.
2. *Benevolentiae captatio,* which made the reader "attentive and well-disposed to the writer" (Conley, p. 94).
3. *Narratio,* which included the facts on which the letter was based.
4. *Petitio,* in which the writer made a request of the reader.
5. *Conclusio,* or the closing.

If you think about much business correspondence today, it follows this same format in many ways.

Perelman (2004) notes that the art of letter-writing was one of the first instances of an applied form of rhetorical practice. Though unique in its form and content, this art was based in many ways on the body of classical theory that was developed by authors such as Cicero in the Roman Republic.

A second major medieval art form was the art of preaching, known as *artes praedicandi*. Conley (1990) points out that despite the importance of preaching in the Middle Ages, there were few textbooks about the subject until 1200. Instructions in preaching before that time focused largely on having students imitate model sermons. Later works on the subject were brief and "primarily practical, not in any significant way theoretical" (p. 96). Cicero, as we have seen, was a strong influence on how the art of preaching was taught.

The sermons described in these textbooks divided into six parts (Conley, 1990):

1. Opening prayer.
2. Protheme, which was an introduction of the topic.
3. Theme, which was the passage from scripture upon which the sermon was based.
4. Division, which was usually divided into three main points and based on key words from the scripture passage.
5. Prosecutio, which is where the main points were developed.
6. Conclusion

A major focus of preaching textbooks was on eloquence and how clergy could amplify their thoughts for their audiences. Conley (1990) notes, "The job of the preacher, after all, was not simply to instruct but to move and edify as well" (p. 97). Like the art of letter writing, the art of preaching in the Middle Ages was a practical art form based on classical rhetorical theory.

Conclusion

Enos (1995) provided a succinct summary of rhetoric's existence and survival in the Roman Empire and Middle Ages: "In essence, rhetoric survived various phases of the Roman Empire and into the Middle Ages because it was perceived as a source of power—whether that power was political, educational, spiritual or cultural" (p. 113). The Middle Ages would be followed by the Renaissance, a period of artistic, scientific, and philosophic discovery. The word renaissance means "rebirth," a fitting term for what Europe experienced during this time.

HUMANISM AND RHETORICAL EDUCATION

The rhetorical practices that developed following the Roman Empire and into the Middle Ages were codified, in some ways, in the sixteenth century. By now, you realize that rhetoric, as it was taught and practiced for nearly thirteen hundred years, was mostly concerned with expressing what had been established as true.

Thus, the focus was on style and delivery. A French philosopher, Peter Ramus (1515–1572) provided an intellectual and academic argument to codify the teaching of rhetoric according to these categories.

Rhetoric, Ramus believed, should consist only of style and delivery. Logic, he argued, should concern itself with invention and arrangement of ideas. Memory, the fifth canon of classical rhetoric, was excluded from the disciplines of both rhetoric and logic. Ramus's most complete elaboration of these ideas is contained in his book *Dialectique*. After the appearance of this book, Audomarus Talaeus, one of Ramus's associates, authored a book called *Institutiones Oratoriae* in 1544, which laid out instruction in rhetoric. Ramus wrote a companion book for logic.

At the basis of Ramus's teaching were the three general laws—truth, justice, and wisdom—contained in Aristotle's *Posterior Analytics*. Ramus used these laws to reform the liberal arts curriculum. The law of truth was used to determine the subject matter of a liberal arts education. That which was not true in every circumstance, according to Ramus, was not a worthy subject of study. Opinions, probabilities, and uncertainties, for instance, were not universally true and should not be part of the liberal arts curriculum. Howell (1961) explained, "Ramus wanted the learned arts to consist of universal and necessary affirmations—of affirmations in which the predicate was true of every case of the subject" (p. 151). Thus, the educational system should teach only universally accepted truths.

The law of justice focused on dividing the subject matter into distinct disciplines. Ramus sought to prevent confusion and intermingling of subjects. That is, rhetoric and grammar were not supposed to teach the same subject matter, according to Ramus's view. The proper subject matter for rhetoric was style and delivery. Invention and arrangement belonged to logic, or philosophy. Finally, the law of wisdom concerned the ordering of propositions with a particular subject of study. Ramus believed that the content matter of a discipline be ordered from general statements to concrete statements.

The influence of Christianity on rhetoric is evident in Ramus's work concerning logic and rhetoric. Howell (1961) wrote that for Ramus, "logic was the center of the program of liberal studies, and the chief instrument of man in his quest for salvation" (p. 153). In fact, noted Howell, Ramus saw God as the only perfect logician and that the ability to reason effectively separated humans from animals, and superior humans for lesser humans.

Ramus's ideas were not well received by all scholars in the European Renaissance. The works of Aristotle and other classical scholars were enjoying a revival in Europe and a great number of "Aristotelians" opposed Ramus. In fact, Ramus was once banned from teaching philosophy by royal edict, yet he has had a profound effect on the practice and theory of rhetoric. Coleman and Corbett (1968) explained, "The most significant effect of this reassignment, however, was that the conceptualizing part of the composition process came to be regarded as an activity of private inquiry rather than one of the steps in the preparation for communicating with an audience" (p. 6). That is, instead of keeping the audience in mind throughout the rhetorical process, speakers would use more dialectical or philosophical methods of invention and arrangement. In this view, the content of a speech was divorced from its actual audience.

BOX 3.3   Internet Activity: The Discipline of Rhetoric

We have just discussed Peter Ramus's view of the distinction between rhetoric and logic. Although Ramus's direct influence waned, his view of the discipline of rhetoric remains with us, in part, today. Do an Internet search (such as with the search engine Google) for "rhetoric" and take note of the various ways that the term is used by educators. Which departments teach courses in rhetoric? What other courses are taught in those

departments? If you can read the syllabi of other rhetoric courses, what information is taught in those courses? Conduct a brief search for "logic" as well. What kinds of departments teach courses in logic? What other kinds of courses are taught in those departments? How does your university handle this distinction? Do you think the distinctions you discovered are useful for understanding and learning about rhetoric?

Ramus's division of rhetoric and logic would inform the thinking of the empirical and scientific philosophers and rhetoricians we'll study in the next chapter. While strict adherence to the writings of Ramus and Talaeus began to subside by the 1700s, Ramus's division between rhetoric and logic exists even today in many academic departments in the Western world (Golden, Berquist, & Coleman, 1976). The Internet Activity, The Discipline of Rhetoric, asks you to assess Ramus's influence on the contemporary rhetoric curriculum (see Box 3.3).

BELLETRISTIC MOVEMENT

At this point in our study, two significant paths emerge in Western rhetoric. On one path, which we will study in the remaining part of this chapter, rhetorical scholars continued to be interested in the style and delivery of rhetoric. Specifically, we'll examine how the belletristic and elocutionary movements in Great Britain furthered the emphasis on style and delivery that had characterized the study of rhetoric since the end of the Roman Empire. At the same time, however, another group of scholars in Great Britain and Europe began studying science, in general, and psychology, in particular, in a systematic, scientific manner. These scholars are often known as the epistemologists. Given the close relationship between psychology and rhetoric, they naturally addressed issues of rhetoric in their study and teaching. Since this type of study is quite different than that of the belletristic and elocutionary movements, we'll study the work of the epistemologists in the next chapter. Refer back to Table 3.1 to see the relationship between the various schools of thought concerning rhetoric during this time period. The work of the epistemologists evolved into a study of argumentation, which we will also take up in the next chapter. For now, let us return to the belletristic movement.

The **belletristic movement** significantly expanded the scope of rhetoric, but maintained the focus on style and delivery. Instead of viewing rhetoric as public speaking, or even sermon making, belletristic rhetoricians also focused on stylistic elements of belles letters, or literature and art. *Belles lettres,* from which the word *belletristic* is derived, literally means "beautiful letters."

Golden and Corbett (1968) defined this movement as follows:

> This approach was based on the concept that rhetoric and related polite arts, poetry, drama, art, history, biography, philology, and so on should be joined under the broad heading of rhetoric and belles letters. Since these disciplines share a common interest in taste, style, criticism, and sublimity, they seek to instruct the student to become an effective practitioner and judge in written and oral communication. (p. 8)

Ferreira-Buckley (1994) explained that belletristic rhetoricians "studied matters now encompassed under such diverse subjects as criticism, grammar, hermeneutics, linguistics, logic, poetics, psychology, rhetoric, and semiotics" (p. 23). The belletristic movement was influenced by Aristotle's *Poetics,* Isocrates' *Antidosis,* Longinus's *On the Sublime,* and Horace's *Ars Poetica.* Thus, these scholars sought to revive classical works concerning style.

The belletristic movement is also credited with developing the practice of rhetorical criticism. Although rhetorical theorists as far back as Aristotle and the Sophists were interested in critiquing rhetorical practice, their focus was clearly on how rhetors could learn the rhetorical principles necessary to give an effective speech. Thus, rhetorical theory—in our previous study—was interested in generating effective rhetorical practice. Belletristic scholars began to use rhetorical theory in a different way, to analyze and critique rhetorical practice for its own sake. Ferreira-Buckley (1994) notes, "As rhetoric's analytic function became more prominent—eventually obscuring its generative function—rhetoric became literary theory" (p. 23). Thus, belletristic scholars used rhetoric to analyze and critique such diverse forms as Shakespeare's plays, sermons, and poetry instead of viewing rhetorical theory as a way to develop effective communication. If you recall our discussion in the previous chapter and that of St. Augustine in this chapter, the goal for many of the theorists was to develop a theory that would lead to effective rhetorical practice. This goal became less important for subsequent theorists.

Adam Smith and Hugh Blair are often credited with being the most influential belletristic scholars. Smith, most acclaimed for his economic work, *The Wealth of Nations,* was a Scottish professor who also delivered a series of lectures on rhetoric. Not generally noted for his rhetorical ability, Smith never achieved the prominence of Blair. An audience member of Smith's, Blair would later gain much more publicity and royal support for his rhetorical teaching. Generally, regarded as the most significant of the belletristic scholars, we'll look at Blair's work in greater detail here. First, though, read more about Blair in Box 3.4, Biography of a Theorist.

Since Blair's work is most representative of the belletristic movement (Warnick, 1993), we'll study his ideas in more depth here. Blair's lectures concerning rhetoric and belles letters were published after his retirement in 1783. The publishing company, by the way, paid him 1,500 pounds for the lectures, making him the highest paid author on rhetoric to date (Ferreira-Buckley 1994, p. 24). His book, *Lectures on Rhetoric and Belles Lettres,* was made up of two volumes of over

---

BOX 3.4   Biography of a Theorist: Hugh Blair

Hugh Blair, one of the great theorists of the belletristic movement, was born on April 7, 1718 in Edinburgh, Scotland. He studied the humanities, Greek, logic, and natural philosophy at the University of Edinburgh. He received a master's degree in 1739, and his study included rhetoric. In October 1741, Blair was licensed to preach by the Presbytery of Edinburgh. He was ordained in 1743 and elected to preach at the Canongate Church. He preached there for eleven years. During this time, Blair studied Shakespeare and the sermons of Frederick Carmichael. He would later preach at Lady Yester's Church and the High Church of St. Giles, the most influential church in Edinburgh. He began conducting lectures on rhetoric. His teaching was so popular that King George III created the Regius Professorship for him; Blair served in that capacity until he retired in 1783. He immediately published his lectures, *Lectures on Rhetoric and Belles Lettres.* Blair died in 1800 and is buried near Greyfriars Church in Edinburgh.

Harding (1965) noted that *Lectures of Rhetoric and Belles Lettres* was "the kind of book Quintilian produced for the first century A.D. Blair selected and restated the teachings of writers like Aristotle, Longinus, Cicero, and Quintilian. He then exemplified their theories by the use of passages from English writers" (Harding, 1965, p. vii). The lectures in this book were printed nearly without revision from when he presented them, in some cases twenty years previously. The book contains forty-seven lectures, which were created for a college-age audience. Keep in mind that during this period, college students were often younger than they are today, some as young as thirteen or fourteen. Harding summarizes Blair's contribution to the study of rhetoric: "It is still certain that he did more to interpret and make known the rhetorical theory of the ancients than any other British or American rhetorical writer" (p. vii).

---

one thousand pages. It contained forty-seven separate lectures, including an introductory lecture, four lectures on taste, four on language, fifteen on style, ten on eloquence, and thirteen on criticism. Potter (1965) noted that for students of rhetoric, twenty-seven lectures hold the most importance. Let's examine Blair's ideas about rhetoric contained in this seminal work. For a summary of the forty-seven lectures contained in this book, consult the website http://www.msu.edu/user/ransford/summaries.html.

Taste

Taste, explained Blair (1965), is "the power of receiving pleasure from the beauties of nature and of art" (p. 16). All people, said Blair, have some sense of taste. He explained, "Nothing that belongs to human nature is more universal than the relish of beauty of one kind of another; of what is orderly, proportioned, grand, harmonious, new, or sprightly" (p. 17). Despite its universal nature, not all people perceive taste in the same way. There are great inequalities in what people consider to be beautiful. Yet Blair believed that taste could be improved with education. He explained, "Taste is a most improvable faculty, if there be any such in human nature" (p. 19). Yet he also observed that there is no one standard of taste for every situation. At the same time, taste is "far from being an arbitrary principle" (p. 34).

The two primary characteristics of taste are delicacy and correctness, according to Blair. Delicacy refers to the ability to see things in beauty that others may not see.

Blair explained that one who has a sense of delicacy "sees distinctions and differences where others see none; the most latent beauty does not escape him, and he is sensible of the smallest blemish" (1965, p. 24). Correctness refers to consistently using the proper standard when evaluating items of beauty. Blair explained, "A man of correct Taste is one who is never imposed on by counterfeit beauties; who carries always in his mind that standard of good sense which he employs in judging every thing" (p. 24). Delicacy is an innate trait, while correctness can be learned.

There are several sources of pleasure, according to Blair. The first is grandeur, or sublimity. Blair saw these terms as synonymous. Though everyone has a conception of these terms, Blair wrote that "it is not easy to describe, in words, the precise impression which great and sublime objects make upon us, when we behold them" (1965, p. 46). The emotion associated with grandeur and sublimity is delightful, but serious with degrees of "awfulness" and "solemnity." Beautiful objects, by comparison, produce a more "gay" or "brisk" emotion. Nature, with its extended plains or boundless oceans, provides examples of grandeur and sublimity. A tall mountain, Blair wrote, is even more grand or sublime than the ocean. Likewise, thunder or the roaring of wind can be sublime because of its sound. In short, "mighty power and strength" account for the sublime.

Writing or speech that references mighty and forceful objects and that affects the imagination achieves sublimity. Blair's view of the sublime differs in some ways from Longinus's view. For Blair, sublime rhetoric must discuss a sublime object. Further, the object must be presented "in such a light as is most proper to give us a clear and full impression of it; it must be described with strength, with conciseness, and simplicity" (1965, p. 60). The rhetor, or poet, must be "deeply affected, and warmed, by" the sublime idea being expressed. Blair noted, "If his own feeling be languid, he can never inspire us with any strong emotion" (p. 60). In particular, the scriptures provide "the highest instances of the Sublime" (p. 61).

Another source of pleasure is beauty. "Beauty, next to Sublimity, affords, beyond doubt, the highest pleasure to the imagination," noted Blair (1965, p. 80). Beauty raises a calmer, more gentle emotion than the sublime. Although sublimity is not lasting, the emotions caused by beauty are of "longer continuance" (p. 81). Color, shape, curves, and motion are all qualities of beauty. In rhetoric, beauty can be achieved by writing or speaking with a certain grace that "neither lifts the mind very high, nor agitates it very much, but diffuses over the imagination an agreeable and pleasing serenity" (p. 90).

Several additional sources of pleasure can be briefly summarized:

- Novelty is noticed by the audience and creates an agreeable emotion.
- Imitation pleases because it reminds us of the original object or idea.
- Melody and harmony, either poetically or musically, delight audience members.

Language

Blair, following his discussion of taste, turned to language. The four lectures on language serve as a precursor to the more lengthy treatment of style. In fact, Blair explained that language "is the foundation of the whole power of eloquence"

(1965, p. 97). Blair defined language as the "expression of our ideas by certain articulate sounds, which are used as the signs of those ideas" (p. 98). Language can be used to communicate "the most delicate and refined emotions" of a person's mind to another. In the four chapters in which Blair discusses language, he focuses on the origin and development of language, the structure, or grammar, of language, and, specifically, the English language.

Style

Language is the means through which a person expresses style, noted Blair. He defined style as "the peculiar manner in which a man expresses his conceptions, by means of Language" (1965, p. 183). Blair offers a particularly vivid illustration of this definition by saying style "is a picture of the ideas which rise" in the mind of the speaker. The style of a rhetor cannot readily be separated from his or her sentiments. Language is but the means through which those sentiments are expressed, in either written or oral form.

Blair explained that style has two qualities: perspicuity and ornament. He explained,

> For all that can possibly be required of Language, is, to convey our ideas clearly to the minds of others, and, at the same time, in such a dress, as by pleasing and interesting them, shall most effectively strengthen the impressions which we seek to make. When both these ends are answered, we certainly accomplish every purpose for which we use Writing and Discourse. (p. 184)

Perspicuity, Blair elaborated, is using language in a way that clearly states the speaker's ideas. He said that rhetoric must be obvious even to negligent listeners and strike them as the light of the sun on their eyes even when they are not looking upwards. He explained, "Perspicuity in writing, is not to be considered as only a sort of negative virtue, or freedom from defect. It has higher merit: It is a degree of positive beauty. We are pleased with an author, we consider him as deserving praise, who frees us from all fatigue of searching for his meaning" (p. 186).

Perspicuity has three qualities: purity, propriety, and precision. Purity refers to using words that are "of the language which we speak" and not "imported from other Languages" (Blair, 1965, p. 187). We might consider this today to mean that a rhetor is to use words that are commonly understood, not exotic words or slang words which do not have designated meanings. Propriety means to use the right word. A rhetor's words should be "correct" and "significant." Propriety, then, refers to the specific words chosen by the rhetor to communicate a specific idea. Precision avoids superfluous words and expressions and gets to the point of the speaker's idea. Blair noted that to "write with precision" one must have "distinctness and accuracy in his manner of thinking" (p. 189). A speaker should avoid saying more than he or she intends to have precision. Blair spends a great deal of time distinguishing between the meanings of words, so as to achieve propriety, and later on how to construct precise sentences.

Read the following passage from Federal Reserve Board Chair Alan Greenspan and consider how he achieved purity, propriety, and precision:

> Partly as a result of the balance-sheet restructuring, business credit quality appears to have recuperated considerably over the past few years. Last year, the default rate on bonds fell sharply, recovery rates on defaulted issues rose, the number of rating downgrades moderated substantially, and delinquencies on business loans continued to decline. The improved balance sheets and strong profits of business firms, together with attractive terms for financing in open markets and from banks, suggest that financial conditions remain quite supportive of further gains in capital spending in coming quarters. (February 11, 2004)

In this passage, Greenspan met each of Blair's standards of perspicuity:

- Despite the highly technical nature of Greenspan's testimony and his position as expert on global economics, Greenspan's speech is not filled with unfamiliar terminology. Although it may require some background in economics to make sense of a few key terms, Greenspan's speech largely has purity.
- In particular, Greenspan's speech reflected the quality of propriety. That is, Greenspan chose very specific words for his ideas. Since the wording he uses in his testimony to Congress influences international economic markets, Greenspan must be careful of his word choice.
- The link between Greenspan's economic mind and his rhetoric is clearly evident in the precision of his language. Greenspan's remarks say no more or less than he intends to say, and he clearly identifies limits and opportunities for the U.S. economy without embellishing or shading his meanings.

A second element of style is ornament. We have previously said that ornament concerns how words are pleasing and interesting for the listener. Ornament is achieved through graceful, strong, or melodious sentences or by figurative language. A graceful sentence has unity, which means that "There must always be some connecting principles among the parts" (Blair, 1965, p. 216). That is, a sentence should discuss one idea, should have a consistent tense and voice, and should be a complete unit of thought. A strong sentence, according to Blair, includes using capital letters for words at places that would make the fullest impression, arranging sentences so that the ideas became stronger from sentence to sentence, and avoiding concluding a sentence with an adverb, preposition, or inconsiderable word. Melodious sentences use pauses—in the form of commas or periods—effectively and they have an imaginative cadence.

The second aspect of ornament is figurative language. We have discussed figures of speech and figures of thought previously— in Chapter 2 and earlier in this chapter, in connection with Longinus. According to Blair, the use of figures enriches language and bestows dignity upon the style of the speaker or writer. Figurative language is also more pleasing for the listener and provides a more striking view of the object being discussed. Blair spent an entire lecture on metaphor, another topic we have discussed previously. The effect of a metaphor, wrote Blair "is to give light and strength to description; to make intellectual ideas, in some sort, visible to the eye, by giving them color, and substance, and sensible qualities" (1965, p. 297). Metaphors should be used "with a delicate hand" to avoid "confusion" and "inaccuracy" (p. 297). Blair then provided several rules for using metaphors effectively. He also discussed several specific figures, including apostrophe, personification, and allegory.

Blair concluded his lectures on style by focusing on different types of style and ways of creating effective style. Some of the rules Blair provided for creating an effective style include:

- Rhetors should have knowledge about the subject of which they are writing or speaking. Blair explained, "The foundation of all good Style, is good sense accompanied with a lively imagination" (p. 402). Blair here reiterated a point made earlier, that to have an effective style, one must have clear thoughts about the subject.

- Rhetors should expose themselves to the best writers and speakers. Blair wrote, "This is requisite, both in order to form a just taste in Style, and to supply us with a full stock of words on every subject" (p. 405). Students of style should not simply imitate the style of the great authors, though.

- Rhetors should adapt their style to the situation and audience. He noted, "Nothing merits the name of eloquent or beautiful, which is not suited to the occasion, and to the persons to whom it is addressed." (p. 406)

Blair's final lecture on style is a criticism of the style used in one of the publications of that time. By focusing on a particular example, Blair sought to illustrate what he had discussed concerning style, to observe any characteristics of style he may not have discussed, and to show the practicality of the subject matter.

Eloquence

Rhetoric, as defined by Blair, comprised a great variety of subjects, including drama, literature, and poetry. Thus, much of what he discussed concerning style focused mostly on written forms of rhetoric. In the twenty-fifth lecture, Blair turns his attention specifically to eloquence, or public speaking. Here, his focus is mostly on delivery of the spoken word. Blair, though, clearly saw style as relating to public speaking. His discussion of public speaking assumes that the speaker has knowledge of style and taste. He defines eloquence as "the Art of Speaking in such a manner as to attain the end for which we speak. Whenever a man speaks or writes, he is supposed, as a rational being, to have some end in view; either to inform, or to amuse, or to persuade, or, in some way or other, to act upon his fellow-creatures. He who speaks, or writes, in such a manner as to adapt all his words most effectually to that end, is the most eloquent man" (Blair, 1965, p. 2).

Blair identified the purpose of speaking as threefold: to inform, to persuade, and to amuse. Of these, he saw persuasion as the "most important subject of discourse" (p. 2). Consequently, Blair defined eloquence as "The Art of Persuasion" (p. 3). Blair distinguished between convincing and persuading, saying that conviction "affects the understanding only; persuasion, the will and the practice" (p. 3).

Thus, persuasion involves the listener taking action on what is said. Convincing is possible based on "mere" reason and argument, but to persuade, the speaker must have passion. Noting that persuasion also requires freedom on the part of the listeners to follow what is said, Blair provided a brief history of rhetoric, from the days of the Greek Republic to the Roman Republic to the "modern times" of eighteenth century Great Britain. Blair noted, "Here, it must be confessed, that, in no European nation, Public Speaking has been considered as so great an object, or been cultivated with so much care, as in Greece and Rome" (p. 37). Blair observed that in all areas of British speaking, from the Parliament to the courts to the pulpit, public speaking did not enjoy the popularity or significance that it did in the ancient Greek and Roman Republics.

The most effective persuasive speaker had a "solid argument, clear method, a character of probity appearing in the Speaker, joined with such graces of Style and utterance, as shall draw our attention to what he says" (Blair, 1965, p. 3). Persuasion begins with good sense and solid argument. Blair also said that "proper method" was important, meaning that everything "should be found in its proper place" (p. 53). Arrangement of ideas, he said, should be done prior to the speech and would help the speaker remember what should be said and help the audience follow without confusion. The speaker must also have passion and use emotion in a way that is consistent with his or her thoughts. Misplaced emotion would create discord with the audience.

Blair also addressed delivery, stating that "the best manner of delivery is the firm and the determined" (1965, p. 60). Arrogant and overbearing delivery should be avoided at all costs; a feeble and hesitating manner indicates that the speaker doubts his or her ideas. However, Blair cautioned that effective delivery is not the most important quality of an effective speaker: "To conclude this head, let every Orator remember, that the impression made by fine and artful speaking is momentary; that made by argument and good sense, is solid and lasting" (p. 61). As he did with matters of style, Blair engaged in criticism of ancient orators to illustrate and further elaborate on eloquence, or oratory.

In subsequent lectures on oratory, Blair further examined arrangement, argumentative appeals, delivery, and improving one's skills in public speaking. A speech, he wrote, contained an introduction, stated the subject and facts associated with it, presented arguments, attempted to touch the audience's passions, and contained a conclusion. In terms of argument, Blair addressed the deductive and inductive arguments and emotional proof. When discussing delivery, Blair touched upon tone, emphasis, use of pauses, and other aspects of delivery.

Criticism

Although Blair devotes much of the last thirteen lectures to criticism, he defines the subject in the third lecture. Criticism, to him, was a way of evaluating beauty by using standards that have been established through experience. Blair's style of criticism is far more formal and systematic than anything we have seen so far. Not only does Blair use criticism to illustrate and further explore the points made in his discussion of style, eloquence, and other topics, but he uses criticism for its own sake to investigate matters such as philosophical writing, poetry, and drama. Blair's systematic approach to criticism today most closely resembles literary criticism, rather than rhetorical criticism. But Blair clearly identified the practices and principles that are used by critics in all aspects of the liberal arts today.

Conclusion

In addition to his focus on criticism, Blair developed a theory of rhetoric that focused on style. Blair's work is illustrative of how rhetorical theory progressed from Longinus in the classical ages to the practice of *artes dictaminis* in the Middle Ages. Like St. Augustine, Blair was interested in how pastors could make effective the word of God for their congregations. From Blair's more comprehensive work on rhetorical style, we move to the elocutionary movement.

ELOCUTIONARY MOVEMENT

At the same time the belletristic movement was gaining prominence in Great Britain, another key rhetorical movement emerged: the **elocutionary movement.** Although the belletristic movement focused on all matters of style in a diverse body of rhetorical and literary works, the elocutionary movement had a single focus: delivery of the spoken word. The elocutionists were also influenced by Ramus's distinction between rhetoric and logic, and most elocutionists specifically focused on delivery. The elocutionary movement sought to teach that eloquent expression was achieved by voice control and bodily action that reflected a conversational pattern of delivery (Golden & Corbett, 1968, p. 8). Thomas Sheridan, one of the principal elocutionists, defined the movement thus: "elocution is the just and graceful management of the voice, countenance, and gesture in speaking" (p. 19). Although focused on delivery, some elocutionists also addressed style and other canons, such as invention (Brown, 1994). The elocutionists also sought to correct the "carelessness in articulation, pronunciation, and action which all too often characterized the speaking of eighteenth century Englishmen" (Golden & Corbett, 1968, p. 7).

Natural versus Mechanical Elocution

Two perspectives developed concerning elocution. One school of thought taught that natural, or conversational, expression was to be desired; the other believed that delivery should be so systematic that certain rules should be used in speaking. Thomas Sheridan, one of the most famous elocutionists, made popular the natural approach in his 1762 book, *A Course of Lectures on Elocution.* His view of delivery is summed up in these words:

> When we reflect that the end of public speaking is persuasion, (for the view of every one who harangues in public is to bring his hearers into his way of thinking); and that in order to persuade others to the belief of any point, it must first appear, that the person who attempts it is firmly persuaded of the

truth of it himself; how can we suppose it possible that he should effect this, unless he delivers himself in the manner which is always used by persons who speak in earnest? How shall his words pass for the words of truth, when they bear not his stamp? (1762/1968, p. 5)

That is, the speaker should appear genuine and without the stylized, systematic mannerisms taught by the elocutionists from the mechanical school.

John Walker, who wrote *Elements of Elocution* in 1781 is often thought to be the champion of the mechanical school. Benzie (1994) notes, "In the end, Walker's influence proved to be far greater than Sheridan's, for the mechanical aspects of the elocutionists' teaching continued to flourish in the nineteenth and twentieth centuries; even by the end of the eighteenth century, Walker's works had virtually become the accepted guides to the art of delivery" (Benzie, 1994, p. 200). Brown (1994) agreed with this assessment, noting that "as the first to develop a systematic, rule-based approach to teaching delivery, he [Walker] powerfully influenced the pedagogy of elocution well into the nineteenth century" (p. 233).

Sheridan's Theory of Elocution

Although his style was generally more conversational than some of the others— and not as accepted in the long-term—Sheridan's view of rhetoric is comprehensive. Sheridan defined good delivery as follows:

A just delivery consists in a distinct articulation of words, pronounced in proper tones, suitably varied to the sense, and the emotions of the mind; with due observation of the accent; of emphasis, in its several gradations; of rests or pauses of the voice, in proper places and well measured degrees of time; and the whole accompanied with expressive looks, and significant gesture. (1762/1968, p. 10)

At the basis of Sheridan's theory of elocution is the idea that the practice of speaking is based, incorrectly, on the practice of reading. Usually when people read, he explained, they do so silently. When we read, explained Sheridan, we learn about only the types of sounds that are to be made—as indicated by letters and words— and pauses—indicated by commas, periods, semi colons, colons, and other markings. In terms of the other aspects of delivery, including "tones, accent, emphases, and gesture, there are no visible marks to serve as guides in these" (Sheridan, 1762/1968, p. 10). In fact, Sheridan explained, "The most essential articles to a good delivery, have been wholly left out of the graphic art" (p. 11).

A speaker must first have the words of the speech "perfectly fixed in their memories; and even then, it is only by repeated trials, and constant practice in rehearsals, that they are able to associate to them, the just tones, looks, and gestures, that ought naturally to accompany them" (Sheridan, 1762/1968, p. 13).

Sheridan's theory can be summarized by his discussion of a few key points:

- *Articulation.* Sheridan defined good articulation as "giving every letter in every syllable, its due proportion of sound" and "making such a distinction, between the syllables" (pp. 19–20). Sheridan taught that by understanding the causes of poor articulation—such as stuttering or lisping—one could learn the proper position of the tongue and lips in making the proper sound.

- *Pronunciation*. Sheridan taught that the preferred dialect was that used in the courts. "All other dialects," he wrote, "are sure marks, either of a provincial, rustic, pedantic, or mechanic education; and therefore have some degree of disgrace annexed to them" (p. 30). By being aware of one's dialect and consciously seek to speak properly, a speaker could be sure to correctly pronounce the words of a speech. Using proper pronunciation, individuals could achieve social advancement within the culture.

- *Accent*. A speaker should be sure to use the proper stress on the correct syllable in a word.

- *Emphasis*. The speaker must also stress the proper word in a sentence. Sheridan explained that emphasis clarifies relationships in a sentence and allows the speaker to communicate the rank of several words—by stressing the most important word. Sheridan provided examples of sentences that have different meanings when emphasis is placed on different words in the sentences.

- *Pauses*. The cessation of sound, Sheridan explained, was necessary so that the speaker can take a breath and so that the listener can understand what is said and see the distinctions between sentences and ideas. Pauses are also used to give meaning to what is said.

- *Tones*. Sheridan explained that the sounds made by the speaker are tones and can communicate a variety of expressions, such as sorrow, lamentation, mirth, joy, and others. The expression of these sounds "requires neither study, art, nor imitation" (p. 105). Instead, they spontaneously break out in "the exactest expressions, nicely proportioned to the degrees of his [the speaker's] inward emotions" (p. 105).

- *Gesture*. Emphasizing the multisensory nature of speaking, Sheridan discusses hand gestures, facial expression, and other body movement. Effective gestures have force, which comes naturally, and grace, which can be learned through art.

Conclusion

The conversational style was accepted by many British and early American practitioners. The movement influenced rhetorical theorists of the day. Golden and Corbett note, "In Blair's brief discussion of delivery, he acknowledged his debt to the [elocutionary] movement by admitting that much of his material was taken from the writings of Thomas Sheridan who had stressed the importance of conversing with the audience in a genuine face-to-face manner" (1968, p. 14).

Much of the teaching of the elocutionists, though, was thought to be artificial and excessive. However, "the excesses, including Sheridan's development of a complex marking system to be used in oral reading and Walker's absurd and ludicrous classification and description of the emotions, brought a charge of artificiality" (Golden & Corbett, p. 8). Blair, for instance, did not condone the "highly

---

BOX 3.5   Internet Activity: The Influence of the Elocutionists

Spend a few minutes considering the impact of the elocutionary movement on the practice of public speaking today. Do an online search using the terms "public speaking delivery" or something similar. Read the advice that is returned on the web pages for the search. Does the advice appear overly mechanical? Are there specific tips given for when and how to gesture? Does the site's author encourage a natural delivery? Overall, how effective are the delivery tips contained on these web pages?

---

artificial teachings of other elocutionists such as Walker" (ibid., p. 14). Richard Whately, whom we will study in the next chapter, offered a "stinging rebuke of the elocutionary movement for its violation of the natural method" in his book *Elements of Rhetoric.*

Despite these criticisms, aspects of the elocutionary movement exist in teaching about public speaking today. Complete the Internet Activity, The Influence of the Elocutionists (Box 3.5), to consider the ways that previous theories influence today's rhetorical instruction.

SUMMARIZING RHETORICAL THEORY

We have surveyed a variety of ideas, principles, and theories in this chapter. To some degree, the chapter has focused on the style and/or delivery of rhetoric, from the Second Sophistic to the elocutionary movement. Let's consider now how rhetorical theory from these time periods intersects with some of our primary topics of discussion; refer to Table 3.2 for reference.

Defining Rhetoric

Although the theorists we have discussed in this chapter took the general approach of focusing on style and/or delivery, they differed significantly on what constituted a rhetorical text. For Longinus and the belletristic theorists, rhetoric included poetry, literature, art forms, oratory, and other expressive forms of communication. St. Augustine was interested in sermons, and Ramus and the elocutionists focused on oratory.

Rhetoric and Knowledge

Overall, the theorists we have looked at took a very different view of the relationship between rhetoric and knowledge than we saw in the previous chapter. St. Augustine elaborates the most on rhetoric's relationship to truth, but he focused on particular ways of reading Scriptures to locate truth and in using faith to find truth. Rhetoric was seen as the way of making truth known to a congregation. The other theorists—Ramus, in particular—sought to distance rhetoric from

Table 3.2 Summarizing Rhetorical Theory

Theorist	Defining Rhetoric	Ways of Knowing	Identity	Judgment
Longinus	Rhetoric equated with the sublime			Preference for those ideas that are sublime
St. Augustine	Making effective the truth of the Scriptures	Invention based on scriptural readings, faith	Created in God's image	Knowledge of truth as revealed through Scriptures
Ramus	Style and delivery; separate from logic	Not concern of rhetoric		
Belletristic movement	Broadly defined as all literature, art, oratory, and expressive forms	Managerial	Tied to beauty	Preference for those ideas that are pleasing, tasteful
Elocutionary movement	Delivery of oral texts		Natural or mechanical	Preference for ideas that are effectively presented

invention. Although the belletristic theorists and elocutionists were, in some ways, interested in invention, their focus was on style and/or delivery. In fact, Warnick (1993) has written that the belletristic movement initiated the beginning of a managerial style of rhetoric, where the speaker, in essence, manages the presentation of rhetoric that has been created by another person.

Rhetoric and Identity

The theorists in this chapter took several different approaches in thinking about human identity. For St. Augustine, humans were created in God's image. A life of faithful devotion meant learning the Scriptures and living in accordance with God's will. For Longinus and the belletristic theorists, ideal forms of humanity were related to beauty. For Longinus, in particular, the genius of a person's mind came across that person's manner of expression. The elocutionists, on the one hand, celebrated the natural talents and abilities of human speakers. On the other hand, they attempted to create systematic, scientific speakers who lacked individuality and creativity.

Rhetoric and Judgment

In short, two standards are used in this chapter to determine what is right from wrong. For St. Augustine, in particular, judgment was based on scriptural reading and location of truth. For the other theorists, the validity and forcefulness of rhetoric depended on its presentation. For Longinus and Blair, the mark of genius was one who can effectively achieve the sublime or has taste. For the elocutionists, effective rhetoric was that which is delivered in a systematic, even scientific manner.

DISCUSSION QUESTIONS

1. Find an example of a sublime speech. Who is the speaker? When was the speech given? How was the rhetoric sublime? Do you think the speech was effective? Why or why not?

2. Evaluate Ramus's argument using your own knowledge of rhetoric, communication, logic, and philosophy. To what degree does each discipline help us understand human experience? How do the disciplines complement each other?

3. What kinds of texts do you consider to be rhetorical? Is your definition as far-reaching as the belletristic theorists? Why or why not?

4. Identify a speaker today who has good taste. What makes him/her effective? Is your judgment about the speaker's taste widely held? Why or why not?

5. Consider the training in speaking and delivery you have received. Have you been taught to use a natural/conversational style of delivery or one that is more rule-based, or mechanical? Which style of delivery do you find more persuasive?

6. Name a speaker today who has effective delivery. What makes the delivery effective? Evaluate the speaker using Sheridan's theory of elocution.

GLOSSARY TERMS

Second Sophistic   The period of time following the fall of the Roman Republic in which traveling teachers of rhetoric focused attention on style and delivery.

sublime   An appeal to the stylistic and aesthetic faculties of the audience.

belletristic movement   A school of thought that studied a wide variety of rhetorical texts and that focused on matters of style and taste.

taste   The ability to receive pleasures from nature and art.

elocutionary movement   A school of thought that focused exclusively on the delivery of spoken words.

4

Rhetoric, Science
and Argumentation

Learning Objectives

After reading this chapter, you should be able to:

1. Describe the influence of science and philosophy on rhetorical theory in the seventeenth, eighteenth, and nineteenth centuries.

2. Distinguish between the belletristic, elocutionary, and epistemological movements in rhetorical theory.

3. Identify the major rhetorical theorists and their contributions to rhetorical theory from the seventeenth, eighteenth, and nineteenth centuries.

4. Construct an argument and identify its elements.

5. Describe key concepts related to the study of argumentation, such as presumption, burden of proof, and refutation.

6. Synthesize the discussion presented in the chapter concerning argumentation and apply these elements to examples of argumentation.

Imagine that it's a Friday night and you and your friends are deciding what to do for the evening. One of your friends would like to go support a charity fund-raiser on campus, while another of your friends would instead like to go to a movie. Each of your friends states their case to the others. Your friend who is pushing for the movie doesn't provide much reasoning for this position. Your other friend, though, offers reasons for going to the fund-raiser and appeals to your group's emotions in supporting the charity. Your friends decide that going to the fund-raiser would be a better way to spend the evening. Whether you realize it or not, the friend that prevailed in the argument made use of several concepts that we'll discuss in this chapter. Specifically, he or she knew what it would take to persuade the others and how to arrange and present arguments. In this chapter, we'll focus on approaches to rhetorical theory based on science and argumentation.

The previous chapter focused on rhetoric's attention to style and delivery during the Second Sophistic, Middle Ages, and Renaissance. Specifically, we addressed the teachings of Longinus, St. Augustine, Ramus, the belletristic movement, and the elocutionary movement. At the same time that the belletristic and elocutionary movements were gaining popularity, the study of science, specifically psychology, and the philosophical school of empiricism took hold in Europe. Thus, we'll begin our study of rhetoric in this chapter in the early 1600s. The scientific study of rhetoric evolved into a systematic study of argumentation; we'll conclude this chapter by looking at two prominent theorists of argumentation from the twentieth century.

THE EPISTEMOLOGISTS

Essentially, the theorists we are about to discuss developed ways of thinking about psychology and reason and put their faith in these theories to explain humanity and rhetoric. Golden and Corbett noted that "Despite the fact that these philosophers and psychologists were essentially nonrhetoricians, they profoundly influenced the direction which rhetoric was to take during the later half of the eighteenth century" (p. 9). Because they used scientific methods of induction and believed that experience was necessary to build knowledge, they are generally called **epistemologists.** We'll briefly examine the cultural influences of the 1600s and then look more closely at the relationship between the epistemologists and rhetorical theory.

Scientific and Philosophic Discoveries

Golden and Corbett (1968) explained that the philosophers and scientists of the seventeenth century found that "the more they studied ancient science, philosophy, and rhetoric, the more they realized man's lack of meaningful insight concerning his basic nature" (p. 9). Humans were able to develop more sophisticated scientific equipment, such as the telescope, and they refined methods of research to be more systematic and generalizable.

Coupled with the surge in scientific thinking and discovery was the diminished power of the church. You'll recall that in the Middle Ages, the Catholic Church exerted a strong influence on what was thought, practiced, and believed in much of Europe. As this influence waned, science became a more significant factor in determining what was considered knowledge and truth. Copernicus discovered that the earth revolved around the sun, for instance, instead of the opposite, which had been the prevailing belief at the time. Additionally, the printing press was invented, which enabled large populations to read Scripture and form their own interpretation of the Bible's meaning. All told, science gained a foothold in Europe, and its influence would only increase as its ability to explain human existence gained followers.

Relationship to the Belletristic and Elocutionary Movements

Take a look at Table 3.1 in the previous chapter to review the chronological relationship between the theorists we are about to discuss with those we discussed in Chapter 3. Specifically, Thomas Sheridan and Hugh Blair were contemporaries with George Campbell. Also, ideas about belletrism, elocution, and science were all being developed at the same time in response to the Renaissance and the revival of classical theories and literature. The views of these three schools of thought were quite different, however.

The belletristic movement, according to Golden and Corbett (1968) "made little visible impact on the treatises of Campbell and Whately" (p. 14), whose work we'll examine in the pages ahead. Additionally, "Campbell, Blair, and Whately supported the emphasis on the conversational pattern of delivery, but deplored the excesses of the elocutionists as a whole" (Golden & Corbett, 1968, p. 14). Though we have classified these theorists based on their primary orientations, keep in mind that all were interested in the same topics and were writing at approximately the same time. You may find it helpful to refer back to Table 3.1 as you read this chapter.

Psychology and Rhetoric

As we examine the specific contributions of the epistemologists, we'll focus on the work of Francis Bacon and John Locke. Bacon's *The Advancement of Learning* was published in 1605 and is available online at http://darkwing.uoregon.edu/%7Erbear/adv1.htm. Locke's principle work, *An Essay on Human Understanding,* was published in 1690. These two theorists are often cited as the most influential of the epistemologists, and their work has significant influence on how rhetoric was viewed and taught at that time.

Both theorists saw the human mind as being composed of two essential categories, the understanding and the will. Bacon explained, "The Knowledge which respecteth the faculties of the mind of man is of two kinds; the one respecting his Understanding and Reason, and the other his Will, Appetite, and Affection; whereof the former produceth Position or Decree, the latter Action or Execution" (p. na). To illustrate this distinction, think of a time when you have been convinced of something but have not acted on it. Perhaps you favored a candidate in a recent political campaign, but didn't vote for the candidate. Or, you joined a gym in order to exercise more, but failed to actually use your membership. In these cases, you might say that you understood that you should do something, but that you did not have the will to do so. Both Bacon and Locke saw understanding and will as the key to explaining human knowledge and action.

Bacon provided what is generally regarded as the key definition of rhetoric to emerge from the epistemologists. He explained that "The duty and office of rhetoric is to apply reason to imagination for the better moving of the will." You can see that his definition for rhetoric reflects the principles of psychology we have discussed previously. For Bacon, rhetoric had to use both creative appeals to the appetite or will along with appeals to the understanding. It isn't enough, he believed, to convince someone of something, you also had to move them to take action. Rhetoric alone was capable of achieving both those goals.

Major Contributions to Rhetorical Theory

Perhaps the most significant rhetorical contribution of the epistemologists is their attack on the syllogism. The syllogism, they argued, did not allow humans to gain new information. Instead, the syllogism simply reconfigured what was already known to be true. Consider the classic syllogism:

All people are mortal. (Generalization)

Socrates is a person. (Specific case)

———————————————

Socrates is mortal. (Conclusion)

The epistemologists would contend that this syllogism doesn't reveal or find any new information, since all of these statements were previously known to be true.

The use of induction, on the other hand, allowed humans to gather experiences and information and gain new knowledge. This observation makes sense when you consider that these were scientists, interested in gathering facts and basing theories on facts. Consider an example of inductive reasoning:

Ships disappear when sailing into the horizon. (Specific case)

The shape cast on the moon during an eclipse is a circle. (Specific case)

When traveling north or south, new stars appear on the horizon. (Specific case)

———————————————————————

The earth is a sphere, it is not flat. (Conclusion)

In this example, new knowledge is created based on the observations of the specific cases. Inductive reasoning follows the scientific approach and was thought to build knowledge in a way that deductive reasoning and the syllogism could not.

Another contribution to rhetorical theory is Bacon's theory of the four fallacies of reasoning. We'll examine how each "idol" helps to explain the limitations people face when choosing a candidate for which to vote.

First, the *Idols of the Tribe* relates to inherent limitations in the nature of humans to reason and attain knowledge. Despite the fact that voters have their own areas of expertise, very few of us have the ability to understand the full range of economic, social, and international issues that are involved in voting for a presidential candidate. We are inherently limited in our ability to understand all the issues of an election campaign.

Second, the *Idols of Cave* pointes to individual traits that prevent knowing. We are biased, prejudiced, and/or incapable of grasping certain concepts and ideas.

For example, we react to wedge issues—such as abortion or gay marriage—and we are influenced by labels such as "liberal" and "conservative." Because we come from our own biases and perspective, our judgment in choosing a presidential candidate is inherently flawed.

Third, the *Idols of the Marketplace* refers to problems inherent in language that prevent clear communication. We'll explore this point in great detail in the next chapter. For now, consider examples of when presidential candidates say they are or are not in favor of affirmative action. This term has a wide variety of meanings within our culture, and not all people may use the term in the same way.

Fourth, the *Idols of the Theatre* refers to fallacies in philosophy and theory that obscure experiential ways of knowing. That is, we are limited by the theoretical and conceptual frameworks we use to make sense of our world. In the United States, many of us are taught that there are two political parties. We often think that only two people are running for the presidency. In fact, there are dozens of candidates from dozens of political parties. The framework we use to think about politics does not always accommodate third parties, and people mistakenly think they only have two choices.

Each of Bacon's idols refers to limitations in our ability to know something. Since Bacon was concerned with how humans understand and act, knowledge about human limitations was fundamental to his theory. Consequently, the idols also describe limitations in the way humans use and are influenced by rhetoric.

Finally, in terms of style, the epistemologists sought to replace a heavily decorated style with one that was clear and simple. They desired that humans have a clear view of reality that was not obscured by needlessly elegant language. You'll recall that several centuries earlier, Longinus and St. Augustine called for a highly elegant style, at least on some occasions. Likewise, the medieval arts that we studied in the last chapter appreciated an elegant and grand style. In the Enlightenment, however, the style of rhetoric used was clear and simple, to more effectively communicate scientific findings and principles. Scientific and medical journals today also use a simple, direct style in order to clearly communicate with the reader.

SHAPING A "NEW RHETORIC"

Perhaps the best example of how the work of the epistemologists influenced rhetorical theory is George Campbell's 1776 book, *The Philosophy of Rhetoric.* According to Bitzer (1963), Campbell's *Philosophy of Rhetoric* ranks among the greatest works in the history of rhetoric, with Aristotle's *Rhetoric,* Cicero's *De Oratore,* Qunitilian's *Institutio Oratoria,* Longinus's *On the Sublime,* and Whately's *Elements of Rhetoric,* which we will discuss later. Ehninger (1950) claimed that Campbell's book "marks the end of one era and the beginning of another. It is the bridge which at once divides and connects the ancient and modern" views of rhetoric (p. 271). You can read more about Campbell in the Biography of a Theorist box for this chapter (Box 4.1).

BOX 4.1   Biography of a Theorist: George Campbell

George Campbell was born on December 25, 1719. The son of a minister, Campbell graduated from Marischal College in 1738, having studied Greek and Latin. Campbell started out studying law and served an apprenticeship in Edinburgh, Scotland. However, Campbell began to study theology and would return to Marischal College and King's College to pursue a degree in theology. Campbell was licensed as a pastor in 1746 and in 1748 was ordained as minister at Banchory-Ternan, Aberdeenshire. He served nine years in the country parish and began his work on the *Philosophy of Rhetoric*. Campbell served as one of the ministers at Aberdeen before becoming the principal at Marischal College in 1759. He was also the minister at Greyfriars Church. Campbell founded and was active in the Aberdeen Philosophical Society. He presented to the society a series of lectures that would become the *Philosphy of Rhetoric*, published in 1776. Campbell published several sermons and scriptural translations before his death in 1796.

Bitzer explained, "The Rhetoric was fully in tune with the leading philosophical ideas current in the middle years of the 18th century, and so we should expect to find that Campbell shares ideas with such thinkers as Bacon and Locke, whose works inspired most of the Enlightenment thinkers of his time" (Bitzer, 1963, p. xii). Campbell entertained ideas about psychology and the nature of knowledge in constructing his theory of rhetoric. As Bitzer noted, "The book's distinctive contributions result from the encounter of a philosophic mind with concepts and problems of rhetoric" (Bitzer, 1963, p. vii). In short, Campbell presented a clear set of principles that explain the art of rhetoric. He merged the best of the classical rhetorical theories with the latest advances in scientific knowledge.

Campbell was also a member of the clergy, and his Christian faith influenced his ideas about philosophy and rhetoric. Bitzer (1963) explained that for Campbell, "all of nature, including human nature, is God's creation" and that "the most important moral and factual truths are vouchsafed by God" (p. xiii). Bitzer concluded, "A critical distinction between the natural world and the supernatural—between what we know upon natural grounds and what we know from revelation—underlies his philosophy and theory of rhetoric" (p. xix). We'll discuss the key points of his book and their contribution to rhetorical theory here. To read the entire book online, go to http://people.cohums.ohio-state.edu/Ulman1/Campbell/.

Defining Rhetoric

Campbell used a broad definition of rhetoric. As Bitzer noted, rhetoric included "any instance of written or oral discourse which aims to inform, convince, please, arouse emotion, or persuade to action, and which has as its communicative content some passion, idea, sentiment, disposition or purpose is an instance of rhetorical discourse" (Bitzer, 1963, p. xix). Campbell thus differed from Aristotle and other classical theorists who focused on only some of rhetoric's functions and purposes, such as public persuasion in a legal or political setting. For Campbell, a broader definition of rhetoric was necessary to account for the epistemologists'

Table 4.1 Campbell's Four Goals of Rhetoric

Goal	Definition
Enlighten the understanding	Provide information upon which the audience can make a decision or take action.
Please the imagination	Use stylistic techniques to keep the audience interested in the rhetoric.
Move the passions	Appeal to the audience's emotions.
Influence the will	Make the audience take action on the topic.

insights into human psychology. Campbell's starting point was the nature of the human mind, as we have previously discussed.

Campbell explained that the four goals of rhetoric are "to enlighten the understanding, to please the imagination, to move the passions, or to influence the will" (Bitzer, 1963, p. 1) (see Table 4.1). The distinctions Campbell identifies are based on psychological theory about the functions of the human mind. Bitzer (1963) explained, "Campbell defines four types of discourses based not on an empirical inspection of instances of messages, but on his conception of the powers, functions, or faculties of the mind" (p. xx). That is, Campbell, unlike Aristotle, did not survey the way that rhetoric was used to derive these distinctions. Instead, he surmised that given what was known of the mind, these distinctions in how humans communicate will naturally follow. Bitzer also observed that Campbell was not consistent throughout the book in terms of referring to these classifications of rhetoric.

Each of these goals of rhetoric builds upon the one that precedes it. At the most fundamental level is understanding, or instructing the hearer. The rhetor may have the goal of informing the listeners or convincing them. Informing audiences requires perspicuity, or being clear; convincing them requires argument. Rhetoric aimed at the imagination presents a "lively and beautiful representation of a suitable object" (p. 3). Poetry, noted Campbell, is a prime example of rhetoric aimed at pleasing the imagination.

A rhetor can appeal to the passions by being sublime, wrote Campbell. Passion is related to "magnitude, or of whatever is great and stupendous in its kind" (p. 3). When properly employed, rhetoric can "have such marvelous efficacy in rousing the passions, and by some secret, sudden, and inexplicable association, awakening all the tenderest emotions of the heart" (p. 4). The goal, he noted, is not to simply create images of greatness, but to influence the listener's emotions.

The final type of rhetoric, according to Campbell, is "the most complex of all" (p. 4). He explained that to move someone to action, the rhetor must combine "that which proposes to convince the judgment, and that which interests the passions" (p. 4). Working together, the three previously discussed types of rhetoric can "constitute passionate eviction" that moves one to act (p. 4). See the Critical Insights box (Box 4.2) for this chapter for an example of how knowledge of these four types of rhetoric can lead to effective persuasion.

Think for a moment about how your use of rhetoric may reflect Campbell's distinctions. If you've ever had to teach someone something, such as in a lecture

---

BOX 4.2 Critical Insights: Campbell's Types of Rhetoric and Effective Persuasion

Examine the advertisement in Figure 4.1. The ad is for EarthShare, an organization that links together the leading environmental organizations from around the world. The ad calls on readers to visit the organization's website and donate money to promote environmental causes. The ad is effective because it appeals to each of Campbell's four types of rhetoric.

The first type of rhetoric, according to Campbell, is reaching the understanding. The ad states that "the world's leading environmental organizations are working together under one name." Readers may not have known this previously and would not have known to which organization to donate money. The ad provides this information.

Second, Campbell wrote that rhetoric should reach the imagination. The advertisement uses pleasing and colorful images of flowers, mountains, and penguins. The copy uses the stylistic device of alliteration, stating that readers could help "protect the prairies and the penguins and the planet." The copy is catchy, encouraging the readers to take notice and pay attention.

Campbell also said that rhetoric should touch the emotions of the audience. Knowing that the reader can help save penguins, such as those pictured, is an emotional appeal. Additionally, the images of the advertisement appeal to the reader's emotions. The images show a pristine wilderness that audience members can help protect.

Finally, Campbell explained that rhetoric should move the will to take action. The advertisement provides the web address of the organization so that the reader can log on to the site and donate money to the organization. While audience members may or may not take action, all of the necessary information has been provided. Although this ad may not entice you to donate money, Campbell's description of the four types of rhetoric helps us to understand the rhetorical messages of the advertisement.

---

or training presentation, you would have had as your goal enhancing their understanding of the topic. You may have used rhetoric designed to please the imagination when you've written poetry or read the creative work of others. Keep in mind that Campbell's view of rhetoric was quite broad, including communication such as poetry and other forms of literature. Rhetoric aimed at moving the passions would include times when you've used rhetoric to reach someone on an emotional level. Finally, you've used rhetoric aimed at moving the will when you have attempted to persuade someone to do something. Convincing your friends to go to a particular movie, for instance, is an example of this use of rhetoric.

You probably also realize from these examples that often when you attempt to achieve one goal, you use rhetoric aimed at one of the other goals to achieve your primary goal. For instance, when attempting to persuade your friends to go to a particular movie—whereby your goal is influencing the will—you may also have to influence their passions or their understanding of the movie you wish to see. Campbell also observed this necessity for a multipronged approach to be true. While a rhetor may have as a goal to enhance the audience's understanding of an idea, for example, the rhetoric may employ imaginative, passionate, or action-oriented rhetoric to achieve the goal of understanding. He explained, "Nevertheless, in discoursing on a subject, many things may be introduced, which are more immediately and apparently directed to some of the other ends of speaking, and not to that which is the primary intention" (p. 1).

FIGURE 4.1   Earth Share Advertisement.

Having looked at how Campbell defined rhetoric and how his definition related to the study of psychology at that time, let's turn to some of Campbell's other unique points about rhetorical theory.

The Role of Invention

Ehninger (1955) believed that Campbell's book represented a fundamental shift in the theory of rhetoric. In particular, Ehninger argued that Campbell—and to some extent Blair (See Chapter 3) and Whately, whom we'll discuss later—shifted their theorizing from the uses of rhetoric by a speaker to how rhetoric was received by a listener. Classical theory, he argued, started with the canon of invention, or finding what may be said by a speaker. Campbell, based on the findings of the epistemologists, instead starts from the perspective of the listener. By focusing on the psychological processes inherent in the reception of rhetorical messages,

Campbell shifted his focus. As a result, his theory is receiver centered instead of speaker centered. Additionally, noted Ehninger, Campbell, Blair, and Whately did not organize their books according to the five canons, which we studied in Chapter 2. Likewise, Campbell, according to Ehninger, blended invention and arrangement so much that each term lost its classical meaning.

Ehninger and others have classified Campbell's rhetoric—because of its approach to invention—as **managerial.** That is, the rhetoric is used to manage claims, proof, and truths developed elsewhere. It is not, according to this view, a method for finding what is fitting and true to say. Ehninger (1955) explained that Campbell most clearly "ruled investigation as a whole out of the province of rhetorical science and assigned it to other substantive and methodological disciplines" (p. 266). Public relations is, in some ways, an example of managerial rhetoric today. Often, public relations practitioners create messages based on research done by the accounting or marketing divisions of an organization. Public relations makes that information effective for the organization's audiences.

However, not all commentators agree with Ehninger's assertions. Bitzer disagreed with Ehninger's conclusion, arguing that Campbell did include invention in his theory of rhetoric. Bitzer (1963) explained, "It seems quite clear that Campbell believed that both logic and grammar are included within the art of rhetoric" (p. xxviii). "In this way," noted Bitzer, Campbell "brought empirical procedures within his theory; that is to say, he included *inventio* while assigning it the essentially empirical mission of accurately drawing knowledge from observation and experience" (p. xxix).

RHETORIC AND ARGUMENTATION

We move now from the nineteenth century to the turn of the century. Our focus shifts now, too, to the study of **argumentation** and its relationship to rhetoric. We might think of argumentation as "the art or activity by which one person, through the use of reasoned discourse, seeks to get other persons to believe or to do what he wants them to believe or to do" (McBurney, O'Neill, & Mills, 1951, p. 1). The key aspect of argumentation is the idea that it involves reasoned discourse, rather than emotional or credibility appeals. That is, argumentation makes use of evidence, reasoning, and systematic thought. Also keep in mind that argumentation is a social process by which people use rhetoric to reach a consensus about what is probably true. That is, argumentation is a conscious attempt to make a good decision based on a systematic discussion of evidence and reasons. Rhetoric, as we have discussed it, is generally thought to be less formal and systematic and is not necessarily based on logic and reasons. Certainly there is overlap between the two practices, but argumentation generally refers to a more specific and focused activity.

The work of the epistemologists and Campbell's discussion of reason laid the groundwork for viewing rhetoric through the lens of argumentation. Yet there is a clear difference between the rhetorical theories of the epistemologists and those we are about to study. Whereas the epistemologists locate truth in the scientific method, argumentation theorists locate truth in the rhetorical process of deliberation. For the epistemologists, rhetoric was a vehicle for communicating truth; for the argumentation theorists, rhetoric is the way that we determine truth.

In some ways, argumentation represents a more narrow focus than what we have seen previously. No longer are we concerned with literature, art, and other expressive forms as we were with the belletristic movement. Nor are we concerned as much with style and delivery. Argumentation involves the canons of invention and arrangement, primarily. However, before we discuss some of the specific contributions made to the study of argumentation by rhetorical theorists in the nineteenth and twentieth centuries, let's review what we have discussed concerning argumentation so far.

In Chapter 2, rhetorical theorists identified many principles that we now consider to be part of the study of argumentation. Aristotle, in fact, has been called the "father of the theory of argumentation" (Perelman, 1982, p. 1). Aristotle developed the idea of inartistic and artistic proof. The ancient theorists developed the syllogism, which was attacked by the epistemologists, who countered it with induction as a way of knowing. We have also discussed the dialectical and persuasive functions of argument.

In the nineteenth and twentieth centuries, argumentation theorists such as Whately, Toulmin, and Perelman, elaborating on concepts we've discussed previously, sought to clarify the relationship between rhetoric, logic, and argumentation. We'll begin our study of argumentation by looking at some of the ideas of Richard Whately, one of the key nineteenth-century rhetorical theorists. Then, we'll move to the twentieth century and discuss some general issues in modern approaches to argumentation. Finally, we'll examine some of the ideas about argumentation of two prominent theorists, Stephen Toulmin and Chaim Perelman.

RICHARD WHATELY

Richard Whately, an Anglican clergyman, was one of the best known of the British rhetorical theorists of the eighteenth and nineteenth centuries. Whately narrowed the focus of rhetoric to a study of argumentation. He wrote, "The art of inventing and arranging Arguments is, as has been said, the only province that Rhetoric can claim entirely and exclusively" (Whately, 1963, p. 40). Logic, Whately explained, is concerned with judging arguments, not inventing them. Additionally, the art of addressing the emotions does not belong exclusively to rhetoric; it is shared with poetry, wrote Whately. Likewise, rhetoric does not concern all types of composition, as did belletrism. Ehninger (1963) summarized Whately's view of rhetoric: "rhetoric is to be regarded as the art of 'reasoned discourse,' as governing that sort of composition in which conclusions are inferred from premises according to the laws of logic" (xiii). Despite the fact that Whately's work expands beyond this narrow definition, he himself insisted that rhetoric should be equated with argumentation and is today "almost universally—indeed, almost automatically—thought of as a treatise on argument" (Enhinger, 1963, p. xiv).

Whately conceived of rhetoric as an "off-shoot" of logic. Ehninger (1963) succinctly states the difference for Whately between logic and rhetoric: "Conceiving of logic as the methodology of proof, he [Whately] consistently treats rhetoric as the application of that methodology in actual attempts to influence, so that while logic is the process of establishing truth by reasoning, rhetoric becomes the process of conveying truth to others by reasoning" (p. xiv). Although Whately includes examples of written argument in his work, he is mostly concerned with rhetoric as oral argumentation. Ehninger clarified: "More correctly, it is a rhetoric of oral argumentation—a rhetoric concerned with argument as it occurs either in the formal speaker-audience situation or in the give and take of face-to-face dispute" (p. xv).

Ehninger (1963) explained that a religious perspective dominates Whately's theory of rhetoric. Thus, concepts such as *presumption* and *burden of proof,* are discussed "to acquaint the Christian apologist with his rights and obligations in controversy" (p. x). Likewise, explained Ehninger, "rhetoric emerges neither as a method for probing judgments nor as an instrument for arriving at collective choices and decisions" (p. xi). Specifically, Whately saw rhetoric as important to clergy members, like himself, who had to convey the "indisputable doctrines of the Christian faith" to an uneducated congregation (Ehninger, 1963, p. x). Additionally, rhetoric was useful for all Christians in order to "defend the evidences of religion against the onslaughts of the sceptic [sic]" (p. xi). Ehninger summarizes Whately's view of rhetoric thus: "With these ends in view, Whately denies the probable or contingent nature of rhetoric, as insisted upon by Aristotle" (p. xi). As we move into the twentieth century, we'll see a loosening of the religious influence on rhetoric; instead, rhetoric will become a way of deciding between possible truths. Despite the limits Whately may have seen for the use of argumentation, his theory provides us with several key concepts that influence argumentation theory today.

Presumption and Burden of Proof

Whately was "the first to transfer from the law of evidence into the general field of non-legal argumentation" the ideas of presumption and burden of proof (Ehninger, 1963, p. xix). Presumption, according to Whately, is a "pre-occupation of the ground" by a side in a controversy. Burden of proof "lies on the side of him who would dispute it" (quoted in Ehninger, 1963, p. 112). For a simple example, you might think of the childhood game "king of the mountain" in which a person stands at the top of a hill until someone else overtakes that position. In the United States legal system, for another example, people are presumed innocent until proven guilty. That means that a person preoccupies the ground of innocence until enough evidence can be presented to prove that he or she is guilty.

Or, you might consider an example in which you want to argue that a certain campus policy should be changed. The current policy—and those who support it—would have presumption, because the policy currently exists. Since you want to change the policy, you would have the burden to prove that it should change. Essentially, these two concepts imply that there is always some kind of advantage to keeping things the same and that before change can take place, a new idea has to be presented that overcomes the advantages enjoyed by the current idea or policy.

Refutation

Ehninger remarked that Whately's discussion of **refutation** is one of the best ever written. Refutation is the practice of countering the claims of an arguer with evidence, reasoning, or other techniques. Whately's ideas influence how refutation is taught and practiced today. Let's look briefly at some of his ideas about the subject.

Whately remarked that if an opponent has recently objected to what will be said, it is advisable to begin with a refutation. But if no one has objected to what will be said, beginning with a refutation may imply "a consciousness that much may be said against it" (quoted in Ehninger, 1963, p. 147). "Sometimes indeed it will be difficult to give a satisfactory Refutation of the opposed opinions, till we have gone through the arguments in support of our own: even in that case however it will be better to take some brief notice of them early in the Composition, with a promise of afterwards considering them more fully, and refuting them" (p. 147). This technique, noted Whately, was Aristotle's "usual procedure" (p. 147).

There are two general methods of refutation. The first, which is "less strictly and properly called Refutation" involves proving the opposite of what one's opponent has stated. Simply offering contradictory evidence accomplishes this method of refutation. Related to refutation is objecting to the opponent's reasoning or identify fallacies present in his or her reasoning. By noting when an arguer has incorrectly used the syllogism, for instance, or by calling attention to an ad hominem argument, an arguer may persuade the audience.

The other type of refutation, which is of greater interest to Whately, is where an arguer "turns the tables" on his or her opponent by showing that what the opponent suggests is a good thing is actually a bad thing or that a bad thing is actually a good thing. A University of Minnesota economist was recently asked to do a study of how much gay marriage would cost the state government in spousal benefit payments. The questioner wanted to argue that gay marriage would be costly to the state. After conducting research the economist learned that gay marriage would generate additional income for the state, instead of costing the state money. The additional income would come from taxes on all the goods and services purchased for marriage ceremonies, for instance. The economist wrote an article in the *Minneapolis Star-Tribune* revealing his research and "turning the tables" on the opponent of gay marriage who had argued that such a policy would cost the state money.

Conclusion

Whately provided a new way of looking at rhetoric and his ideas about presumption, burden of proof, and refutation remain with us today. Whately's *Elements of Rhetoric* and *Elements of Logic* equated rhetoric with argument and unified again what Ramus had separated. Stimulated by Whately's work, rhetorical theory's interest in argumentation today remains an important part of the study of rhetoric.

RHETORICAL APPROACHES
TO ARGUMENTATION

In the final part of this chapter, we'll examine the work of two influential theorists concerning argumentation, Stephen Toulmin and Chaim Perelman. These two European theorists—Toulmin was English and Perelman Belgian—provide us with three new ways of thinking about argumentation.

First, Toulmin and Perelman split with the traditional study of logic. To put it simply, Toulmin and Perelman sought to study and understand argumentation as it actually occurred instead of as it should occur. At the heart of Toulmin's (1969) theory of argumentation is what he sees as a divergence between "the practical business of argumentation" and "the corresponding analyses of them set out in books on formal logic" (p. 147). Perelman added, "As a consequence, it is necessary that we clearly distinguish analytical from dialectical reasoning, the former dealing with truth and the latter with justifiable opinion" (Perelman, 1982, p. 3). Ramus—who said that invention and arrangement belonged to logic—failed to see this distinction, making an error that was "fatal for rhetoric" (Perelman, 1982, p. 3). Although logic may appropriately deal with deciding questions of truth based on systematic reasoning, modern argumentation theorists believe that the task of creating and evaluating statements that can be considered reasonable for a particular audience should fall to rhetoric.

Second, Toulmin and Perelman—Toulmin, in particular—emphasized the linguistic nature of argumentation, an approach that is directly related to their practical focus. Because arguers use words and because words have ambiguous meanings, we must also include the words arguers use in any kind of study or description of argumentation. In the next chapter, we'll take up in more detail what is meant by the "linguistic turn" in rhetoric and its impact on rhetorical theory. You'll see that this idea has had a great deal of influence on rhetorical theory in the twentieth century.

Finally, Toulmin and Perelman focused on audience response to arguments. In so doing, they split with the traditional study of argumentation from a philosophical perspective and paved the way for rhetorical theorists to use their theories to learn about rhetoric. Until the introduction of Toulmin to U.S. rhetorical scholars, these scholars had largely ignored the study and practice of argumentation (Brockriede & Ehninger, 1960).

THE LAYOUT OF ARGUMENTS

Perhaps the most useful tool of rhetoric to emerge from the study of argumentation is Toulmin's map of an argument's structure. Brockriede and Ehninger (1960) noted that Toulmin's classification of arguments provides a way of diagraming and critiquing arguments. You can read a lengthy biography of Toulmin online at http://www.neh.gov/news/humanities/1997–03/wartofsk.html. Let's examine the components of an argument, according to Toulmin's theory. We'll begin with the three basic components of an argument: claim, data, and warrant.

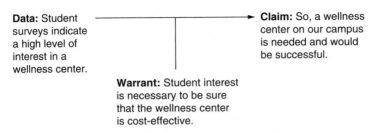

FIGURE 4.2   Diagram of an Argument According to the Basic Elements of Toulmin's Model.

According to Toulmin (1958) a **claim** is the "conclusion whose merits we are seeking to establish" (p. 97). Brockriede and Ehninger (1960) explained that the claim "is the explicit appeal produced by the argument, and is always of a potentially controversial nature" (pp. 44–45). The statement, "Our campus should build a wellness center" is an example of a claim, since it asserts a conclusion, or answer, to the question about whether a wellness center should be built on campus.

Data are the "facts we appeal to as a foundation for the claim" (Toulmin, 1958, p. 97). Brockriede and Ehninger (1960) elaborated, "Data may report historical or contemporary events, take the form of a statistical compilation or of citations from an authority, or they may consist of one or more general declarative sentences established by a prior proof of an artistic nature" (p. 44). You might think of data as the evidence used to support a claim. Data that could be used to support the construction of a campus wellness center might include statistics about student interest, financing options, or examples of how the wellness center could support the campus's academic programs.

Brockriede and Ehninger (1960) explained that "Data and claim taken together represent the specific contention advanced by an argument, and therefore constitute what may be regarded as its main proof line" (p. 45). The claim contains or implies the word "therefore," according to Toulmin. Thus, we might say "Students are very interested in a wellness center; therefore, our campus should build a wellness center."

The third component of Toulmin's model is the **warrant.** Toulmin explained that an arguer needs to explain how he or she moved from the data to the claim. He explained, "Our task is no longer to strengthen the ground on which our argument is constructed, but is rather to show that, taking these data as a starting point, the step to the original claim or conclusion is an appropriate and legitimate one" (Toulmin, 1958, p. 98). Thus, we use a warrant, which functions as a bridge to "authorize the sort of step to which our particular argument commits us" (p. 98). The warrant in our wellness center example could be: "Student interest in a wellness center is necessary to make sure the center is cost-effective and needed." This statement provides a justification or rationale for the claim. A diagram of these three elements of an argument is provided in Figure 4.2.

We have discussed the main components of the Toulmin model of argument: data, warrant, and claim. However, because Toulmin was interested in how people

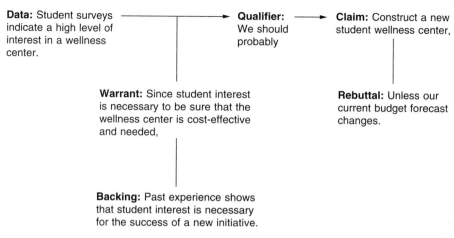

FIGURE 4.3   Complete Model of an Argument.

argue, as opposed to more formal logic, he included additional elements in his model: qualifiers, rebuttal, and backing. A *qualifier* is a statement that we make about the strength of the argument. Toulmin (1958) explained that it is used to "register the degree of force which the maker believes his claim to possess" (p. 45). When you use the words "probably" or "certainly" in an argument, you are using a qualifier.

A *rebuttal* expresses some kind of exception that would negate the argument being made. Toulmin provided some analogies: "The rebuttal performs the function of a safety valve or escape hatch, and is, as a rule, appended to the claim statement" (1958, p. 45). The rebuttal "recognizes certain conditions under which the claim will not hold good or will hold good only in a qualified and restricted way" (p. 45). Consider this statement: "Unless our budget forecast changes significantly, we should build a new student wellness center." The rebuttal in this case is the phrase, "unless our budget forecast changes significantly." The qualifier, to accommodate this uncertainty, is the word "probably."

The final element of Toulmin's model is the *backing,* which consists of "credentials designed to certify the assumption expressed in the warrant" (1958, p. 45). The backing is the reason the warrant is valid. The backing is often a scientific study or a law or some other form of proof for the warrant. The backing should not be confused with the data, which is the initial observation or support for the claim. Toulmin explained that "Backing must be introduced when readers or listeners are not willing to accept a warrant at its face" (p. 45). For the wellness center example, backing might include a statement that "Past experience shows that initiatives that lack student interest generally don't succeed, while those that are backed by the students are successful."

Toulmin's model allows us to visualize how arguments are created and used. The model also helps us to critique arguments, because it allows us to see if parts are missing or unsubstantiated (Brockriede & Ehinger, 1960). To see a complete picture of Toulmin's model, see Figure 4.3. This argument, when stated, would be,

---

BOX 4.3   Internet Activity: Diagramming an Argument

Read a letter to the editor in your local newspaper or locate one online. You can do a Google search for "letter to the editor" or "editorial" to quickly find a wide range of articles. Find one or two arguments in the article and outline them using Toulmin's model. Does the author's arguments fit the Toulmin model? Why or why not? Is the argument effective, according to the model? If there are parts of the argument missing, supply them in order to bolster the author's claim.

"Student surveys indicate a high level of interest in a wellness center. Since student interest is necessary to be sure that the wellness center is cost-effective and needed, we should probably construct a new student wellness center, unless our current budget forecast changes." Now, complete Internet Activity, Diagraming an Argument (Box 4.3), and diagram an argument contained in a recent letter to the editor.

Toulmin's model also helps to diagram and make sense of Aristotle's artistic proofs: logos, ethos, and pathos (Brockriede & Ehninger, 1960). Recall that logos refers to reasoning, ethos to proofs based on credibility, and pathos to those based on emotions. According to Brockriede and Ehninger (1960), Toulmin provided us with a methodology by which we can chart these types of arguments as well. You'll also recall that Aristotle discussed inartistic proof, which refers to data that are themselves conclusive, according to Brockriede and Ehninger. In the case of inartistic proof, we don't need a warrant to move from the data to the claim. The physical presence of an object, for instance, would serve as data, but also as the claim that the object exists. We are interested here in how artistic proof can be expressed in Toulmin's model of an argument.

Substantive Arguments

What Aristotle referred to as logos, Toulmin calls substantive arguments. According to Brockriede and Ehninger (1960), a substantive argument contains a warrant that "reflects an assumption concerning the way in which things are related in the world about us" (p. 48). The warrant in our previous example—that student support is necessary for a successful wellness center—is a substantive warrant, for example. There are several types of relationships that can exist between ideas. We'll divide these into two broad categories: inductive and deductive. See Table 4.2 for a list of these types of argument.

Inductive Argument Forms   There are three types of inductive arguments: argument by example, argument by analogy, and argument by causal correlation. *Argument by example* "examines one or more cases within a specific class and reasons that if these cases have certain features then other, as yet unknown, cases in the class will also have those features" (Hollihan & Baaske, 1994, p. 76). In other words, we use argument by example when we generalize to a population after examining a sample of that observation. Whenever you infer about a larger group

Table 4.2 Types of Arguments and Examples

General Type	Specific Type
Inductive	Example
	Analogy
	Correlation
Deductive	Generalization
	Sign
	Classification

of objects, people, or events based on a few examples of that group, you're using argument by example. An advertisement for Hilton Hotels pictures five women and states "It's wonderful to share dreams. It's even better to own them." The conclusion is that these women are examples of the "diverse ownership of hotels within the Hilton Family." Thus, opportunities exist for women and minorities to buy into Hilton Hotels.

Argument by analogy says that what is true of one object, person, or event will also be true of other objects, people, or events that are essentially the same. Of course, it's important that the two items being compared are truly similar. For example, the state of California may be seen as a microcosm of the United States: both have similar geographic diversity, population diversity, and population density. Should California adopt a single-payer system of health care as has been proposed and should the system prove effective, one could argue that a similar system would be effective throughout the entire United States. An advertisement for the Jeep Liberty Renegade shows an image of a man's tie being untied. Another image shows the Jeep Liberty Renegade tearing through the countryside. The implied analogy supports the claim is that driving a Jeep Liberty Renegade is as relaxing as untying a tie.

Argument from causal correlation infers that similarities (or differences) between object, people, or events can be attributed to whatever characteristic is shared (or not shared) between the objects, people, or events. The correlation suggests that there is some kind of causal relationship between the two compared objects, events, or people. For example, we might infer that children who grow up being exposed to violence on television and then participate in violence themselves are proof for the claim that "television causes violence." The particular elements of acts of violence and television viewing are correlated and a cause-effect relationship is established.

Argumentation scholars largely draw on the work of John Stuart Mill, who identified three procedures that can be used to discover causal relationships. The *method of concomitant variation* is used to identify similar variations in two elements. One might say that as the amount of legal gambling in a city increases, so does the crime rate. As one increases (or decreases), so does the other compared object. *The method of agreement* looks for a common element among essentially dissimilar situations. For example, if a group gets food poisoning, identifying a similar food that each member ate would indicate the cause of food poisoning. The *method of differences* looks at one difference between two similar cases. If one member of a group of people became sick following a dinner and no one else did, doctors may try to determine if the person ate anything that was different than what the others ate.

An advertisement for Wal-Mart features a statement from Cynthia, a Wal-Mart employee. She states: "I spent 15 years of my life working in the vision field as an assistant, for another company. But, within two years of working for Wal-Mart, I furthered my education, got my optician's license, and began my career as a specialist...." This statement shows the difference between Wal-Mart and another company and implies that Wal-Mart allowed Cynthia to have a better career.

Deductive Reasoning Deduction is a process in which one "generalizes from theories or principles believed to be true to claims about individual cases" (Hollihan and Baaske, 1994, p. 81). Deductive arguments often may be reduced to syllogistic form, which we have discussed previously. Freeley (1993) contended that deductive reasoning is used to establish the "certainty" of a conclusion (p. 163). Ziegelmueller and Kay (1997) added to this discussion by arguing that deduction is primarily an analytic process—it breaks down generalizations and applies them to specific cases.

There are three major types of deductive reasoning. The first is *causal generalization*. Unlike causal correlation (the inductive argument type), causal generalization looks at known cause-effect relationships and establishes that such relationship holds true for a particular case that is part of that class (Hollihan & Baaske, 1994, p. 82). An advertisement for Sally Hansen Nailgrowth Miracle states the generalization that "Soy protein, vitamins, and keratin help stimulate healthy growth." Evidently, these products cause nail growth. This statement also implies that the specific case—Nailgrowth Miracle—is included in the generalization, meaning that using this product will lead to nails that "become longer and stronger."

Argument by sign involves tying certain observed characteristics to a generalization and making a claim about the particular case. If for example, I have a runny nose, sore throat, and fever, I can be said to have a cold. Thus, the sign of a cold consists of the symptoms I described (the generalization) and if I have those symptoms (a particular case), then it can be assumed that I have a cold (the claim). An advertisement for Coca-Cola pictures a woman at her birthday party. She is surrounded by smiling friends, an expensive kitchen, and, of course, Coca-Cola. The ad asks, "Who's counting?" In other words, the advertisement suggest that signs of happiness don't include being young, but they do include drinking Coca-Cola.

In argument from classification, explain Brockriede and Ehinger (1960), the statement of data is "a generalized conclusion about known members of a class of persons, objects, events, or conditions" (p. 50). The warrant, they explained, "assumes that what is true of the items reported in the data will also be true of a hitherto unexamined item which is known (or thought) to fall within the class there described" (p. 50). In other words, an employer in your town might have had excellent experience hiring students from your school. When you apply for a job with this employer, they might use an argument from classification to

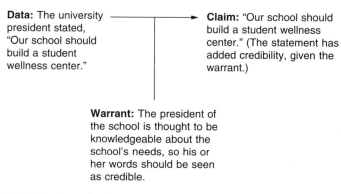

FIGURE 4.4   Authoritative Argument, According to Toulmin's Model.

assume that you—like other alumni from your school—would be a good employee. The employer assumes that people from your school are hardworking, well trained, and competent; since you are member of that group of people, the employer might think that you would also possess those characteristics.

An important point to note is that deductive arguments can generally be said to fit the form of a classic syllogism:

All people are mortal; (Major premise)

I am a person; (Minor premise)

Therefore, I am mortal. (Conclusion)

The syllogism provides the structure and rules for a deductive argument. If one of the premises is false, the claim is questioned. The claim might still be true, but the syllogism doesn't allow one to make that judgment. Likewise if the particular case does not fit the generalization, the claim can be disputed. Again, it may or may not be true, but the claim doesn't necessarily follow from the reasoning presented. Although Toulmin—like Campbell, Locke, Bacon, and Whately—was generally skeptical that all arguments could be classified by the syllogism, this classic form of reasoning can be used in deductive arguments.

Authoritative Arguments

Toulmin's model also helps us diagram appeals to ethos, which he called *authoritative arguments*. In an authoritative argument, the data consists of testimony from some person. The warrant "affirms the reliability of the source from which these are derived" (Brockriede & Ehinger, 1960, p. 51). The claim "reiterates the statement which appeared in the data, as now certified by the warrant" (p. 51). A statement from the university president affirming the need for and feasibility of building a campus wellness center would likely be accepted since the president has the credibility to make such a statement (see Figure 4.4).

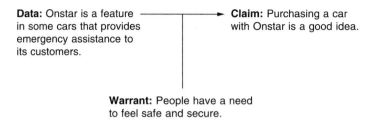

FIGURE 4.5   Motivational Argument, According to Toulmin's Model.

Motivational Arguments

Finally, Toulmin allows us to diagram emotional appeals, or pathos. A motivational argument is very similar to an authoritative argument. However, the warrant in this case "provides a motive for accepting the claim by associating it with some inner drive, value, desire, emotion, or aspiration, or with a combination of such forces" (Brockriede & Ehninger, 1960, p. 51). In other words, data are offered that refer to some value, need or emotion humans experience. The warrant affirms the presence of this value, need, or emotion and supports the claim that the data should be accepted based on their appeal to a genuine human need, value, or emotion. Consider Onstar, a tool that provides emergency assistance to drivers of certain General Motors vehicles. OnStar advertisements typically refer to the need for safety and thus build support for the claim that the reader should purchase a car with OnStar (see Figure 4.5).

CHAIM PERELMAN'S "NEW RHETORIC"

The Belgium theorist Chaim Perelman was also interested in developing a way to critique arguments as they appeared in actual discussion. Perelman believed that the way to more accurately discuss argumentation was to focus on its audience. For Perelman (1982), argumentation necessarily involved an audience, which made it different from formal logic, "in which no attention is paid to the meaning of the symbols" (p. 13). Argumentation, though, requires a relationship between the speaker and the audience. Ray (1978) explained, "Since it is the audience that the speaker seeks to influence by argument, all argumentation is developed in relation to an audience" (p. 362). In Perelman's (1982) words, "all argumentation aims at gaining the adherence of minds, and, by this very fact, assumes the existence of an intellectual contact" (p. 14). The audience, he explained may not be the person or people physically present to hear the speaker. It is even more difficult to locate the exact audience for written rhetoric, since writing spreads to many audience members unknown to the writer. Perelman (1982) defined the audience as "the ensemble of those whom the speaker wishes to influence by his argumentation" (p. 19).

Perelman (1982) noted that the "audience" is always a "more or less system-atized construction" (p. 19). That is, the audience is an idea the speaker considers as he or she prepares arguments and techniques of argumentation. Too often, wrote Perelman (1982), rhetoric had become an "academic exercise" in which it addressed "conventional audiences" (p. 20). He was concerned that rhetoric was not taught in a way to address a meaningful audience, but one that was instead invented for the rhetorical exercise at hand. Such a view limited rhetoric and made it an artificial art, according to Perelman.

In argumentation, he explained, "care must be taken to form a concept of the anticipated audience as close as possible to reality. An inadequate picture of the audience, resulting either from ignorance or an unforeseen set of circumstances, can have very unfortunate results" (Perelman, 1982, p. 20). Without a clear under-standing of the audience, a speaker who thinks he or she has constructed effec-tive arguments, may find the opposite when confronted by a real audience. Perelman advised, "Accordingly, knowledge of those one wishes to win over is a condition preliminary to all effectual argumentation" (p. 20). In fact, Perelman advised arguers that "the important thing is not knowing what the speaker regards as true or important, but knowing the views of those he is addressing" (pp. 23–24). While Plato lamented the rhetor's flattery of the audience, Perelman observed that no orator can "afford to neglect this effort of adaptation to the audience" (p. 24).

Perelman identified a distinction between persuading and convincing to help rhetors consider the audience they are addressing. Persuasion, he wrote, is a form of argumentation that claims validity only for a particular audience, while con-vincing is a type of argumentation that holds true for an audience of "every rational being" (1982, p. 28). The former type of argumentation is aimed at a par-ticular audience, the latter at the universal audience. The **particular audience** is composed of those in attendance at a rhetor's speech; the **universal audience** is composed of "all normal, adult persons" (p. 30).

Perelman explained that "Argumentation aimed exclusively at a particular audience has the drawback that the speaker, by the very fact of adapting to the views of his listeners, might rely on arguments that are foreign or even directly opposed to what is acceptable to persons other than those he is presently address-ing" (1982, p. 31). That is, when you argue an appeal for more money for your student organization in front of the student government, you might use different appeals than if you presented your organization's alumni with similar arguments. Perelman was concerned that you would use faulty arguments if you only consid-ered the immediate audience.

The importance of the universal audience, on the other hand, is to provide a "norm for objective argumentation" (Perelman, 1982, p. 31). "Argumentation addressed to a universal audience must convince the reader that the reasons adduced are of a compelling character, that they are self-evident, and possess an absolute and timeless validity, independent of local or historical contingencies" (Perelman & Olbrechts-Tyteca, 1969, p. 32). The strongest arguments, he thought, were those that had a timeless appeal to a universal audience.

SUMMARIZING RHETORICAL THEORY

Despite their diversity, the theorists we have discussed in this chapter all sought to develop a deeper understanding of humans and how they made decisions. In general, we focused first on the epistemologists and then on theorists interested in argumentation. Let's review their positions on certain key terms.

Defining Rhetoric

Whereas Bacon, Locke, and Campbell include appeals to the imagination in their definition of rhetoric, Whately, Toulmin, and Perelman are mostly interested in reasoning. In fact, even credibility and motivational arguments could be described with a reasoning model, according to Brockriede and Ehninger (1960).

Rhetoric and Knowledge

Both approaches to rhetoric that we examined earlier largely concerned epistemological questions. However, each approach took a different path to knowledge. The epistemologists—Bacon and Locke, in particular—sought to use the methods of science to determine what was true. The modern rhetoricians—Toulmin, and Perelman—relied on people's ability to systematically form reasonable opinions about questions by using argumentation.

Rhetoric and Identity

This chapter marks a significant break with the previous two chapters in terms of identity. The epistemologists present us with scientific conceptions of what it means to be human. They studied the human mind and they explored humans' place in the universe. For the first time, science was able to more or less correctly conceive of the relationship between humans, their own planet, and the planets of this universe. Additionally, the argumentation theorists focused on humans as reasoning animals. Toulmin and Perelman both assign humans the value of reasoning, which is new to our discussion and elevates the status of what it means to be human above what we have seen previously.

Rhetoric and Judgment

The argumentation theorists also present us with a clear view of the relationship between rhetoric and judgment, promoting the idea of reasoned judgment grounded in probability. Perelman perhaps has provided the best example of this view with his concept of the universal audience. He seeks to develop a theory by which valid and ethical arguments can be created and presented to audiences.

DISCUSSION QUESTIONS

1. How were the epistemologists different from the ancient scientists such as Aristotle? How were they similar?

2. Do you agree with Bacon's and Locke's description of the human mind? Are there other important qualities to consider?

3. Recall an example of rhetoric that effectively convinced you of something but failed to move you to take action. Account for the rhetoric's failure. What would have made the rhetoric more effective?

4. Consider a current court trial. Who has presumption? Who has the burden of proof? Do you think the side with burden of proof will be able to overcome the presumption of the other side? Why or why not?

5. Read a transcript from a political debate and locate instances of refutation. Did either of the debaters "turn the tables" on the other? Was the argument effective? Evaluate the overall quality of refutation in the debate.

6. Refer to an advertisement in a magazine or newspaper. Locate a motivational argument present in the advertisement. Diagram the argument using Toulmin's model. Is the argument effective? Why or why not?

7. Refer to an authoritative argument in a political speech. Diagram the argument using Toulmin's model. Is the argument effective? Why or why not? How does your rationale for the argument's effectiveness differ from the rationale you used in the previous question?

GLOSSARY TERMS

epistemologists   A school of thought that believed experience, scientific study, and induction were effective ways of learning about the world.

argumentation   The systematic use of reasoning to support claims.

managerial rhetoric   A view of rhetoric that sees reduced emphasis on invention. According to this view, rhetoric is used to communicate what is discovered through different disciplines or methodologies.

refutation   Countering the claims of an arguer with evidence, reasoning, or other techniques.

claim   The explicit appeal produced by an argument.

data   The facts that serve as the foundation for the claim.

warrant   The systematic rationale for moving from data to claim.

particular audience   The audience that is physically present for a speech.

universal audience   The theoretical audience of all rational people who may potentially be an audience for the speech.

PART III

Linguistic Reflexivity

5

Rhetoric and Meaning

Learning Objectives

After reading this chapter, you should be able to:

1. Explain the reflexive nature of language and its impact on rhetorical theory.
2. Explain the relationships between symbols, objects, and thoughts.
3. Identify ways of using rhetoric clearly.
4. Explain how society and the self are constructed through rhetoric.
5. Discuss ways that language may be incapable of expressing ideas.
6. Identify how language oppresses.
7. Describe how rhetoric moves a culture to its tyrannizing image.
8. Explain how rhetoric is epistemic.

President Bill Clinton, when facing allegations that he had an inappropriate sexual affair with White House intern Monica Lewinsky, made this statement:

> It depends on what the meaning of the word "is" is. If the—if the—if "is" means is and never has been, that is not—that is one thing. If it means there is none, that was a completely true statement. . . . . Now, if someone had asked me on that day, are you having any kind of sexual relations with Ms. Lewinsky, that is, asked me a question in the present tense, I would have said no. And it would have been completely true.

Clinton was saying that when asked whether he was having an affair, he had said that there "is" no affair, indicating that at the present time, he was not involved in an affair. He did not believe, according to this statement, that he had lied because he did not deny that there had been, at one time, an affair. In any case, Clinton's statement received a great deal of criticism because it seemed that he was "splitting hairs" about the meaning of words and that he was using language to obfuscate his involvement with Lewinsky. Though impeached, Clinton was not removed from office. The scandal, however, clouded his presidency and legacy.

Interestingly, rhetorical theorists made a similar observation about the ambiguity of language in the early 1900s. Whether they would have agreed with Clinton's argument, we'll never know. More than likely they would have agreed with the general public who saw Clinton as taking advantage of the language. In either case, a group of rhetorical theorists argued that our language and symbol systems—the foundation of rhetoric—had arbitrary meanings that resulted in confusion and ambiguity about what they meant. Not all theorists saw ambiguity as a negative aspect of rhetoric. Kenneth Burke, whom you will meet in the next chapter, identified ambiguity as a key resource for rhetors. In any case, we hereby recognize that symbols do not have a necessary, natural, or logical connection to what they represent

The theory from this period—and that discussed in the next chapter—has also been called New Rhetoric. Richards (1936) explained, "The old Rhetoric was an offspring of dispute; it developed as the rationale of pleadings and persuadings; it was the theory of the battle of words and has always been itself dominated by the combative impulse" (p. 24). In place of the old rhetoric is a New Rhetoric, that focused primarily on language as the source of human meaning, expression, and motivation. The theorists we study in the next chapter extend the New Rhetoric envisioned by Richards.

Our focus in this chapter is on the symbols of rhetoric and how those symbols suggest meaning for audiences. The theorists we discuss in this chapter make the argument that rhetoric has multiple meanings and that misunderstanding can result when humans share symbols with each other. Ogden and Richards (1928) explained, "Words, as every one now knows, 'mean' nothing by themselves, although the belief that they did . . . was once equally universal" (pp. 9–10). We'll begin by briefly surveying the culture of the 20th century.

THE CULTURAL MILIEU

We begin this chapter at the turn of the twentieth century. The United States was becoming a world superpower, in much the same way as had Greece, Rome, and Great Britain previously. Western nations were beginning to become industrialized and enjoy the prosperity brought about by newly found wealth. Not all members of society, however, shared equally in this wealth. Those who worked long hours in the factories for low wages were alienated by the new economic system. Rhetorical theorists, such as Kenneth Burke, theorized how rhetoric led to alienation but also how rhetoric could be used to give voice to the disenfranchised in society.

In 1914, World War I broke out in Europe, and soon the United States was involved as well. Over the next thirty years, the world fought two major wars, and many of the world's nations faced a severe economic depression. Rhetorical theorists were influenced by these events and sought to create a view of rhetoric that would help unite the world's citizens. One of the leading theorists we'll study, Alfred Korzybski, fought in World War I and reflected on these experiences as he created the theory of general semantics.

New media of communication will also influence our study in this and the next chapters. If you'll recall from our previous chapters, oral and print communication were the primary media of rhetoric during the time periods we have discussed. Although the ancient theorists (Chapter 2) had printing capabilities, they relied primarily on oral communication. The printing press, developed in 1436, influenced the practice and theory of rhetoric during the time periods examined in the third and fourth chapters. In this chapter, though, we'll see an even greater emphasis on the role of media in rhetoric. The twentieth century saw the development of radio and television and their assimilation into the U.S. household. Their presence in Western culture certainly changed the nature of rhetoric and its theory.

Our discussion in this chapter will end with a publication from 1967. The decade of the 1960s was marked by widespread distrust of government and the presence of activist movements for a number of causes, including civil rights, women's rights, and peace. We don't know the degree to which these activists were aware of advances in rhetorical theory, but the same ideas that influenced rhetorical theorists no doubt affected the activists as well. Specifically, both were influenced by the idea that our language was more than a simple container for ideas. Language and other symbols were instead seen as vehicles for the creation of social truth and knowledge (recall our earlier discussion in Chapter 1). The activists, for example, used symbols to question the "truths" provided by the government and attempted to persuade the American public to accept a different view of truth. We'll study Robert L. Scott's view of "rhetoric as epistemic" to understand how this same thinking pervaded rhetorical theory.

LINGUISTIC REFLEXIVITY

The ideas we discuss in this chapter are often referred to as **linguistic reflexivity.** Celeste Condit (1995) and other rhetorical theorists use the term *linguistic reflexivity* to refer to the "intellectual orientation that entails constant reflection on the forces of language as they are at work in what one hears and what one speaks" (p. 209). In other words, rhetorical theory turns its attention in this chapter to the role and influence of language in how we communicate. In earlier theories of rhetoric, language plays a secondary role to speakers, the world, and listeners. But now, for the first time, theorists systematically investigate symbols and their influence on us.

The classical view of language is best captured by statements made by Plato and Aristotle. Both theorists believed in the natural relationship between symbols and their referents and sought to align rhetoric with reality. As Condit (1995) has explained, "Plato does not understand language as a system of usage, and hence he does not understand language as having its own independent 'force' " (p. 211). When language was misused, Plato believed that it was due to evil individuals, not due to the inadequacies in language itself, claimed Condit. While not holding out hope for absolute truth, Aristotle, like Plato "maintains an attitude that sees language as tied to some objective, external set of meanings, and hence not as the locus of its own force or a process with its own distinctive characteristics" (Condit, 1995, p. 212). Neither theorist saw in language an inherent power to create understanding, misunderstanding, or cultural relations.

The scientific approach to rhetoric that we studied in the past chapter, Condit noted, viewed rhetoric as "an annoying little Bee that got in the way of the search for knowledge" (1995, p. 212). These theorists wanted to put aside language and rhetorical training and simply allow the science to "speak through" the rhetor (p. 212). She noted that in the early part of the twentieth century, theorists began to shift their focus from the philosophical or psychological aspects of communication to the linguistic.

Condit (1995) outlined the premises of linguistic reflexivity. First, language has its own distinctive structure (p. 209). That is, we have nouns, verbs, adjectives, and so forth, and how these parts of speech are arranged and structured suggest meaning and allow language to be used to communicate effectively. Some theorists take this idea one step further, saying that our language also creates rules for conduct and aids our perception of the world.

Second, "this structure exerts powerful influence on us to say, see, and understand things in particular ways that are consonant with this structure" (Condit, 1995, p. 209). Our grammar, for instance, includes past and future tense, along with several other tenses. These tenses shape how we talk and think about events. Likewise, the English language is marked by dichotomies that influence how we think. You can either be right or wrong, true or false, male or female, and so on. It is difficult in the English language to carve out a middle ground between dichotomous words.

Finally, "in particular instances it is in some ways better to speak in ways that are not dictated by this structure, but that are responsive to other factors" (Condit, 1995, pp. 209–210). When we discuss rhetorical theory from other cultures, for instance, or when we discuss cultural criticism, you'll see how theorists suggest that we should reject at least parts of our language system in order to achieve equality.

The concept of linguistic reflexivity pervades a great deal of rhetorical theory that we'll study in the rest of this book. Let's look more closely now at how words obtain meaning and the implications of linguistic reflexivity for how we communicate with rhetoric.

MEANING

The study of meaning is often traced to two British theorists, Charles Kay (C. K.) Ogden and I. A. Richards (1928). You can read more about them in Box 5.1. Their book, *The Meaning of Meaning,* is the prime source for understanding their theory of language. Ogden and Richards were some of the first theorists interested in how language led to miscommunication and how it could be used more effectively. Their focus was on the "fundamental characteristics of language" (Condit, 1995, p. 214). Ogden and Richards "hoped that if individuals knew the likely pitfalls of language, they could speak more accurately and thereby communicate more effectively"

BOX 5.1   Biography of a Theorist: Ogden and Richards

Charles Ogden was born June 1, 1889. As an undergraduate at Cambridge University, he was interested in the study of language and would become an author, editor, and translator later in life. I. A. Richards was born on February 26, 1893 in Cheshire, England. Like Ogden, he studied at Cambridge University. Richards was interested in history and philosophy and planned to become a psychoanalyst.

In 1918, Ogden and Richards began work on *The Meaning of Meaning*, which was published in a series of journal articles. In 1923, the work

was published as a book. They also developed the theory of Basic English—a limited set of words that should be used in order to reduce confusion. Ogden worked for a variety of publications and continued to promote the study of Basic English. Richards held a variety of academic positions and continued to collaborate with Ogden on several additional works. In 1939, Richards came to the United States to teach at Harvard University, where he developed textbooks to help teach Basic English. Ogden died on March 21, 1957; Richards lived until Sept. 7, 1979.

(Condit, 1995, p. 214). In a series of lectures at Bryn Mawr College in 1936, Richards defined rhetoric as "a study of misunderstanding and its remedies" (1936, p. 3). He explained further, "We struggle all our days with misunderstandings, and no apology is required for any study which can prevent or remove them" (p. 3).

Richards argued that it was important to focus on the language of rhetoric in its own right. We could not, he explained, focus simply on the thoughts, ideas, or "bare notions" about which language discusses. Richards (1936) explained, "The trouble is that we *can* only 'collect the whole sum and tenor of the discourse' from the words, we cannot 'lay aside the words'; and as to considering 'the bare notions themselves'" (p. 5). Richards was reacting to thinking similar to that of Plato, who wanted to separate the words used in rhetoric from the "true" thoughts the words expressed. For Richards, the words were part of the equation and ideas could not be studied apart from the language through which they were expressed. Thus, a study of language and meaning was necessary to understanding rhetoric.

An important aspect of his and Ogden's work was Basic English, an 850-word vocabulary of English words that they believed could be used by anyone in any situation to communicate clearly. By using only a few, clearly defined words, it was thought that people could more easily reach understanding. Richards spent time in China teaching Basic English while Ogden founded the Orthological Institute to promote the spread of Basic English. British prime ministers Neville Chamberlain and Winston Churchill, who provided government funding for the project, supported the movement. A list of the 850 words in Basic English is available at http://ogden.basic-english.org/words.html. Despite their efforts, Basic English never really gained popularity, and it lost government support in Great Britain when Churchill left office in 1945.

The Semantic Triangle

We can begin to understand Ogden and Richards' view of meaning by studying their concept of the **semantic triangle** (Figure 5.1). The semantic triangle outlines the relationship between the three elements of meaning: symbols (words or

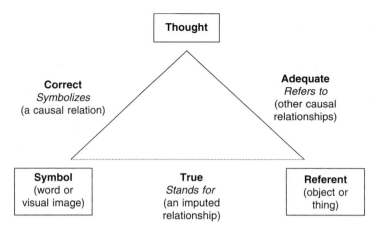

FIGURE 5.1   Semantic Triangle.

Adapted from C. K. Ogden and I. A. Richards, *The Meaning of Meaning* (New York: Harcourt, Brace, and Company, 1923). Author rendering.

images), thoughts (the ideas we have about symbols), and referents (the objects referred to by symbols). By understanding the relationship between these elements, we can better understand Ogden and Richards' theory of meaning.

Ogden and Richards (1928) explained that symbols cause certain thoughts, and, reciprocally, certain thoughts cause the use of certain symbols. Thus, the relationship between symbols and thoughts is causal in nature. They explained that "When we speak, the symbolism we employ is caused partly by the reference we are making and partly by social and psychological factors—the purpose for which we are making the reference, the proposed effect of our symbols on other persons, and our own attitude" (pp. 10–11). That is, if you are to persuade someone, you are likely to use particular symbols to do so. Your intent causes you to use one symbol over another. Likewise, if you are nervous in a communication situation, your symbol use may be affected. Your nervousness and uncertainty may cause you to say particular words.

Conversely, when we are the receiver, our thoughts are caused by the symbols others communicate to us. Ogden and Richards (1928) explained, "When we hear what is said, the symbols both cause us to perform an act of reference and to assume an attitude" (p. 11). When you see a car commercial on television, for instance, you might recall a similar feeling of freedom and escape depicted in the commercial. Or, when a politician appeals for your vote, he or she may say something that causes you to support their candidacy.

On the other side of the triangle in Figure 5.1, there is a similar type of relationship. When we physically see the referent, such as the book you are reading or the chair in which you are sitting, we think of that book or chair or you can think of objects, or referents, that are not in your immediate presence. You can recall a high school teacher or a loved one or a favorite pet even if they are not present or if the symbols for those objects are not present. In either case, you can

---

BOX 5.2   Internet Activity: Decoding Meaning

Locate a speech in *Vital Speeches,* using your Infotrac College Edition account. Identify a word in the speech that has contested meanings. That is, find a word that has controversial meanings or meanings that people do not agree upon. Using the semantic triangle, diagram this symbol and its relationship to a thought and object. Which meaning is suggested by the speaker? Did the speaker attempt to persuade the audience to accept a particular meaning for the term? Who is the audience? Do you think the audience agreed or disagreed with the speaker's meaning for the term? How significant was agreement about the meaning of the term to the speech?

---

bring them to mind, and their presence or memory causes you to have particular thoughts.

The interesting relationship for rhetoricians is that depicted by the bottom dashed line on the triangle in Figure 5.1. According to Ogden and Richards (1928), "there is no relevant relation other than the indirect one" (p. 11). The symbol and the referent, they explained, are not "connected directly" (p. 11). The relationship is only implied or imputed. The word we use for chair could just as easily be the word we use for book. There is nothing natural about calling a book, a book, or a chair, a chair. These relationships are subjective and arbitrary. We agree upon their meanings through social interaction. The Internet Activity for this chapter in Box 5.2 asks you to use the semantic triangle to uncover meaning in a controversial speech.

The following observation may seem fairly obvious to you, but for the readers of Ogden and Richards, it was a profound observation. Ogden and Richards noted that saying a symbol *means* something implies a direct and simple relationship between the symbol and the referent. However, such thinking creates misunderstanding and confusion because the symbol never truly means its referent. In the Critical Insights feature for this chapter (see Box 5.3), we'll consider an example from contemporary culture to explore more fully the relationship between symbols, thoughts, and objects.

The Role of Context in Meaning

Ogden and Richards (1928) identified context as being one of the key reasons why people have different interpretations of symbols. They explained that "the peculiarity of interpretation being that when a context has affected us in the past the recurrence of merely a part of that context will cause us to react in the way in which we reacted before" (p. 53). A sign is a specific kind of stimulus that causes us to react in a particular way to another stimulus we have previously experienced. In other words, if you eat something exotic and don't enjoy the experience, the mere sight of that food in the future or even a symbol for the food will cause you to react negatively to either the object or the symbol. Your future thoughts about that object/symbol have been influenced by your previous experiences with the object. Thus, your interpretation of the symbol or object is shaped by the context in which you previously experienced that object.

BOX 5.3   Critical Insights: The Meaning of School Mascots

The use of Native American nicknames and mascots for high school, college, and professional athletic teams is controversial, to say the least, because of the multiple meanings those symbols may have. The University of North Dakota (UND), for instance, is known as the Fighting Sioux. The word "Sioux" and the Indian head logo used by UND are the symbols involved in this controversy. To those who support the nickname, the symbols cause thoughts of pride—usually in the school's athletic success. Or, for alums, the symbols may cause thoughts of nostalgia for the Alma matter. The object referred to may be a particular UND student athlete or a general image of athletics at the school. For supporters of the nickname and logo, the relationship between the symbols used to support the teams and the teams themselves seems natural and beyond questioning.

However, opponents of the Sioux nickname and logo have different thoughts because of these symbols. For them, the symbols represent the oppression of Native American culture by the white people and the U.S. government. The object, in this case, is generally thought to be a Native American person. Interestingly, the relationship between the symbol and object in this case is more complicated. In fact, the word "Sioux" is a general term, referring to any number of Native American tribes, the Lakota, Nakota, and Dakota. It may be difficult to determine exactly which Native person is being referred to by the word "Sioux." Additionally, the word "Sioux" originated when the French named the native peoples with a word that referred to "enemy" or "snake." Thus, it may not be a flattering symbol to use to refer to a Native person. Of course, the perspective of the symbol user is what determines the kind of implied or imputed relationship between a symbol and an object. The point here is that for supporters of the use of Native American nicknames and logos, the relationships in the semantic triangle seem to be quite stable and natural. For opponents, on the other hand, these relationships are thought to be highly subjective and potentially offensive. As Ogden and Richards (1928) explained, "The fundamental and most prolific fallacy is, in other words, that the base of the triangle given above is filled in" (p. 15).

Let's return to the example of Native American mascots (see Box 5.3). If the context in which you have previously experienced a mascot was purely in an athletic setting, you will have a meaning for the mascot tied to that experience. On the other hand, if the context in which you experienced the word "Sioux" was situated in the struggle between Native and white cultures, then you may have a different meaning for that symbol. The context, here, controls how you ascribe meaning to the symbol.

If you think back to the ancient Greek rhetors and rhetorical theorists, you'll remember that given the oral nature of their culture, they could only speak about events that were present in time and space. That is, they more or less shared in the same context for determining the meaning for words. Thus, their interpretations of symbols were no doubt similar. As time progressed, mediated forms of rhetoric were developed—the printing press in the fifteenth century and radio by the early twentieth century—that changed the contexts in which rhetors and their audiences experienced symbols. People had different contexts for determining meaning, resulting in misunderstanding and, consequently, theories about linguistic reflexivity such as Ogden and Richards'.

BOX 5.4 Biography of a Theory: Alfred Korzybski

Korzybski was born in 1879 in Warsaw, Poland. When he was thirty-five, he joined the Second Russian Army for World War I. He was injured several times before coming to Canada and the United States as an artillery expert for the Russian Army. When the Russian army and government fell to the Bolsheviks, Korzybski traveled the United States to promote the sale of war bonds to the U.S. population. The war played a pivotal role in Korzybski's thinking about humanity and its use of symbols.

His primary publication was *Science and Sanity: An Introduction to Non-Aristotelian Systems and General Semantics*, published in 1933. His primary argument, as far as rhetoric is concerned, was that human symbol use allowed us to achieve progress, but it also caused many problems as well. A more deliberate and careful use of language, he wrote, would help us to achieve greater cooperation and happiness. The use of mathematical devices would be a key way to help improve language use.

AVOIDING MISUNDERSTANDING: GENERAL SEMANTICS

The General Semanticists, a loose collection of theorists, sought to create a way of using language clearly. Proponents of the **general semantics** movement included its founder Alfred Korzybski and its primary proponents, Irving Lee and S. I. Hayakawa. You can read more about Korzybski in Box 5. 4. Condit (1995) wrote, "Korzybski sought to make human beings use their language reflectively, and to build that reflection into a reflex as natural and automatic as the language tendencies that they sought to counter" (p. 215). Though general semantics is no longer a predominant theory, it remains a guiding force for many followers who believe that its principles can help them live a more fulfilling life. The website for Korzybski's organization, the Institute of General Semantics can be found at http://www.general-semantics.org/.

General Semantics is the theory developed by Korzybski to help humans understand how they can avoid behaving like animals. Humans often impose on themselves "silly and harmful" conditions that make us similar to animals in many respects (1958/1933, p. 8). "Verbal issues," noted Korzybski, "seem to pervade all human problems to some extent" (1958/1933, p. 10). By addressing the "linguistic and semantic issues and their physiological and psycho-logical aspects," Korzybski believed we could avoid animalistic behavior. Effective language use, he explained, is a key component of a more enlightened existence and can allow us to achieve what Korzybski called "sanity."

Korzybski called his theory "non-Aristotelian." Aristotle, Korzybski wrote, was interested in creating a general method for all forms of scientific discovery. Keep in mind that Aristotle's theories of rhetoric, to which we have often referred, are only a small part of his life's work. Aristotle also taught and wrote about science, mathematics, politics, and aesthetics. He used similar techniques, such as classification and taxonomy, in all of his discovery and writing. These techniques, Korzybski explained, were no longer completely valid in the twentieth century. For instance, Aristotle saw the world as more or less stable and unchanging; Korzybski's theory is grounded in a dynamic world that is constantly marked by change. Where Aristotle saw "either-or" dilemmas, Korzybski sees infinite possibilities. He explained, "The aim of the work of Aristotle and the work of the non-aristotelians is similar, except for the date of our human development and the advance of science" (1958/1933, p. xi). General Semantics seeks to preserve the aims of Aristotle, while incorporating the latest scientific techniques, according to Korzybski.

Negative Premises

One of the key differences between Aristotelian theory and General Semantics, and the fundamental premise of General Semantics, is the idea of **negative premises.** Whereas Aristotle sought to determine what things "are," Korzybski sought to show that they "are not." Korzybski explained, "If we start, for instance, with a statement that 'a word is not the object spoke about,' and some one tries to deny that, he would have to produce an actual physical object which would be the word—impossible of performance, even in asylums for the 'mentally' ill" (1958, pp. 10–11). Refer to our discussion of Ogden and Richards. They have said that the object is not the same as the word; this is the same point that Korzybski made. He also noted that we can use language to reflect upon language. In this sense, language is reflexive, as we have seen.

Another important feature of language is its ability to be abstract. The word "mammal," for instance is more abstract than the word "person" which is more abstract than the word "Susanne," which refers to a specific person. Words vary in their level of abstraction. Some words, such as "true," "love," or "yes" could be used to refer to objects at various levels of abstraction. For instance, it is true that a creature standing before you is a mammal, it is also true that this creature is a person, and it is true that the creature's name is Susanne. Thus, the word "true" in this sense refers to any of the various abstract terms. Such a word was termed **multiordinal.** Knowing that words like "true" were multiordinal allows us to be more clear in our communication. Korzybski thought that "this semantic freedom does not result in confusion" because such terms are "devoid of meaning outside of a context" (1958, p. 14). It was futile and illegitimate to speculate about the meaning of terms such as "reality" and "fact" because they were multiordinal terms that had no general meaning.

Maps

Ultimately, Korzybski links language to the structures of our existence, such as our laws, institutions, and ways of thinking. "Languages," wrote Korzybski, "must be considered only as maps" (1958, p. 58). A map represents an object or place, but it is not that object or place. Korzybski remarked, "A map is not the territory it represents, but, if correct, it has a similar structure to the territory, which accounts for its usefulness" (p. 58). The structure he is referring to is that of the "world, ourselves and our nervous systems included" (p. 59). Essentially, Korzybski argued that the map of language, as outlined by the classical theorists such as Aristotle, is no longer effective for humans to use because it doesn't reflect the structure of our twentieth-century experiences or thought processes.

Table 5.1 Remedies for Misunderstanding

Remedy	Definition	Example
Indexing	Use of subscript numbers to indicate the uniqueness of two objects, people, or things.	$Chair_1$: Chairs in your classroom $Chair_2$: The chair at which you study $Chair_3$: Chair in which you watch television or relax
Chain-indexing	Use of subscript numbers to refer to different states of the same object, person, or phenomenon.	$Weather_1$: Rainy weather $Weather_2$: Sunny weather $David_1$: David when he is happy $David_2$: David when he is mad
Dating	The use of superscript numbers to indicate how people, objects, or phenomena change over time.	$Computer^{1974}$: Large and slow. $Computer^{2005}$: Fast and portable.
Etc.	Indicates that we can never say all there is to say about a subject.	Rhetoric deals with symbols, people, truth, etc.
Quotes	Used when the meaning of a term is doubtful, misleading, or dangerous or when the meaning is not widely understood.	"Political correctness" is a way of using language to promote equality.
Hyphens	Used to unite terms that have been separated.	Body-soul Mind-body

To restore sanity, he argued, we must use language in a way that represents the structures of our experience. He explained, "All our doctrines and institutions depend on verbal arguments. If these arguments are conducted in a language of wrong and unnatural structure, our doctrines and institutions must reflect that linguistic structure and so become unnatural, and inevitably led to disasters" (1958, p. 59). Korzybski turned to the language of mathematics to suggest ways of using language more clearly. A complete account of his rationale and method for doing so is beyond the scope of this chapter. Instead, we'll turn to the outcomes of his study and discuss some of the specific ways that Korzybski thought we could use language more scientifically.

Extensional Devices

The General Semanticists developed a series of **extensional devices**—communication techniques designed to clarify meaning. Specifically, these devices make conscious the abstracting that we do when we communicate. In our previous discussion of abstracting, we saw how we cannot help but make abstractions when we communicate. The techniques we'll discuss here help to bring that process of abstraction into the open (see Table 5.1).

Indexing is the use of index numbers to indicate the uniqueness of two objects, people, or things. If a person uses the word "chair" in conversation with someone else, he or she may be referring to any of a number of different types of chairs. With indexing, however, the person might use different symbols—$chair_1$, $chair_2$, and chair$_3$—to refer to different chairs. Chair$_1$ may be the chair in a classroom in which you take texts and notes, chair$_2$ may be the chair at which you study, and chair$_3$ may indicate the chair in which you watch television or socialize with friends. By distinguishing between the different chairs using index numbers, the communicator is able to identify the uniqueness of a variety of chairs.

Chain indexing is a more specific type of indexing in which the same object, thing, or phenomenon is shown to be in any of several environmental, social, or psychological states. The weather, for instance, regularly changes, except if you live in certain geographic locations. One day it might be rainy (weather$_1$) and the next day sunny (weather$_2$). People, too, regularly change states. A person named David can be said to be David$_1$ when he is happy, David$_2$ when he mad, or David$_3$ when he is in sad. Simply referring to him as David is not sufficient, the General Semanticists believe, because it does not specify his current condition. You can apply this same technique to any kind of object, person, or idea.

Dating is a third type of extensional device. This technique is similar to the other forms of indexing we have discussed, but is concerned with how people, objects, or things change over time. For example, Theresa[2004] has had more experiences and is presumably a different person that Theresa[1984]. In other situations, dating is used to specify between objects of different time periods. Computer[2005] is much faster and smaller than computer[1974].

Another device is the use of *etc.,* which helps communicators realize that there is more to the subject than can be discussed. Using *etc.* helps to illustrate that a statement is incomplete and bound by space-time restrictions. I might add *etc.* to the end of each chapter of this text to indicate that there is more to the subject than I am able to cover in the space provided. Additionally, *etc.* helps communicators to avoid the either-or distinction that General Semantists believe plagues Aristotelian thinking. By introducing the possibility that a third aspect to a discussion exists, the rhetor allows for a variety of positions on a topic.

Quotes should be used when the meaning of term is doubtful, misleading, or dangerous. For Korzybski, terms such as "body," "soul," or "emotion" were troublesome and should be included in quotation marks because of their ambiguous meaning. Quotation marks can also be used to indicate terms that are used in a specific way that may not be widely understood.

Hyphens should be used, according to the General Semanticists, to unite terms that have been separated under Aristotelian logic. Body-soul are examples of such terms, indicating that two terms should be understood together. Another example cited by Kozybski (1951) is organism-as-a-whole-in-an-environment to indicate that people cannot be viewed separate from their environment.

The six extensional devices discussed here indicate the abstract nature of language and the difficulties posed by Aristotelian elementalism. You can learn more about extensional devices by accessing the site for the European Society for General Semantics at http://www.esgs.org/uk/ext.htm.

Although there are still many who use the general semantics theory to communicate more effectively, the theory is often reduced to a set of rules and guidelines and has lost its theoretical focus. Condit (1995) argued the techniques of effective rhetoric use were presented in textbooks as "cookbook procedures that were expected to protect the language user in an almost automatic fashion" (p. 216). That is, the

Table 5.2 Mead's Theory of Symbolic Interaction

Term		Definition
Mind		The ability to use significant symbols, words that have shared meanings.
Self		Ability to reflect on ourselves as objects.
	I	Impulsive and active aspect of the self
	Me	The aspect of the self that controls the I by using societal rules and expectations as a guide for behavior.
Society		The shared set of meanings and rules that exist with a culture.

theory of the General Semanticists lost its focus on reflection and became a set of rules to be followed.

THE MIND, SELF, AND SOCIETY

Ogden, Richards, and Korzybski are frequently cited in rhetorical textbooks such as this one for their theories concerning language. They were not the only theorists interested in meaning at this time, however. As far back as the mid-1800s, the American Charles Peirce was writing about meaning and in 1916, a collection of lectures by the Swiss linguist Ferdinand de Saussure, was published as the *Course in General Linguistics*. Charles Morris published *Foundations of the Theory of Signs* in 1938, a treatise largely influenced by Peirce. Peirce and Saussure are considered to be the founders of semiotics, which is the study of signs. Semiotics differs in some ways from how rhetorical theorists study signs and meaning, but there are some striking parallels. In fact, semiotics is often used in cultural studies, which, as we'll see later in this book, has much in common with contemporary rhetorical theory. We'll return again to semiotics later in this book. Our focus in this chapter will be on the work of George Herbert Mead, one of the followers of Peirce.

Mead's theory (1934) is often referred to as **symbolic interaction.** Essentially, he explained how language creates personal identities and social collectivities. Through our symbolic interaction with others, we learn who we are and we learn about the culture in which we live. The focus of symbolic interaction is on symbols; particularly, on how individuals and cultures are formed by the symbols that are used within the culture. To understand his theory, we'll look at its key components, including the mind, self, and society (see Table 5.2).

Mind

Humans, to function in a society, must have the ability and knowledge to use symbols that have common meanings. Mead refers to this as the **mind.** We're not born with the capability to use and understand symbols. Instead, we develop the mind through the process of language acquisition. In other words, the mind is the process by which we use **significant symbols,** a sign that arouses meaning in self and others. If I would say to you the word "junfre," you would have no idea of what I am referring. That's because the "word" that I typed was just a random set of letters typed on my keyboard. However, if I would say the word "cat," you and I would likely form an image of a four-legged creature with a long tail. We have previously discussed symbols and meaning; the idea of a significant symbol reflects the same ideas we have discussed previously. Mead, however, takes this idea further by showing the implications of the significant symbol.

Let's look at this further by using another example. At your school, no doubt, there are significant symbols whose meaning is known only to those who go to the school. At my school, for instance, students live in "the beer can," they dance at the "Underground," and they ask for help from a "SOC." Students on our campus know that the "beer can" refers to the tall, cylindrical-shaped dormitory on campus, the Underground is a dance club in the student union, and a SOC, or student orientation counselor, provides registration and other campus information during their first few days on campus. When first-year students come to campus for the first time, they no doubt are confused by some of the references to these terms. Through their interaction with other students, they quickly come to understand the meanings of these significant symbols and they are able to freely communicate within the universe of discourse. While Mead wasn't necessarily the first theorist to discuss culture, he did have a significant impact on how we think about the process of culture formation and maintenance.

Self

Perhaps even more significant than Mead's conception of symbolic interaction within a culture is his view of how we use symbols to interact with ourselves. "The language process," he explained, "is essential for the development of the self" (1962/1934, p. 135). For Mead, the **self** is our ability to respond to ourselves as objects. When we communicate, we can consider how others will respond to what we have said because we can consider how they assign meaning to the significant symbols we use. In other words, Mead realized that we can talk to ourselves and that we can react to ourselves in much the same way that others can react to us.

The self is developed through time, said Mead, and is not present when someone is born. It arises through the interactions we have with others and is shaped by the kinds of relationships with have with other people. Mead explained, "In the conversation of gestures what we say calls out a certain response in another and that in turn, changes our own action, so that we shift from what we started to do because of the reply the other makes" (1962/1934, p. 141).

Specifically, we react to the **generalized other,** a perception we have of how we think others see us. The generalized other refers to the collection of all the individuals in society. When you communicate in ways that reflect a common set of rules, you are reacting to the generalized other. For instance, raising your hand in class before you speak or not talking to someone else while the instructor is lecturing are examples of how the generalized other influences how we communicate. A **significant other** is a particularly influential person in your life who gives feedback to you about your self. Our romantic partners, parents, close friends, and siblings may all serve as significant others. You may be a confident communicator, for instance, because of the positive feedback you receive from the significant others in your life. Their affirming messages give you a high sense of self-esteem.

There are two aspects to the self: the I and the me. The I is the unpredictable and impulsive aspect of the self. Mead explained, "The 'I' is the response of the organism to the attitudes of the others; the 'me' is the organized set of attitudes of others which one himself assumes" (1962/1934, p. 175). Basically, the "me" is the information a self has about how it should respond in a given situation. The "me" is based on previous encounters and interactions with others. The "I" is the specific response to a given situation. It is not completely predictable and may go against the beliefs the self has about how it should act in a situation. After the "I" takes action, the "me" considers the action and its response from others and stores the information for later use. You've probably heard the expression, "putting your foot in your mouth." This means that you said something that you immediately regretted. Using Mead's terminology, the "I" puts the foot in the mouth; the "me" remembers what it tastes like. The self is created through the constant interaction of the "I" and the "me."

Society

When we share significant symbols within a culture, we create a universe of discourse. Mead explained, "A universe of discourse is simply a system of common or social meanings" (1962/1934, pp. 89–90). He further elaborates that "This universe of discourse is constituted by a group of individuals carrying on and participating in a common social process of experience and behavior, within which these gestures or symbols have the same common meanings for all member of that group" (1962/1934, p. 89). In very general terms, everyone who speaks the same language shares in a universe of discourse. In a more specific sense, people who share more particular meanings for words are said to share a universe of discourse. The students at your school, for instance, share a universe of discourse consisting of the key symbols of your school. Citizens of the United States share a universe of discourse that is different from citizens of Great Britain, even though they speak the same language. Thus, we are members of multiple and overlapping universes of discourse.

Conclusion

By focusing on the symbols used by members of a society, Mead greatly expanded our ability to consider the power of symbolic activity. Symbols are not simply vessels that transport meaning, instead they are the very means by which we create ourselves and the world in which we live.

BROADENING CONCEPTIONS OF MEANING

Whereas many of the theorists we have discussed studied how words mean, Susanne Langer studied the inability of words to convey certain types of meanings. Language, she wrote, is "our most faithful and indispensable picture of human experience, of the world and its events, of thought and life and all the march of time" (1960, p. 80). However, language is not capable of expressing all aspects of human experience. Rhetorical forms such as music or art, she explained, have meanings that are not reducible to words. Langer's theory of rhetoric sought to identify a more complete way that meaning can be explained.

Discursive and Presentational Rhetoric

Langer (1960) distinguishes between discursive and presentational forms of rhetoric. The discursive form of language is reflected by the "linear, discrete, successive order" of words (p. 80). She explained that "We must name one thing and then another, and symbols that are not names must be stuck between or before or after, by convention" (p. 80). If you recall your training in grammar, you learned the discursive form of language. You learned that nouns are people, places, and things and that verbs name actions or states of being. Adjectives modify nouns and adverbs modify verbs. You may have even learned how to diagram sentences discursively by showing the different parts of a sentence and how they relate to each other.

The discursiveness of language, wrote Langer, means that "only thoughts which can be arranged in this peculiar order can be spoken at all; any idea which does not lend itself to this 'projection' is ineffable, incommunicable by means of words" (1960, p. 81–82). Langer directly addressed the epistemological function of rhetoric. She explained that a statement about the nature of something that does not fit within a language's particular set of rules cannot be verified as being true or false. In fact, such a statement would be "unthinkable" because it falls outside of our normal symbolic practices (1960, p. 83).

The prevailing thinking, according to Langer, was that if something could not be expressed discursively, it was a feeling, or an expression of some kind of emotion or inner feeling. Langer argued that this view limits what we consider to be intellectual activity. In particular, this view of symbolism favors scientific thought, because it can be expressed discursively. Artistic forms of expression, such as music, poetry, or painting, were not seen as intellectual or substantive counterparts to discursive forms of language.

Langer explained, "I do believe that in this physical, space-time world of our experience there are things which do not fit the grammatical scheme of expression. But they are not necessarily blind, inconceivable, mystical affairs; they are simply matters which require to be conceived through some symbolistic schema other than discursive language" (1960, p. 88). Language, she explained, "is by no means our only articulate product" (p. 89). Recall for a moment some piece of music or art that struck you as beautiful or sublime. You may not have been able to express the feelings you had about the object, but you knew that it caused you to have certain thoughts, feelings, or emotions. For Langer, that inability to express with words the feelings we have when we encounter a symbol was evidence that there exists symbols and meaning that escape our discursive ways of expression.

Our sense organs—such as eyes and ears—perceive in ways that are not reducible to symbolism. When you see something, for instance, your first perceptions of that object may not be linguistic. It is possible to perceive relationships between visual forms, such as lines, color, or proportions. But Langer said that these relationships are "altogether different from the laws of syntax that govern language" (1960, p. 93). Visual forms are not discursive: "They do not present their constituents successively, but simultaneously, so the relations determining a visual structure are grasped in one act of vision" (p. 93). "Their complexity, consequently, is not limited, as the complexity of discourse is limited, by what the mind can retain from the beginning of an apperceptive act to the end of it" (1960, p. 93). Discursive expression, explained Langer, is limited in its ability to project complex ideas into discursive form.

Consider now a visual image, such as a photograph. The symbolic elements of a visual image—lighting, colors, and so forth—might appear to be similar to language, but, in reality, they function quite differently. Langer explained that the areas of light and shade in a photograph help us to see what is pictured in the photograph, but beyond that, they have no independent meaning. She considered that they would simply be a "blotch." Additionally, there is not one kind of shading for the nose and another for a mouth. Instead, the meaning of the blotches is determined by how that blotch is positioned next to other blotches. Finally, a photograph conveys a great deal of information; more than we could convey through discursive representations. She wrote that this is why passports contain pictures, not descriptions of the individual holding the passport. Imagine the difficulty in identifying someone if their driver's license contained a verbal description of them and not their picture. Pictures and other nondiscursive forms of rhetoric require that they be viewed in totality in order to understand their meaning.

A photograph—and other nondiscursive symbolic forms—has no vocabulary, at least not in the same sense as discursive symbolic forms. "Since we have no words, there can be no dictionary of meanings for lines, shadings or other elements of a pictorial technique. We may well pick out some line, say a certain curve, in a picture, which serves to represent one nameable item; but in another place the same curve would have an entirely different meaning. It has no fixed meaning apart from its context" (Langer, 1960, p. 95).

In essence, presentational forms, such as art and music cannot be adequately expressed using a discursive language. Langer summarizes:

> The meanings given through language are successively understood, and gathered into a whole by the process called discourse; the meanings of all other symbolic elements that compose a larger, articulate symbol are understood only through the meaning of the whole, through their relations with the total structure. Their very functioning as symbols depends on the fact that they are involved in a simultaneous, integral presentation. This kind of semantic may be called 'presentational symbolism,' to characterize its essential distinction from discursive symbolism, or 'language' proper. (1960, p. 97)

Langer takes up one last topic when she discusses the discursive nature of feelings. Like art, our feelings are not immediately reducible to words. How we feel, in fact, depends on the symbol system we have to express them. Langer elaborates:

> Everybody know that language is a very poor medium for expressing our emotional nature. It merely names certain vaguely and crudely conceived

states, but fails miserably in any attempt to convey the ever-moving patterns, the ambivalences and intricacies of inner experience, the interplay of feelings with thoughts and impressions, memories and echoes of memories, transient fantasy, or its mere runic traces, all turned into nameless, emotional stuff. (pp. 100–101)

Langer's ideas about the nature of language as a means of expressing a variety of topics is important for our discussion, as they highlight some of the limitations of language to express presentational experiences, such as art, music, or emotions. Keep in mind her ideas as we further explore linguistic reflexivity.

RHETORIC AND OPPRESSION

Later on in the book we'll discuss the relationship between power and rhetoric and approach this subject from a variety of angles. Here we'll simply identify some specific ways that language enters a discussion of power. Many theorists have discussed this relationship; for now, we'll turn to noted feminist theorist Cheris Kramarae. Feminist theorists such as Kramaerae, are interested in how the world has been shaped and influenced by men, which has silenced women and the expression of their interests. We'll study their ideas in Chapter 8. For now, let's return to the direct link between language and power.

Muted Group Theory

Kramarae (1981) explained that a woman's presence as a rhetor is not "always fully acceptable" (p. xiv) and that women face disadvantages when they communicate with men. Kramarae said women are a "muted group" because the language of our culture does not serve women as well as it does men. Women cannot express themselves as easily as men because the words we use have been formulated based on the male experience. That is, women are "muted" in our culture. Women, she argued, have different experiences and require different words than our language contains in order to express themselves. Because of language, women are forced to see the world through the experiences of men and communicate using male words. Women are "muted" because they cannot easily express their perspective and experiences.

Kramarae (1981) identified several hypotheses that result from women being muted by male language.

- Females are more likely to have difficulty expressing themselves fluently within dominant (public) modes of expression" (p. 4). Because females have different experiences than men, they are likely to have difficulty translating their experiences into words based on male experiences.

- Males have more difficulty understanding females than females do understanding males. Females are used to seeing the world through the eyes and language of men, but men seldom are forced outside of their experience.

- Females seek ways to express themselves outside of the male experience. Women seek alternative forms of expression that do not always take the form of traditional ways of communicating.

- Women are more likely to state their dissatisfaction with dominant modes of public discourse. Because those modes do not fit with female experiences, women will call attention to the inadequacy of male language. Literature, wrote Kramarae, is often used to voice this dissatisfaction.

- Women will seek to change "dominant public modes of expression" when those modes do not allow for female expression.

- Women are not as likely to create words that become highly recognized and used by both men and women. Women are often excluded from the production of new words.

The Rhetoric of Childbirth

Two examples can help explain muted group theory and illustrate Kramarae's arguments. First, consider how we typically talk about childbirth. Cosslett (1994) explained that childbirth is often described from the male point of view, using a masculine vocabulary. She noted, "As a central, life-changing event for many women, childbirth needs to be made visible, written about, from a woman's perspective. Too often, the story has been taken away from women by the 'audience perspective' accounts of fathers, or, more influentially, doctors" (p. 2). That is, mothers have been muted in their ability to describe childbirth in their own terms. In fact, noted Cosslett, women often have to translate their experiences into the language of science. If you think about it, the terms we use to describe childbirth—the fact that a doctor "delivers" the baby, for instance—almost make invisible the central role of the mother in the event. For a contrary view, consider the vocabulary used by midwives. They don't "deliver" a new baby, they "catch" the baby, for instance. This terminology positions the mother as the central figure and opens up new ways of talking about childbirth from her perspective.

Cosslett (1994) sought to bring to light the women's perspective of childbirth. By relating the narratives of three women, Cosslett sought to make public what had been muted. The Internet also provides the opportunity for women to challenge the dominant modes of rhetoric about childbirth. Numerous websites provide the diaries or journals of women who describe childbirth from their perspective using terminology not derived from the medical profession. What follows is an excerpt from a journal at www.unassistedchildbirth.com.

> I was so in awe of my body's efficient work. Everything was so primal, so natural, so calm, so healing. This really was the birth I'd always dreamt of. No one to talk to me or ask questions. No one to distract me or stress me. Just me and baby. Alone together. My focus was total and unbroken. I felt strong and rewarded. It was the most empowering moment of my life. (http://www.unassistedchildbirth.com/marley.htm)

Keep in mind that this woman had her child at home without doctors present. The resulting experience was empowering for the mother, and her vocabulary reflects this sense of empowerment and lacks the traditional medical terminology used to describe childbirth.

In short, by using nontraditional venues to describe childbirth from the mother's perspective, women are able to challenge the traditional rhetoric surrounding childbirth. The act of becoming a mother is told through rhetoric that reflects the mother's perspective and doesn't necessarily use words that reflect the masculine, scientific perspective. For women, the act of challenging the power arrangement solidified by traditional terminology is empowering.

Sexual Harassment

For another example of muted group theory, consider sexual harassment. By most reports, women were propositioned, threatened, and sexually abused long before there was a term to describe these kinds of inappropriate behaviors. The 1964 Civil Rights Act, for the first time, named this abuse and declared it to be against the law. In 1972, Title IX of the Education Amendment made sexual harassment illegal in educational institutions. Prior to these laws, sexual harassment may have been considered a "joke" and wasn't taken seriously by men. Despite the psychological and physical harm resulting from sexual harassment, women lacked a name for it and struggled to have their voice heard in society at large.

Despite the eventual confirmation of Clarence Thomas to the United States Supreme Court in 1991, allegations that he had sexually harassed one of his former employees, Anita Hill, sparked a flood of sexual harassment suits (Figure 5.2). After hearing Hill's story, other women were willing to come forward and express their experiences with sexual harassment. The prominence of the Thomas nomination hearings provided a way for women to discuss sexual harassment in ways that they had not previously.

In sum, without a term to describe sexual harassment, the abuse of women remained something that was unspeakable. Even after legislation codified the term, women were often quiet about their experiences. Public venues were needed to free women from the constraints of masculine rhetoric that downplayed sexual harassment and its effect on women. We'll return to similar ideas about rhetoric and power in Chapters 7-9. Keep in mind what we have discussed here—that ambiguity in the meaning of symbols is related to how power is managed in a culture.

WEAVER: MEANING AND VALUES

Richard Weaver was an American theorist who provided a linguistically based theory of the role of rhetoric relative to truth and culture. He sought to identify ways that rhetoric could be used to promote the truth in a culture and drive people to their ideals. Weaver was very much influenced by Plato; you'll see much in common with Plato's theory of rhetoric. Let's begin our discussion of Weaver by looking at his distinction between dialectic and rhetoric.

Dialectic and Rhetoric

Plato's influence on Weaver's theory of rhetoric can be seen in how Weaver defined rhetoric. Weaver defined rhetoric as "truth plus its artful presentation" (1953, p. 15). Before we discuss rhetoric in greater detail, we must see how Weaver thought rhetors arrived at truth. To determine truth, a rhetor must first engage in the process of

FIGURE 5.2 Anita Hill testifies to the Senate Judiciary Committee in 1991 about sexual harassment. Hill's rhetoric brought to light an experience that has been muted for women and led to an increase in sexual harassment suits by women.

dialectic, which Weaver defined as "a method of investigation whose object is the establishment of truth about doubtful propositions" (1953, p. 15). Dialectical inquiry will seek to determine what is good or just. But dialectic is limited in its usefulness. Dialectic may be able to *convince* an audience that something is true, but it cannot *move* the audience to take action on the topic. For example, you might be convinced you should exercise but have failed to act on that conviction. That is, the facts and research may have convinced you to exercise, but you have yet to be presented with compelling rhetoric that would move you to take action.

This is where rhetoric enters the picture. We have just said that rhetoric involves the artful presentation of truth. Weaver was influenced by the classical theorists, such as Aristotle and Plato, and wrote about many of the same rhetorical techniques they discussed, such as reasoning and style. Rhetoric, to him, consisted of the use of these techniques to convey to an audience what was found to be true through the dialectic. Weaver (1953) explained, "Rhetoric moves the soul with a movement which cannot finally be justified logically" (p. 23). Weaver further elaborated that understanding—the role of dialectic—logically precedes actualization—the role of rhetoric. Weaver summarized, "There is, then, no true rhetoric without dialectic" (p. 17).

Several additional points about Weaver's definition of rhetoric are worth noting. First, rhetoric concerns real people and their world. Dialectic, on the other hand, refers only to intellectual arguments that are not immediately applicable in real situations. Weaver (1953) explained, "That is why rhetoric, with its passion for the actual, is more complete than mere dialectic with its dry understanding. It is more complete on the premise than [sic] man is a creature of passion who must live out that passion in the world" (p. 21).

Related to this, Weaver noted that a rhetor's choice of artistic appeals and techniques would vary from audience to audience. The rhetor had to be sensitive to the audience when choosing rhetorical techniques. What may be effective for one audience, may not be effective for another audience. Although the conception of truth—found through dialectic—would remain constant, the rhetoric used in different situations may be different.

Third, in actual practice, the line between dialectic and rhetoric may be blurred. Weaver uses the example of a "fact-finding" committee that might be used by Congress or on your university campus. In purely dialectic terms, this committee would be only concerned with discussing universal principles and not with making its findings appeal to a public audience. Weaver notes, however, that committees such as this often fulfill both functions. Dialectically, the committee uses information to determine what is right or wrong; rhetorically, the committee is sensitive to how it artfully presents its findings to the public.

Finally, you might recall Plato's earlier fears about rhetoric obscuring what was true and leading audiences to make poor decisions. Weaver puts his faith in the dialectical process as a valid source of what is true. Johannesen, Strickland, and Eubanks (1970) note, however, that it is never clear upon what Weaver places this faith. They explained, "What the ultimate Good was and how it is known through intuition, Weaver never really made clear. What comprised his ultimate Good was likewise unclear" (p. 12).

Rhetoric and Knowledge

Rhetoric fulfills an important function when it moves audiences to accept what is true, which leads us to a discussion of knowledge. Weaver noted that "Rhetoric passes from mere scientific demonstration of an idea to its relation to prudential conduct" (1953, p. 21). He identified three different orders of knowledge: "First, there is the order of facts about existing physical entities. These constitute the simple data of science" (1953, p. 30). The statements "It is currently 30 degrees outside" or "This chair is black" or "My dog is running" are statements that exist at the first order of knowledge. At the second level of knowledge are "statements about these facts; these are the propositions or theories of science" (1953, pp. 30–31). A meteorological theory of why it is thirty degrees—because of an approaching cold front—or an explanation of why my dog is running—to chase a rabbit—would be considered a statement at the second level of knowledge.

Knowledge at the third level consists of statements about statements, or statements about the theories described in the second level. Weaver (1953) explained, "A statement about the value or implications of the theory of this placement would be knowledge of the third order; it would be the judgment of a scientific theory" (p. 31). Knowledge of this type would include a statement about the accuracy of a weather forecast or the implication of why my dog is running. Weaver was interested in how ideas, universals, and first principles were formed at the third level of knowledge. He distinguished the third level from the previous two by noting that the others are statements about particulars, not statements about universal principles.

Importantly, dialectic is used at this level to determine the nature of universal principles. Since statements at the first two levels of knowledge concern facts and may be refuted by additional facts, there is no need for dialectic or rhetoric. At third level, though, dialectic is needed to determine what is right and wrong.

Our discussion of dialectic, rhetoric, and the three levels of knowledge contained in Weaver's theory points to a powerful role for rhetoric in the world. The important information in life concerns values, not the observation of facts, and rhetoric guides us in making decisions about those values. Weaver thought that "The duty of rhetoric is to bring together action and understanding into a whole that is greater than scientific perception" (1953, p. 24).

Types of Argument

Having established that dialectic is useful for locating universal principles and rhetoric is useful for presenting these principles, we now turn our attention to some of the specific ways that rhetoric can be used to guide audiences to make ethical decisions. Weaver argued that certain types of arguments were inherently more truthful and ethical than others. Argument from definition, or principle, was seen to be the most ethical while argument from situation, or circumstance, was thought to be the least ethical.

Additionally, he believed that a person's view of the world could be seen by the kind of arguments he or she used. A person who typically uses arguments from definition, he believed, was an idealist, a quality Weaver believed was desirable. A person who argues from situation was a liberal, and was not concerned with universal principles. Let's explore in more detail how Weaver viewed these two types of arguments—based on circumstance and on principle—and the rhetors who use them.

The least ethical type of argument was that of circumstance, said Weaver. In this form of reasoning, a rhetor uses the specific situation as the basis to make decisions and guide action. Weaver explained that argument from circumstance "is the least philosophical of all the sources of argument, since theoretically it stops at the level of perception of fact" (1953, p. 57). If you were to appeal to an instructor to change a grade that you have received on a test, you might be tempted to use argument from circumstance. You might explain that you had to work late the night before the test and didn't have a chance to study. You might also explain that you need to pass the test and the course in order to graduate that semester. Weaver would say that these were ineffective arguments because they did not rely on a fundamental truth developed through the dialectic.

The most desirable form of argument, according to Weaver, is argument from definition. This type of argument reasons from the nature or essence of things. It assumes that there are universal truths upon which people can make decisions. These principles result from the dialectic and are statements at the third level of Weaver's theory of knowledge. Returning to the grade appeal example, you would be better off arguing from principle. You might explain that the instructor's test was unreasonable according to some principle or standard. You might, for instance, compare the instructor's test with those of his or her colleagues. Or, you might contend that it is unreasonable to expect students to remember so much detail. According to Weaver, these arguments would be more effective, because they are based on principles or definitions developed through careful inspection and research.

Ultimate Terms

Another rhetorical device suited to promoting that which is ethical is the use of ultimate terms. An **ultimate term** is a word or name that has a great deal of power to move human impulse. Weaver explained that a "god term" is an "expression about which all other expressions are ranked as subordinate and serving dominations and powers" (1953, p. 212). That is, a god term subsumes all other terms as the rallying cry for a culture. Weaver saw "progress" as the god term of his day (the 1950s). This term, and related terms such as "progressive," had the most force in culture. He wrote, "It would be difficult to think of any type of person or of any institution which could not be recommended to the public through the enhancing power of this word" (1953, p. 212). Thus, politicians claimed they were "progressive," public policy was developed for the sake of "progress," and scientific study was promoted for the "progress" it could provide. Some other ultimate terms, according to Weaver, included "efficiency," "science," and "fact." Are these still valid ultimate terms in our culture today? Since the September 11, 2001 terrorist attacks, "homeland security" might also join this list.

Ultimate terms can also unite a culture *against* a group or idea. Weaver refers to these as **terms of repulsion.** The counterpart of a "god term" is the "devil term." The word "communist" has long been the devil term in U.S. culture. With the fall of communism in the 1980s, though, this term has lost its sense of potency. We might think of "terrorism" as the new devil term in culture today. When rhetors speak of terrorists, they unite their audience to take action to keep the nation secure and free.

The categories of ultimate terms and terms of repulsion allow us to study the history of a term's usage and understand how it became potent in a culture. Weaver identifies a third group of terms, which he calls **charismatic.** These terms gain their power in mysterious ways, appearing "to have broken loose somehow and to operate independently of referential connections" (Weaver, 1953, p. 227). Additionally, "Their meaning seems inexplicable unless we accept the hypothesis that their content proceeds out of a popular will that they shall mean something" (p. 227). That is, the meaning for charismatic terms is generally agreed upon by a given culture.

Weaver explained that "freedom" is a good example of a charismatic term. This term often demands contradictory actions. One person's freedom, for example, impinges on another's freedom. Or the freedom to protest a war is often met with criticism that the war is being fought for the cause of freedom. In any case, "freedom" remains a potent term in our society in a way that defies rational thought or discussion. Weaver noted that "democracy" is also a charismatic term in our culture.

Weaver cautioned against careless use of ultimate terms, whether they are positive or negative. He wrote, "The ethics of rhetoric requires that ultimate terms be ultimate in some rational sense" (1953, p. 232). Weaver was especially cautious of charismatic terms: "They often sound like the very gospel of one's society, but in fact they betray us; they get us to do what the adversary of the human being wants us to do" (p. 232). To prevent becoming a victim of our own "thoughtless rhetoric," Weaver advised students of rhetoric to use the dialectical method to determine the true nature of the rhetoric we employ. Doing so would ensure that we use rhetoric for ethical ends.

RHETORIC AS EPISTEMIC

Meanings, we have said, are contextual. They are based on how a particular group of people assign meaning to a symbol because of their shared experiences with that symbol. The meaning for a symbol varies from group to group, culture to culture. Each of these groups develops knowledge about meaning based on what they believe the symbol to mean. Except for Weaver, we have, in this chapter, rejected Plato's idea that symbols have one true meaning. We have said that symbols can have any number of meanings. Ultimately, the idea of linguistic reflexivity leads to the idea that rhetoric creates knowledge.

That is, we say that rhetoric is epistemic, an observation that Robert L. Scott made in 1967. He explained, "In human affairs, then, rhetoric, perceived in the frame herein discussed, is a way of knowing; it is epistemic" (p. 17). Explaining further, he wrote, "Man must consider truth not as something fixed and final but as something to be created moment by moment in the circumstances in which he finds himself and with which he must cope" (p. 17). In the first chapter, you'll recall, we previewed this observation about rhetoric by saying that it establishes what is probably true in a given situation. Scott was not the first to hold the view that rhetoric is epistemic. He noted, "I merely hope to clarify through a fresh analysis a way which has always been open and sometimes chosen, but seldom in a clear, incisive manner" (p. 10). Let's look more closely at Scott's rationale for taking the view that rhetoric establishes knowledge.

Scott (1967) outlined the two prevailing views of the relationship between truth and rhetoric. The first view, most clearly espoused by Plato, is that truth can

FIGURE 5.3 Juries use rhetoric to make decisions about the guilt or innocence of the accused. Research suggests that jurors make these decisions as they discuss the issues and do not always have previous ideas about guilt or innocence. Jurors use rhetoric to determine truth, which is the premise of Scott's theory.

be known to some individuals, who then use rhetoric to enlighten those who do not possess truth. He labeled this approach as being "undemocratic" (p. 10) and leaving no substantive role for rhetoric.

The other view, of course, is that rhetoric can be used to offer positions and reasons and to determine what is probably true for a given audience at a given time. Scott (1967) explained that

> By "truth" one may mean some set of generally accepted social norms, experience, or even matters of faith as reference points in working out the contingencies in which men find themselves. In such cases the word might be better avoided, for in it the breath of the fanatic hangs threatening to transmute the term to one of crushing certainty. (p. 12)

Scott explained that we may not always know what we believe before using rhetoric in an uncertain situation. Instead, it is through speaking and acting that we come to know.

Research on how juries deliberate, for instance, shows that generally there are large numbers of undecided jurors at the start of deliberations (Figure 5.3). As the jurors talk about the evidence and the witnesses, though, they come to develop positions about the guilt or innocence of the suspect. After spending time using rhetoric, then, the jurors form a belief about what is true in that situation. In a similar way, our political process is structured to allow opportunities for voters to express themselves prior to casting their vote in the election. The DebateWatch program, sponsored by the Commission on Presidential Debates, is a good example of this idea. DebateWatch encourages community members to watch the presidential and vice-presidential debates with each other and talk about what they learned. The program is designed to reduce the effect of the media and provide opportunities for voters to use rhetoric to determine for whom they should vote. Thus, by going to a DebateWatch event, you might not have an opinion about who should be elected. By engaging in discussion with others at the event, though, you may able to determine who should get your vote.

Scott also highlighted how viewing rhetoric as epistemic can lead to ethical action on the part of rhetors. If we hold this view of rhetoric, he explained, we are forced to tolerate the diverse opinions of others. For in their opinions, we may find that which we believe. Viewing rhetoric as epistemic also prompts us to act. Scott explained, "If one cannot be certain, however, then one must either withdraw from the conflicts of life or find some way to act in the face of these conflicts" (p. 16). Inaction, he argued, "ought be considered ethical failure" (p. 16). Likewise, when we seek to use rhetoric to determine what should be accepted, we are responsible for our actions and the result of our actions. Scott's view of rhetoric is a natural outgrowth of the linguistic reflexivity we have discussed in this chapter. The relative nature of meaning and the ability to reflect on symbols lead to a way of viewing rhetoric as epistemic.

SUMMARIZING RHETORICAL THEORY

As we discussed at the beginning of this chapter, the study of linguistic reflexivity, to which each of the theorists we have discussed in this chapter contributed, ushered in a new way of thinking about rhetoric that forever changed the nature of the discipline. Condit (1995) identified linguistic reflexivity as "the dominant intellectual development of the twentieth century" (p. 209). We will continue to understand the impact of reflexivity on rhetorical theory as we move through our study of the twentieth century. Let's summarize our discussion in this chapter by addressing the key elements of rhetorical theory we have just examined.

Defining Rhetoric

The theorists presented in this chapter mostly focus on verbal rhetoric that is linguistically –based, that is, on oral and written forms of rhetoric. Langer, of course, explores ways that symbolism is produced in nondiscursive forms such as art and music. Her focus, though, is to reconcile these forms with more discursive forms of rhetoric.

Weaver provides the most succinct definition of rhetoric: truth plus its artful presentation. This definition reveals his epistemological orientation toward rhetoric and emphasizes the stylistic features of rhetoric. His theory includes a great deal of discussion of the linguistic elements of rhetoric.

Richards argued for broadening the scope of rhetoric beyond words. He believed that rhetoric should not just include persuasion, but expository discourse as well. He explained that persuasion "is only one among the aims of discourse" (1936, p. 24).

Rhetoric and Knowledge

We saw two clear orientations toward knowledge in this chapter. The minority view is expressed by Weaver, who holds out faith in the process of dialectic to determine truth. Thus, truth is determined prior to the use of rhetoric and rhetoric simply makes known what is true. Keep in mind, though, that Weaver believed that the powerful role of rhetoric was to *move* audiences. Dialectic, he believed, was insufficient to move audiences.

The majority of the theorists discussed in this chapter take the view that rhetoric is epistemic. That is, rhetoric is tied to how we know. This view is most clearly stated by Scott, who counters the view posited by Plato (and Weaver) that rhetoric makes the truth known. For Scott, the role of rhetoric as epistemic makes the practice of rhetoric necessary and ethical. Linguistic reflexivity makes this view possible, since we are able to reflect on the power of language to control our perceptions and beliefs.

Rhetoric and Identity

Another common thread through this chapter has been that rhetoric shapes how we see ourselves, others, and the world in which we live. Mead stated this mostly clearly in his theory about the mind, self, and society. For Mead, we are who we are because of how others react to us. That is, we gauge our perceptions of ourselves based on the rhetoric we encounter from others. We can also conceive of the self through rhetoric. Finally, for Mead, society is made meaningful because of the rhetorical interactions that we share with others. How we think and believe is related to how we have interacted with others.

A significant part of the General Semanticists' theory was to create a use of language that closely mirrored the world in which we live and, importantly, the psychology of individuals in that world. They saw ontology directly tied to the way we use language. By matching the words we use with our internal maps, we would be healthy and productive humans. For them, the question of what it means to be human was inextricably tied to the rhetoric we use.

Rhetoric and Judgment

Finally, we saw in this chapter that ethics is shaped in implicit ways by language. Previously, we viewed ethics as existing apart from rhetoric. That is, we did not see ethics as arising from the words we use. In this chapter, though, we learned that how things are said and the words we use have ethical dimensions. Weaver pays the most attention to this topic. For him, rhetoric leads to the tyrannizing image of a culture. In particular, the use of god and devil terms carry with them implicit ethical statements. When we use particular words, we are calling on particular values and normative ways of seeing the world. Scott, too, addresses ethics. His view of rhetoric as epistemic implies the need to be ethical. If we believe that through rhetoric we find contingent truths, then we must question our beliefs and those of others. We must also be open and responsible to the rhetoric of others.

DISCUSSION QUESTIONS

1. How do you view language? Do you think that language is a transparent medium that transmits thoughts and ideas? Do you see language as a barrier to communication? What techniques do you use to communicate clearly?

2. Choose a controversial term in our culture today, such as affirmative action, feminism, or political correctness. Use the semantic triangle to diagram the possible thoughts people have for these terms.

3. Think of an experience you've had recently. Using extensional devices, communicate that experience to someone else. How did the extensional devices help your communication? Did they hinder your communication in any way?

4. What are some terms that are commonly known to the students on your campus but aren't widely known outside of campus? How do these terms create a culture on your campus?

5. Have you ever had an experience that you could not put into words? What was that experience? How do we express ourselves if we cannot use words to do so? Do you think some experiences truly escape language or do we need to simply think more about the experience to express it linguistically?

6. Evaluate Kramaraes muted group theory. Do any of her hypotheses ring true with your experiences? How might language be changed to give more voice to muted groups?

7. What are some god terms in use in our culture today besides those cited in the text? Some devil terms? Some charismatic terms? Locate a magazine advertisement and/or a presidential speech. Which of these terms do you see used there?

8. Do you view rhetoric as epistemic? Why or why not? How do your views of the relationship between rhetoric and knowledge shape how you respond to the rhetoric of others?

GLOSSARY TERMS

linguistic reflexivity   An orientation that requires reflection on the forces of language.
semantic triangle   A method of identifying relationships between words, thoughts, and things.
general semantics   A theory of language that seeks to clarify meanings and that includes the use of extensional devices.

negative premise   Defining a term by distinguishing what it is not.

extensional devices   Techniques that can be used to clarify the meaning of a statement.

symbolic interaction   A theory that says personal identities and social collectivities are made meaningful through sharing symbols.

significant symbol   A symbol that evokes the same meaning in others as it does in the self.

self   The ability to respond to ourselves as objects.

dialectic   The process of abstract thinking about truth.

ultimate term   A word or name that has a great deal of power to move human impulse.

term of repulsion   A word or name that moves people to reject a particular idea.

charismatic terms   Terms or words that get their meaning in mysterious ways.

6

Dramatism

Learning Objectives

After reading this chapter, you should be able to:

1. Distinguish dramatism from other rhetorical theories.
2. Explain the implication of the negative for how humans construct their worlds through rhetoric.
3. Describe and apply the concepts of identification, the pentad, cycles of redemption, and form to rhetorical practice.
4. Describe and apply Fisher's narrative perspective on rhetoric.
5. Describe and apply Bormann's symbolic convergence theory.
6. Explain the epistemological, ontological and ethical dimensions of dramatism.

Throughout the 2004 presidential campaign, Democratic challenger Senator John Kerry argued that President George W. Bush had not done enough to help Americans. Kerry alleged that Bush had led the country into a war that would be difficult to win and squandered the budget surplus by giving a tax break to the rich. Kerry used a rhetorical technique that we'll discuss in this chapter, *scapegoating*. By portraying Bush as the source of problems in our country, Kerry was hoping that voters would decide to remove Bush from office and give our nation a "fresh start." On a broader level, each of the candidates tried to create a reality for voters with their rhetoric. Bush wanted the nation to think that he was the strongest choice to protect the country, whereas Kerry wanted voters to select him to correct the problems caused by Bush. We mentioned this view—that rhetoric creates reality—in our last chapter and will examine it in further detail in this one. Specifically, we'll address dramatistic theories of rhetoric in the next few pages.

Our discussion in the previous chapter focused on the ambiguities of language and how they influence human interaction. Language will be a central theme in this chapter as well; however, language—and other types of symbol use—will be viewed as a far more powerful force on human interaction than we have previously discussed. Kenneth Burke, one of the most significant rhetorical theorists of this century, explained that rhetoric "is rooted in an essential function of language itself, a function that is wholly realistic, and is continually born anew; the use of language as a symbolic means of inducing cooperation in beings that by nature respond to symbols" (1969, p. 43). For Burke, language—and other symbols—is the central focus of rhetorical theory.

Burke's theory of rhetoric and the theories related to it are often called dramatism, which is the study of how language and other symbol systems create the rhetorical worlds in which we live. Burke (1968) defined the central tenet of the theory as follows: "Dramatism is a method of analysis and a corresponding critique of terminology designed to show that the most direct route to the study of human relations and human motives is via a methodical inquiry into cycles or clusters of terms and their functions" (p. 445). In other words, dramatism is interested in how language functions to create and maintain communities of individuals. Burke was the "philosophical and inspirational source" of dramatism, but it is important to note that a wide range of dramatistic theorists have contributed to the rhetorical perspective (Brock, Scott, Chesebro, 1990).

In this chapter, we'll survey the key concepts of several dramatistic theories. Specifically, we'll study how Burke defined rhetoric and how rhetoric relates to identification, guilt, and motives. Then, we'll discuss two additional dramatistic approaches: the narrative paradigm and symbolic convergence theory. First, however, let's learn a little more about Kenneth Burke to understand how he came to his views on rhetoric. Read Box 6.1, Biography of a Theorist, to learn more about him.

THE NATURE OF RHETORIC

Previous rhetorical theorists studied rhetoric to understand its effects. For Burke, the influence of language goes far beyond its persuasiveness. He viewed rhetoric as creating realities in which we must operate. In fact, he explained, we use rhetoric to navigate our way through these rhetorically created social structures and rules. Burke offered this glimpse of what it means to live in a rhetorically constructed world:

And however important to us is the tiny sliver of reality each of us has experienced firsthand, the whole overall "picture" is but a construct of our symbol systems. To meditate on this fact until one sees its full implications is much like peering over the edge of things into an ultimate abyss. And doubtless that's one reason why, though man is typically the symbol-using

---

BOX 6.1   Biography of a Theorist: Kenneth Burke

Kenneth Burke, one of the most important rhetorical theorists since Aristotle, developed his theory of dramatism to challenge many prevailing ideas about rhetoric, literature, and social criticism. In his seventy-five years as a writer, Burke published eighteen books and numerous academic and popular press articles. Burke's theory has been influential in several disciplines: rhetoric, English, sociology, philosophy, and linguistics. Burke's theory stems, in part, from his life experiences. Phyllis Japp noted in 1999: "Burke often experienced life as one at odds with his world, chronically unable or unwilling to march in step with the academic drumbeats of any era, frequently challenging those comfortably empowered by prevailing intellectual hierarchies" (p. 116). The result was a body of ideas that provided a counterstatement to the prevailing theories of his time.

Burke was born in Pittsburgh, Pennsylvania, in 1897. He attended Peabody High School in Pittsburgh, Ohio State University, and Columbia University. Burke never received a formal university degree because "every course I wanted to take was for graduate students only" (qtd. in Chesebro, 1993, p. ix). He educated himself, learning three languages other than English—Latin, French, and German—and read the great literature of the world (Rueckert, 1993, p. 3).

For a period of time, Burke lived in the Greenwich Village part of New York City and wrote for the literary magazine *The Dial*. He served as managing editor of the magazine until 1929. Burke taught at a number of institutions, including the University of Chicago, Bennington College, Princeton University, Kenyon College, Indiana University, Drew University, Pennsylvania State University, the University of California at Santa Barbara, Harvard University, and the University of Pittsburgh. Burke was awarded numerous honorary degrees and received the National Medal for Literature in 1981.

Burke's major works include *Counter-Statement* (1931), *Permanence and Change* (1935), *Attitudes Toward History* (1937), *The Philosophy of Literary Form* (1941), *A Grammar of Motives* (1945), *A Rhetoric of Motives* (1950), and *The Rhetoric of Religion* (1961). He never completed an eighth major work, *Symbolic of Motives*. Burke also wrote poetry, short stories, and musical lyrics.

Burke married twice and had five children. Among his grandchildren was the singer Harry Chapin. Burke wrote the words to at least one Chapin song, *One Light in a Dark Valley*. Burke died on November 19, 1993 at his farm in Andover, New Jersey. As today's theorists and critics contemplate the usefulness of Burke's theories in today's mediated, multicultural world, Brock (1999) believed that his "ideas will continue to be taken seriously" (p. 13.). To learn more about Burke, visit the Web site for the Kenneth Burke Society at http://www.home.duq.edu/~thames/kennethburke/about.html.

animal, he clings to a kind of naïve verbal realism that refuses to realize the full extent of the role played by symbolicity in his notions of reality. (LSA, p. 5)

A good starting point for Burke's theory of dramatism is his definition of humans (Burke, 1966), which he revised several times and composed in poetic form:

Being bodies that learn language
thereby becoming wordlings
humans are
the symbol-making, symbol-using,
symbol-misusing animal
inventor of the negative
separated from our natural condition

by instruments of our own making
goaded by the spirit of hierarchy
and rotten with perfection.

This definition provides the foundation upon which many of his ideas of dramatism are based. Interestingly, Burke elaborated on his definition of humans after he had already written much of the work that now comprises dramatism. We'll start our discussion of dramatism by focusing on what is, perhaps, its most central element: symbols.

Symbol Use

For Burke, the essential difference between humans and animals is that humans have the capacity to create, use, and misuse symbols. In the first chapter, we explored briefly the idea that symbols represent something. Words, for instance, are symbols for ideas; a stop sign is a symbol for a particular traffic law; and a picture is a symbol for a previous experience. Symbols allow humans "to imagine, to select, to create, and to define situations to which they respond" (Gusfield, 1989, p. 8).

Implicit in our symbol use is the concept of *naming*. When we use symbols, we identify a person, place, object or event in such a way as to distinguish it from something else. We can never be completely objective when we do this because language is not neutral. Burke suggested that naming is a "magical" act that only approximates the relationship between the named and what it truly represents. Burke explained that symbols are "screens" that separate us from a nonverbal world (1966, p. 5). As a result, Burke explained that our names contain "attitudes" toward the objects of what we name. These attitudes suggest our position toward the object as well as suggest how others should view the object. Burke explained that rhetoric is the "dancing of an attitude" (1973, p. 9).

A few examples can help to illustrate this point. Consider the names that are used for various ideological positions in contemporary cultural debates. In the abortion debate, those who are in favor of abortion call themselves "pro-choice" while those who oppose abortion are "pro-life." Each label suggests a way of looking at the issue of abortion. Each label also suggests a way of viewing the other side: proponents for legalized abortion become "pro-death" or "anti-life" while opponents of abortion are "anti-choice." Consider, too, the debate over "affirmative action." As the name implies, this policy attempts to provide equal opportunities for all people, no matter their race, sex, or sexual orientation. Yet, opponents of affirmative action refer to the policy as a "quota system," which means that someone unqualified for a job may be hired for that job because of their cultural background. In each case, the names used by those involved in these debates controls public perception of the issue.

Given the capacity to use symbols, Burke claimed, we also have the capacity to misuse symbols, and do so quite regularly. Sexual harassment is an example of the use of symbols to inflict psychological harm. Sexual harassment can occur solely through symbol use. That is, physical contact is not necessary for sexual harassment to occur. Those who use symbols to sexually harass others exercise power over their victims and use symbols to unfairly manipulate circumstances—asking for sexual favors in exchange for promotion, for instance. Victims of sexual harassment experience a wide range of psychological harm as well as discrimination if they do not go along with the harasser's demands. Sexual harassment is a striking example of how symbols can be used to exercise power in an illegitimate and unjust way.

Negative Symbols

A particular type of symbol is the negative, representing the idea of "no" or "not." Burke explained that the negative is inherent in language use. Before we were able to create and use symbols, for instance, humans could only make gestures to items in their physical presence. Our gesturing, and its accompanying thought processes, could not accommodate the idea of "no." As humans began to develop symbols to represent abstract objects, they also developed the idea of "no" or "not." Burke explained that the negative serves definitional and moral functions in rhetoric.

When we define things, wrote Burke, we define them in terms of what they are not. Our symbol use, noted Burke, is marked by "the paradox of substance:" To say what something is, we have to say what it is not. We distinguish, for instance, between a cat and a dog by noting that a dog is *not* a cat and that a cat is *not* a dog. A dog is not a bird, either; nor is it a mouse. Thus, we can't use symbols without implicitly referencing what the symbol is *not*. At the same time, Burke wrote, we must be careful to realize that the word is not the thing it names. Although the definitional function of the negative is an important distinction between the type of symbols humans and animals use, Burke was more interested in the moral function of the negative.

Burke argued that instead of simply defining objects in our world, the negative is used to create moral rules for how we should act. In other words, the negative allows us to say "Thou *shalt* not." In fact, Burke stressed the point that not only did humans invent the negative, but language and the negative "invented" us as well (1966, p. 9). By this, he is referring to the moralizing aspect of the negative. When *we* are invented *by* the negative, we become moral agents, capable of making choices about what we should do and not do. Inevitably, Burke contends, we violate moral laws, creating guilt.

Guilt is an important concept in dramatism that we'll address throughout much of this chapter. We've already discussed how the negative implies certain moral laws or rules; in the next few paragraphs we'll discuss additional ways that guilt is created through language. Guilt is a sense of disorder, imbalance, or remorse that individuals and groups feel because of symbol use. Guilt is experienced at different degrees, or levels. You might feel guilt if you forget a meeting with a friend, you might feel guilt if you fail a test because you did not study long enough for it, or you might feel guilt if you cheated on a test and were placed on academic suspension. Additionally, Burke identified categorical guilt, which is experienced by a group of people. When a child commits murder, many members in society feels guilt because such action is out of the ordinary and is a sign that something is wrong with the social order. When political leaders do something wrong, many members in society also feel guilt. Thus, guilt is experienced by both individuals and groups. We'll discuss ways of using rhetoric to remove guilt later in the chapter. For now, let's discuss further ways that guilt is created through the use of rhetoric.

Hierarchy

Another of the clauses in Burke's definition of humans is that we are "goaded by the spirit of hierarchy." Implicit in our symbol use is the idea of hierarchy. Humans use words to arrange themselves in structures, organizations, and social orders. Consider the various levels of government. The ultimate position in the United States government is president. That position, with all its attendant rights and responsibilities, is created and perpetuated by our laws and customs, which depend on rhetoric. Although the hierarchy disturbs some people's notions of democracy and human freedom, humans seek the order it provides. Burke explained that we are also "moved by a sense of order" in the same way that we are goaded by hierarchy (1966, p. 15).

Hierarchy, or a sense of order, is another source of guilt that results from our rhetoric. Despite attempts to minimize differences between individuals, guilt results when we operate in structures that allow privileges to some, but deny those same privileges to others. Burke explained, "Those 'Up' are guilty of not being 'Down,' those 'Down' are certainly guilty of not being 'Up'" (1966, p. 15). Consider your experiences in the hierarchy of your college or university. After a point, students not advancing in class standing because they have repeatedly withdrawn from classes, for instance, are denied access to scholarships or financial aid, a form of punishment for not completing course work. Likewise, a junior or senior might feel bad for first- or second-year students who cannot register for classes early and thus fail to be able to take the classes they wish. The expectations of our society that people will be gainfully employed and not dependent on the social welfare system also exemplifies how guilt permeates our social hierarchies.

Another concept is implicit in hierarchy as well, according to Burke: mystery. In some ways, hierarchies depend on mystery. Burke explained that "King and peasant are 'mysteries' to each other" (1966, p. 15). As an example of how mystery preserves hierarchy, let's consider your experience with famous actors or actresses. Despite everything we think we might know about our favorite movie or television stars, we can never know everything there is to know about them or their daily activities. Though we might read in a magazine about their homes, vacations, and love lives, we can never really know about their lives. They often live in seclusion and carefully manage their personal lives. Mystery is part of the difference in status between them and us and, in part, preserves that distance.

Perfection

Finally, Burke believed that we are "rotten with perfection." He explained that central to rhetoric is the desire by humans to seek perfection. We seek to use "proper names" or we try to live the "perfect life" (1966, pp. 17–18). Burke pointed out that perfection, ironically, could be very destructive. Think of how we use the term "perfect fool" or "perfect villain." These terms indicate that evil can be achieved perfectly. As a result, trying to live the perfect life often causes us, or our society, great suffering in the process. Consider professional athletes, business executives, or entertainment celebrities who are able to negotiate the "perfect" contract, entitling them to millions of dollars in compensation. Meanwhile the poorest members of our society are barely able to feed or shelter themselves. Our pursuit of perfection may result in a rotten society, so to speak, which leads to its members experiencing guilt. Here again, we see how rhetoric results in guilt, a concept we will explore in greater detail in subsequent sections of this chapter.

ACTION AND MOTION

Understanding the central elements of Burke's theory of dramatism, we can now use these elements to understand the nature and implications of rhetoric. Burke distinguished between motion and action. Motion is nonsymbolic, whereas action is based on symbols, or rhetoric. The growth of a tree, for instance, is purely biological, which makes it a form of motion. Your saying the word "tree," on the other hand, is a form of action. Burke wrote, "'Things' can but move or be moved. 'Persons' by definition can 'act'" (1970, p. 187). In this book, as you should realize by now, we are concerned with action.

Burke presented three postulates that further describe the relationship between action and motion. First, "There can be no action without motion" (1968, p. 447). Speaking—a symbolic activity—requires that you move your mouth and other physical features to make a word. Even thinking, Burke explained, requires some type of neurological motion. That is, something happens in your nervous system that makes speech possible. Second, "there can be motion without action" (1968, p. 447). Consider again the growth of a tree. A tree will continue to grow despite the type of symbols that surround it. The tides and sunrises are also examples of motion that does not require action. Third, "action is not reducible to terms of motion" (1968, p. 447). Consider this sentence that you are reading. Certainly motion contributed to the production of its message. When I pressed the computer keys, words appeared on my computer screen through mechanical movements, or motion. As the words you are reading were printed on the page, motion again was required. However, without understanding the meaning of the words, the physical representations of the letters on the page are meaningless. That is, the action of my writing cannot be reduced to the simple marks that appear before you. You must understand the English language to understand what I have written.

Besides allowing us to communicate, action involves choice. A tree has no choice but to grow. Humans, however, can choose when and how to use symbols. As Burke explained, "If one cannot make a choice, one is not acting, one is but being moved, like a billiard ball tapped with a cue and behaving mechanically in conformity with the resistances it encounters" (1970, p. 188). Because rhetoric provides the opportunity for humans to act, moral rules, and laws exist to govern the choices we make. Here again, we encounter in Burke's theory the idea that rhetoric leads to moral choices and, consequently, makes guilt a part of our social system.

IDENTIFICATION

Before we again encounter the idea of guilt, we should understand how rhetoric leads to identification. Burke (1969b) explained **identification:** "A is not identical with his colleague, B. But insofar as their interests are joined, A is identified with B. Or he may identify himself with B even when their interests are not joined, if he assumes that they are, or is persuaded to believe so" (p. 20). Burke explained that when two individuals identify with each other, they are consubstantial. Cheney (1983) explained that this means there is a degree of overlap between the individuals and that this overlap can be real or perceived. Elaborating upon what may be shared by two individuals who are consubstantial, Burke listed sensations, concepts, images, ideas, and attitudes (1969b, p. 21). We use rhetoric to identify with a variety of "targets," including other people, families, groups, values, goals, knowledge, activities, or objects (Cheney, 1983, p. 145). So, if you share attitudes with a roommate, significant other, or family member, you identify with that person. Or, if you have had similar experiences with someone, you could be said to identify with that person. Or, maybe you have been on vacation and have seen someone wearing a sweatshirt from your college or hometown. You identify with that person because of what they are wearing.

Because of rhetoric, we experience division and conflict; consequently, we seek to identify with others to overcome this division. Hierarchy, as we have previously discussed, promotes the differences between people. We do not wish to be isolated from individuals, however, so we must use rhetoric to identify with them. Mystery is another factor of symbol use that causes us to seek identification; we try to identify with others to reduce the mystery that separates us from them. Because we seek out identification, it follows that rhetors may also use rhetoric strategically to convince us that we are like them. A politician, for instance, will talk about shared experiences with an audience, or an advertiser will show how the company shares the same values as the consumer. There is a fine line, however, between cooperation and exploitation. Ultimately, rhetoric, seen as the desire to identify with others, is a moralizing force in our culture. The desire to identify with others leads us to conform to what is accepted in society. Keep in mind that in unity, there is also division. Burke (1969b) wrote, "In being identified with B, A is 'substantially one' with a person other than himself. Yet at the same time he remains unique, an individual locus of motives" (p. 21). That is, we can never really identify completely with someone else.

In some cases, identification leads us to take on names or titles and to join with other individuals in groups or organizations with whom we share interests and values. In this sense, our identity is related to how we identify with other people. If you attend the University of Nebraska, for instance, you might call yourself a "Husker." If you attend the University of Oklahoma, you might consider yourself a "Sooner." Cheney (1983) noted that sometimes our group identities are at odds with one another. For instance, you might call yourself a "Republican" but were opposed to the war with Iraq. As a Republican, you might have felt pressure to support President Bush, a fellow Republican. However, being opposed to the war, you identified with another group, the "war protestors," who were seen as being opposed to President Bush and many Republican ideas.

Rhetoric as Identification

In Chapter 2, we equated rhetoric with persuasion, a definition stemming from Aristotle. Burke's definition of rhetoric as identification marks a significant departure from our previous thinking in several ways. First, identification is related to cooperation and highlights the role that audience members play in persuasion. Aristotle showed how rhetors can appeal to audience members, but Burke was interested in how audience members persuade themselves to identify with a rhetor. Second, the concept of identification allows for the possibility for unconscious persuasion to occur as we persuade ourselves of something without being explicitly persuaded to do so by others. Finally, rhetoric as identification involves a degree of self-persuasion. We have said that rhetoric lies at the intersection of a rhetor and an audience. Burke concluded that we can be our own audiences and act upon the messages of our "secret thoughts" (1969b, p. 38). The words of others are only effective, wrote Burke, when they can "speak in the language of a voice within" (1969, p. 39). Persuasion is only complete when an audience member convinces himself or herself of what has been said by others. Aristotle's view of rhetoric does not go this far.

Types of Identification

Identification is achieved when rhetors use one or more of three broad types of identification. For each one, we'll discuss ways that a university tries to identify with prospective students or employees. The first type of identification is obvious and direct. "It flowers in such usages as that of a politician who, though rich, tells humble constituents of his humble origins" (Burke, 1972, p. 28). A popular event on my campus is the opening academic convocation. Attended by nearly all the new freshman, this event features a recent alum, who addresses the new students. The alum speech typically explains that he or she comes from a similar background as the new students and identifies some of the similarities between what the new students will experience and what he or she has experienced. Importantly, the alum shows that attending the university can lead to great things. This year's speaker—though not even thirty years old—is a popular anchor of one of the local television news programs. Her speech inspires the new students to identify with the university and what it has to offer.

The second type of identification uses antithesis, creating an us-versus-them distinction. In other words, a rhetor identifies a particular person, object, or situation as an enemy of the audience being addressed. Those who are opposed to that person, object, or situation thus identify with the rhetor. For instance, each year the university plays our cross-town rival in football. The bookstore sells shirts each year that disparage the opponent in a humorous way. By showing what the students should be against, the t-shirts are designed to cause students to identify with their own school.

The third type of identification "derives from situations in which it goes unnoticed" (Burke, 1972, p. 28). For instance, using the word "we" to unite audience members with the rhetor is a powerful, yet subtle, type of identification. The condensed version of the mission statement for the university is simply: "We develop knowledge, talent, and skills for a lifetime of learning, service, and citizenship." The word "we" reinforces the idea that all of the university community is united in its effort to accomplish these goals. Thus, the statement encourages identification between the university members and those who might join the university as students or faculty members.

FRAMING SYMBOLIC EXPERIENCES: THE PENTAD

Burke was interested in the relationship between thought and words. When we conceive of a situation, we communicate to others how we see that situation through the rhetoric we use. Recall our prior observation that the words we use are not neutral, objective references to objects or ideas. Instead, our rhetoric is always subjective; but at the same time, we cannot escape the rhetorical worlds we inhabit. The strategies we use to frame situations are based on motives, or situations. "Situation," wrote Burke, "is but another word for motives" (1973, p. 20).

The **pentad** is a tool of analysis that lets us trace how our worlds are constructed through rhetoric. In so doing, we also understand the various motives, or situations, that determine how individual rhetors size up the situations they face. Five terms comprise the pentad: act, scene, agent, agency, and purpose. Burke provided a succinct description of how these terms are used to identify a rhetor's motives for framing a situation in a particular way. Burke wrote,

> In a rounded statement about motives, you must have some word that names the *act* (names what took place, in thought or deed), and another that names the *scene* (the background of the act, the situation in which it occurred); also, you must indicate what person or kind of person (*agent*) performed the act, what means or instruments he used (*agency*), and the *purpose* (1969a, p. 1).

The pentad is a method of analysis that focuses the critics attention on the types of words used to describe "what people are doing and why they are doing it. (1969a, p. 1)

Because individuals have different philosophies about the world, they are predisposed toward featuring one or two pentadic terms when they use rhetoric. We'll explain the elements of the pentad, discuss pentadic ratios, and then see an example of how the pentad can be used to interpret a rhetor's communication. See Table 6.1 for a summary of these concepts.

Elements of the Pentad

We have briefly identified five elements of the pentad. Let's now examine them in a bit more detail.

- Rhetors will undoubtedly discuss some kind of *act* when they communicate. In fact, Burke believed the act to be the central term of the pentad. What is significant, however, is how the act is reinterpreted by how rhetors feature the other elements of the pentad (Tonn, Endress, & Diamond, 1993).

- The *scene,* according to Burke, refers to the background of the act or the situation in which the act took place. Rhetors who feature the scene see the

Table 6.1 Burke's Pentad

Term	Definition	Example from Bush's Speech
Act	What happens or takes place	Military action against Iraq
Scene	Context or background of the action	Danger posed by Hussein
Agent	Person or persons who peform the act	Saddam Hussein, who had the choice of peaceful resolution or war
Agency	Means through which action takes place	United States, who would be enforcing international law
Purpose	Reason an action took place	Iraqi liberation

world as relatively permanent and deterministic (Tonn et al., 1993). That is, the situation is thought to control the actions of agents for rhetors who feature scene.

- The *agent* is the person who performed the act. Rhetors who feature the agent, see people as rational and capable of making choices. Agents, some rhetors contend, have the power to overcome scenic elements that limit their choices or actions.

- *Agency* refers to the means through which an action takes place. People who feature agency in their rhetoric are pragmatic; they are concerned with how to accomplish particular acts.

- Finally, some rhetors feature *purpose* when they talk. That is, rhetors sometimes focus on the reason for doing something.

It is important to note that the pentad should not be used descriptively to simply identify the various elements in rhetoric, but rather to interpret the motives of a particular rhetor. For instance, an agent can be labeled as responsible for a particular act, or the act may be portrayed as stemming from a particular scene. For example, if you agree to meet a friend at the library at a particular time to study and your friend fails to show—your friend fails to act, in other words—you can identify your friend—the agent—as responsible or you can say that something in the scene—car trouble, for instance—is being responsible for your friend's tardiness.

Additionally, the pentadic terms can be used strategically by rhetors to influence how their audience sees a particular situation. Rhetors can choose which pentadic terms to emphasize in order to influence the thinking of an audience. In a few paragraphs, you'll read about an important speech given by President Bush. Bush framed the debate over going to war with Iraq very carefully, emphasizing the role of Saddam Hussein as agent and the United States as agency in the confrontation.

Ratios

The relationship between two pentadic terms is called a **ratio.** It is often useful to explore the ratios apparent in a rhetor's discourse. Gusfield (1989) explained that a lack of balance between the two terms of a ratio can help critics understand the relationship between the two terms. One element of the pentad, for example, can be explained by the other element. In our previous example about your friend being late to meet you, the two ratios we discussed were act-agent and act-scene. In one scenario, you might label your friend—the agent—as being responsible for the act. In another scenario, you might identify the scene as being responsible.

Let's consider another example. Proponents of a federal welfare system often use a scene-agent ratio in their rhetoric to justify social welfare. They argue that social structures and systems have led to the need to support people who do not make enough money to escape poverty. That is, welfare advocates argue that economic realities, business practices, and educational opportunities prevent some people from gaining the kind of employment they need to escape poverty. In this case, the scene is the controlling term of the scene-agent ratio; the scene constrains the actions of the agents, welfare recipients. You probably realize from this example that the counterratio, used by those who oppose welfare, is an agent-act ratio. That is, individuals are responsible for their own actions, and the government should not support individuals who do not achieve success in our economic system. In this case, the agents, welfare recipients, control the act, earning enough money to support themselves. This example illustrates the powerful differences that can emerge when rhetors use pentadic terms to manage rhetorical situations.

Applying the Pentad to Rhetoric

To better understand how critics use the pentad to understand how rhetoric size up situations for audiences, let's consider President Bush's speech on March 17, 2003. In this speech, Bush gave an ultimatum to Iraqi President Saddam Hussein to leave Iraq or face a U.S. military invasion. The central pentadic term in the speech is *act*. President Bush used the speech to justify military action against Iraq. Bush said, "We are now acting because the risks of inaction would be far greater." In addition, Bush warned, "Yet, the only way to reduce the harm and duration of the war is to apply the full force and might of our military, and we are prepared to do so." Related to the act is the *scene*. In referring to the scene, Bush noted the danger posed by Hussein. He said, "The [Hussein] regime has a history of reckless aggression in the Middle East. It has a deep hatred of America and our friends. And it has aided, trained and harbored terrorists, including operatives of al Qaeda." Additionally, Bush spoke of the *purpose* of military action: "The tyrant will soon be gone. The day of your [Iraqi] liberation is near."

What was most significant about Bush's speech was how we framed the justification for U.S. action. Two ratios are key to Bush's strategy: act-agency and act-agent. The U.S. was acting without the complete support of world nations at the time. Despite an earlier resolution in the United Nations authorizing force to remove Hussein if he failed to comply with international law, the current U.S. action failed to have the support of France, Germany, Russia and many other world nations. Bush had to frame his actions to justify immediate U.S. action. To do so, Bush strategically framed the situation for his worldwide audience.

Instead of portraying the U.S. as the agent, he framed the U.S. as the *agency,* enacting the will of the United Nations. Bush said, "We believe in the mission of the United Nations," evoking the idea of the U.N. as the agency for world peace and cooperation. Given the lack of U.N. support for immediate military conflict, Bush adopted the role of agency by saying, "The United Nations Security Council has not lived up to its responsibilities, so we will rise to ours." Thus, Bush transferred the agency of the United Nations to the United States. The *agent,* according to Bush's rhetoric, was Hussein. Bush said, "Should Saddam Hussein chose confrontation . . ." and "If Saddam Hussein attempts to cling to power . . ." Further Bush said that the attacks weren't "inevitable," but they were "possible" if Hussein did not leave the country. Bush effectively shifts the responsibility for the attack to Hussein, while at the same time makes the United States the agency for previously decided U.N. action. By isolating the terms of the pentad and highlighting the ratios between selected terms in the speech, we can gain insight into Bush's strategy as he attempted to win world support for military action against Iraq.

REDEMPTION FROM GUILT

Recall the concepts of guilt, perfection, and identification that we have discussed. Guilt, as you'll recall, is an ever-present part of symbol use which results from the negative, our quest for perfection, and our hierarchical social arrangements. One of our most important uses of rhetoric is to suggest ways of managing guilt. Burke suggested several ways that we can manage guilt, two of which are tragically or comically.

Tragic Redemption

When we experience *guilt,* we are induced to seek the *perfect* redemption from the guilt. As we seek redemption, we look for symbolic sacrifices. Burke explained that

> a dramatistic analysis shows how the negativistic principle of guilt implicit in the nature of order combines with the principles of thoroughness (or "perfection") and substitution that are characteristic of symbol systems in such a way that the sacrificial principle of victimage (the "scapegoat") is intrinsic to human congregation. The intricate line of exposition might be summed up thus: If order, then guilt; if guilt, then need for redemption; but any such "payment" is victimage (p. 450)

Let's look at this process in a bit more detail.

Terms for Order   Humans tend to naturally seek order, given our drive for perfection and hierarchy. As we have seen, however, our quest for order is constantly polluted because of guilt that results from the negative. When the guilt becomes significant enough, an individual rhetor or a community of rhetors seeks to remove that guilt. Recall our previous discussion of guilt and how both individuals and groups experience guilt when the social order is disrupted. Burke (1970) outlined the process through which guilt is created and removed. He called this process **terms for order.**

Rhetoric leads to guilt, but rhetoric is also the way of removing guilt from the social system. In order to remove guilt and restore order, some kind of redeemer is needed. Two general strategies of purification may be used, mortification and scapegoating. Mortification occurs when the guilty individual or group admits their guilt and ask for forgiveness. The guilty are often punished and sometimes driven from the community. President Clinton apologized for his affair with Monica Lewinsky and was punished by being impeached, but he was not removed from office. In this case, public opinion was in favor of some time of punishment, but against removal from office. We may assume, then, that Clinton's apology and impeachment were sufficient to achieve redemption for his guilt.

The other type of purification is scapegoating. A scapegoat, explained Burke, is "the 'representative' or 'vessel' of certain unwanted evils, the sacrificial animal upon whose back the burden of these evils is ritualistically loaded" (1973, pp. 39–40). Burke explained that this step involves substitution: "one character may be redeemed through the act or agency of another" (1970, p. 176). We try to create a worthy, or perfect, scapegoat, to refer back to our previous discussion of perfection. In fact, a scapegoat who is less than perfect will not suffice to remove the guilt from a society.

Burke explained that scapegoats can be made worthy in three ways. The scapegoat can be legally responsible for the guilt and subject to the laws of the society. For example, court trials are rituals designed to legally endow a scapegoat with the guilt of a crime. Second, the scapegoat can be assigned in a fatalistic sense, such as the character Oedipus in Greek tragedy. Fatalistic scapegoats may have a personal flaw or too much pride. Third, a scapegoat can be a worthy vessel for guilt by being "too good for this world" (Burke, 1973, p. 40). Here, Burke used the religious example of Jesus Christ, a scapegoat who was killed because he was thought to be above the social order. Ultimately, the scapegoat has to be removed from the social order. As Carlson and Hocking (1988) have explained, "when the scapegoat is destroyed, the 'sins' are cast out" (p. 206).

The sacrifice of the victim—through mortification or scapegoating—must be sufficient in order for redemption to occur. The acquittal of O. J. Simpson in his criminal trial, for example, was insufficient to remove the guilt that he was perceived to have caused. Thus, society did not collectively achieve redemption because he was declared not guilty. A friend that does not forgive you for doing something wrong would be denying redemption because your apology was insufficient. However, if your apology was sincere enough, your friend might forgive you, restoring order to the relationship. Redemption, though, is only temporary, as "there is always something wrong in the world, always a new source of guilt" (Carlson & Hocking, 1988, p. 206).

An Example of Tragic Redemption   A. Cheree Carlson and John E. Hocking (1988) examined the letters, notes, and other messages left by visitors at the Vietnam Veterans Memorial to understand how visitors achieved redemption from their guilt caused by the Vietnam War. In their rhetorical criticism, Carlson and Hocking were interested in how rhetoric, left behind at the wall served to achieve redemption for its visitors.

Carlson and Hocking (1988) write that the Memorial suggests that pollution has disrupted the social order: "The seemingly endless list of the dead, rising on a granite wall from a gash in the ground, conveys the idea that something terribly wrong has

FIGURE 6.1 The Vietnam Veterans Memorial in Washington, D.C., invites several types of rhetorical responses from its visitors. Through rhetoric, visitors to the memorial achieve redemption, either by scapegoating the dead or mortifying themselves.

happened" (p. 206). Americans feel guilt "about American involvement, the disastrous outcome and the lives lost in vain" (p. 204). Because the Vietnam Memorial is symbolic, it suggests several different strategies of victimage for those who view it. Carlson and Hocking explain that viewers of the Memorial use either scapegoating or mortification strategies to rid themselves of guilt associated with the Vietnam War.

Remember that a scapegoat is a vessel, according to Burke, that is filled with guilt and removed from the social order. Carlson and Hocking (1988) suggest that scapegoats are not always viewed negatively by those who would fill them with guilt. Sometimes, the authors explain, victims are sacrificed in order to create a positive meaning for the community. In the case of the Vietnam Memorial, visitors redefined the war's victims as "sacrificial victims who died for our sins" (p. 207). The fallen are heroic, cleansing the nation of the sins of the war. Redemption is achieved, through scapegoating, because the visitor transforms the war into "a positive event of heroism and bravery" (p. 206).

For other visitors, the wall calls on them to come to terms with their own actions during the war or their own feelings about the war. The messages these visitors leave behind illustrate that they are seeking penance as part of a mortification process. Visiting the Memorial and responding to it are ways of apologizing to those who died in the war and whose names are memorialized on the black granite surface. Redemption is achieved in this case, because the visitor can leave with a sense of peace because his or her guilt about the war has been reduced by paying respects at the Memorial. Carlson and Hocking provide an illuminating view of how rhetoric can achieve tragic redemption.

Comic Enlightenment

The "'other' way of dealing with guilt" is comedy (Brummett, 1984). When guilt is experienced, rhetors can choose to manage guilt tragically or comically. In tragic redemption, the guilty is removed from the rhetorical community through either scapegoating or mortification. Comic redemption, conversely, holds that all individuals, at times, are guilty of foolish actions. Instead of removing them from the social order, comic redemption is achieved by belittling the fool, welcoming the fool back into the community, and learning from the foolish action. Carlson (1986) explained that "The comic frame identifies social ills as arising from human error, not evil, and thus uses reason to correct them" (p. 448). The result of comic redemption is that the social order learns from the mistakes of its members. By piecing together the work of Burke; Hugh Duncan, a Burkean sociologist; and other scholars, we can identify a path to comic redemption that is similar in form to that Burke identified for tragic redemption. The three stages to comic enlightenment include incongruity, belittling, and enlightenment.

Incongruity One of the fundamental differences between tragic and comic redemption is the nature of the guilt. In tragic redemption, you'll recall, guilt arises when we morally fail due to the negative, hierarchy, or perfection. Rhetors pursuing the comic route focus on the *mistakes* of a fool in the rhetorical community. Or, to think of it another way, rhetors identify "the incongruities between what people say they will do in society and how they actually behave" (Brummett, 1984).

Belittling The comic counterpart to purification is belittling. Tragic purification is designed to punish and remove the guilty; comic belittling pokes fun at the comic scapegoat, teaching him or her a lesson from which all in the community can learn. When you consider that all humans potentially make mistakes, you realize that all of us are potential comic scapegoats. Duncan explained that the comic scapegoat "can be laughed at but he is also being laughed with. We are laughing at him to purge him—and ourselves—of folly, not to torture and kill him" (1962, p. 395).

Enlightenment The end result of tragic redemption is that the order is restored when the guilty are removed from the social system. In comic redemption, the end result is enlightenment, or learning from our mistakes. A particularly important lesson we learn from comic redemption is that our taken-for-granted way of thinking is flawed in some way. Burke encouraged individuals to see the world from different perspectives, and comic redemption is one way for us to escape the dominant perspective we have of situations.

Limitations of Comic Redemption Despite Burke's "hankering after a comic perspective on human affairs" (1972, p. 29), the comic method of redemption may not be sufficient in many cases of guilt. Though victimage is "not inevitable,"

Burke noted that there are tremendous pressures toward tragic redemption. He noted that "There are also comic victims, the 'butts' of humor—but will things stop there?" (1972, p. 29). Ultimately, the source of incongruity may grow so large that tragic redemption is necessary to restore order.

An Example of Comic Redemption Although we often think of rhetoric as taking place in important speeches or political events, popular culture, including television sit-coms, is a powerful source of rhetoric in our society as well. The television show *Friends* often used comic redemption to teach its audience a lesson. In the seventh season, one episode explored how each of the six friends dealt with turning thirty. Each character's actions in the episode highlighted what they perceived to be a problem, or an incongruity, with growing older. In particular, Ross's character rejected the notion of getting older by buying a small red sports car.

Throughout the episode, Ross was belittled by the others for buying this impractical car, which was clearly aimed at restoring his youthful vitality. This exchange illustrates how Ross was belittled by the others but also how he belittled himself:

Monica: Well, doing nothing on your thirtieth is better than doing something stupid, like Ross.

Ross: Hey! That was a practical purchase! I needed that car for transportation! Okay? I—I have a child!

Ross: "That's not what this is about okay? I . . . I am a sports car enthusiast. I have *always* been into cars."

Joey: "Hey, what's the horsepower on this thing?"

Ross: "I don't know, but . . . but look how shiny!"

Joey makes fun of how little Ross knows about the car, but Ross admits, in a comedic way, how he really doesn't know much about sports cars. The ultimate joke in the episode is that the car is parked so tightly in its parking space, that Ross can't back out until the cars around him leave. As they finally are able to go for a ride in the car, they see an older man driving the same model of car. The car suddenly loses its appeal as a fountain of youth.

We learn, through the characters on *Friends,* that turning old isn't so bad. In fact, the episode questions our society's obsession with youth. Each of the characters is shown to do something beyond reason in the episode. Upon reflection, the characters realize that their actions have been foolish, and they come to terms with aging. Of course, a critic could also interpret the episode as meaning that we haven't really achieved enlightenment, since we only experience a narrow view of aging.

Redemption, either comic or tragic, is one of the most important aspects of Burke's theory of dramatism. As we use rhetoric to achieve redemption, we encounter each element of dramatism that we've discussed. Symbol use, the negative, hierarchy, and perfection all give rise to guilt. How a rhetor chooses to approach guilt can be revealed by which pentadic term he or she features. Identification helps us to

---

BOX 6.2   Critical Insights: Hunting and Heritage On Trial

Rhetorical critics frequently focus on one aspect of Burke's rhetorical theory, such as identification or the pentad. Mari Boor Tonn, Valerie A. Endress, and John N. Diamond, however, integrated Burke's many ideas as they studied the arguments surrounding a murder trial in Maine. Their study is published in the May 1993 issue of the *Quarterly Journal of Speech*. This article is an excellent example of the insight offered by Burke's rhetorical theory.

Tonn, Endress, and Diamond (1993) studied the debate surrounding the killing of Karen Wood. In 1988, Donald Rogerson was hunting deer in a wooded area near Herman, Maine. Nearby lived Karen Wood, who had recently moved to Maine from Iowa. Believing he had seen the tails of two deer, Rogerson fired twice. Instead of shooting a deer, he shot and killed Wood, who was in her back yard. Two buff-colored mittens lay at her side (Tonn, Endress, and Diamond, 1993, p. 165). A grand jury failed to indict the hunter for the death. A Burkean analysis helps us to understand why.

Tonn, Endress, and Diamond (1993) use the pentad and tragic redemption to explain public response to the death. The key terms of the pentad are *act*, the shooting; *agent*, either the hunter or the victim; and *scene*, the physical setting of the incident and the perceived assault on the heritage of hunting in the state. In public discussion, Rogerson, the hunter/agent, was exonerated for his act because of the way the scene was depicted: the victim, while on her property, was not in her "back yard," but was instead in a wooded area behind her house. Also, it was growing dark and difficult for him to see her.

Yet the guilt caused by the act, the shooting, needed to be removed. Since the hunter was not a suitable scapegoat, public discussion transformed the victim/agent, Wood, into the scapegoat. Talk show hosts castigated Wood for not wearing orange—a color easily seen by hunters—while walking in the woods. Wood was also attacked for not exercising common sense the afternoon she was shot. In fact, some public rhetoric argued the victim "tempted" the hunter to shoot her by waving her white-mittened hands in the air. In essence, Wood was portrayed as violating the established norms and disrupting the social order of Maine's hunting community. The shooter, and all other hunters, were transformed into the victims of Wood's actions. Thus, Wood was the perfect scapegoat to purify the pollution caused by the shooting.

Tonn, Endress, and Diamond (1993) explained that by transforming the scene, public rhetors also transformed the actions of the hunter, turning his shooting into motion for which he could not be accountable. Additionally, the physical scene of the shooting was seen as less important than the larger context, controversy over hunting in Maine and the "invasion" of outsiders, such as Wood, that threatened the traditional norms and customs of Maine's residents. From this analysis, we can appreciate how Burke's theory helps us to understand the motives and redemptive processes inherent in a community's rhetoric.

---

determine if redemption, or enlightenment, has been achieved. Box 6.2 shows how these elements come together in a Burkean rhetorical criticism.

NARRATIVE

A number of rhetorical theorists other than Burke also approach rhetoric from a dramatistic perspective. We'll study Walter Fisher's narrative paradigm and Ernest Bormann's symbolic convergence theory. Each of these theories shares with Burkean dramatism ideas about the social construction of knowledge, the influence of symbols on how we perceive the world, and how a dramatic metaphor can be used to understand human motivation. We'll first address Fisher's narrative paradigm and apply it to contemporary rhetoric.

Understanding the Narrative Paradigm

Fisher (1987) proposed a theory of rhetoric in which dramatic stories take on the role of arguments. He claimed that all people are essentially storytellers and that we constantly evaluate and choose from the stories we hear. Thus, a television commercial can be viewed as a story told to consumers, for example. This is not to say that the rhetoric lacks substance or that it is "mere rhetoric." In fact, the contrary is true. Like Burke, Fisher argued that our world is created through symbols and thus by using symbolic structures—stories—we can induce others to see the world through our eyes. Stories, according to Fisher, have substance and weight because they reflect how we see our world.

Fisher says, humans are "essentially storytellers" (1987, p. 64). That is, our rhetoric can be considered a story, with a plot, characters, and other attributes of good fiction. Second, instead of using strict rules of logic, such as inductive and deductive reasoning, Fisher writes that we use "good reasons" when making decisions and persuading others. Good reasons use traditional ideas about logic, from Chapters 2 and 4, along with ideas about the values the storyteller shares with his or her audience. What is meant by "good reasons" varies—to some degree—among situations, genres, and media of communication (Fisher, 1987). Finally, "the world as we know it is a set of stories that must be chosen among" (Fisher, 1987, p. 65). Viewing communication as a narrative is meaningful for people in a wide variety of cultures and communities because "we all live out narratives in our lives and because we understand our own lives in terms of narratives" (p. 66).

Humans use *narrative rationality* when evaluating the stories they hear, which is based on two standards: narrative probability and narrative fidelity. **Narrative probability** asks whether the story is consistent with itself. **Narrative fidelity** evaluates the degree to which the individual components of the story "ring true" with the audience. Narrative rationality depends not entirely on rules of logic but also on the values that are a part of decision making. This is an important part of Fisher's theory. Let's consider these standards in greater detail.

Narrative probability concerns the degree to which the story "hangs together." In other words, this standard looks at whether the story makes sense by itself. Fisher (1987) argues that stories must have structural coherence, material coherence, and characterological coherence. *Structural coherence* refers to whether the story contradicts itself. A witness who testifies in court and says something different than he or she had previously said would not have structural coherence. The story would not "hang together." *Material coherence* refers to how well the story accounts for facts that are known to be true. A witness who testifies that the car in the accident was green, when all the other witness claim it was red would not have material coherence. *Characterological coherence* questions the reliability of the characters in the story. A witness accused of murder but who is claiming innocence would be difficult to believe if he or she did not display some emotion about being accused.

Presidential campaigns are often viewed from a narrative perspective. In essence, each candidate is telling a story to voters and they will choose which story to believe when they vote. Let's examine how these standards we just discussed might be used to assess 2004 Democratic presidential candidate Howard Dean's rhetoric in his candidacy announcement speech of June 23, 2003.

First, we'll assess his rhetoric from the standpoint of narrative probability. Does it have structural coherence, or internal logic? Dean's overall message was that he wished to "restore all that it means to be an American." As audiences assessed his story, they determined to what degree his policy proposals reflected this theme. For instance, Dean made the argument that the current administration's tax cuts "are designed to destroy Social Security, Medicare, our public schools and our public services." In other words, Dean's opposition to the tax cuts would restore the American institutions that he mentioned. Next, does Dean's rhetoric meet the standard of material coherence, adequately reflecting the audience members' perception of reality? Dean implies that his message should pass this test: "From New Hampshire to Texas I met Americans doubting the words of our leaders and government in Washington." How about characterological coherence of his message, or the believability of the characters involved? Dean asserted, "I am a doctor and I was proud to be Governor of Vermont: where we balanced budgets, where we made sure that nearly every child in our state had health care coverage." The audience was left to evaluate Dean's qualifications to be president and how much he should be trusted.

The second standard of Fisher's (1987) narrative paradigm is *fidelity*. Whereas coherence refers to the integrity of the story, fidelity refers to the individual components of stories and the degree to which these components make sense to the audience. Thus, probability concerns the story itself and fidelity refers to the connection between the story and the audience. Fisher explained that fidelity questions "whether they represent accurate assertions about social reality" (p. 105). Fidelity can be understood by looking at five concepts—fact, relevance, consequence, consistency, and transcendent issue. For each, we'll cite examples of how Howard Dean attempted to meet the standard of fidelity in his announcement speech.

- The question of *fact* explores the values that are embedded in a story. Dean's overall campaign message was to "unite and empower" people everywhere to take back their country. This was Dean's value: empowering people.

- The question of *relevance* concerns the appropriateness of the values to the nature of the decision. By empowering his audience, Dean believed that they would restore America to greatness. He closed his announcement speech by saying, "You have the power to reclaim our nation's destiny. You have the power to rid Washington of the politics of money. You have the power to make right as important as might." This call to the audience reinforced his value of returning the nation to its people, asserting its appropriateness.

- The question of *consequence* examines the effects of adhering to a particular value set when making a decision. Dean contended that if Americans were not empowered, the current president would continue to divide the nation. If he were elected, on the other hand, Americans would have a reason to vote again.

- The question of *consistency* asks if the values of the story confirm one's personal experience. Dean tried to assert that his story was representative of a voter's experiences: "The Americans I have met love their country. They believe deeply in its promise, our values and our principles. But they know something is wrong and they want to take action." No matter what Dean said, though, passing the test of consistency ultimately depends on the audience to judge whether the story fits with their experience.

■ The question of *transcendent issue* asks if the values in question "constitute the ideal basis for human conduct" (Fisher, 1987, p. 109). Dean argued that if Americans engaged once again in politics, the United States can once again return to its "high moral purpose."

Although Dean makes the case for narrative fidelity, remember that Fisher says it is up to the audience member to determine if the story makes sense.

Fisher's narrative paradigm provides us with another way to examine rhetoric from a dramatistic perspective. He claimed that rhetoric is similar to a story and that humans make judgments about stories based on narrative probability and narrative fidelity. In the next section, we'll examine a final dramatistic theory, symbolic convergence theory.

SYMBOLIC CONVERGENCE THEORY

A final dramaturgical approach we will discuss is symbolic convergence theory. Ernest Bormann (1972) and his colleagues at the University of Minnesota used a dramatic metaphor to explain how individuals use rhetoric to form common ways of seeing the world. Like Burke's theories and Fisher's narrative paradigm, Bormann's theory focuses on how "Individuals in rhetorical transactions create subjective worlds of common expectations and meanings" (Bormann, 1972, p. 400). We'll examine the basic framework of symbolic convergence theory and then see how it can be used to explain the recent low-carb dieting craze. An extensive bibliography of sources about symbolic convergence theory can be found at http://rhetjournal.net/SCT_FTABiblio.html.

Understanding Symbolic Convergence Theory

Bormann found that when individuals in small groups communicate, they essentially create and share stories, or **fantasies,** to fulfill some need (Bormann, 1985). The word *fantasy* is not used here in a conventional sense. Fantasies, according to this theory, are very real events that happen to people and groups. In essence, a fantasy can be defined as a shared experience between people. Thus, a fantasy may include experiences you and some friends had on a recent trip together, the image that your university projects to others, or the ideas and stories told by candidates in a political campaign.

Fantasy sharing is used to deal with conflict, solidify relationships, or express emotion. Stories also help the group create a shared culture, or way of seeing the world. Some fantasies are told so often, that only a word or two is needed for the group to burst into laughter or understand what was meant. Thus, the simple act of storytelling is an important tool for group communication.

Table 6.2 Symbolic Convergence Theory

Term	Definition	Example
Fantasy theme	Shared experiences or stories retold among a group of people	Eating foods that are low in carbohydrates can lead to sustained weight loss.
Fantasy type	Common stories told over and over again	The latest diet will help people lose weight quickly and easily.
Chaining out	The process by which fantasy themes or types are spread through a group or culture	The appearance of diet books in bookstores, new foods in grocery stores, and media representations (such as comic strips).
Rhetorical vision	Common way of seeing the world that results when many people share in a fantasy theme	Diets that are low in carbohydrates are healthy and useful for managing weight.

Bormann theorized that group fantasy sharing can be used to explain how larger groups of people create shared visions of reality based on the stories they share. A political campaign, for instance, can be viewed as a set of stories that are shared among voters. Members of a rhetorical community view an unfolding fantasy much as they would a movie or play. **Fantasy themes** are the contents of the story that are retold by group members. Sometimes, the group develops particular fantasies that have similar plot outlines, scenes, and characters (Bormann, 1985). These repeated patterns of exchanges are called **fantasy types.** As the fantasy themes "chain out" among the group members, the group forms a **rhetorical vision,** which is a common way of seeing the world based on the process of sharing fantasies. Bormann (1972) believed that "A rhetorical vision is constructed from fantasy themes that chain out in face-to-face interacting groups, in speaker-audience transactions, in viewers of television broadcasts, in listeners to radio programs, and in all the diverse settings for public and intimate communication a given society" (p. 398). Table 6.2 depicts the various components of the theory.

Rhetorical visions are based on typical characterizations and plot lines. In fact, future fantasy themes can be based on existing rhetorical visions to spark predictable emotional responses (Bormann, 1972). Rhetorical critics using symbolic convergence theory to understand must examine a number of rhetorical artifacts related to a dramatic incident. Then, the critic looks for patterns of characterizations, dramatic situations, and settings. The critic then reconstructs the chaining-out process to understand how rhetorical vision came to be believed. Use symbolic convergence theory to understand a contemporary social issue by completing the Internet Exercise, Social Issues and Rhetorical Fantasies (Box 6.3).

Applying Symbolic Convergence Theory

Symbolic convergence theory can help us understand the latest trend in dieting: the low-carbohydrate diet (see Table 6.2). Although the most popular of these diets, the Atkins Diet, was first introduced in 1972, it has only been in the last five to ten years that low-carb dieting has enjoyed widespread popularity. Joining the

---

BOX 6.3   Internet Exercise: Social Issues and Rhetorical Fantasies

Symbolic convergence theory states that individuals "chain out" views of reality until they become widely shared in society. The chaining-out process occurs through face-to-face communication and media channels. Newspaper and magazine coverage of topics is good example of media that chain-out fantasies. Use your Infotrac College Edition account to look up a series of news articles about a controversial social issues, such as affirmative action, racism, or capital punishment. Identify the fantasy or fantasies that are chaining out in the articles. Who are the good characters? Who are the bad characters? What fantasy types are evidence? What is the dominant rhetorical vision about the issue?

FIGURE 6.2   Think for a moment about how you first heard about low-carb dieting: was it in the media, in a grocery store, or through a friend? How did you participate in the chaining-out process?

CATHY © 2004 Cathy Guisewite. Reprinted with permission of Universal Press Syndicate. All rights reserved.

Atkins Diet are a host of similar diets, such as the South Beach Diet and the Zone. Each diet is accompanied by a book, often near the top of the best-seller lists. These diets play into a popular fantasy theme: that losing weight can be quick and easy if one has the right diet. Often these diets are portrayed as allowing people to lose weight without a lot of exercise or sacrifice.

The fantasy theme chained out in a variety of ways. The diets became the topic of media reports and new stories as well as people's everyday conversations. Former President Bill Clinton received attention for losing weight on the South Beach Diet, and comic strips, such as Cathy (see Figure 6.2) exploited the dieting trend. Grocery stores introduced low-carb food sections, and many restaurants provided low-carb menu options for people. Scientific studies that supported these types of diets also contributed to their popularity.

Although not all dieters have success with these diets and despite arguments that they may not healthy, low-carb dieting has resulted in a widely held rhetorical vision: that foods high in carbohydrates lead to weight gain, but that low-carb eating can be a healthy way to maintain a person's ideal body weight. At least in part because so many people have adopted this rhetorical vision, food companies, such as Krispy Kreme and Hostess, experienced slumps in their sales. Some experts even attributed a drop in beer consumption to low-carb dieting. The low-carb dieting fantasy resulted in a rhetorical vision for some people that made them careful of what they eat.

SUMMARIZING DRAMATISTIC THEORY

As in previous chapters, we'll summarize our findings. We'll now review the primary approaches of dramatistic theorists to defining rhetoric and how they view epistemology, ontology, and ethics, our key themes we have studied so far. Finally, we'll review their primary theoretical contributions.

Defining Rhetoric

For dramatists, rhetoric is the use of symbols to create common ways of identifying. Their definitions of rhetoric imply that meaning is created cooperatively through the exchange of symbols. In the last chapter, we discussed the linguistic turn in rhetorical theory; here the dramatists take this linguistic turn one step further and fully explore its implication for how we know and experience the world.

Rhetoric and Knowledge

In dramatistic theory, knowledge is created through the interaction of human rhetors and the symbols they use. "Truth" for a given community is created through the exchange of symbols. This is probably most apparent with symbolic convergence theory, where the chaining out of rhetorical fantasies leads to the creation of a rhetorical vision. Burke's theory of dramatism is a bit more implicit, but in some ways, more profound. He argues that our entire way of knowing is based on the rhetoric we use.

Rhetoric and Identity

In Burke's later writing (1968), he explained that dramatism was literal, not metaphorical. In doing so, he shifted his focus from epistemology to ontology (Brock, Scott, & Chesebro, 1990). Quite literally, rhetoric creates a structure through which we know and experience the world. He also defines humans as "bodies that learn language." In this sense, we are literally products of the linguistic systems in which we operate. As mentioned earlier, Condit (1995) explained that, dramatism comes from a perspective in which language is seen as influencing how we see, understand, and experience the world.

Rhetoric and Judgment

The concept of the negative is clearly a moralizing force in Burke's theory of dramatism. The negative creates standards for what we should and should not do. Burke also theorizes that the negative creates hierarchies, which, in some cases, serve as structures that guide a culture's view of morality. The concept of guilt is another important aspect of how rhetoric creates and enforces specific moral standards. When guilt is apparent, rhetoric is used to remove the guilt and restore the social order, which, again, is a moralizing force. Likewise, Fisher's concept of narration includes a moral component. For Fisher, rhetoric consists of stories about values. Rhetoric, to him, is often a struggle to determine which values should hold the most weight for a given audience.

DISCUSSION QUESTIONS

1. Which element of Burke's definition of human do you think is the most significant? Why?

2. To what extent do you think hierarchies exist in cultures? Are there some cultures that lack hierarchies? If so, how might those cultures experience rhetoric?

3. How useful is Burke's theory of dramatism in a world marked by mediated and visual messages? How useful is Burke's theory of dramatism in a multicultural world?

4. Identify some type of cultural guilt that is currently being experienced in a particular rhetorical community? How do you think that guilt will be expunged, tragically or comically? What steps will be taken, do you think, to remove the guilt?

5. To what degree do you think humans tell and evaluate rhetoric as stories, as Fisher suggests? What are some examples of rhetoric you have analyzed from the narrative perspective?

6. Identify a fantasy theme being "chained out" in a particular community. What is the plot of the fantasy? Who are the characters? Has the fantasy theme created a rhetorical vision? What is that vision?

GLOSSARY TERMS

identification Real or perceived overlap of two individuals' perspectives or ways of seeing the world.

pentad Model for locating the motives in a rhetorical text. Includes the terms of act, agent, agency, scene, and purpose.

terms for order The stages through which tragic redemption occurs. Includes guilt, purification, and redemption.

ratio The relationship between two pentadic terms.

fantasies Stories shared by groups of people.

narrative probability One of the standards by which receivers evaluate narrative rhetoric. Includes structural, material, and characterological coherence.

narrative fidelity   The standard used to evaluate the validity of the individual elements of narrative rhetoric.

fantasy themes   The contents of stories that are retold by group members.

fantasy types   Fantasies that have similar plot outlines, scenes, and characters and that are repeated patterns of exchanges.

rhetorical vision   The result of fantasy sharing, in which members of a culture, community, or group share a similar way of understanding reality.

PART IV

Rhetoric, Culture, and Power

7

Critical Approaches
to Rhetoric

Learning Objectives

After reading this chapter, you should be able to:

1. Describe the nature of critical studies of rhetoric.
2. Explain ideology and hegemony.
3. Locate ideographs in rhetorical texts.
4. Explain how rhetoric can liberate.
5. Describe the critical rhetoric perspective.

Pick up a magazine and flip through it, paying attention to the advertising. How would you evaluate the advertisements you see? Using the rhetorical principles covered in previous chapters, you could evaluate the effectiveness of an advertisement in persuading the target audience to purchase what is advertised, and you might consider how the ad uses reasoning or credibility appeals, for instance. Our focus in this chapter will take us in a different direction. Instead of judging the effectiveness of a rhetoric, we will look more at the link between rhetoric and power. We'll be asking questions such as:

- Is there anything wrong with an advertisement?
- What is the ideology behind an advertisement?
- Are the actions requested by an advertisement harmful or beneficial to audience members?

Our previous discussion of rhetorical theory did not address these sorts of issues. Much of our discussion in the first four chapters was aimed at clarifying how rhetorical messages are effective. In Chapters 5 and 6, we started to look at language and its reflexive nature and we began to understand how rhetoric creates reality. To some degree, these theories extend our understanding of the impact of magazine advertisements. The theories in this chapter, though, will take us a step further toward answering the questions in the previous paragraph. We'll begin to study how power and ideology are expressed through rhetoric and how rhetoric may be used to empower and disempower certain groups of people.

In this chapter, we'll discuss what are referred to as *critical* approaches to rhetoric. The word "critical," in this sense, refers to a concern for power and ideology as expressed through rhetoric. Don't confuse the concept of critical in this chapter with its more common meaning of "negative." Instead, the theorists in this chapter are interested in identifying how we can critique the ways that rhetoric influences power relationships in society. We should note that not all critiques are negative. A great deal of critical work focuses on how rhetorical messages are liberating, as well.

We'll begin our discussion by identifying some of the differences in how we'll study rhetoric in this chapter and then discuss more precisely what is meant by *critical studies*. After surveying some of the most significant contributions to modern rhetorical theory, including the work of Antonio Gramsci, Michael Calvin McGee, Jurgen Habermas, and Raymie McKerrow, we'll conclude the chapter by pointing out their impact on our study of rhetoric and knowledge, identity, and judgment.

SHIFTING EMPHASES IN RHETORICAL THEORY

In this chapter we'll start to see some subtle shifts in our study of rhetoric that will carry through to the end of the book. First, rhetorical criticism will become more prominent in our discussion. In the first chapter, we discussed the relationship between practice, theory, and criticism. In each chapter since, we have discussed specific examples of rhetorical criticism that stem from theory. In the remaining chapters, we'll see that criticism is tightly integrated with theory and practice. Many of the theories will offer a methodology for critics. Building theory will become less significant; using critical practice to critique rhetoric's role in a culture will become more significant. As Lucaites and Condit (1999) have explained, "Whereas previously theory, criticism, and history stood as starkly different dimensions of rhetorical studies, henceforth they would become increasingly implicated in and by one another" (p. 14).

Second, we'll begin to focus our attention increasingly on nonoratorical rhetorical artifacts. In fact, twentieth-century theorists and critics often use the term "text" to refer to rhetoric. A **text** is a set of symbols that can be seen to produce meaning. A book, for instance, fits this definition. Its pages contain symbols that produce meaning for the reader. Likewise, a film can be said to contain multiple symbols, including dialogue, images, editing effects, and music, that contribute to the meaning of the film. Theorists/critics of contemporary rhetoric may also see clothing, lifestyles, or architecture as rhetorical texts that can be read for their meaning(s).

Finally, we'll focus less on how rhetorical theory helps to create effective communication and more on the influence of rhetoric on the world in which we live. From our earlier discussion, it should be clear that many of the theorists we have discussed were interested in helping rhetors create effective presentations. Now, theorists and critics will be interested in how rhetoric shapes the cultures in which we live.

CULTURAL INFLUENCES

We are covering about 150 years in this chapter. The historical foundation of critical studies can be traced back to the work of Karl Marx, Frederick Engels, and Antonio Gramsci, all of whom wrote during the mid-1800s to early 1900s. We'll end the chapter by looking at one of the most popular rhetorical theories today, critical rhetoric. We'll find that the cultural influences on rhetorical theory are similar to those we discussed in Chapters 5 and 6. Here, though, we'll focus more on the political climate of the time, exploring how politics in the early 1900s influenced the development of critical rhetorical theories.

You'll recall that the Industrial Revolution that brought a great deal of wealth to individuals in industrialized nations by the early part of the twentieth century did not empower all members of society. Workers were being subject to machines and to powerful political forces that they did not or could not influence. In short, people were alienated by economic "progress" and the political systems that enabled these new economies. Consequently, they turned to new political ideas to find ways of liberating themselves of oppression. In Russia, the Bolshevik Party came to power in 1917 following a violent revolution against the monarchy. Led by V. I. Lenin, the Bolsheviks instituted a communist government that lasted until the 1980s.

Lenin had been influenced by the *Communist Manifesto,* a book written by Karl Marx and Friedrich Engels, who had explored the alienation of the working class and its need to revolt against the ruling class. Communism spread throughout the world. In China, Mao Tse-tung came to power. We'll discuss the impact of Chinese communism on rhetorical theory in Chapter 9. Communism, or a variant of communism, also spread to several European countries.

In Germany, Adolf Hilter led the revolt against the republican form of government instituted by the Treaty of Versailles. He claimed that communists and Jews were taking over the country, winning support from thousands of like-minded Germans. After gaining political office as a member of the Nazi party, Hitler led the nation in its attacks on other European nations. The annihilation of millions of Jews and other groups is widely documented; we'll discuss the influence of the Nazis on rhetorical theory when we study the work of Habermas.

The political turmoil of Europe following World War I and World War II led to intellectual activity in Europe, most notably in Germany and France, that questioned government policies. Drawing on the work of Marx, theorists such as Jurgen Habermas in Germany, Antonio Gramsci in Italy, and Louis Althusser in France, theorized about the relationship between rhetoric, protest, and government activity. Wander (1984) explained that these scholars believed that under certain conditions, people should "not only oppose the state, but also undermine the existing order" (p. 197). By grounding their protest in intellectual theory and practice, these theorists have provided a model of what is commonly called "critical practice" that guides rhetorical theorists and critics to this day.

To summarize, the early part of the twentieth century saw a variety of attempts to reshape national and international politics. Many of these attempts centered on the need to restore meaning to the lives of working people and empower them in a time when power was being stripped from them. This line of thought will pervade our discussion in this chapter as we examine how rhetorical theory has developed to investigate how power is managed in modern culture.

THE IDEOLOGICAL TURN

The ideological nature of rhetorical theory is addressed by a series of articles published in the *Central States Speech Journal* during 1983–1984. Sparked by Philip Wander's writings, scholars questioned to what degree rhetorical theorists and critics should concern themselves with questions of ideology. Previously much of the discipline did not seek to question the underlying motives or intentions of rhetors, in the belief that rhetorical critics should provide objective descriptions and evaluations of rhetorical practice using rhetorical theory as a guide and model. According to Cloud (1994), Wander and his supporters "argued that it would be productive for rhetoricians to view discourse as an agency of economic and political power, and to bring rhetoric's considerable repertoire of textual analysis skills to bear on understanding how political and economic power is mediated, reinforced, perpetuated, and challenged in the texts we study" (p. 143).

Wander developed the idea of the Third Persona to clarify the nature of ideological rhetorical criticism. The First Persona refers to the speaker and his or her intent , and the Second Persona concerns the audience. The **Third Persona,** explained Wander (1984), refers to what is negated in rhetorical practice. According to this view, in one sense, people are negated when rhetoric communicates what we are to "avoid becoming" (p. 210). Wander also means that rhetoric can create standards against which people are measured. Those who do not measure up to these standards are negated. Wander explained that when rhetoric negates the experiences of individuals, they are denied their full range of rights and they are denied the ability to use rhetoric to influence public affairs. Ideological rhetoric, according to Wander, should address how rhetoric negates the experiences of individuals in society.

As you consider the advertising contained in magazines, let's use a more spe-cific example to illustrate Wander's idea. The text of an advertisement for Seiko watches reads, "It's not your handbag. It's not your neighborhood. It's not your boyfriend. It's your watch that tells most about who you are." After considering this statement, think about who or what is negated. The advertisement implies that the watch a person wears is indicative of his or her intelligence, compassion, and personality. The essence of who we are, it says, is revealed on our wrists. Con-sider what else the advertisement is saying. Is the advertisement saying that those people who can't afford a stylish watch don't have as much to say about who they are? The ad also seems to imply that where you live, whom you date, and what you carry with you also say something about who you are. An ideological critic would explain how rhetoric sets standards—wearing a stylish watch is equated with a desirable personality—and how that standard influences how we think about people in our culture. The Third Persona, then, is a way of reading a rhetor-ical text with an eye to what is left out or excluded from the text and the impli-cations of that exclusion.

CRITICAL APPROACHES TO RHETORICAL THEORY

Wander identified what is now generally referred to, collectively, as the critical approach to rhetoric. Despite the fact the theorists in this chapter have different and even conflicting views of rhetoric, they all take critical approaches to rhetor-ical theory. Often, they are grouped under the classification of **critical studies.** Before we proceed, it is necessary to define what is meant by this term. Brummett (1994) defines critical studies as a group of theories that are critical in attitude, methodological, concerned with power, and interventionist. Let's briefly survey these characteristics, keeping in mind that these are generalizations that are not true of all critical theorists.

The Critical Character

First, critical approaches to rhetoric are interested in looking beneath the surface of a rhetoric text. Brummett (1994) explained that critical theories assume "that things are often other than (or more than) they seem" (p. 72). Critical theorists are not necessarily hostile, negative, or destructive toward rhetoric, they only "want to know what else is going on besides the obvious" (p. 72). You might think about this process as "making visible the invisible" (Wilson, 2003).

A critical approach to the movie *American Beauty,* for instance, might look at how the movie portrayed American culture and whether this portrayal was accu-rate. Kevin Spacey's character would be seen as representing Americans who seemingly have fulfilled the American dream but feel alienated by contemporary culture. A critical theorist might say that his rejection of American culture is heroic and that we shouldn't assume that prosperity leads to happiness.

Critical Methodology

To uncover these deeper meanings, critical approaches to rhetoric are methodological in nature. That is, critical theories are designed to investigate the meaning of a rhetorical text and the complex relationship it has to its context as well as make judgments about the meanings or influences of the text (Brummett, 1994). First, critical methodologies are designed to uncover the meaning(s) of a rhetorical text. In many cases, critics do not seek to uncover a single meaning for a text, but rather to show how that text might mean different things to different people.

Second, critical theories seek to explore the complex relationship a rhetorical text has to its context. The methodology of critical theories does not seek to establish a simple cause-effect relationship between rhetoric and its impact. Instead, critics try to uncover the multiple ways that meanings arise and how audience members are influenced by them. For example, critical theory methodology is not necessarily interested in whether television shows cause violence in society. Rather, they are concerned with how culture is influenced by the presence of violence on television and the meanings that exist in a culture about violence.

Third, critical theories seek to evaluate rhetoric. Critics judge whether rhetoric—its meanings and effects—are good or bad, positive or negative, or desirable or undesirable. Early critical approaches that we discussed were more concerned with the effectiveness of a rhetorical text. That is, critics employing an Aristotelian methodology might be interested in whether a speech, or some other rhetorical form, was effective in achieving its goal. Critics working from a critical studies perspective would be less likely to say that a magazine advertisement, for example, was effective. Critical theory methodology would instead be interested in how a rhetorical text creates expectations and norms in a society about what is desirable or undesirable.

Concern with Power

As we have noted, critical theories are concerned with power. Brummett (1994) explained, "Critical studies examines what power is or what it has been understood to be, and how power is created, maintained, shared, lost, and seized" (p. 76). Typically, we think of power that is exercised through political means or force. For instance, the president of the United States has a great deal of political power, able to enact laws and take actions that most Americans could not do. Critical studies, however, is also interested in the more subtle forms of power managed through rhetorical texts. Brummett explained, "power is seized and maintained in other, less obvious ways: in architecture, in classroom layouts in public schools, in social norms for proper behavior during movies and sporting events—in other words, in all the experiences of popular culture" (p. 76).

For critical theorists, power is most interesting when it concerns the empowering and disempowering of large groups of people, that is, when it is seen to relate to groups of people—referring to characteristics such as race, class, or gender—rather than to individual persons. A critical theorist might study a magazine advertisement, for instance, to understand how it privileges the experiences and meanings of a particular group of people. Our focus in this chapter will be on how rhetoric is used to manage power in society.

BOX 7.1   Critical Insights: A Critical Perspective on Disney's *Pocahontas*

Ono and Buescher's (2001) analysis of how Disney marketed the movie *Pocahontas* provides an example of the characteristics of critical studies we have just discussed. They argue that Disney used Pocahontas, a figure from Native American history, as an effective way to market the movie. We said that critics first explain the meaning of a rhetorical text. Ono and Buescher note that "when Disney imported the figure of Pocahontas into mainstream commodity culture and reshaped it, new meanings were ascribed to the figure of Pocahontas and most older meanings were lost" (p. 25). Specifically, Disney "transformed the story of a real person into a line of marketable objects" (p. 25).

Ono and Buescher (2001) do not settle for a simplistic analysis of Disney's strategies, instead they note the complex relationship that exists between the Pocahontas character and popular culture. The authors uncover a range of marketable objects featuring Pocahontas, discuss the meaning of these objects for popular culture, and describe the historical meaning of Pocahontas. Essentially, the authors uncovered a web of meanings related to the Disney character. Additionally, the authors evaluate Disney's strategies and their impact on power relationships in our culture. Disney, they argue, used utopic images of the struggle between Native Americans and whites, diverting attention from the true social problems that existed. At the same time, Disney created a sexualized and exotic image of Native American women. Ono and Buescher (2001) conclude, "Disney appropriates the experience of oppression as if to end it, while simultaneously creating and sustaining new ways to oppress" (p. 35). Finally, Ono and Buescher offer several intervention strategies that readers can use to better understand how power is managed through contemporary rhetoric.

Critical Intervention

Critical theorists do not restrict themselves to examining power relationships in society, but instead they try to play an active role in intervening where there is disparity in power. Brummett (1994) explained that critical theorists are interested in "getting involved in problems in order to change the world for the better" (p. 76). He explained that this perspective assumes people have choices about how to live their lives and that rhetoric is the means through which we learn about our choices. Critical theorists seek to explain the consequences of particular choices and in doing so, they influence how people make them. At a higher level, critical theorists are involved in politics and persuasive movements, and they communicate their ideas about power through the popular and news media.

Critical approaches to rhetorical theory are united by a concern for critical character, power, and intervention. For an example of an application of the critical approach in the light these issue, read Box 7.1, Critical Insights.

RHETORIC AND MARXISM

Critical approaches to rhetoric often use Marxism as a theoretical basis for making observations about ideology and power. Based on the work of Karl Marx and Frederich Engels, Marxism is a theoretical approach to society that can be used to explain a variety of disciplines, including economics, philosophy, politics, history, and rhetoric. Marxism is based on the perspective of materialism, which contends that real, physical objects or conditions give rise to culture and our experiences. Marx made this distinction by defining two key concepts: the base and the super-structure. The **base** refers to the actual practices and products of capitalism, including land, buildings, and money. These material objects lead to a **superstructure,** which includes the social, political, and religious institutions of a culture as well as the social consciousness of its people. Culture, in this view, is dependent on the material economic forces within the culture.

Marxism is also concerned with class struggle. For the early Marxists, the struggle was between the bourgeoisie, or capitalists, and the proletariat, or workers. Marx and Engels explained, "Owing to the extensive use of machinery and to division of labor, the work of the proletarians has lost all individual character, and, consequently, all charm for the workman. He becomes an appendage of the machine, and it is only the most simple, most monotonous, and most easily acquired knack, that is required of him" (1955, p. 16). They continued, "Not only are they slaves of the bourgeois class, and of the bourgeois state, they are daily and hourly enslaved by the machine, by the overlooker, and above all, by the individual bourgeois manufacturer himself" (p. 17).

Because they controlled the capital and the modes of production, the bourgeois controlled the superstructure of the society. Marx and Engels observed, "No sooner has the laborer received his wages in cash, for the moment escaping exploitation by the manufacturer, that he is set upon by the other portions of the bourgeoisie, the landlord, the shopkeeper, the pawnbroker, etc." (1955, p. 17).

Marx and Engels called on the proletarians to band together and take power from the bourgeois. In Marx's thinking, this revolution would replace the existing order with one that was more egalitarian and just. Versions of Marxism as a political practice lives on in some countries, most notably Cuba and China. Marxist thinking also influences a great deal of intellectual activity in the world today, including that of contemporary rhetorical theorists and critics.

Revising Marxist Theory

Adherents of Marxist ideology have broadened and significantly revised Marxist theory for their use. Cloud (1994) has identified three main strains of Marxist ideology that are present in rhetorical theory and criticism: materialist, idealist, and relativist (see Table 7.1). The *materialist* view of rhetoric focuses on how rhetoric conceals or reveals political or economic forces. This view, which never loses sight of what is tangible or material and seeks to reconcile rhetoric with the reality that people regularly witness and experience, is aligned most closely with traditional Marxism. Cloud examined rhetoric surrounding the Persian Gulf War in 1991 to illustrate different approaches to Marxist rhetoric. Using the materialist approach, she explored how phrases such as "collateral damage" justified the actual killing of Iraqi civilians.

A second Marxist approach is labeled *idealist* by Cloud (1994). In this view, rhetoric is viewed as a material force that determines the ideas that people have about their world and culture. Theorists adopting this perspective see rhetoric as existing in the clothing, advertising, television shows, and so forth, of a culture. These rhetorical texts create ways of thinking within the culture that lead to

Table 7.1 Marxist Approaches to Rhetoric

Approach	Nature of Reality	Function of Rhetoric
Materialist	Reality exists apart from rhetoric.	Real economic or political interests motivate rhetoric.
Idealist	Reality exists, but our perception of it is influenced by rhetorical texts.	Rhetoric determines material relations.
Relativist	Reality is determined through symbolic action and subject to interpretation.	Rhetoric creates reality.

material relations. Cloud identified McGee's work (1990) as indicative of and influential in the development of this school of thought. McGee wrote that people assemble fragments of rhetoric into texts that make sense to them. That is, people are exposed to numerous rhetorical texts. Using these texts, people create highly subjective views of the world. According to Cloud (1994), the idealist approach would have focused on the various texts of the war: yellow ribbons and euphemistic terminology (such as "collateral damage"), for instance, and how these people used these texts to justify their view of the war.

A third Marxist approach is what Cloud called the *relativist* approach. In this view, rhetoric creates reality. Cloud (1994) explained that from this approach, "The critic is not in a credible position to adjudicate the truth or falsity of discourse, or to speculate about whose interests are served by a particular set of texts" (p. 153). Cloud argued that by taking a view of reality that is based on rhetorical texts, theorists and critics cannot adopt a moral or political critique toward rhetorical practice. In fact, she noted, one critic whom she labeled a relativist argued the Persian Gulf War never happened, but was only manufactured by the media. Cloud argued that despite the mediated nature of the war and whatever effects that may have had on viewers' apprehension of its events, real people died in the war and it is important to remember that real fact. According to Cloud, the relativist approach is exemplified by Raymie McKerrow's concept of critical rhetoric, which we will explore later in the chapter.

IDEOLOGY, POWER, AND HEGEMONY

With this background in Marxism generally and Marxist rhetorical theory and criticism, specifically, we can turn to some of the key terms in Marxist though. We'll focus in this section on ideology, power, and hegemony.

Ideology

Ideology is a central concept in our discussion in this chapter. Brummett (1984) defined **ideology** as "an interrelated system of meanings that are generated by the system of artifacts that comprise a culture" (p. 25). This definition identifies several key aspects of ideology. First, an ideology is a *system of meanings*. Meaning, we have said, is based on perception. What something means to me may be different from what it means to you. An ideology, then, is a set of *related perceptions* that people have about their world. These perceptions, or meanings, are related to each other in that they are concerned with the same general ideas, or principles. A political ideology will have similar ways of giving meaning to political problems such as budgeting, crime and punishment, and defense. That is, Republicans, for example, will generally perceive such issues in similar ways, in distinct contrast to Democrats.

Second, an ideology is generated by a *system of artifacts.*, which refers to a set of symbols that have powerful meanings for a group of people. An American flag, the Statue of Liberty, and the Star Spangled Banner are part of a system of artifacts that refer to American culture. Your school mascot, school colors, and school song are part of the system of artifacts that comprise your school culture. Taken together, a system of artifacts suggests a way of thinking or believing. When you see the American flag and hear the Star Spangled Banner, you may think about the Revolutionary War that won freedom for the early American colonists. From an early age, we're taught the meaning of these symbols and what they represent. These meanings help us form beliefs about freedom that cause you to perceive events or ideas in a particular way. You might, for instance, believe that going to war with Iraq was justified because it would protect our freedom, which was in jeopardy.

Finally, ideology is related to *culture*. That is, an ideology is held by a group of people who are similar in some way. As we have previously discussed, cultures may be broad or narrow in scope. They may include national groups, racial groups, gender groups, or organizational groups. In each case, the group, or culture, of individuals will likely have similar ways of seeing themselves and others because of how they have learned to perceive the objects in their environment. You will probably share with the students at your school similar ways of viewing the students, programs, and alumni of your rival school. Republicans will share ways of seeing political events with each other, and they will differ from Democrats in how they see those same events. How we learn to perceive symbols is based on the meanings we have for the artifacts in our culture. To learn more about ideology, complete the Internet Activity, Investigating Ideology, in Box 7.2.

Power

With an understanding of ideology, we can look to how ideology is related to **power,** or the ability to control meanings within a culture, and to rhetoric. A culture will only rarely have a single set of beliefs about the meaning of artifacts that exist within that culture. Instead, there will exist a dominant way of generating meaning that is not shared by all within the culture. Consider the Confederate flag that is widely displayed in the South, including on some public buildings in some states. The dominant meaning for this artifact is that it is a reminder of the South's rise prior to the Civil War. The flag represents at once pride and heritage and a particular ideology. However, this is not the only meaning that exists for the flag. To some, the flag represents slavery and oppression during a time that is best forgotten. The extent to which either of these views is accepted by the members

---

BOX 7.2   Internet Activity: Investigating Ideology

You have just read that ideology is created through the meanings associated with a series of cultural artifacts. Log on to the website for your school and investigate its ideology by answering the following questions. What are some of the dominant symbols on the school's website? What are the meanings of these symbols? What ideology or ideologies are present in their meanings? How does this ideology create a culture for your school? Does the intended ideology that stems from the website square with your view of the school's culture? Why or why not?

---

of the culture is determined by the relative power of the proponents of each view. Members of a culture gain power in ways that we will discuss shortly.

Initially, though, let's briefly discuss the role of rhetoric in as it relates to ideology and power. Rhetoric enters the picture in several ways. First, the artifacts upon which ideology is based are largely rhetorical in nature. Flags, statues, advertisements, clothing, and so on, are all artifacts that give rise to ideology. Each of these artifacts can be viewed rhetorically. Second, rhetoric is used to manage the meaning of those artifacts; that is, rhetoric is used to gain, manage, and negotiate power.

Hegemony

Hegemony is a concept that appears in a great deal of critical theory, but is most often traced to the work of Antonio Gramsci, an Italian communist who wrote in the early 1990s. Hegemony is the subtle control exerted over a culture's ideology by the dominant class. The rule by hegemony is so subtle that those who are oppressed by others willingly allow themselves to be oppressed.

A current television commercial for a credit card illustrates the concept of hegemony. A man is shown enjoying consumerism: he has a new car, a golf club membership, a large house, and a riding lawn mower. However, the man admits that he is "in debt up to his eyeballs." Because he has bought into the idea that it is important to own consumer items, he has taken on a lot of debt and cannot fully enjoy economic prosperity. The commercial is for a credit card company that can consolidate his debt, resulting in lower monthly payments. The real point, however, is that the man and his family are victims of hegemony: they have freely and willingly allowed themselves to be controlled by the dominant class. Not only have they sacrificed their economic prosperity for these needless consumer goods, but they will also have to make high interest payments as a result.

Gramsci identifies different ways that control is exerted within a culture and gives examples of coercive control as it is exercised by means of legal institutions, laws, and even authorized physical force. One form of oppression is through rigid control over information. By limiting the kind of knowledge that exists in the culture, the ruling class can influence the beliefs and values of citizens. Another type of control, as we have just seen, is hegemony, or the subtle control over common sense. Gramsci points out that the dominant class uses rhetoric in such a way as to make certain beliefs and values appear to be common sense. In our society, it makes sense—to many people—to have a beautiful house and car, a well-manicured lawn, and fashionable clothing. These beliefs that we take for granted have some very real consequences, however: we pile up consumer debt, we pollute the environment, and we subject ourselves to the rules of others because we have to work to pay off our credit and bills. For Gramsci and other critical theorists, that ideological control is exercised in such a way within culture is very troubling. It is important to note that in fact hegemony is not necessarily a tool used by those holding political power. Gramsci points out that the oppressed classes can also use hegemony to influence the dominant classes in a culture. Rhetorical theorists attempt to explain how and why hegemony occurs.

IDEOGRAPHS

We said earlier that rhetorical artifacts (such as flags and statues) give rise to ideology but also that power is managed through rhetorical texts. Here we explore in greater detail some of the ways rhetorical theorists have discussed the relationship between rhetoric, power, and ideology.

McGee (1980) explained that myths, or ideologies, are present in the words we use to communicate. He defined an ideology as "a political language, preserved in rhetorical documents, with the capacity to dictate decision and control public belief and behavior" (p. 5). Short slogans, phrases, or what he calls ideographs, characterize political language, or ideology. **Ideographs** are words or phrases that are "pregnant" with ideological commitment—for example, "liberty," "rights of privacy," or "religion." Ideographs suggest to their audience a vast set of meanings about what is valuable or appropriate within a culture. These meanings control "power" and influence the shape and texture of each individual's reality. McGee explained that ideographs function as guides, warrants, reasons, or excuses for behavior. Because of their potent expression of cultural orientation, we do not question their fundamental logic.

Political candidates use ideographs to engage the beliefs, values, and behaviors of their audiences. Democratic presidential candidate Wesley Clark's speech of October 22, 2003 was punctuated by ideographs. Here are some excerpts (in which italics have been added to highlight ideographs):

> First, I believe in *economic opportunity* for all Americans.
>
> I believe there are few things more important to a person's *dignity*, to a family's *security,* and to our nation's *prosperity* than the chance to engage in honest labor and to earn a decent living doing it. That is why we need to do whatever is necessary to create jobs and restart America's economic engines.
>
> Second, I believe in *economic growth* that benefits all Americans.
>
> I believe we should pursue pro-growth policies that value what actually drives growth-not consumption by the wealthy, but meeting the needs of ordinary Americans driven by the *hard work,* energy, and *innovation* of highly

skilled Americans, in a climate that rewards investment and *entrepreneurship,* and promotes the R&D, the innovation and risk-taking, that is the engine of economic growth.

You'll note that some ideographs, such as "economic opportunity," "prosperity," "and innovation" may be seen as slightly more powerful than some of the others.

McGee's (1980) theory of the ideograph is a useful way to locate the ideological statements expressed in a rhetorical text. In the next section, we move our discussion away from ideology to focus on the process by which power is communicated.

THE PUBLIC SPHERE

The theorists we have discussed so far identify the primary ways that power and ideology are embedded in rhetoric. The theories we have yet to examine—those of the public sphere and critical rhetoric—explore how rhetoric can be used to question these power arrangements.

Lifeworld and System

To begin our discussion of how rhetoric can be used to ensure democracy, we'll briefly explore Jurgen Habermas's idea of the distinction between the "lifeworld" and the system. Habermas believes that there should exist two realms of human interaction. The first is the system, in which money and power dominate. The system includes businesses and commercial enterprises as well as the government, which codifies the interest of capitalists. Opposed to the system is the lifeworld, which is the realm of human social interaction. Our relations with our family and friends occurs within the lifeworld. Habermas believes that the system "colonizes" the lifeworld; that is, our social interactions are being influenced and framed by the interests of capitalism. For instance, people are forced to work long hours instead of spending time with their family and friends. More significantly, Habermas believes that our political discussions are influenced by the interests of business. In fact, capitalism controls the kinds of political and personal decisions people make. He sees this as being harmful to democracy and sought to develop ways of freeing our personal interests from that of business and the government. You can read more about Habermas in the Biography of a Theorist box for this chapter (see Box 7.3).

Defining the Public Sphere

To counter the colonization of the lifeworld, Habermas researched what has been called the **public sphere,** which Hauser (1998) defined as "a discursive space in which individuals and groups associate to discuss matters of mutual interest and, where possible, to reach a common judgment about them. It is the locus of emergence for rhetorically salient meanings" (p. 21). The public sphere, according to

---

BOX 7.3   Biography of a Theorist: Jurgen Habermas

Jürgen Habermas was born in Düsseldorf, Germany, on June 18, 1929. As a youth, he had served in the Hitler Youth and fought for the Nazis during the final months of World War II. Following the war, Habermas watched closely the Nuremburg Trials in which Nazi officials were tried for war crimes. Habermas realized, for the first time, the despotic nature of the Hitler regime, and he embraced the nature of critical theory throughout his education. He studied at universities in Göttingen, Zurich, and Bonn where he studied philosophy, history, and economics. Max Horkheimer and Theodor Adorno were influential professors. Habermas served as a research assistant to Adorno at the Institute for Social Research in Frankfurt, or the "Frankfurt School," as it was called. Habermas's teaching career took him to the University of

Heidelberg, Frankfurt am Main, the Max Planck Institute in Starnberg, The New School for Social Research in New York, Princeton University, and the University of California Santa Barbara. He has also held an appointment at the University of Frankfurt, from which he retired in 1994.

A proponent of the Frankfurt School, Habermas embraced critical theory that questioned the influence of science and technology on democratic governments. Habermas's key works include *Theory and Practice* (1971), *Communication and the Evolution of Society* (1976), *The Theory of Communication Action: Volume I* (1984), and *The Theory of Communication Action: Volume II*(1987). Habermas continues to write and respond to reviews of his work.

---

this view, involves the use of rhetoric between people who presumably have interest and knowledge in what is being discussed. Additionally, the individuals are able to reach some kind of consensus about the issues, and their decision is reflected by some kind of action. For most public sphere theorists, the judgments of the public sphere are carried out by government officials, who act in the best interests of the public.

Let's examine an example of a group who is working to fulfill the goals of the public sphere. Democracy for America (DFA) is a political action committee inspired by the 2004 candidacy of Democratic presidential Howard Dean. As stated on its website, the group is

> dedicated to supporting fiscally conservative, socially progressive candidates at all levels of government—from school board to the presidency. DFA fights against the influence of the far right-wing and their radical, divisive policies and the selfish special interests that for too long have dominated our politics.

The group makes extensive use of a blog, which allows group leaders to communicate with the group's members. At the same time, the blog allows group members to communicate with each other about issues that concern them. Using the company MeetUp.com as an organizing tool, Democracy for America sponsors monthly face-to-face meetings at more than five hundred locations across the United States. At these meetings, Democracy for America members discuss issues of local and national concern and organize events to communicate the DFA's message. Though not entirely deliberative in nature, Democracy for America is a group of individuals who have similar concerns and who meet to discuss and determine the best course of political action to implement their ideas about government. You can find out more about DFA by going to their website, http://www.democracyforamerica.com. Keep this example in mind as we pursue our discussion of the public sphere.

History of the Public Sphere

Hauser (1998) makes the distinction between civic virtue and civil society. By understanding this difference, we can better understand the role of the public sphere in contemporary society. In ancient Greece and Rome, Hauser explains, influential men gained political power by being skillful at public speaking. The only political rhetoric that mattered was that conducted in the legislative and legal assemblies by the men who were skillful rhetors. There was no recognition that private communication had any influence on the political decisions of the government. As a result, there was a strong connection between individuals fortunate enough to have powerful positions in government and the government itself. Keep in mind that slaves and women were excluded from participating in Greek and Roman public life and thus could not influence the decisions made by the government.

Following the fall of the Roman Empire, the church countered the government as strong institutional forces in the lives of European citizens. Additionally, locally powerful feudal lords exercised power that checked the power of the government. The result, explains Hauser was the development of civil society: "a network of associations independent of the state whose members, through social interactions that balance conflict and consensus, seek to regulate themselves in ways consistent with a valuation of difference" (1998, p. 26). Hauser notes that an important aspect of civil society is that it was necessary to manage the diverse numbers of opinions and perspectives that resulted from new national borders and trading practices. Politically, civil society members discussed important issues in spaces other than the legal and political assemblies. Hauser explains that politics was discussed in newspapers, personal conversations in coffeeshops, and political clubs: "These were sites for open dialogue in which reasons for and against an idea were elaborated, tested, refuted, extended, and, ideally, resolved" (p. 27). In essence, civil society led to the development of a public opinion that was formed in spaces other than the parliament or court (Hauser, 1998).

The practices of the European civil society in the seventeenth and eighteenth centuries served as the model for Jurgen Habermas's view of the public sphere. He envisions a bourgeois public sphere that would rationally discuss issues of importance to a society and advise the government on making decisions that were in the public's best interest. Asen and Brouwer (2001) explain Habermas' view: "As a historical concept, the bourgeois public sphere describes the emergence in civil society of a realm in which citizens came together as private citizens to form a public that, acting in an advisory capacity, debated the activities of the state" (p. 4). The public sphere acts as check on the autocratic activities of the government and ensures that the people's rights are protected.

It's important to note that Habermas believes that the public sphere will carry out its deliberations using open debate in which citizens have the ability to express themselves. But it's also important to note that Habermas's view of the public sphere is based on one that includes only a very limited number of public citizens, notably the bourgeoisie. These members of society are in the middle to upper classes and typically are capitalists. That is, they own businesses and are responsible for production in the society. The public sphere that serves as the basis for Habermas's theory, is exclusionary toward women and other members of society. His theory also seeks a clear distinction between the public affairs of the state and the private affairs of individuals. The public sphere, he believes, existed in the realm between the private and the public.

Redefining the Public Sphere

Contemporary public-sphere theorists are reconsidering the idea and its implication for contemporary democratic culture. Asen and Brouwer (2001) offer three ways of rethinking Habermas's original notion of the public sphere. Keep in mind that these ideas are thought to provide models through which public discussion can be encouraged in order to develop a democratic practice that is free of controlling interests, such as that of consumerism. In short, the public sphere is seen by rhetorical theorists as a way of preventing special interests and commercial interests from dominating public life and public discussion about important issues.

First, Asen and Brouwer envision a *multiplicity of publics,* rather than a single public, as Habermas has. The exact nature of how these multiple publics may be configured and how they may actually deliberate important issues is not clear. Some theorists see the public sphere as being composed of organizations like Democracy for America, which we discussed earlier. Through various organizations such as this, public debate takes place in multiple forums and for multiple purposes. But each group desires to influence the public good and public discussion.

Another way of thinking that has gained popularity is by viewing the public sphere as being composed of any number of counterpublics. Asen and Brouwer (2001) explained that **counterpublic** spheres attempt to "disrupt the homogenizing and universalizing processes of global mass-communication culture that promotes an uncritical consumerism" (p. 7). Also, counterpublics appeal to the needs and values of specific groups of people, such as sex, race, class, or sexuality.

The Queer Public Sphere Project is an example of a counterplublic. According the organization's website, the group is designed to provide access to resources for "lesbian, gay, bisexual, transgendered, two-spirit, queer and other sexually dissenting constituencies" and critique heteronormative culture. Through discussion and dissemination of ideas concerning this group's interests, The Queer Public Sphere Project hopes to influence public debate and discussion of important issues.

Second, Asen and Brouwer (2001) see permeable boundaries between the public and the private. Previously, public sphere theorists were concerned with public discussion of the public good. The public sphere was not thought to concern the private matters of citizens. Now, though, public sphere theorists see that important public decisions often result from private matters. Discussion about sexuality, for instance, has both public and private dimensions. Additionally, the end result of the public sphere discussions is not necessarily seen today as resulting in consensus. Asen and Brouwer (2001) note that "expressing identity, raising awareness, celebrating difference, and enabling play" may all be goals of the public sphere.

Finally, Asen and Brouwer (2001) examine the link between the public sphere and the government. In Habermas's original view, the public sphere is thought to exist between the private lives of citizens and the government. The public sphere serves to advise the government on important issues. Critics of this view contend that the public sphere is thus weak, with a great deal of deliberative ability but little authority to influence the actions of the government. A number of ways that the public can more directly influence the government have been offered. Ackerman (1993), for instance, has explained that voters could be given vouchers by the government to spend on political candidates during a campaign. Some theorists contend that the Internet presents a valuable opportunity for various publics to become more actively involved in government decisions.

Universal Pragmatics

In addition to Habermas's view of the public sphere, which, as we have said, is the subject of much controversy and revision, his theory of universal pragmatics describes how individuals can reflect on their language use and use rational argument to protect the lifeworld from the encroachment of money and power. According to Habermas, "The task of universal pragmatics is to identify and reconstruct universal conditions of possible understanding" (1979, p. 1).

At the core of universal pragmatics are speech acts and how those speech acts can be challenged to come to rational understanding. A speech act is a statement that accomplishes something or does something. A threat is an example of a speech act. When you make a threat, you enter into an implicit contract by which you pledge to take some action if someone else doesn't take one. Habermas (1979) outlined three types of speech acts: *constatives, regulatives,* and *avowals.* Constatives are used to assert the truth or falsity of something. When you say that it is cold outside, you are using a constative. Regulatives are used to influence someone else. You use regulatives when you make a promise or issue a command. Avowals are used to express the speaker's feelings or emotions, such as saying "I am sad."

Constatives, regulatives, and avowals are measured against certain standards. Constatives must be *truthful.* Habermas (1979) wrote that the intention of the speaker does not matter. What matters is the "truth of the proposition" (p. 58). Regulatives must be *appropriate* given the interpersonal relationship between the speaker and listener. A student, for example, cannot demand that an instructor give a certain grade for an assignment. Such command is not appropriate for the relationship. Avowals must be *sincere* expressions of a speaker's feelings. If I say that I am sad, that statement must be a genuine reflection of my mood.

Habermas fears a society in which audience members take a rhetor's words for granted. He argues that audience members should question what a rhetor says and does. When we question the statements of a source, we engage in discourse.

There are different types of discourse, depending on which type of statement—constative, regulative, or avowal—is questioned.

Constatives, or truth claims, are resolved through theoretic discourse, which uses evidence to support arguments. *Theoretic discourse* is the search for evidence to support a statement concerning truth; it is a "claim of validity" (Habermas, 1973, p. 18). Democratic presidential candidate Howard Dean used theoretic discourse in this statement from a September 25, 2003 debate: "We cannot afford all of the tax cuts, the health insurance, special ed and balancing the budget, and we have to do those things. The fact of the matter is that 60 percent of Americans at the bottom got $325." Since he used specific facts to support his position, he used theoretic discourse. Dean's statement would have been stronger had he cited a source for his statistics, but the fact that he cited evidence qualifies the statement as discourse.

Practical discourse is used when appropriateness is questioned. Habermas wrote that practical discourse offers justifications for the use of regulatives, statements that are used to influence others. We'll use another example from the 2004 presidential campaign to illustrate this point. When Dean made a statement saying the Democratic party should try to seek the votes of those in the South who fly the Confederate flag on their pickup trucks, he was asked to apologize by several of his Democratic rivals. In other words, Dean's opponents used a regulative in asking him to say he was sorry for making what appeared to be insensitive comments. One Democratic candidate, Al Sharpton, also used practical discourse in a November 5, 2003 debate in Boston. He said:

> And you can't misquote Martin Luther King like that. I come out of the King movement, I didn't just read him. He talked about us leaving racism there. And I think that Maynard Jackson said that the Confederate flag is America's swastika. If a Southern person running, if John Edwards, a Bob Graham had said that, they'd have been run out this race.
>
> I don't think you're a bigot, but I think that is insensitive, and I think you ought to apologize to people for that.
>
> When Bill Clinton was found to be a member of a white-only country club, he apologized. You are not a bigot, but you appear to be too arrogant to say "I'm wrong" and go on."

Thus, Sharpton offered a rationale for his use of a regulative.

Sincerity is not usually resolved through discourse, but rather through continued communicative action. When we doubt the sincerity of a speaker, for instance, we examine their nonverbals or we ask questions that probe their sincerity.

As arguers attempt to resolve their differences over truth claims, they may not agree on standards for their discussion. Thus, they turn to *metatheoretical discourse* to argue about what constitutes good evidence or reasonable standards. Since there is often confusion about the reliability of economic statistics, presidential candidates might agree to accept statistics from one source, for example. Finally, speakers may resort to *metaethical discourse* to argue about the nature of knowledge itself. Metaethical discourse is a philosophical argument about how knowledge is generated. Thomas A. McCarthy (1978) explained, "For here we must consider the question, what should count as knowledge?" (p. 305). Traditionally, knowledge is produced by scientific inquiry. We might assume that evidence from scientific study is the most reliable, but Habermas would caution us to also consider other ways that knowledge is created.

CRITICAL RHETORIC

Habermas grounds his theory in the idea that a reasoned, rational approach to language use can lead to liberation. Another approach to liberation that has been offered is that of **critical rhetoric**. According to Raymie McKerrow (1989), "As theory, a critical rhetoric examines the dimensions of domination and freedom as these are exercised in a relativized world" (p. 91). He sees in rhetoric the possibility to interrogate the ways that power is embedded in culture and to continually reflect on the kinds of power relationships that rhetoric creates. He explains, "In practice, a critical rhetoric seeks to unmask or demystify the discourse of power. The aim is to understand the integration of power/knowledge in society—what possibilities for change the integration invites or inhibits and what intervention strategies might be considered appropriate to effect social change" (McKerrow, 1989, p. 91). Whereas Habermas's theory is grounded in the stability of rationality and reason, critical rhetoric rests on the assumption that power relations are always changing and must be constantly evaluated. To learn more about critical rhetoric and its practice, visit Michael Calvin McGee's website, Fragments, at http://www. mcgees.net/fragments/.

Defining Critical Rhetoric

McKerrow (1989) has identified four features of critical rhetoric. First, it has "critical spirit;" that is, critical rhetoric, like the theories of Gramsci, McGee, Foucault, and Habermas, is concerned with power, ideology, and rhetoric. Second, critical rhetoric attempts to demystify sources of power in society by revealing ways that rhetoric conceals its relationship to knowledge and power. Third, a critical rhetoric critique "is not detached and impersonal" but it serves to provide an argument against something (p. 92). Finally, critical rhetoric must have consequences. The critic using this perspective must suggest ways to redistribute power more equitably or suggest possibilities for future actions available to those involved in the rhetoric. To clarify our terminology in this section, we will use the term *critical practice* to denote rhetorical criticism that uses the perspective of critical rhetoric.

To give a brief example, critical rhetoric might be used to critique advertising featuring women in popular magazines. The critic may observe that women featured in advertisements are thin, positioned in subordinate postures, and seen as sexual objects. The critic might argue that the ideology of consumption that is supported by these advertisements disempowers women by transforming them into objects that can be consumed. The critic would clearly take a position that this is harmful for women and may suggest ways that women can personally resist the images of advertising or ways that the industry can be changed. We'll discuss a more complete example of critical rhetoric toward the end of the chapter. Now let's explore the theory in more detail.

Theoretical Aspects of Critical Rhetoric

The task of critical rhetoric is to "constantly challenge the status quo to be other than it is" (McKerrow, 1991, p. 75.) To see how it achieves this purpose, we'll briefly survey the theoretical basis for critical rhetoric and then turn to more practical considerations. There are two processes inherent in critical rhetoric: a critique of domination and a critique of freedom. The critique of domination seeks to demystify the conditions of domination that are present in discourse. The critique of freedom refers to a never-ending skepticism on the part of the critic to examine and re-examine conditions of power and domination. McKerrow (1991) notes that in any critique, one or both of these process may be present.

The first process—the critique of domination—focuses on the rhetorical practices that control the dominated. McKerrow (1989) has explained that "The critique is directed to an analysis of discourse as it contributes to the interests of the ruling class, and as it empowers the ruled to present their interests in a force-ful and compelling manner" (p. 93). We have discussed ideology and hegemony previously; critical rhetoric seeks to find ways to liberate those who are oppressed by the dominant culture. In particular, critical rhetoric seeks to give voice to those members of society who are not privileged to speak out in other ways. McKerrow also points out that power relationships should not be seen in simple, oppositional ways. That is, there is no simple way of viewing the powerful and powerless. People shift their positions relative to ideology; a critique of domina-tion must be mindful of this idea and not take anything for granted. McKerrow even observes that there are "multiple classes, groups, or even individuals with varying degrees of power over others" (p. 96).

The second process inherent in critical rhetoric is the critique of freedom, which McKerrow (1991) explained as being "the freedom to pursue other power relations" (p. 75). This process makes clear that the critique of power is ongoing: "Results are never satisfying as new social relations which emerge from a reaction to a critique are themselves simply new forms of power and hence subject to renewed skepticism" (McKerrow, 1989, p. 96). McKerrow (1991) offers an example:

> Having instantiated a new set of power relations (e.g., The Republic) Plato would then be content in having finished his task. A critical rhetor would experience no such contentment. There is an ever-present tension between one's life at a moment in time, with a set of power relations relatively intact, and the possibility of constant challenge that would revise that set. One takes a stand from where one is in the present, looking forward to a future yet unrealized. (p. 76)

Critical rhetoric is concerned with creating a new way of looking at the world—of creating a new social truth. Although truth is a problematic term—we have discussed it throughout this book—McKerrow is most interested in using critical rhetoric to challenge the rhetorical structures in society that contribute to unequal power relations. By challenging these structures, a new "truth" is created until it is again critiqued by critical rhetoric.

Critical Rhetoric in Practice

Critical rhetoric offers us a new way of thinking about the role of the rhetorical critic. The critic, from this perspective, is seen as the inventor of the rhetorical text. A text is not viewed as being complete but is instead thought to be comprised of a collection of fragments from culture. The critic interprets for the reader the meaning of these fragments and identifies how they have been arranged in a meaningful way. For instance, a critic may study an advertisement that contains a variety of slogans and symbols. Since the meaning of these slogans and symbols exists outside the advertisement, the critic would identify their meaning and show the relationship of the advertisement to culture. Texts are viewed as never being complete; there is always more to a rhetorical text than is present in the words and images of the text. Compare this view with that of a more traditional approach to rhetorical criticism, in which the critic may examine a speech. By and large, the speech is seen as a complete document and the critic analyzes what is there. More often than not, critical rhetoric is interested in what is not present as well as what is present in a text.

Additionally, critics who use critical theory are not necessarily academics. Rhetorical criticism, or critical rhetoric, becomes a practice that is carried out by a number of individuals through a number of communication media. A rhetorical criticism published in an academic journal may be an example of critical rhetoric, but so too may be a newspaper editorial by a local resident or a commentary in *Time* magazine by a regular columnist.

Let's turn now to eight principles of critical rhetoric to see how this theory is used (McKerrow, 1989, pp. 101–9). First, critical rhetoric is not a method, but a perspective, that a critic takes toward a rhetorical text. Some methods of rhetorical criticism lay out a step-by-step procedure for doing a criticism. There is no such procedure for critical rhetoric. The critic uses an inventive approach in uncovering how power is embedded in a rhetorical text. In the Ono and Beuscher study discussed previously (Box 7.1), the authors invent their own way of looking at Pocahontas; they do not follow a rigid step-by-step procedure.

Second, critical practice views the discourse of power as material. That is, power manifests itself in tangible rhetorical texts such as television shows, films, magazine advertisements, speeches, or other similar texts. Because it is easily accessed by the popular culture, these material texts have a profound effect on ideology and power.

Third, "rhetoric constitutes doxastic rather than epistemic knowledge" (McKerrow, 1989, p. 103). Throughout this book, we have explored the relationship between rhetoric and knowledge. You'll recall that Plato, for instance, saw rhetoric as obscuring what was true, whereas Scott argued that rhetoric helped determine what was true in a culture. Critical rhetoric takes a slightly different approach to this topic. McKerrow has explained that critical rhetoric views rhetoric as doxastic: "Rather than focusing on questions of 'truth' or 'falsity,' a view of rhetoric as doxastic allows the focus to shift to how the symbols come to possess power—what they 'do' in society as contrasted to what they 'are'" (McKerrow, 1989, p. 104). The focus, then, of critical rhetoric is to explain how symbols come to have a meaning that is more or less widely shared within a culture. Refer back to the Pocahontas example. It provides a clear example of how the Pocahontas figure from history was given new meaning by Disney.

Fourth, critical practice sees the process of naming as a central symbolic act. The labels we create for objects should not be seen as fixed or permanent or natural. Instead, these labels constantly change in their meaning and their relationship to other objects; their meanings are contingent on context. In addition, there is great power in naming objects with symbols. The names we use for objects influence how we view those objects and respond to them. The Ono and Beuscher (2001) study, again, illustrates how Disney was able to name Pocahontas and give her meanings consonant with contemporary culture and the marketing objectives of the Disney company.

Fifth, the critical rhetoric perspective does not assume that influence is the same as causality— that, as McKerrow (1989) has explained, a symbol "impacts" upon other symbols. An important aspect of this idea is the *potential* for influence that exists through symbol use. McKerrow uses this example: "The potential for images of crime to influence the social reality of the elderly is present through the depiction of such symbolic acts on nightly crime drama" (1989, p. 106). Returning to our previous example, we might say that Disney's portrayal of Pocahontas has the potential to influence how audience members view Native American women—as sexualized objects. We wouldn't make the claim that it *causes* viewers to make those associations.

Sixth, absence is as important as presence in understanding and evaluating symbolic action from a critical rhetoric perspective. A critic employing a classical theory—Aristotle's or Cicero's, for instance—would be interested in what a rhetor communicated. A critical rhetor, though, would also examine what was not communicated. The idea here is that what's not communicated often makes what is communicated more powerful or meaningful. An advertisement of a mother playing with her children might imply several ideas, from a critical perspective. The lack of an observable job for the mother and the absence of the father, might be said to imply that women are responsible for child rearing and that their careers are not important.

A seventh principle of critical rhetoric is that meanings are multiple, or polysemic, rather than singular, or monosemic. This means that a rhetorical text may mean different things to different people. Particularly, critical rhetoric seeks to find the meaning that exists in a text that subverts or rejects the prevailing ideology of a culture. Although there may exist in the text a more obvious view that supports the prevailing power structure, critical rhetoric is more interested in the identifying the subversive meanings. Ono and Buescher (2001) exemplify this idea by claiming that the Pocahontas movie and its promotion offers ways to question the dominance of the Disney marketing machine and its reshaping of historical figures.

Finally, critical rhetoric sees criticism is a performance. McKerrow (1989) explains that "the critic as inventor becomes arguer or advocate for an intepretation of the collected fragments" (p. 108). The point is that rhetoric criticism should not be seen as something that is written, published, and filed away for future readers. Instead, critical practice—a form of rhetorical criticism—should be presented to the public to prompt action.

Critical Rhetoric: An Example

The Ono and Buescher example from Box 7.1 is an example of critical rhetoric. The authors identified how Disney created meaning for Pocahontas in a way that managed power relations. They argued that Disney appropriated the historical character and manipulated her in ways that promoted their movie— and at the expense of certain groups in society, such as women and Native Americans. Lucaites (2001) provides another example when he analyzes the rhetoric of affirmative action. Lucaites examines how we talk about affirmative action in our culture. Although a complete summary of Lucaites' arguments is beyond the scope of our discussion here, he concludes that what is most important from an analysis of affirmative action rhetoric is how we talk about racism and affirmative action. He explains, "To that extent, whether our concern is with the old racism or the new racism, it is *how* the *topos* of "race" adorns our public talk that must concern us, for it is precisely at that site of engagement that the successful existence of our collective life as "one people" resides, whatever other differences might separate us." For additional examples of critical rhetoric, visit Michael Calvin McGee's website at http://www.mcgees.net/fragments/essays/guests/index.html.

SUMMARIZING APPROACHES TO POWER AND IDEOLOGY

The theorists we have discussed in this chapter have all been concerned with the ways that rhetoric is used to manage, reinforce, or change ideology and power relationships in society. Let's summarize what we've discussed about some key issues.

Defining Rhetoric

None of the theorists we have discussed offered a formal definition of rhetoric. Rather, they have focused on the implications of rhetoric and not necessarily on the construction of rhetorical texts. Critical rhetoric comes closest to discussing rhetoric in the ways that early theorists did. However, the critical rhetoric approach blends rhetorical practice and rhetorical criticism. Performing rhetoric, in the traditional sense, should also be the performance of a rhetorical critique of power, according to McKerrow.

Rhetoric and Knowledge

The relationship of epistemology to rhetoric and ideology has been the central concern of this chapter. Habermas is concerned that the knowledge produced in Western cultures reflects the desires of capitalism. He seeks to find ways that the public could better discuss what should constitute knowledge and how they could carefully deliberate what is true in the culture. McKerrow identifies rhetoric as doxastic, meaning his concern is with how symbols come to have meaning in a culture. He's not as interested in what is true or false, but rather how a belief becomes true or false in a culture.

Rhetoric and Identity

As we have seen, ontology is a focus of concern for the theorists we have been studying. According to Habermas, people's identities are too closely tied to their work. He wishes to free individuals from the constraints imposed on their identities by work. To the other theorists, such as Gramsci, McGee, and McKerrow, ontology is directly related to how we see ourselves within the power structure of society. Our status influences our conception of our identity; for these theorists, our status is inextricably linked to power, ideology, and hegemony.

Rhetoric and Judgment

Each of the theorists we have discussed at length here—Gramsci, McGee, Habermas, and McKerrow—treat the ethical use of rhetoric. Their concern is to liberate those who are oppressed so all may enjoy freedom. Each has developed theoretical frameworks that allow them to talk about how ethical decisions may be made in a free society.

DISCUSSION QUESTIONS

1. Locate your school's mission statement. You may find it in a course catalog or on the school's Web site. What is the ideology in the mission statement? How is that ideology apparent in your school's culture? What are some ideographs in the mission statement?

2. Recall an episode of a popular television show. How was the show hegemonic? What are some examples of "common sense" beliefs that may disempower some groups in society? How might the hegemonic message of the show be opposed?

3. Consider again the issue you discussed in the previous question. Does public discussion about this issue meet the requirements of the ideal speech situation? Why or why not?

4. Find a magazine advertisement. Conduct a critical rhetoric analysis of the ad. What power relationships are hidden in the ad? What signs are apparent in the ad? How do those signs come to have meaning? What might be some of the influences of this ad?

GLOSSARY TERMS

text   A set of symbols that can be seen to produce meaning.

Third Persona   Perspective toward rhetoric that considers what is negated.

critical studies   The body of rhetorical theory that is critical in character, concerned with power and interventionist.

base   The real objects of our culture, such as money, land, tools, and machines.

superstructure   The institutions and ideas that result from material practices in a culture.

ideology   An interrelated set of meanings that are generated by the system of artifacts that comprise a culture.

hegemony   Subtle control exerted over a culture's ideology by the dominant class.

power   The ability to control meanings in a culture.

ideographs   Words or phrases that suggest ideology.

public sphere   The process by which free people may deliberate public issues without undue influences.

counterpublic sphere   A view of society that runs contrary to the prevailing beliefs; based on the needs of specific cultural groups.

ideal speech situation   A theoretical construct that ensures that the public sphere adequately discusses an issue.

critical rhetoric   A perspective that requires constant reflection on the power structures created by rhetoric.

8

Gendered Rhetorical Theories

Learning Objectives

After reading this chapter, you should be able to:

1. Define sex, gender, and feminism.
2. Describe efforts to include the public and private rhetoric of women in academic study.
3. Identify some of the distinctive styles of gendered rhetoric.
4. Explain the gender diversity approach to rhetoric.
5. Discuss some of the ways that rhetoric oppresses women and how it can liberate them.

Senator and former first lady Hillary Clinton often tops the list of "most popular female politician" in the United States. As a senator from New York and as the wife of former president Bill Clinton, Hillary has been able to use rhetoric to influence policy and shape American attitudes. Many political pundits think that she will one day run for U.S. president. However, Senator Clinton is not viewed favorably by all Americans. In fact, her popularity provides us a way to think about the public's attitudes toward women politicians. Her popularity raises questions that we will address in this chapter: How should we judge female rhetors? Do females use different rhetorical techniques than men? What is the role that women should play in the public sphere? As we discuss gendered rhetorical theories, we'll focus on these questions, and more, in our analysis.

Our previous discussion of rhetorical theory and practice has centered, in large part, on the experiences of men. Initially, we focused on rhetorical practice in ancient Greek and Roman civilizations, where only male landowners were recognized as using rhetoric. Our focus then shifted to European rhetoric, which, again, examined how men used rhetoric to preach, teach, and make known scientific findings. Our discussion of meaning in Chapters 5 and 6 introduced the possibility that multiple meanings may exist for words and that not everyone shares in the same social reality. Most recently, in Chapter 7, we looked at how power is managed through rhetoric. In this chapter, we take our conversation one step further by beginning to explore the rhetorical theories of different cultures. Here, we focus on women and the ways that gender influences rhetoric and rhetorical theory. In the next chapter, we'll look at African, Chinese, and Native American approaches to rhetoric.

We'll begin this chapter by defining some key terms—sex, gender, and feminism—and then survey a brief history of women's movements. Then we'll look at efforts to include the rhetoric of women in the academic study of rhetoric. Following that, we'll describe some of the distinctive styles of gendered rhetoric. Finally, we'll look at one theorist who describes ways that rhetoric is used to oppress women, but also how rhetoric can be used to liberate.

DEFINING GENDER AND FEMINISM

Since the meanings of the terms *sex, gender,* and *feminism,* which are basic to our further discussion, are not immediately clear, we'll begin by defining them.

Sex and Gender

Sex and *gender* are terms that are often confused in our culture. Sex is biological. Men and women have distinctive characteristics because of sex. Women have the capability of giving birth, men cannot. Women have certain hormones in their body, men have others. Additionally, social structures and laws often treat men and women differently. Usually we think of two sexes—male and female. However, Condit (1997) explains that certain genetic combinations make possible a greater number of sexes than just two.

Gender, on the other hand, is socially constructed and not given at birth. We usually think of gender as a continuum, with masculine on one end and feminine on the other. A person may be more or less masculine than another; a person may be more or less feminine than another. A woman can be more masculine than a man. Our gender identity is determined by a number of factors, including how we've been socialized to think about our gender roles. In this chapter, we'll pay particular attention to how rhetoric creates expectations about gender.

Foss, Foss, and Griffin (1997) have explained the influence of gender, rather than sex, on rhetoric:

> We believe that some biological differences between women and men (such as menstruation, which most women experience) affect individuals' life

experiences. But we see the differences between women's and men's communication as attributable primarily to socialization practices—which construct men and women differently—and to the different power positions that sexes are accorded in society. (p. 120)

The term "gendered" in the title of this chapter indicates the focus of our discussion.

Feminism

In previous chapters, we discussed the ambiguity in rhetoric and how words can have multiple, contested, and even contradictory meanings. The term **feminism** is a striking example of this point. Throughout history, it has been assigned a variety of meanings. The ability to control the meaning of this term, in fact, has played a significant role in how people respond to feminist theory and feminists. We'll use a fairly broad definition in this chapter, adopting that provided by Campbell (1989): "My use of 'feminism' here is inclusive and catholic, referring to all those who worked for the legal, economic, and political advancement of women, beginning in the 1830s" (p. 3).

The chapter title uses the words "rhetorical theories" to indicate that there is not agreement about the nature of feminist rhetorical theory or practice. In fact, there are several interpretations of how rhetoric is practiced by women and many ideas about what should be included in a theory of feminist rhetoric. We'll see some diverse approaches in this chapter, but there are two threads that unite them. First, the theorists discussed in this chapter are concerned with how women have been included or excluded in the study and practice of rhetoric. Second, they are interested in minimizing the power differences between men and women that result from rhetorical practice, theory, and criticism.

A SHORT HISTORY
OF WOMEN'S MOVEMENTS

There have been at least three significant waves of women's rights movements. The first wave, which took place in the late 1800s and early 1900s, resulted in women gaining the right to vote. The second-wave, which took place in the sixties and seventies, sought equal rights for women in a variety of areas. The third-wave is thought to have started in the mid-1980s and is ongoing. We'll briefly survey the three waves of the women's rights movement here so you have some idea of the culture in which the theories we are going to explore in this chapter emerged.

First Wave Feminism

We will examine the first wave of the women's rights movement in more depth in the next section of this chapter, so we'll only briefly highlight some of its features here. The first wave is thought to have originated with the Women's Rights Convention in Seneca Falls, New York, in 1848. The movement faded from the public's view following passage of the Nineteenth Amendment in 1920 that gave women the right to vote.

A primary goal of the first wave was to win the right to vote for women, but there were many other goals of the women's movement of this time. For instance, the feminists of the first wave also sought to gain freedom for blacks from slavery. The abolitionist movement, as it was called, included many women who also spoke out for the rights of women. Ironically, one of the first women orators, Sarah Grimké, faced opposition from male abolitionists. In addition to lobbying against slavery and for the right to vote, women also rejected pressure on them to fulfill certain stereotypical roles. Laws at that time also treated women as the property of their husbands. Additionally, women worked long hours in such places as textiles factories.

In 1848, a group of women met at Seneca Falls, New York. Participants signed the "Declaration of Sentiments and Resolutions," which spelled out some of the issues and causes of the movement. The Civil War disrupted the women's movement, but eventually led to the abolition of slavery. Elizabeth Cady Stanton and Susan B. Anthony formed the American Equal Rights Association in 1866. Its goal was to bring about the goal of suffrage for all. Two years later, the Fourteenth Amendment to the Constitution was passed, which gave black men equal rights with white men, but denied equal protection to women, black or white. In fact, the law clearly specified that it was referring to men.

The women's movement split into two divisions in 1869. Elizabeth Cady Stanton and Susan B. Anthony formed the National Woman Suffrage Association (NWSA). Lucy Stone, Henry Blackwell, and Julia Ward Howe formed a more conservative organization, the American Woman Suffrage Association (AWSA). Also in 1869, Wyoming was organized as a territory. Its organization included the right to vote for women. The Fifth Amendment was passed in 1870, which formally gave the right to vote to black men. The amendment further divided the suffrage movement.

In the years following, women attempted to use the legal system to gain the right to vote. In fact, Anthony was arrested in Rochester, New York, for voting. Her fine was never enforced, as you'll read about later. In 1890, the NWSA and the AWSA merged to form the National American Woman Suffrage Association. Wyoming was also admitted to the union, with a law granting women the right to vote. Other states would adopt the same law. In addition, more organizations were formed nationwide to urge the federal law be changed. Under the leadership of Carrie Chapman Catt, the NAWSA finally was able to unite the nation's suffragists, and the Nineteenth Amendment was adopted in 1920. Three years later, the Equal Rights Amendment for women was proposed. Despite efforts of second- and third-wave feminists to pursue its passage, the amendment has never been adopted.

Throughout this period, there was a great deal of rhetoric practiced by women. Retors such as Anthony gave speeches, engaged in protest, and lobbied government officials. However, little rhetorical theory and criticism from a feminist or woman's perspective was developed until the 1970s and 1980s. In fact, the speeches of the early feminists are difficult to locate today, and many were not recorded.

We'll survey theoretical and critical approaches to the rhetoric of first-wave feminism in a few pages. Let's now glance at what many have called the second-wave of the women's rights movement.

Second-wave Feminism

Betty Friedan presented a view of the culture of the 1960s in her 1963 book, *The Feminine Mystique,* which many have said started the modern feminist movement, or second-wave feminism. Friedan's book discussed the "problem that had no name." She argued that working at home exclusively did not fulfill some women. As her ideas spread through society, more clearly developed theories, or ideologies, about feminism were developed, although no single ideology prevailed. Radical feminists were interested in the ideas of androgyny and feminism. The socialist ideology sought to educate women to be agents of change in society. The liberal ideology attempted to eliminate barriers to equality by focusing on changing the laws and policies of societal institutions, including government, business, and education. There were many women as well, who did not support the ideas of the movement and, in fact, started movements countering those of the second-wave feminists.

Consequently, the issues of the second-wave feminist movement were varied, as the activists sought to influence the public on a variety of topics. Feminists wished to eliminate pornography, which they said encouraged violence against women. Many feminists sought to expand reproductive rights, demanding access to safe and legal abortions. The feminist movement also addressed workplace issues, such as equal pay for equal work and sexual harassment. The feminist movement sought to reduce violence against women in all forms. In short, the feminist movement of the 1960s and 1970s was not a unified movement aimed at achieving a particular goal. The movement consisted of multiple rhetors using a variety of persuasive strategies to reach audiences. Likewise, opponents of the movement used rhetoric to convince audience members to oppose the efforts of the feminists.

The feminist movement employed rhetorical strategies and a decision-making style that were unique to the movement. The movement did not want to simply replace one hierarchical system for another, equally oppressive one. The women, and men, of the movement sought to reduce hierarchies in society, promoting freedom of opportunity for all. The National Organization for Women, NOW, was started in 1966. The group remains to this day a powerful voice for women. Another influential group was the National Women's Political Caucus, under the leadership of Gloria Steinem. NOW adopted an organizational style that gave great autonomy to its local chapters (Davis, 1991).

A widespread rhetorical strategy was consciousness raising. Consciousness-raising groups were formed on the local level, encouraging personal redemption (Linden-Ward & Green, 1993). Through rallies, discussion forums, and meetings, feminists sought to raise society's knowledge of inequality and promote solutions. Women developed counter-institutions, such as women's clinics that served female audiences. The feminist movement also supported legislation, such as the

Equal Rights Amendment (ERA), which would ensure equality through the law. The feminist movement used a variety of strategies to persuade society to change its attitudes and laws concerning women. In addition, according to Davis (1991), the media "brought about" widespread transformation in how Americans thought about women. She argued that books, articles, films, and television shows helped to spread feminist ideas.

The feminist movement achieved success on some issues, but not on others. Politically, the ERA must be ratified in three more states before it becomes part of the constitution. Yet many laws concerning affirmative action and sexual harassment were passed as a result of the movement. Davis (1991) notes that, "Between 1960 and 1990, feminists achieved half a revolution. Laws were passed, court decisions were handed down, and sex discrimination was officially prohibited" (p. 16). Davis noted that the single greatest achievement of the movement was that it "transformed most people's assumptions about what women were capable of and had a right to expect from life" (p. 16).

Third-Wave Feminism

Today, however, feminists are still concerned about a variety of issues, including salary equity, childcare, and domestic abuse. Third-wave feminism, as it is often called, is more complex than the previous two waves. In fact, third-wave feminism is often identified for its contradictory messages and its seeming rejection of first- and second-wave feminist principles. Baumgardner and Richards (2003) explained Third-wave Feminism is "the thousands of little girls with temporary tattoos on their arms, and Mia Hamm soccer jerseys on their backs" (p. 17). Third-wave Feminist activism takes the form of "the single mother who organizes the babysitting chain on Election Day so that all the housebound mothers can vote" (p. 17). At the same time, women regularly face discrimination in the justice system, at work, and at school. Additionally, some women who call themselves feminists take pride in practices that seemingly construct them as objects in a patriarchal world. They wear makeup and designer clothing and enjoy listening to Brittany Spears or Shania Twain. The Cathy cartoon in Figure 8.1 represents the tension between second- and third-wave feminism.

Baumgardner and Richards (2003) summarize the various and contradictory approaches to feminism today:

> Most young women don't get together to talk about "Feminism" with a capital F. We don't use terms like "the politics of housework" or "the gender gap" as much as we simply describe our lives and our expectations. To a degree, the lack of a Third-wave feminist terminology keeps us from building a potent movement, which is why we need to connect our pro-woman ethics to a political vision. (p. 48)

The rhetoric of the feminist movement continues, even if the messages, leadership, and cultural beliefs have changed. To learn more about the women's movement, visit an online archive of documents compiled by researchers at Duke University at http://scriptorium.lib.duke.edu/wlm/.

FIGURE 8.1 This Cathy cartoon illustrates some of the differences between second- and third-wave feminists.

CLASSIFYING GENDERED RHETORIC

With this introduction to gender, feminism, and the three waves of the women's rights movement, we can now turn to some specific theories about rhetoric. As you read these theories, keep in mind four primary frameworks:

1. Inclusion
2. Reconceptualization
3. Gender diversity
4. Oppression and liberation

The theories that correspond with these frameworks are outlined in Table 8.1. We'll briefly explore each of these frameworks in greater detail before discussing the theories that make up each framework.

Inclusion

Spitzack and Carter (1987) suggest that by focusing on rhetors who had public power and managed power through rhetoric, women have often been excluded from rhetorical history. Feminist rhetorical theory seeks to uncover not only public female rhetors but also those who have used rhetoric privately. A great deal of the scholarship about women's rhetoric has taken the form of rhetorical criticism.

Table 8.1 Summary of Feminist Rhetorical Theories

Theme	Theory/Theorist	Summary	View of Gender
Including the rhetoric of women	*Man Cannot Speak for Her* (1989)–Campbell	Female orators face special obstacles, different from those of their male counterparts.	Men and women are different because they face different rhetorical problems.
	Women Speak (1991)–Foss and Foss	Women's rhetoric includes nonpublic tests, such as cooking and sewing.	Men and women are different because they have different experiences.
Reconceptualizing differences between men and women	*The Rhetoric of Women's Liberation*–Campbell (1973)	Rhetoric of women's liberation is a distinct but unified genre of rhetoric.	Given differences in power status, women have had to develop alternative modes of rhetorical expression.
	The Womanizing of Rhetoric–Gearhart (1979)	Rhetorical theory should focus on listening, receiving, and collaboration, not conquering.	Men and women are essentially different; men are more confrontational, which is harmful.
	Beyond Persuasion: Invitational Rhetoric–Foss and Griffin (1991)	Rhetoric should be seen as an invitation, and the rhetor should take care to create an atmosphere of trust and equality	Gender is socialized, but invitational rhetoric can be used by men and women.
	Feminine Style–Campbell (1989)	Women's rhetoric has a distinct style that has emerged from their experiences as women.	Men and women are different because they have had different experiences.
Creating a theory of rhetoric that is gender neutral, but compatible with feminist goals	*Gender Diversity Perspective*–Condit (1997)	Rhetoric creates gender while embracing multiple criteria to judge rhetoric.	"Man" and "woman" is a false dichotomy; there exist multiple genders.
Viewing ways that rhetoric oppresses and liberates women	Mary Daly	Examines how rhetoric can be used to oppress or liberate women.	Men and women are different; men collectively victimize women.

As such, it has been largely inductive in nature—building theory from specific examples. Much rhetorical criticism of women's orators has not immediately adopted the terminology or theories that we have discussed so far. Feminist critics have instead sought to create their own methods and theories for the criticism of feminist rhetoric. We'll survey some of their work in the next section.

Reconceptualizing

The projects of Campbell and Foss and Foss argue that women should be studied as rhetors and that there may be some differences in how women use rhetoric. Additionally, they believe, along with other theorists, that conceptualizing rhetoric from a feminist perspective will empower women. The theorists we will study in this section seek to create a theory of gendered rhetorical theory; they have sought to redefine rhetorical constructs from a feminist perspective. In this section we'll look at the three of the most significant reconstruction projects, beginning with Campbell's initial observations that there exists a distinct feminist rhetorical genre.

Gender Diversity

Celeste Condit (1997) argues that the reconstruction approaches we have just discussed, or as she calls it, the *dichotomous* approaches, are based on the basic distinction between men and women. Condit claims that "Such feminist criticisms misrepresent the history of rhetoric and rest on untenable and counterproductive notions of human gender" (p. 92). Instead, she seeks to develop a model of rhetoric that appreciates gender diversity "in order to reconstruct an understanding of the rhetorical tradition that is compatible with feminist goals while appreciative of human eloquence" (p. 92).

Oppression and Liberation

Finally, we turn to the radical feminism of Mary Daly. She has identified ways that rhetoric oppresses women, but also some ways that rhetoric can be used to free women's voices. She explains that "Patriarchy appears to be 'everywhere.' Even outer space and the future have been colonized" (1978, p. 1). We'll turn to her theory of how rhetoric oppresses and liberates at the end of the chapter. As you read along, refer back to Table 8.1 to keep in mind the distinctions between the various theoretical approaches.

THE PUBLIC RHETORIC OF WOMEN

Karlyn Kohrs Campbell has sought to make known the voices of women orators. One of her most ambitious projects is a book titled *Man Cannot Speak for Her: A Critical Study of Early Feminist Rhetoric* (1989). Campbell explains the nature of this book thus: "As a rhetorical critic I want to restore one segment of the history of women, namely the rhetoric of the early woman's rights movement that emerged in the United States in the 1830's" (p. 1). She further explains that "Men have an ancient and honorable rhetorical history. Their speeches and writings, from antiquity to the present, are studied and analyzed by historians and rhetoricians" (1989, p. 1). Women, she notes, "have no parallel rhetorical history" (p. 1). Her book outlines the general challenges facing women orators and the ways that feminist orators confronted those challenges. Campbell analyzes the speeches of several

---

BOX 8.1 Spotlight on a Theorist: Karlyn Kohrs Campbell

Karlyn Kohrs Campbell's work in the area of feminist rhetoric has greatly shaped and influenced its study. Campbell is currently chair of the Communication Studies department at the University of Minnesota. She is the author or editor of eight books, including *Man Cannot Speak for Her: A Critical Study of Early Feminist Rhetoric*, which was published in 1989. She has published scholarly work in journals such as *Quarterly Journal of Speech, Philosophy and Rhetoric, Rhetoric and Public Affairs, Women's* *Studies in Communication,* and *Communication Education.* She is currently the editor of the *Quarterly Journal of Speech.* Campbell has received the *Francine Merritt Award* for contributions to women, the *National Communication Association Distinguished Scholar Award*, the *Ehninger Award for Distinguished Rhetorical Scholarship*, the *Winans-Wichelns Book Award*, and the *Charles Woolbert Award for Scholarship of Exceptional Quality and Influence.*

---

feminist orators, including Sojourner Truth, Sarah and Angelina Grimké, Lucretia Coffin Mott, and Elizabeth Cady Stanton. You can read more about Campbell in Box 8.1, Spotlight on a Theorist.

At the beginning of her work, Campbell explains in detail the reasons women have been excluded from rhetorical study and the implications of their exclusion. First, and perhaps most significantly, Campbell notes that women have been prohibited from speaking and when they did speak, "their words often were not preserved" (Campbell, 1989, p. 1). We have a rich heritage of male speakers—as has been evident throughout this book—but we lack a similar history for women. Campbell believes that any study of rhetoric must include the study of women if we are to "understand human symbolization in all its variety and to identify touchstones that illustrate the peaks of human symbolic activity" (Campbell, 1989, p. 9).

Additionally, women orators face stiffer standards than men when their rhetoric is analyzed and evaluated by critics. Since a great deal of rhetorical criticism is interested in evaluating the effectiveness of rhetoric and since women orators have faced long odds in persuading their audiences, their work is often overlooked because it hasn't been successful. Yet Campbell notes, "Critics must judge whether the choices made by rhetors were skillful responses to the problems they confronted, not whether the changes they urged were enacted" (Campbell, 1989, p. 3). We'll briefly survey some of Campbell's observations about feminist oratory from the women's suffrage movement.

Campbell's work focused on early women orators who spoke against slavery and subsequently in favor of the women's right to vote. Initially, women faced great obstacles in even being able to speak in public about the slavery and women's suffrage. According to Campbell (1989), to overcome these obstacles, early orators focused on audiences of women and sought to convince other women of "the need to convince members of a fledgling movement of the rightness of their cause, and the need to persuade women with little power and few resources that they can be effective in working for social change" (p. 34).

In particular, Angelina Grimké was able to "subtly appropriate the language of the Bible in order to assume a persona that transcended male-female roles and legitimated her rhetorical action" (p. 34). As such, Grimké created a conflict for her audience and contributed to the construction of her character as a speaker. Campbell notes, "Her use of this sophisticated strategy enriches critical understanding of the role of character in persuasion, because it illustrates the relevance of social role relationships and of the dramatic concept of personae in explaining how influence occurs" (p. 34). This statement illustrates how the critic builds theory from particular examples of feminist oratory.

When faced with opposition, feminist orators developed complex responses. One typical argument was that the Bible prohibited women from speaking and that a woman's true destiny was not compatible with rhetoric. Coffin Mott was one speaker who responded to this argument. According to Campbell, she was effective in doing so because Mott "fulfilled traditional rhetorical requirements, usually perceived as outside the capability of females" (1989, p. 47). Additionally, Coffin Mott was seen as a credible speaker—a Quaker minister who showed that women could "move into the public sphere and retain their moral character and commitment to humane values" (Campbell, 1989, p. 47).

The Declaration of Sentiments of Seneca Falls was a rhetoric document produced to identify the vision of the women's suffrage movement. Although the document was not immediately recognized as an ideological document, Campbell (1989) notes that the document "accurately reflected the views of those whose principles it expressed" (p. 69). In fact, the document was rhetorically sophisticated, explains Campbell: "In espousing natural rights principles, woman's rights advocates reaffirmed their commitment to the values of the nation, and as the movement developed, they saw themselves as perfecting, not overthrowing, the democratic republic they loved as Americans" (p. 69).

Susan B. Anthony was arrested in November 1872 for voting in Rochester, New York. She then embarked on a three-week speaking tour to influence jurors who might decide her case. Using evidence and deductive arguments, Anthony made the case that although she voted, such action wasn't criminal. The principles upon which she based her speech were all supported in written law or one of the founding documents of the nation. The speech was highly structured and used a great deal of examples and analogies. Its close comparison to traditional forensic oratory made Anthony's speech unlike others that had been presented by feminist orators. She was effective. Despite losing the case, she was fined $100, which was never collected by the state.

As you can see from this discussion, early feminist orators used diverse rhetorical approaches to achieve their goals. Some orators were deductive, others inductive. Some used a high style of speaking, others a simple style. Some used evidence while others used numerous examples. Importantly, Campbell observes that "analysis of early movement rhetoric uncovers unusually revealing examples of a style rarely taught and infrequently recognized, a style particularly suited to women speakers and women audiences" (p. 190). Specifically, a "feminine style" emerged from Campbell's analysis. Not all women speakers used this style, but there did appear to be something in common with how many of the rhetors approached their subject and audience. We'll take up the subject of the feminine style later in this chapter. Campbell concludes her analysis by stating, "Contemporary feminists can learn much from early rhetoric, not just about women's history, but about the issues that persist, the dilemmas women have faced through time, and the irreducible elements of a feminist program" (p. 190).

THE PRIVATE RHETORIC OF WOMEN

Having briefly surveyed Campbell's analysis of feminist rhetoric that has occurred in public situations, we will now turn our focus to the study of women's rhetoric that has taken place in more private settings. Keep in mind that in previous chapters we have studied rhetoric as the public, strategic discourse of powerful individuals. Sonja Foss and Karen Foss (1991) have studied women's rhetoric that does not fit this criterion in their book *Women Speak*. They explain, "we consciously sought to expand the scope of significant women communicators beyond those active in movements or involved in political activities by privileging ordinariness over noteworthiness" (p. 5). As a result, Foss and Foss believe that their analysis will subvert the dominant culture's way of thinking about rhetoric—a way that privileges the male perspective while disempowering women's voices: "We see *Women Speak* as offering a subversive alternative to traditional approaches to public address that have privileged male communication precisely because it asserts the inherent value of women's expression and declares it eloquent on its own terms" (p. 22).

Like Campbell, Foss and Foss avoid using traditional rhetorical theory to analyze the rhetoric in their study. Instead, feminism—"the belief that men and women are entitled to equal opportunities for self-expression" (p. 20)—plays a central role in their analysis. Three assumptions guide their analysis of women's rhetoric. First, they contend that gender filters all experiences that we have as social beings. Understanding the influence of gender on women's communication is a central goal of their study. Second, Foss and Foss believe that women's experiences are different from men's. Consequently, theories of rhetoric that have developed with men as subjects would not be useful for women's rhetoric. Finally, borrowing from the critical approach that we discussed in the previous chapter, Foss and Foss explain that "feminist scholarship is done to improve women's lives" (p. 21). In other words, understanding how and why women use rhetoric is seen as central to the task of improving women's lives. With this orientation to their work in mind, let's turn to some of their observations about women's rhetoric.

Foss and Foss (1991) examine a wide range of women's communicative experiences, including those concerning architecture, baking, shopping, journal writing, newsletters, comedy, and dress. Each chapter focuses on one of these activities and is written by a woman who describes her experience. Foss and Foss do not summarize the experiences or try to speak for the women featured in the book. Instead, the women are permitted to communicate on their own terms and in their own ways about their subject. Their words reveal on their own the rhetorical characteristics of their experiences.

The following examples serve to illustrate the the rhetorical implications of Foss and Foss's study.

- In describing shopping, Kanengieter notes, "We exchange. We linger. We return. Communion with one another and necessary anonymity, not possessions, are what we seek" (p. 310). This description highlights the importance for women of connecting with others and forming opinions through interaction. These motivations characterize both the shopping experience and the language used to describe it (its rhetorical dimension).

- In another chapter, Myers describes what she has learned from motherhood: "I am less single minded, better able to see wholes—whole time, larger chunks of future imposed on each now. Streamlined mother life. I am a better observer of humans for being a mother, and more tolerant of others— especially other mothers" (p. 230). Again, the author of this chapter alludes to key elements of gendered rhetoric: its holistic nature, tolerance, and sensitivity to the needs of others.

- In the chapter on baking, Williams explains that, "the process of making a new cheesecake begins by thinking about the recipient. Does she like graham-cracker crust, a pastry crust, or a chocolate-pecan crust? What is his taste in foods—does he like sweet or tart foods?" (p. 41). The chapter considers how women's rhetoric takes into account its effect on the audience.

Like rhetoric, the experiences of women—including shopping, motherhood, and cooking—offer a particular way of seeing the world. In fact, some feminist scholars see very little difference between the formal practice of rhetoric—in the form of speeches, for instance—and the day-to-day kinds of activities in which women engage. In other words, language and experience are tightly interwoven.

CAMPBELL AND THE WOMEN'S LIBERATION MOVEMENT

Our previous discussion in this chapter has focused on ways that theorists have included women in the study of rhetoric. We turn now to the second main category in Table 8.1. Here and in subsequent sections, we'll look at how theorists have tried to explain differences in how men and women communicate. We return again to the study of Karlyn Kohrs Campbell. In her 1973 article, "The Rhetoric of Women's Liberation: An Oxymoron," which analyzes the rhetoric of the women's movement in the seventies and eighties, she identifies a style of rhetoric that she considers unique: "I conclude, then, that women's liberation is a unified, separate genre of rhetoric with distinctive substantive-stylistic features" (Campbell, 1973, p. 84). Foss, Foss, and Griffin (1997) note that "Campbell's article constituted the first effort to reconceptualize rhetorical constructs from a feminist perspective, a focus of feminist scholarship that would not appear again for many years" (p. 15). Let's look more closely at Campbell's observations and arguments about women's rhetoric.

Initially, Campbell notes that the rhetorical requirements of those arguing for women's rights were different from similar movements conducted by African Americans or students in the 1960s. She notes that "Feminist advocacy unearths tensions woven deep into the fabric of our society and provokes an unusually intense and profound 'rhetoric of moral conflict'" (p. 75). Particularly she notes that the sex role requirements for women contradict those that we celebrate in American culture. Our cultures teaches that self-reliance, independence, and achievement are important values. Traditionally, however, these values have defined roles played by men; women have been forced into roles that are very different from these more valued roles. According to Campbell, "Consequently, feminist rhetoric is substantively unique by definition, because no matter how traditional in its argumentation, how justificatory its form, how discursive its method, or how scholarly its style, it attacks the entire psychosocial reality, the most fundamental values, of the cultural context in which it occurs" (p. 75).

For instance, Campbell points out that legal decisions of 1874 and 1961 affirmed that in marriage, women were more or less viewed as the property of their husbands. Husbands enjoyed protections under the law that their wives did not have. This legal situation creates a moral dilemma: one must admit that our culture doesn't respect equal rights or that women should be treated unequally within this culture. In either case, arguing against the current situation presented a dilemma for women because doing so seemed revolutionary and radical. Women rhetors were faced with having to challenge the fundamental values upon which the culture is based, something they could not do using traditional rhetorical techniques.

Initially, women's movement advocates had difficulty getting other women to support the cause. Since women were isolated and under the influence of men, liberation rhetors had to devise nonpublic ways of communicating to them. Leaders of the women's movement had to create a sense of "sisterhood" and give women a sense of autonomy, according to Campbell (p. 79).

One rhetorical strategy that was used to counter isolation and alienation was consciousness raising. Campbell explains that this technique involved "meetings of small, leaderless groups in which each person is encouraged to express her personal feelings and experiences" (p. 79). The goal was to bring to light the common perceptions and feelings that women had about their culture. Rhetorically, consciousness raising resulted in a new rhetorical framework: "affirmation of the affective, of the validity of personal experience, of the necessity for self-exposure and self-criticism, of the value of dialogue, and of the goal of autonomous, individual decision making" (p. 79). This form of rhetoric, notes Campbell, is far removed from traditional rhetorical theory.

Additionally, the rhetorical qualities of group consciousness raising sessions was also present in more public rhetorical venues. Although this type of communication may make you think of a group therapy session, Campbell is adamant that such style is "rhetorical rather than expressive and public and political rather than private and personal" (p. 81). Importantly, this way of speaking positions the participants' problems as resulting from society; these are not pathologies peculiar to individual women.

Finally, the rhetorical style of the women's movement was "confrontative" and "violated the norms of decorum, morality and 'femininity' of the women addressed" (p. 81). Specifically, two rhetorical devices—the attack metaphor and symbolic reversals—were used. The attack metaphor shocks the audience into questioning sexism. An example would be a drawing of Rodin's "The Thinker" as a woman or stating that "Trust in God; *She* will provide." Symbolic reversals "transform devil terms society has applied to women into god terms and always exploit the power and fear lurking in these terms as potential sources of strength" (p. 82). Using the word "bitch" in a positive way, for instance, would be an example of symbolic reversal.

We have been discussing the stylistic features of the women's liberation rhetoric. Campbell notes that there was an interdependent relationship between the style and substance of women's rhetoric. Specifically, the rhetoric of women's liberation contained many implicit arguments against the culture's values. The substance of the rhetoric took on the stylistic features that we have previously discussed. For example, "consciousness raising require[d] that the personal be transcended by moving toward the structural, that the individual be transcended by moving toward the political" (Campbell, 1973, p. 83).

In short, the rhetoric of women's liberation is at once personal and political. Using a unique rhetorical style that was very personal, women were able to communicate to a broader audience important political issues. Womens' rhetoric set up a contrast between public, structural problems and the statements of personal experience and feeling that extend beyond the traditional boundaries of rhetorical acts. Campbell concludes that "Traditional or familiar definitions of persuasion do not satisfactorily account for the rhetoric of women's liberation. In relation to such definitions, feminist advocacy wavers between the rhetorical and non-rhetorical, the persuasive and the non-persuasive" (p. 84).

THE WOMANIZATION OF RHETORIC

Sally Miller Gearhart (1979) offers another way to reconceptualize women's rhetoric. Traditionally, she argues, rhetoric has been equated with persuasion and has been based on a masculine view of the world in which "any intent to persuade is an act of violence" (p. 195). She argues, therefore, that rhetoric must be womanized. By this she means that rhetoric should not be seen as a way to conquer. Instead, rhetorical theory should focus on atmosphere, listening, receiving, and a collective rather than competitive mode (p. 201). Let's discuss in more detail Gearhart's thoughts about the womanization of rhetoric.

Initially, Gearhart condemns the traditional theory and practice of rhetoric: "The patriarchs of rhetoric have never called into question their unspoken assumption that mankind (read 'mankind') is here on earth to alter his (read 'his') environment and to influence the social affairs of other men (read 'men')"

(Gearhart, 1979, p. 195). Specifically, Gearhart addresses the idea that rhetoric is designed to effectively change the audience. Traditional rhetorical theory assumes that it "is a proper and even necessary function to attempt to change others" (Gearhart, 1979, p. 195).

The view that rhetoric should be used to change others creates an oppressive practice that privileges some members of society while disempowering others. The traditional view of rhetoric holds that the speaker possesses knowledge and uses rhetoric to convey that knowledge to less knowledgeable audience members in order to influence their views. Gearhart argues for a different conception of the speaker-audience relationship.

However, Gearhart does not deny that changes in humans take place. What concerns her is the *intent* to convert: "To change other people or other entities is not in itself a violation. It is a fact of existence that we do so. The act of violence is in the intention to change another" (Gearhart, 1979, p. 196). The intent to change leads to what Gearhart calls the conquest/conversion model of rhetoric. The conquest model is based on the mentality of "invade or violate" (1979, p. 196). The conversion model is more subtle and, she adds, more insidious because it has the appearance and earnestness of having integrity. When someone is converted, they feel it is for their own benefit. Gearhart, however, sees no benefit to the converted.

Consequently, Gearhart examined alternatives to a rhetoric aimed at changing people, offering the following definition: "Communication can be a deliberate creation or co-creation of an atmosphere in which people or things, if and only if they have the internal basis for change, may change themselves; it can be a milieu in which those who are ready to be persuaded may persuade themselves, may choose to hear or choose to learn" (1979, p. 198). She identifies two types of rhetorical situations: learning and conflict encounter. Rhetoric that occurs in a learning situation would serve to generate energy so that the individuals involved may grow; that which takes place in a conflict encounter would be characterized by dialogue, she explained.

No matter the type of rhetorical situation, five qualities must be present:

1. No one involved in the rhetorical situation should intend to persuade or enlighten the others. Instead, all should be committed to creating an atmosphere in which change for both or all individuals can take place.

2. All involved must understand that there are differences among those who participate. The parties will either have differing levels of knowledge about the topic or they will have disagreements about the matter at hand.

3. Those involved must feel equal in power, even though there may be differences among them.

4. Each individual must work at communication, since it is a difficult achievement.

5. All individuals must be willing to yield their position to the others.

Gearhart's call for a new way of thinking about rhetoric reflects the principles of feminist communication practices. She explains that "Feminism is at the very least the rejection of the conquest/conversion model of interaction and the develop-ment of new forms of relationship which allow for wholeness in the individual and differences among people and entities" (Gearhart, 1979, p. 201).

INVITATIONAL RHETORIC

Foss and Griffin have envisioned a view of rhetoric that is compatible with femi-nist goals as well as with the goals of other ideologies that promote equality. Specifically, they promote the view that rhetoric does not necessarily have to be persuasive. They argue that viewing rhetoric only as persuasive leads to rhetorical practice that devalues the lives, experiences and knowledge level of the audience member (Foss & Griffin, 1995). To counter this view and to promote the status of the audience in the rhetorical interaction, they present the idea of *invitational rhet-oric,* which focuses on the choices that audience members make and the idea that rhetors should create situations in which audience members are free to make choices about what they hear and read.

Defining Invitational Rhetoric

Foss and Griffin's (1995) work seeks to establish a better relationship between rhetor and audience, one built upon principles of equality, the immanent value of human life, and preservation of self-determination. In their own words, their the-ory of **invitational rhetoric** is "an invitation to understanding as a means to cre-ate a relationship rooted in equality, immanent value, and self-determination" (1995, p. 5). A key concept in their idea of rhetoric is the word "invitation." Through invitation, Foss and Foss contend that the rhetor does not denigrate the perspec-tives of the audience member but instead tries to appreciate and respect those per-spectives. In addition, by offering an invitation, the rhetor realizes that not all in the audience will accept or respond to the message, a position that is acceptable to an invitational speaker.

An invitational speaker has two primary objectives in mind: offering perspec-tives and creating "external conditions that allow others to present their perspec-tives in an atmosphere of respect and equality" (Foss & Griffin, 1995, p. 7). Offering perspectives is the "giving of expression to a perspective without advocating its support or seeking its acceptance" (p. 7). The speaker might use narrative, for instance, not so much as a persuasive tool, as we have discussed, but rather as a way to articulate the perspective of the speaker. It is important that the invita-tional speaker question his or her own beliefs in the process of speaking.

The second primary objective of invitational rhetoric is creating an atmos-phere in which audience members feel comfortable offering their own perspec-tives. In particular, this atmosphere involves safety, value, and freedom. The speaker develops safety by making the audience members feel that their perspectives will be received with respect and care. Value is achieved when the speaker allows each person to feel like they are a unique individual. The speaker may, for instance, seek to see the world from the perspective of the audience member. Finally, freedom is apparent when the audience members can develop and choose options from the alternatives suggested by the speaker. Fundamentally, freedom results when the audience member does not feel pressure to accept the ideas of the speaker.

An Example of Invitational Rhetoric

Although both men and women may use invitational rhetoric, we'll examine a speech by a woman, Oprah Winfrey, as an example of this theory. On May 30, 1997, the popular talk show host and actress addressed the graduating class at Wellesley College. Winfrey used several methods of inviting her audience to hear her perspective on life. For example, Winfrey stated, "You all know this, that life is a journey and I want to share with you just for a few moments about five things (aren't you glad there aren't ten) five things that have made this journey for me exciting." By using the word "share" Winfrey was making clear that she is offering an invitation and doesn't wish to impose her guidance on the audience.

You'll recall that in addition to offering an invitation to the audience, the invitational rhetor seeks to offer perspectives and create an atmosphere of respect and equality. At the heart of Winfrey's speech are five tips that she wished to pass along to her audience. These tips were her perspectives on life, which she wished to convey to the audience. Additionally, Winfrey addressed her audience's beliefs, including their spiritual beliefs. Winfrey didn't impose her beliefs, though, instead creating an atmosphere of respect and equality. She defined a higher source as "God" but said "you can call it whatever you want to, the force, nature, Allah, the power." Winfrey allowed her audience to hear her speech through the perspective of their own spirituality. In doing so, she extended to her audience respect for their various religious views.

FEMININE STYLE

We have previously discussed Campbell's work in bringing to light the voices of women from the suffrage movement. As part of her study, Campbell (1989) identified a unique way of using rhetoric in these speakers that she called the "feminine style." **Feminine style** "emerged out of their experiences as women and was adapted to the attitudes and experiences of female audiences. However it was not, and is not today, a style exclusive to women, either as speakers or as audiences" (Campbell, 1989, p. 12). As Dow and Tonn (1993) have explained, "Campbell's theory of feminine style, developed through her analyses of historical and contemporary feminist rhetors and their distinctive audiences, has provided an alternative critical orientation with which to understand the source, form, and function of female communicative strategies and their effectiveness in women's movements" (p. 286).

Feminine style is based on women's experiences in learning crafts such as cooking, cleaning, canning, sewing, childbearing, child rearing, and the like.

Campbell provides a lengthy explanation:

> Such discourse will be personal in tone (crafts are learned face-to-face
> from a mentor), relying heavily on personal experience, anecdotes, and
> other examples. It will tend to be structured inductively (crafts are learned
> bit by bit, instance by instance, from which generalizations emerge). It will
> invite audience participation, including the process of testing generalizations
> or principles against the experiences of the audience. Audience members
> will be addressed as peers, with recognition of authority based on experience
> (more skilled craftspeople are more experienced), and efforts will be made
> to create identification with the experiences of the audience and those
> described by the speaker. The goal of such rhetoric is empowerment,
> a term contemporary feminists have used to refer to the process of
> persuading listeners that they can act effectively in the world. (Campbell,
> 1989, p. 13)

It is important to note that feminine style is not based on sex, but rather the gendered experiences of women: "There is nothing inevitably or necessarily female
about this rhetorical style, it has been congenial to women because of the accul-
turation of female speakers and audiences" (Campbell, 1989, p. 13).

Dow and Tonn (1993) have explained that the socialization of women has led
to the use of several rhetorical techniques by women rhetors. The feminine style
includes the use of narrative, concrete examples, analogies, and anecdotes as the
primary evidence for claims (p. 287). That is, women are likely to tell stories, use
personal examples and anecdotes, and make analogies to prove their point than
they are to use evidence such as statistics or deductive reasoning. Additionally, the
feminine style also has a personal tone that encourages the audience to participate
in the rhetorical event (p. 287). Women are likely to be more open and offer their
perspective to the audience. Read more about feminine style and one rhetor's use
of it in Box 8.2, Critical Insights.

Dow (1995) cautioned against using the feminine style as a way to characterize the rhetoric of all women. She explained that rhetorical theories such as
feminine style can "unwittingly elide differences among women, falsely universalizing women's experience according to a model based on the lives of white,
middle-class women. Simultaneously, they exaggerate differences between men
and women, often promoting a false biologism that feminist scholars refer to as
'essentialism'" (p. 109). Instead, Dow sees rhetoric as a product of power as
much as it is a product of gender. That is, women in particular positions of
power may use rhetoric in similar ways, but they may use rhetoric in quite a
different way than other women in different positions of power. Dow (1995)
explains that what is important is the *"interaction of powerlessness and gender"*
[emphasis original] (p. 109). That is, Dow and Tonn's analysis of Ann Richards
(see Box 8.2) should be seen as illuminating a particular type of rhetoric used
by a woman in a particular position of power. Dow makes it clear that not all
women use rhetoric in the feminine style and that there may be different feminine styles for different rhetors.

BOX 8.2 Critical Insights: Ann Richards's Feminine Style

Dow and Tonn (1993) use Campbell's theory of feminine style to study the rhetoric of former Texas Governor Ann Richards (Figure 8.2). They observe that

The synthesis of formal qualities of feminine style evidence in Richards's rhetoric (use of narrative, concrete examples, analogies, and anecdotes as primary evidence sources; personal tone, and encouragement of audience participation) with an alternative political philosophy reflecting feminine ideals of care, nurturance, and family relationships functions as a critique of traditional political reasoning that offers alternative grounds for political judgment. (p. 289)

Specifically, Dow and Tonn focus on how Richards tested argumentative claims, privileged personal grounds for public knowledge, and created a unique rhetor-audience relationship.

Richards used numerous personal examples as the basis for her political arguments. She spoke of letters received from constituents, for example, as the basis for her support or opposition to particular public policy. Instead of using deductive reasoning, which is traditionally used in political argument, Richards gave numerous examples, using an inductive style. In addition, Richards's rhetoric celebrated the values of feminism. She focused on how women have overcome obstacles posed by masculine culture and how relationships are an important part of public life. She also used a style of rhetoric that promoted identification with the audience. Dow and Tonn note that "she acknowledges the audience in her inclusive pronouns, she encourages audiences to draw their own conclusions from the examples she offers, and she self-discloses, a strategy that presupposes the trust among peers" (1993, p. 296).

In sum, Dow and Tonn believe that Richards' use of a feminine rhetorical style has important implications for the practice of rhetoric. By using this style in mainstream political addresses, Richards challenged previous ways of thinking about rhetoric. Additionally, a feminist ideology is implicit in this rhetorical style. Dow and Tonn also comment on how Richards's rhetoric creates an alternative sphere for public rhetoric. This observation is based both on Habermas's ideas about the public sphere and McKerrow's concept of critical rhetoric that we surveyed in the previous chapter. In terms of the public sphere, the feminine style can be used to promote a partial or counter–public sphere. That is, gendered rhetoric can help particular members of the public communicate in ways that promote rational understanding of emancipation. In terms of critical rhetoric, the feminine style offers a "positive alternative to the discourses of power" and points to how rhetoric can be used to resist the dominant power structure (Dow & Tonn, 1993, p. 300).

GENDER DIVERSITY PERSPECTIVE

We are now moving on to another perspective of gendered rhetoric, the **gender diversity perspective.** Condit has developed this perspective to be compatible with other feminist projects and ideology, and at the same time seeking to distinguish between rhetoric and ordinary communication, a line that has been somewhat blurred in our previous discussion. Condit defines rhetoric as persuasion that takes place in the public sphere. In doing so, she embraces the practice that is seen by many theorists, such as Gearhart, as being coercive, violent, and patriarchal. For Condit, rhetoric-as-persuasion does not have to be seen as patriarchal.

A central component of Condit's theory is that there are multiple genders, not just two. She explains that "Gender is culturally constructed" and "disrupting the

FIGURE 8.2   Former Texas Governor Ann Richards speaks at the 1992 Democratic National Convention.

traditional categories of male and female is a useful way to liberate women from the strictures of oppression that have, historically, been assigned to the category 'woman'" (Condit, 1997, p. 96). Condit also incorporates race and class into her theory: "The category of 'woman' is not in any way monolithic, but varies dramatically by race and class" (Condit, 1997, p. 97). In essence, she asserts that the rhetoric one uses is determined less by a male-female distinction and more by the kind of male or female you are and by how race and class intersect with your perspective of the world. Let's examine her premise in more detail.

The first step in studying a theory of gendered rhetoric is to erase the idea that gender is split along a male-female line. Condit explains, "Women cannot be oppressed as women if they are not recognized as such with traditional/dominant sex relations" (p. 97). Thus, women can only be perceived as "the other" if they are included in "the other" category. It may seem odd to you to think of other configurations for gender than male/female, so we'll explore this point further. Although it may seem to you a rather simple observation that women give birth and men don't, Condit points to numerous examples to make her case that gender is a more complicated distinction than the one we usually make. For one, biological tests on men and women show more biological overlap than differences (Condit, 1997). When differences are found, they are often due to statistical factors that represent some women and men, but not all men or women. As Condit points out, biological measures of differences often don't study *essential* differences between men and women, only *average* differences. Condit also refers to her work in genetics to show that "all efforts to use biological categories to dichotomize human gender ultimately break down" (p. 98). Further, she notes that women of color have observed that race and class influence their view of the world in addition to gender.

Despite her efforts to break down the male-female distinction, Condit observes that there are differences between men and women and that these differences have been used as the basis for discrimination. For example, "informal rules that require sixty hours of work per week for a professional career during the child-bearing years discriminate against most women in a society where most women provide most of the child-rearing labor" (p. 100). Thus, it is important to retain the concept of gender but do so without the simple male-female dichotomy.

Condit asserts that "A gender diversity perspective would thus encourage us to go beyond the observation that rhetoric historically has been practiced primarily by males to explore the multiplicity and contradictions of the gendering of that practice" (1997, p. 101). Similarly, she argues that "The portrait of human gender is much richer than it has been drawn thus far, and it would be more interesting to explore the range of human styles than simply to lump women in a single box" (p. 103).

At the heart of Condit's theory is the idea that gender is constructed through rhetoric, rather than being a product of gender: "A gender diversity perspective treats rhetoric as the grounds of the construction of gender, rather than as the product of an already constructed essentialist gender" (Condit, 1997, p. 103). She rejects the more simplistic view of gender and rhetoric presented by Dow and Tonn (see Box 8.2). Instead, Condit explains that it would be helpful to look at how speakers such as Ann Richards have used masculine and feminine rhetorical qualities, for example: "Instead of explaining continually that Ann Richards, or Geraldine Ferraro, or Barbara Boxer had gender 'against' them as speakers, we might begin to ask how these speakers, all enormously successful, constructed their genders in positive ways" (Condit, 1997, p. 104).

Not only is gender constructed through rhetoric, but so too are social relationships, according to Condit. Unlike Gearhart—who sees intentional persuasion as violence—Condit sees rhetoric as necessary for social interaction, whether intentional or not. She maintains that cooperation, which can be seen as a feminine value, is dependent on rhetoric's ability to make known options and choice in a society.

Condit also believes that not all rhetors are created equal. That is, some rhetors have a special ability to use eloquence. She rejects the view that rhetoric is private and equally practiced by all who participate. She summarizes, "All human beings can communicate, and all human beings employ rhetoric. However, most of us lack the eloquence of an Elizabeth Cady Stanton or a Sojourner Truth" (p. 106). Condit defines eloquence thus: "Eloquence is not a simple property. Its fundamental task is to take an incompletely spoken, fragmentary set of experiences and to articulate those experiences in a coherent set of relationships that nourish a particular audience in a particular context, perhaps even moving them to new visions from old ones" (Condit, 1997, p. 107). That is, rhetoric requires skill in order to move individuals to see their world in new ways.

Condit ultimately proposes some specific guidelines for a gender diversity rhetorical theory. First, she recommends appreciating multiple sets of fluid criteria for judging rhetors. That is, rhetorical critics must understand and recognize the techniques of women—as identified by Campbell, for instance. Importantly, Condit argues that critics should not reject a standard of excellence completely. That is, she believes it was possible to judge the effectiveness of a speaker despite the fluidity of criteria that may be used to do so. Additionally, a gender diversity perspective sees rhetors not as "all-powerful father figures," but as servants and leaders (p. 109). Also, we must disentangle social structure to make it more equalitarian. You'll note that Condit does not provide a step-by-step outline of the gender diversity perspective. Like critical rhetoric, her theory is best thought of as a perspective by which we can study rhetoric.

To exemplify Condit's idea of gender diversity in rhetoric, we'll examine how presidential candidate Howard Dean and his wife, Judy, responded to reporter Diane Sawyer's questions during a February 2004 interview on the ABC show *Primetime Live* (Figure 8.3). The Deans argued throughout the interview that traditional assumptions about gender did not apply to their marriage and relationship. In essence, they sought to present a compelling and effective rhetorical performance while at the same time renegotiating the gender standards that are used to evaluate presidential candidates and their wives.

In short, political wives are traditionally expected to join their husbands on the campaign trail and support the husband's efforts to win office. Judy Dean, however, continued to practice medicine in the family's hometown of Burlington, Vermont, while her husband, Howard, attempted to win the Democratic nomination throughout 2003 and 2004. Howard Dean faced questions because of the apparent lack of support given by his wife. Further, after appearing with her husband at a stop in Iowa, Judy Dean then faced scrutiny for appearing with him as a political prop in a last-ditch effort to save his candidacy. The interview with Sawyer occurred prior to the New Hampshire primary at a time when Howard Dean was trailing in the polls and as the couple faced questions about Judy Dean's role in the campaign. Let's examine a few exchanges from the interview:

Diane Sawyer: But I've heard people say it and they're just baffled, mainly, because they've said running for the President is a really important thing and people in this country consider the presidency enormously important thing. They would assume that however much you love your practice and heaven knows, everybody wants their doctor to love their practice that you would, for this time say, "Well, the most important thing is for me to be with him out there doing this which he believed in for the country."

Judy Dean: I think they're both important and I think they're all important. And I think, um, I think I support Howard totally in what he's doing and I think he'd make a great president and I often I would like to be there more when I talk to him every night. I would like to be there, just for myself. I'd like to share some of the ups and the downs and I certainly (Inaudible) them. But I . . . I just, you know, I have a primary first practice.

FIGURE 8.3 Presidential candidate Howard Dean and his wife, Judy, appear on the ABC show *Primetime Live* to discuss her role in the campaign.

It's . . . it's . . it's my own private practice and my patients are my patients and they really depend on me and I really love it. It's not, it's not something I can say "Oh, you can take over for a month." It just doesn't work like that. And and you know, (Inaudible) and I support him totally and I will do interviews so people can find out what I'm like. But I'd love to be closer to him and and travel with him at times. But it's . . . it . . . but home and my practice is very, very important. Trying to balance and (Inaudible) and that's the way it is.

Diane Sawyer: (Overlap) Do you think, for instance, the Clintons who had a young daughter at the time that they campaigned, do you think that they didn't respect family and . . .

Howard Dean: I think that's different. Every family has to work these things out for themselves. And this is the way we've looked at our marriage and it's been a great marriage. Best thing that's ever happened to me, plus having kids.

Howard Dean: There's really another side to this. I have women, my age, coming up to me in the campaign trail saying "Thank God your wife is like that." We just got a bunch of letters at home saying "Thank God.

Hallelujah. A woman who has her own career and doesn't get dragged around." Some people would say "Where has she been?" Other people would say "Thank heavens. A different kind of first lady."

To summarize, the Deans faced scrutiny in the public and media because they did not embody the rhetoric of a traditionally gendered couple. They had to use this rhetorical opportunity to present a convincing performance—an eloquent performance—that argued there should be multiple standards for the rhetoric of political spouses. They argued there should be multiple sets of standards, including the supportive wife on the campaign trail as well as the supportive wife who stays home with the family. Additionally, Howard Dean presented himself not as the "all-powerful father figure," but as a servant who was fully aware of the choices he made as he campaigned for president. Ultimately, the Deans argued for new ways of seeing the relationship between political candidates and their spouses. In essence, they used an eloquent performance before a public audience to create a new view of gender.

RHETORIC AND OPPRESSION/LIBERATION

Mary Daly, you'll recall, wrote that rhetoric has been largely controlled by men, at the expense of women: "The facts is that we live in a profoundly anti-female society, a misogynistc 'civilization' in which men collectively victimize women, attacking us as personifications of their own paranoid fears, as The Enemy. Within this society it is men who rape, who sap women's energy, who deny women economic and political power" (1978, p. 29). For Daly, though, women can use rhetoric to free themselves from the oppression of a patriarchal rhetoric. For more information about Mary Daly and her work, visit her website at http://www.mdaly.com/.

Daly identifies two literal spaces that are important to the study of rhetoric and gender. The **foreground** is the space where rhetoric is used to oppress women and the **background** is a space where women use specific rhetorical techniques to free themselves from oppression. A central term to her theory is *spinning,* which is a manner of seeking out the ways that rhetoric has been used to oppress women. Spinning requires that women explicitly study language: "These deceptive perceptions were/are implanted through language—the all pervasive language of myth, conveyed overtly and subliminally through religion, 'great art,' literature, the dogmas of professionalism, the media, grammar. Indeed, deception is embedded in the very texture of the words we use, and here is where our exorcism can begin" (1978, p. 3). We'll examine here her ideas of the foreground and background and how rhetoric is used in each.

Foreground

The foreground is the world many of us experience. It is characterized by rhetorical practices that oppress women, making them subordinate to men. Daly defines foreground as "surface consciousness" (1978, p. 26), explaining that "Objectification and alienation take place when we are locked into the male-centered, monodimensional foreground (1978, p. 2). Foss, Foss, and Griffin (1999) have identified six rhetorical techniques that are used to keep women in the foreground:

1. Ritualistic violence
2. Silencing women's voices
3. Fixing women's images
4. Refusing to see the problem
5. Reversal
6. Elementary terms

We'll examine three of these rhetorical techniques here.

Ritualistic Violence In cultures throughout the world, violence is inflicted upon women in ways that are taken for granted. Daly has identified five violent rites that take place in the world's cultures: Indian *suttee,* Chinese footbinding, African female genital mutilation, European witch burning, and American gynecology (1978, p. 111). Indian *suttee* is a ceremony that burns alive Indian widows on the funeral pyre of their husbands. Daly explains, "Since their religion forbade remarriage and at the same time taught that the husband's death was the fault of the widow (because of her sins in a previous incarnation if not this one), everyone was free to despise and mistreat her for the rest of her life" (1978, p. 115). The widow would either feel compelled to throw herself on the funeral fire or would be forced to her death. Through rhetoric, notes Daly, each of these violent customs becomes embedded in a culture so that both victims and victimizers perform these rituals uncritically (1978, p. 109).

Silencing Women's Voices Daly has observed that women's voices have been silenced in many ways. The use of the generic pronoun "he," for instance, functions both to include women and men in the same category and to exclude women, making them seem like the "other." When we use the word "chairman," for instance, we might be referring to a man or woman. It does not call attention to the sex of the person. However, the word "chairwoman" calls attention to the fact that person is a woman. She is then thought to be out of the ordinary, or different, than any other "chairman."

Fixing Women's Images The patriarchy also manipulates how women are viewed in a culture. For example, when women models are airbrushed and edited in publications such as *Cosmopolitan, Glamour,* or *Playboy,* they appear thin, sexual, and available for male viewing. Daly explains that a "Paradise" is established that allows women to view women in "domesticated" and "pleasurable" ways: "Thus, the monitors of the foreground, the male myth-masters, fashion prominent and eminently forgettable images of women in their art, literature, and mass media—images intended to mold women for male purposes" (pp. 2–3). What is necessary, wrote Daly, is to break through the foreground of the "Playboy's Playground" and let out the "bunnies, the bitches, the beavers, the squirrels, the chicks, the pussycats, the cows, the nags, the foxy ladies, the old bats and biddies" and allow women to name themselves, instead of be named by men.

Background

The background is the space where women can achieve liberation by rejecting patriarchy and bonding with other females. Daly defines the background as the "divine depth of the Self" (1978, p. 26). By reflecting on language and how it is used to oppress, Daly believes that women could be free from patriarchy. Foss, Foss, and Griffin (1999) identify eight rhetorical options that lead to liberation:

1. Metaphor
2. Redefinition
3. Capitalization
4. Spelling/Be-spelling
5. Grammar/Sin-tactics
6. Pronunciation
7. Spooking/Sparking/Spinning
8. Be-laughing

We'll focus on the first three of these options.

Metaphor A *metaphor,* as we noted earlier, is the use of one term in the place of another. In Daly's theory of rhetoric, metaphors are used to "evoke action, movement" (Daly, 1984, p. 24). They also introduce a new logic, or a new way of using rhetoric to challenge the rhetorical system of the patriarchy. They allow users to "transform/transfer our perceptions of reality" and enable women to "break out of linguistic prisons" (Daly, 1984, p. 26).

Redefinition Another rhetorical option is *redefinition,* which is featured prominently in Daly's work. Daly believes in changing the meaning we have for oppressive words so that they can be used to liberate. For instance, the word "spinster" has usually had negative meanings for women. For Daly, the meaning of spinster is "a woman whose occupation is to spin" (p. 3). That is, a spinster is one who engages in the process of spinning, which we have said leads to freedom and liberation. So, instead of "spinster" being negative, "spinster" is redefined by Daly as a positive, liberating term. This is one example of how Daly reexamines rhetoric and proposes changing it to better serve the interests and needs of women.

Capitalization A final rhetorical technique used by Daly is selective capitalization of particular words that reinforce her meaning for them: "I capitalize Lesbian when the word is used in its woman-identified (correct) sense, but use the lower case when referring to the male-distorted version reflected in the media" (1978, p. 26). Additionally, the word "foreground" is not capitalized, but the word "Background," because it relates so directly to the Self, is capitalized. Daly's choices for

---

BOX 8.3   Internet Activity

Visit the website for *Glamour* magazine at http://www.glamour.com/. Using Daly's ideas of the foreground and background, identify some of the rhetorical techniques used at the *Glamour* site. Which foreground techniques are used? Which background techniques are used? Do you think the *Glamour* site liberates women or does it continue to oppress them?

---

capitalizing some words and not others relates to the way she evaluates those words.

Daly's reflexive and inventive use of rhetoric allows her to see how rhetoric can serve an emancipatory function for women. You'll see how to apply her theory to a website when you complete the Internet Activity for this chapter (Box 8.3).

SUMMARIZING GENDERED RHETORICAL THEORIES

We have surveyed a number of approaches to rhetoric and gender in this chapter. Although their theories may differ, the theorists here are united in identifying the relationships between rhetoric and oppression and rhetoric and liberation. Each seeks, in her own way, to highlight the importance of rhetoric in how men and women are socialized into gender roles. Let's summarize their views by returning to our key concepts.

Defining Rhetoric

The theorists in this chapter are not unified in defining rhetoric. For some, such as Campbell, rhetoric is public, intentional, and persuasive. Condit adds to this an emphasis on eloquence. For Campbell and Condit, rhetoric is an art that gifted rhetors use to move audiences to particular ends. Gearhart, however, sees this type of rhetoric as violence. You'll remember that she is concerned with the intent to persuade. Foss, Foss, and Griffin alert us to an invitational rhetoric that can be used to offer perspectives. Although persuasion may result, what is more important from their perspective is making audience members feel safe to question the rhetor's beliefs. Additionally, Foss and Foss believe that the private communication between women have serves a rhetorical function.

Rhetoric and Knowledge

Feminist rhetorical theory asserts that a more accurate perspective of the world is gained by including the experiences and voices of women in an account of rhetorical theory. Implicit in these theories is the assumption that epistemology and conceptions of truth are linked to the rhetoric we use to describe the world. Thus, men and women may have different conceptions of what is true because they have different rhetorical practices that cause them to see the world in different ways. However, these theorists disagree about where to start in creating a gendered epistemology. Some would look to differences between men and women, whereas others would focus on multiple genders. Fundamental to their theories, though, is a belief that knowledge is linked to gendered ways of experiencing the world.

Rhetoric and Identity

Likewise, these theorists see that ontology is linked to rhetoric and that men and women have different ways of experiencing reality. They recognize that there are masculine and feminine identities, not just masculine. Again, there is little agreement among these theorists about how to theorize a feminist identity.

Daly's theory is the most explicitly ontological. She views rhetoric as being intimately connected to how women see themselves and experience their worlds. As women are able increasingly to use rhetorical techniques of background, they become more liberated and free.

Rhetoric and Judgment

Despite the disagreement among feminist theorists about epistemic and ontological concerns, almost all agree that the goal of rhetoric should be to create a society in which all persons are seen and treated as equals. There is a strong ethical dimension to each of these theorists' work.

DISCUSSION QUESTIONS

1. What is your experience with gender? How does gender play a role in your life? Have you noticed different rhetorical styles between men and women?

2. How are your everyday communicative experiences rhetorical? To what extent does rhetoric pervade your day-to-day activities such as shopping, cooking, and relaxing?

3. Who are some examples of famous women rhetors today? What obstacles do they face? Find an example of a speech given by one of them and analyze it using feminine style. Was the speech effective? Why or why not?

4. How do you view the intent to persuade? Can you think of an example when you have been offended by someone's intent to persuade you? Why was the event offensive?

5. From your own experience, cite an example of when you used invitational rhetoric. Describe the experience. Were you successful? Why or why not?

6. Find an example of a recent speech by a woman. Using what we have discussed of the gender diversity perspective, analyze the speech. How was gendered constructed by the speaker? What stylistic techniques were used by the speaker? Was the speaker effective? Were there any techniques used by the speaker that were particularly unique to that speaker? What? How successfully did the speaker use those techniques?

GLOSSARY TERMS

gender   How we conceive of ourselves as masculine or feminine.

sex   A biological trait.

feminism   A concern for the legal, economic, and political equality of women.

feminine style   A rhetorical style that uses narratives, examples, and analogies and that seeks to create a personal relationship with the audience.

invitational rhetoric   A way of using rhetoric that invites understanding by creating a relationship with the audience based on equality, value, and self-determination.

gender diversity perspective   A perspective on rhetoric that recognizes the values of feminism while at the same time appreciating human eloquence.

foreground   The rhetorical practices that oppress women.

background   Rhetorical practices that can empower women.

9

Non-Western
Rhetorical Theories

Learning Objectives

After reading this chapter, you should be able to:

1. Identify various ways of thinking about culture and components of culture.
2. Describe ways that rhetoric is related to culture.
3. Identify key components of an African model of culture.
4. Identify various forms of Chinese rhetoric and major Chinese theorists.
5. Describe the uses of rhetoric and its limitations in confrontational settings for Native Americans.

Hip-hop is a popular genre of music today. Music sales, clothing styles, and linguistic practices are all evidence of its popularity. Because we have broadened our definition of what constitutes rhetoric, you probably realize that we could view various hip-hop texts, such as music or movies, as rhetoric and can imagine the various ways we could study them. In particular, you might be interested in addressing how these texts communicate power and ideology. In this chapter, we'll discuss another way to study rhetorical texts: through the perspective of culture. In fact, we'll use those of the rapper Nelly to illustrate this approach later in this chapter.

In the previous chapter, we explored some alternative theories and practices of rhetoric, specifically those of women. In this chapter, we focus on rhetoric and theory produced by members of various racial or ethnic cultures. At the same time that Plato and Aristotle began to systematically study and teach about rhetoric in their culture, people were using rhetoric and theorizing about its effect in other cultures in different parts of the world. The history and account of these alternatives theories has largely been obscured, at least in Western approaches to rhetoric.

CULTURE-CENTERED RHETORICAL THEORY

Before examining rhetorical theory from the perspective of culture, let's briefly survey the nature of culture and its key components.

Defining Culture

Culture refers to two different, but related concepts. In one sense, it refers to the certain types of products produced by people in a particular society (Williams, 1977). These products include art, literature, television shows, films, and architecture. Culture also refers to the "whole ways of life" of a society (Williams, 1977). Culture is, in this case, the "active process of generating and circulating meanings and pleasures within a social system" (Fiske, 1989, p. 23). This sense of the word includes the beliefs, norms, and values developed by a group of people in response to the demands of their day-to-day existence. Laws, educational systems, and ways of believing operationalize these beliefs and values. Brummett (1994) combines these two meanings by claiming that cultures are complex organizations of beliefs, values, and practices. Cultures are made up of "food, clothing styles, ways of walking and sitting, architecture, forms of entertainment, sayings and expressions, moral and ethical norms, religious practices, and other artifacts" (Brummett, 1994, p. 22). In short, culture refers to the process by which meanings are created in a society of people as well as the products of this process.

Rhetoric and Culture

We have seen throughout this text that rhetoric is related to culture. In Chapter 2, we saw that one type of rhetoric grew out of the specific and unique cultural beliefs, values, attitudes, and behaviors of the Greek and Roman cultures. In Chapters 3 and 4, we saw how rhetoric responded to changing cultural beliefs and values regarding religion and science. Chapters 5, 6, and 7 demonstrated that the new industrial age created new demands for rhetoric to address ideology, alienation, and human cooperation. In future chapters, we'll explore further the relationship between rhetoric and culture. Here, as we have noted, we will examine the relationship of rhetoric to non-Western cultures, including African, Chinese, and Native American.

Benson (1998) has posed a question that will help guide our discussion: "Is rhetoric a universal discipline, present in every culture and time, or is it a unique, historically situated invention that appeared in Greece and worked its way into a fitful relation with Western culture?" (p. ix). For the most part, we'll find that rhetoric is a universal discipline used in cultures throughout the world but that its forms and purposes are different from those we have discussed previously.

For instance, Garrett (1993) claims that Chinese culture is "one of the handful of instances of a mature civilization developing a sophisticated practice of argumentation unrelated to the Greco-Roman tradition" (p. 105). She elaborates on the significance of such a practice: "Such cultures are of special value in illustrating how argumentation and theories of argumentation may develop in a variety of linguistic, social, political, and cultural contexts" (p. 105).

Not only does rhetoric respond to and is developed because of specific cultural practices, but rhetoric has a reciprocal relationship with culture. Rhetoric shapes culture, reinforcing particular beliefs, values, and behaviors within it. The use of Greco-Roman rhetoric in Western democracies, for instance, privileges and emphasizes the values of freedom of speech, debate, and majority rule. But in a culture where group needs take priority over those of the individual, freedom of an individual's speech may be less crucial rhetorically than negotiated agreement. Likewise, as we have learned, rhetorical practices are often hegemonic, perpetuating particular ideological positions within a culture.

Culture-Centered Criticism

We should briefly comment on the critical implications of culturally based rhetorical theory. Throughout this text, we have referred to rhetorical criticism as a method of using rhetorical theory to understand and critique rhetorical practice. In this chapter, we discuss culture-centered criticism as a method of analyzing rhetoric from the perspective of the culture that produced the rhetoric. Thus, using a Western-centered rhetorical theory, such as Aristotle's ethos, pathos, and logos or Burke's pentad, *may* lead to skewed and unreliable results. In the final part of this chapter, for instance, we'll look at how judgments of Native American rhetoric often fail to take into account the actual purpose of the culture's rhetorical practices. When measured against the wrong yardstick, rhetorical criticism fails to offer insight into the interplay of rhetoric and culture. We'll discuss here some alternative methods that may be more suitable for rhetoric produced by members of non-Western cultures.

Like the feminist theorists in the previous chapter, the theorists we are going to study believe that by engaging in theory building and criticism based on alternative cultural perspectives, we can better understand other cultures. The members of those cultures will be empowered, it is thought, because their rhetoric will be understood on their own terms. Thus, many of the theorists in this chapter have a political agenda for their work that's not unlike those we met in the previous two chapters. We'll begin our discussion by looking at a popular theory of African-centered rhetorical theory, Afrocentricity.

AFROCENTRIC RHETORICAL THEORIES

A great deal of recent thinking about African rhetoric has been centered around the term **Afrocentricity**. This term, made popular by Temple University professor Molefi Asante (1987), refers to placing African culture and experiences at the center of one's critical and theoretical perspective. According to Asante, "The crystallization of this critical perspective I have named Afrocentricity, which means, literally, placing African ideals at the center of any analysis that involves African culture and behavior" (1987, p. 6). Asante goes on to explain that "The Afrocentric analysis re-establishes the centrality of the ancient Kemetic (Egyptian) civilization and the Nile Valley cultural complex as points of reference for an African perspective in much the same way as Greece and Rome serve as reference points for the European world" (1987, p. 9). It is important, argues Asante, that "any interpretation of African culture must begin at once to dispense with the notion that, in all things, Europe is teacher and Africa is pupil. This is the central point of my argument" (1987, p. 59). By placing African customs, traditions, and rhetorical principles at the center of a rhetorical theory, Asante hopes to empower African people and liberate the voices of African orators. In essence, Afrocentricity suggests that critics may study African rhetoric by looking at how rhetors seek to achieve African values such as harmony and balance. You can read more about Asante and Afrocentricity by accessing his website at http://www. asante.net/.

Defining Rhetoric

Rhetoric, according to Asante, is "the productive thrust of language into the unknown in an attempt to create harmony and balance in the midst of disharmony and indecision" (1987, p. 35). This definition highlights several key concepts that we will discuss in greater detail later. First, rhetoric is thought to address topics about which the truth is not known. We use rhetoric to arrive at truth. Second, Afrocentric rhetoric addresses harmony and balance. The African rhetor attempts to create harmony where there is disharmony; order where there is disorder. In fact, the unique style of African oratory includes the creative efforts of both the speaker and the audience to ensure that harmony is created in the rhetorical situation. However, as Asante has explained, rhetoric is, at least in part, the product of a skillful rhetor. He wrote, "In this sense, rhetoric is not a science; it is an art. That is to say, a certain inventive skill is needed in managing words and sentences to be effective as a communicator" (1987, p. 35).

Let's briefly examine how Martin Luther King Jr.'s "I Have a Dream Speech" exemplifies an African approach to rhetoric. King's purpose clearly fits with that of Afrocentric rhetoric. He sought to create harmony where there was disharmony and bring justice to the nation's African Americans. King used his speech to question the truth of the time: that segregation was natural and necessary. He offered a competing view of truth and invited his audience, and the public at large, to join in his view of reality. A skillful rhetor, King clearly involved his audience. Through the pacing of his speech and the rhythm he created with his voice, the audience applauded, shouted its approval at times, and was clearly moved at the end of the speech. Audience response to the speech is a sign that King was effective. You can read and hear selections from King's speeches at the King Papers Project at Stanford University. The website is located at http://www.stanford.edu/ group/King/.

Table 9.1 Components of African Rhetoric

Factor	Definition	Techniques
Frame of mind	The speaker's and audience's social, creative, and psychological influences.	*Rhythm*: To create a relationship with the audience. *Styling:* To convey status or create identification between speaker and audience
Context	Social realities and constraints of the rhetorical event, including slavery and discrimination.	
Linguistic code	Historical methods of conveying information.	*Lyrical quality*: Narrative quality of rhetoric and musical attitude of the speaker. *Vocal artifact*: Using the voice as a communicative medium. *Indirection*: Circular style of speaking that avoids directness.
Delivery	Performance where audience is invited to participate.	

Theorizing African Rhetoric

Asante identified four factors to consider in the construction of an Afrocentric rhetorical theory: frame of mind, context, structure of code, and delivery of message (see Table 9.1). Initially, Asante explained that rhetoric is related to its users' social, creative, and psychological factors. The *frame of mind* of African rhetors and audience members is reflected by the rhythm and styling of African speakers. *Rhythm* refers to how well the speaker can regulate the flow of words by using pauses. This capacity may seem to relate to rhetorical delivery, but, according to Asante, rhythm is an essential skill used by the speaker to create a relationship with the audience. By using pauses and rhythm, the speaker is able to "keep" the audience and allow the audience to define the boundaries for the rhetorical event. Thus, the use of rhythm influences the frame of mind of both the speaker and audience member.

Likewise, **styling** reflects the frame of mind of African rhetors and audiences. Asante defines styling as "the conscious or unconscious manipulation of language or mannerisms to influence favorably the hearers of a message" (1987, p. 39). Styling relates in two ways to the frame of mind of the speaker and audience. Various forms of visual styling, such as clothing or gesture, can give the speaker an elevated status in the eyes of the audience. Additionally, varying the pronunciation of certain words or giving emphasis to particular words creates a bond between speaker and audience. The chorus to the rap song "Nellyville" (see www.sing365.com) includes styling.[*]

[*]All lyrics from "Nellyville," by Haynes Cornell and Yaghnam Waiel, are reprinted with permission. © 2002 BMG Songs, Inc. (ASCAP)/Jackie Frost Music, Inc. (ASCAP). All rights for the US on behalf of Jackie Frost Music, Inc. (ASCAP) administered by BMG Songs, Inc. (ASCAP).

Nelly, the rapper, emphasizes words in particular ways in order to connect with his audience:

> There's no . . . way . . . I . . . I could explaiiiiin . . .
> the way I feel right now
> There's no . . . way . . . I . . . I could explaiiiiin . . .
> the way I feel about livin in Nellyville

Though it's difficult to capture the full impact of this technique in written form, listening to the song reinforces the style of Nelly's delivery.

Asante offers another example from a speech:

> In an education meeting at a university, where a young speaker gave his view of education, he began by saying "Education is for the C-O-M-M-U-N-I-T-Y. I mean com-mu-ni-ty." He was styling, and every person familiar with the "tradition" knew that the speaker had seized upon this stylistic device to have an impact. Between the speaker and the audience was an authentic bond, created by the spoken word. (1987, p. 40)

The second aspect of an Afrocentric rhetorical theory is the *context* of the rhetorical event. Asante asks two questions about context: "What are the social realities governing the development of black language? And what are the constraints upon black speakers against creating new rhetorics?" (1987, p. 40). Both history and the current situation influence the context in which Afrocentric rhetoric is used. Asante notes, "Black language and communication are framed by characteristic practices that are products of a special experience, environment, and heritage" (1987, p. 43). In other words, black rhetoric is shaped by experiences of slavery, segregation, and discrimination. This is true not only of the African American experience in the United States, but also in places such as South Africa.

Context is an important part of the rap song "Nellyville." In describing a community far removed from the crime that blacks may experience, Nelly raps:

> Imagine blocks and blocks of no cocaine, blocks with no gunplay.
> Ain't nobody shot, so ain't no news that day.
> Ain't nobody snitchin, they refuse to say."

Audience plays an important role in determining the context of rhetoric. According to Asante, "Black audiences demand to hear certain expressions, to see certain things, and to enjoy certain kinds of humor" (1987, p. 41). Also, the same rhetorical techniques used by a black speaker with a black audience may not be as effective with a white audience.

A third consideration in developing a theory of African rhetoric is the *linguistic code* of the culture: "How ideas have been structured in the past dictates, to a large extent, how they will be structured in the future" (Asante, 1987, p. 43). African rhetoric has been shaped by three primary approaches to language: lyrical quality, vocal artifact, and indirection.

Lyrical quality refers to the narrative structure of African rhetoric as well as the musical attitude the speaker takes in delivering the rhetoric. A narrative organizational pattern means that the speaker tells a story, so to speak, in chronological fashion.

But the story also has poetic qualities to it, with rhythm, repetition, and other stylistic devices. The song "Nellyville" reflects this component of African rhetoric. The song starts with the words "Welcome to Nellyville," indicating that the song will resemble a story. As a piece of music, the song also has musical qualities.

Asante traces the lyrical attitude taken by African rhetors to the oral nature of traditional African culture. The lyrical quality of African rhetoric is reinforced by the call-and-response relationship the speaker has with the audience. Black audiences often give their approval to what the speaker is saying by calling out during the speech with words such as "Amen," "Preach the truth!" and "Yes, Lord." The oral tradition and the call-and-response practices have established the lyrical quality of African rhetoric.

The speaker also uses his or her voice in traditional ways that reflect the linguistic code of Afrocentric rhetoric. In Western rhetorical theory, we often distinguish between delivery and content. For African rhetoric, these aspects are unified. Asante explains that "in the African culture, voice is an instrument just as significant as the lexical items spoken. Some lexical items cannot be powerful until they are powerfully spoken by the orator" (1987, p. 48). Thus, what is said cannot be separated from how it is said. But the speaker must have the skill to know when to use intonation and tonal styling. Likewise, emotion is an important part of using the voice to achieve effective rhetoric. The rapper Nelly uses his voice to reflect particular emotions such as anger, indifference, and humor. The voice of the rapper is a key ingredient in how well he or she connects with the audience.

A third component of the linguistic code of African rhetoric is *indirection*. Western rhetoric teaches its users to be direct and to the point. Asante explains that the opposite is true of African rhetoric: "By 'stalking' the issues, the speaker demonstrates skill and arouses hearers' interest. The person who goes directly to the issues is said to have little imagination and even less flair for rhetorical style" (1987, p. 51). The style of indirection is one of deduction and enthymeme, and Asante points out that this is the style of rhetoric that was brought to America by Africans from Africa. Rap music is often characterized by indirection. Rappers frequently talk around an issue instead of directly confronting it. The audience for rap music is counted upon to make the connection between the song and their own lived experiences.

We have discussed the rhetorical attitude, context, and linguistic code of African rhetoric. The final aspect of an African rhetorical theory is *delivery*. Afrocentric rhetoric is viewed as a performance in which the audience is invited to participate by offering its approval of the speaker's message. We have previously discussed this as the call-and-response pattern. The speaker must use a speaking style to facilitate this kind of relationship. The rapper Nelly uses lyrics that involve the audience in his song "Nellyville," encouraging their participation with lines such as "now everybody say" and "help me out now."

Asante characterizes the African delivery style thus: "Our speakers generally prefer the extemporaneous mode of delivery, characterized by lively speaking and the coining of exact language at the moment of utterance" (1987, p. 54). As with jazz, Asante notes, the African style of speaking is one of improvisation. Rap music is another example of an art form that is highly improvisational. Rappers make up their songs and lyrics as they perform.

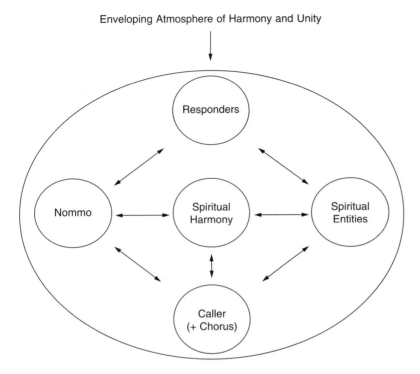

FIGURE 9.1 Model of Afrocentric Rhetoric.

A Model of African Rhetoric

A model of African rhetoric proposed by Knowles-Borishade (1991) exemplifies Afrocentricity and Asante's ideas about what is needed in a theory of African rhetoric. She confirms Asante's view of the necessity of an Afrocentric approach to African rhetoric, asserting, "Rhetorical standards emanate from ancient African traditions, such that the form, content, and dynamics of African-American oratory can be validly analyzed only within the parameters of African cultural ideals" (Knowles-Borishade, 1991, p. 488).[*] Additionally, "African orature is culturally idiosyncratic and does not conform to the Western style of speech-making. The understandings, assumptions, expectations, and symbolic meanings are drawn from the African belief system and traditions" (pp. 488–489). As a result, she explains, "African oratory has been erroneously held under the critical scrutiny of European rhetorical values. Such limited, provincial analyses are destined to arrive at distorted, pejorative conclusions because of the categorical cultural differences that exist between the two rhetorical styles" (p. 489). To counter the inaccurate view of African rhetoric, Knowles-Borishade has developed a model of African rhetoric that effectively demonstrates African rhetorical practice. See Figure 9.1 for a depiction of the various elements.

---

[*]All quotations from A. F. Knowles-Borishade (1991), "Paradigm for Classical African Orature: Instrument for a Scientific Revolution?," *Journal of Black Studies* 21(4):488–500, are reprinted with permission of Sage Publications, Inc.

Components

According to Knowles-Borishade, Western rhetoric contains three primary components, the speaker, speech, and audience, whereas African rhetoric consists of five components: caller-plus-chorus, spiritual entities, Nommo, responders, and spiritual harmony. You should not necessarily view these components as being part of linear model, as you would with speaker-speech-audience. Instead, the first four elements work together to achieve the final element, spiritual harmony. Let's look more closely at the five elements of this model of African rhetoric.

The Caller Like the Western speaker, the African caller is the primary creative element and initiates the rhetoric (Knowles-Borishade, 1991). The *caller* has high moral character and must be skilled in the art of oratory: "If classical artistry is to be attained, the Caller must become a poet-performer and direct her/his creative powers toward a higher level of consciousness by activating spiritual and psychic powers" (Knowles-Borishade, 1991, p. 491).

The caller enacts a ritualistic format at the beginning of the oratorical event by invoking spiritual entities. The oratorical event involves assumptions about the nature of the universe and human beings' place within the universe, beliefs about human's relationship to God, and beliefs about humans' relationship to each other. Through the caller, African oratory uses spiritual forces to achieve a higher consciousness. Knowles-Borishade explained, "As a spiritual force, the Caller is seen as having the ability to tap the cosmic forces for a higher truth by merging his/her vibratory forces with the rhythmic vibrations of the universal cosmic energy" (Knowles-Borishade, 1991, p. 491).

The spiritual and secular are combined in African rhetoric (Knowles-Borishade, 1991). Rhetorical events often begin with prayer, giving a sense of "depth and mystery to the occasion" (p. 493). Knowles-Borishade vividly explains the process by which the caller creates a spiritual environment for the rhetorical event:

> The Caller usually begins in a typical ritualistic fashion. First, having marshaled her/his psychic powers, the Caller often pauses to command a pregnant silence. S/he then breaks that static stillness to give birth to the Word through utterance. This beginning pause is highly symbolic in the act of creation. It represents the spiritual force of the human being who possesses the power literally to speak creation into being and to create order and harmony from chaos through the force of the spoken Word. (p. 493)

In addition to creating a spiritual environment for the rhetoric, the caller must elevate his or her status as a skilled rhetor. Voice, movement, and articulation are some of the means by which the caller demonstrates his or her rhetorical skill. Knowles-Borishade (1991) notes that artistry is an important element of rhetorical skill: "The artistic creation cannot be static in style, content, and function" (p. 493). Innovation is prized in artistry of the rhetoric.

The objective of the caller is to present solutions to the social and political problems of the audience. In particular, social justice, morality, and human welfare are often the subjects of African oratory. African morality, explains Knowles-Borishade, is grounded in a humanistic orientation. That which is good "brings dignity, respect, contentment, prosperity, joy" to humans (1991, p. 493).

The Chorus The second element of African rhetoric is the *chorus*. The chorus combines its voice with that of the caller to "bear witness to the truth of the Word" (Knowles-Borishade, 1991, p. 494). The chorus is a small group of audience members that contribute to the caller's message. They are the first to respond to the caller and even anticipate to some degree the caller's message. They will typically shout out "Amen" or "that's right" or "Go ahead on" while the caller is speaking. The chorus can be located in several physical locations, but often appears at the back or sides of the caller. Or, the chorus is located among the audience at large.

Spiritual Entities You may recall that the rhetorical event is initiated by the caller invoking spiritual entities. Knowles-Borishade (1991) notes that these may include the "creator God, lesser deities, angels, the Holy Spirit, ancestors, the (living) dead, and the (living) unborn" (p. 495). By invoking the names of spiritual entities, the caller creates a spiritual environment for the rhetoric and illustrates "the African belief in the existence, influence, and power of Spiritual Entities of various types" (p. 495).

Nommo The content of the rhetorical event is revealed through **Nommo,** which Knowles-Borishade (1991) defines as "the Word pregnant with value-meanings drawn from the African experience which, when uttered, give birth to unifying images that bind people together in an atmosphere of harmony and peace" (p. 495). In African rhetoric, the word, or nommo, refers not just to the force of particular words that are included in the speech but also to how those words sound to the audience. Words have particular sounds or rhythms. Or, to put it another way, words create particular kinds of vibrations. According to African beliefs, these vibrations are what allow listeners to experience the essence of that which is communicated. We have said that the content of African rhetoric is spiritual in nature. Thus, the vibrations of the caller's words bring the audience closer to spiritual harmony. Through the vibratory force of the words used by the speaker—the nommo—the audience is led to experience the Spirit. Knowles-Borishade notes, "Nommo activates Spirit through vibratory sound or vocal rhythms" (p. 496).

In essence, "the Caller takes on the role of human conduit who draws upon the Cosmic Energy of Spirit in the creative discursive act and effects change through the faculties and power of Nommo" (Knowles-Borishade, 1991, p. 497). Specific types of distinctively African words and phrases give rise to the most forceful vibrations. What is often referred to as "Black English" or "Ebonics," for instance, represent phonological, syntactic, and tonal patterns that "pierce the deepest structure of the African spirit and psyche" (p. 497).

The Responders The audience for the rhetorical event is referred to as the *responders,* according to this Afrocentric model of African rhetoric. In Western rhetoric, the audience is often thought to be passive, not playing a significant role in the rhetorical act. In African rhetoric, audience members are "secondary creators in the event, containing among them a vital part of the message" (Knowles-Borishade, 1991, p. 497). The responders sanction or reject the message based on the caller's character and rhetorical skill as well as the relevance of the message.

The responders voice their approval or rejection of the caller's message through a practice known *as call-and-response*. Keep in mind that the respondents are a larger group than the chorus (see earlier discussion) whose members, unlike the respondents, work in connection with the caller. Like the chorus, the respondents use their voices while the caller is speaking to reinforce, support, or reject what is said. The caller's message is thought to be tentative, depending on audience response. According to Knowles-Borishade (1991), "Call-and-response is more complex than merely a matter of group structure and reciprocal communications. As a process, call-and-response promotes levels of perfected social interaction through these verbal checks and balances as the event progresses" (p. 498).

Spiritual Harmony Spiritual harmony, as we noted earlier, is achieved through the interaction of the other four components. As Knowles-Borishade (1991) explains, "A new creation comes into being, with an attending mystical kind of joy, celebration, and sharing in Spirit" (p. 498). Harmony among those attending the event empowers them to act on the solutions offered by the caller. By implementing the solutions discussed, injustices may be corrected and order restored. The validity of the solutions, however, is considered secondary to considerations of harmony. If harmony is not achieved, solutions cannot be enacted. A speech that offers excellent solutions but does not move its audience would fail, according to the African model.

We can use Knowles-Borishade's model to analyze Illinois Senate candidate Barack Obama's keynote address at the 2004 Democratic National Convention. An Afrocentric analysis focuses on how Obama moved his audience to look beyond political differences to find national unity. Read about his speech in Box 9.1, Critical Insights.

Conclusion

Afrocentrism is the belief that African culture and ideals should be used to explore African rhetoric. We have seen that African people have a rich tradition of rhetoric that is dependent on the mutually creative and artistic powers of the caller and responders. The ultimate goal of African rhetoric is to create harmony where there is disharmony.

CHINESE THEORIES OF RHETORIC

A common perception is that Asian cultures do not have a rich rhetorical history. Numerous contemporary scholars, however, have uncovered evidence that Asian cultures, such as China, Japan, and India, do indeed have a rhetorical history to rival that of the Western cultures we have discussed. In fact, Lu (1998) claims, "Evidence uncovered during the course of my research, along with a few previous studies, strongly indicated that China possesses a rich rhetorical tradition. Moreoever, while retaining certain characteristics uniquely Chinese, Chinese rhetoric appears to share many striking similarities with the Greek rhetorical tradition" (1998, p. xi).* Lu's study is historical, but she explains that historical theories

---

*All quotations from X. Lu, *Rhetoric in Ancient China Fifth to Third Century B.C.E.*
(Columbia, SC: University of South Carolina Press, 1998) are reprinted with permission.

BOX 9.1   Critical Insights: Obama's 2004 Keynote Address

In his keynote address to the 2004 Democratic National Convention, Obama was the caller in the speech, using his high moral character and exceptional rhetorical skill to move the audience. Because many Americans did not know of Obama before the speech, he introduced himself by providing some personal background. The son of a black father from Kenya and a white mother from Kansas, his parents "imagined me going to the best schools in the land, even though they weren't rich, because in a generous America you don't have to be rich to achieve your potential." In the spirit of Afrocentric discourse, Obama invoked the presence of his deceased parents: "They're both passed away now. And yet, I know that, on this night, they look down on me with pride." By referring to his home state as the "Land of Lincoln," Obama also reminded his audience of one our nation's most popular presidents.

The chorus for the speech—those who anticipated Obama's remarks and supported his message—wasn't necessarily apparent to those watching the speech. Yet the Democratic Party leadership clearly gave their support to Obama in choosing him to give an important, prime time keynote address at the conference. Additionally, television cameras panned to key Democrats and African Americans in the audience, such as DNC Chair Terry McAuliffe and Jesse Jackson, who were clearly pleased with Obama's speech and its reception. Also on the stage were a group of delegates who applauded and offered their support for each of the speakers, including Obama. Finally, some audience members were given signs featuring Obama's name (see Figure 9.2). These supporters provided visual support for his message.

Obama's speech was rich with nommo. Although he did not rely on traditional African vernacular or phrasings, his words created imagery and they provided a powerful rhythm for his delivery. Nearly every paragraph of the speech used an image or creates rhetorical style. The speech was filled with repetition, alliteration, antithesis, and other rhetorical figures that we discussed in Chapter 2. Here are a couple of examples:

- *Antithesis:* "My parents shared not only an improbable love; they shared an abiding faith in the possibilities of this nation."
- *Repetition:* "If there's a child on the South Side of Chicago who can't read, that matters to me even if it's not my child. If there's a senior citizen somewhere. . . ."

Importantly, these rhetorical devices provided a cadence and rhythm to Obama's speech that allowed his voice to powerfully affect his listeners. Obama's voice echoed the verbal message. His delivery had energy, forcefulness, and sincerity.

The responders, including the thousands in the convention hall and the millions watching on television, were moved by the speech. Delegates in the convention hall applauded loudly when he finished. Commentators noted the success of his speech, and bloggers gave their endorsement as the speech was taking place.

The highlight of Obama's speech was his call for harmony and unity. In numerous ways, Obama called on Americans to unite and avoid a politics of division:"The pundits, like to slice and dice our country into red states and blue states; red states for Republicans and blue states for Democrats. But I've got news for them, too. We worship an awesome God in the blue states, and we don't like federal agents poking around our libraries in the red states." He repeatedly asked audience members to support John Kerry, the Democratic candidate, who Obama believed would allow the nation to "reclaim its promise."

Most critics of the speech agree that Obama was effective. From an Afrocentric perspective we might say that he achieved spiritual harmony. Obama's words, the audience response, and the political support he received following this speech are all evidence that he achieved harmony.

FIGURE 9.2   Barack Obama's 2004 Democratic National Convention Keynote Address.

of rhetoric in China influence the communication patterns that are used today. In this section, we'll survey her research about Chinese rhetorical theory, exploring briefly Chinese history and culture, various definitions of rhetoric and related activities, and some of the primary values and assumptions of Chinese rhetoric.

Chinese History and Culture

Lu (1998) has noted that as in Western cultures, Chinese culture developed particular needs for rhetoric, language, and discourse. To better understand the similarities and differences between the two cultures, let's look briefly at several important time periods in Chinese history.

The period between the Xia and Shang dynasties, approximately from the twenty-first to eleventh century B.C.E., was marked by the oral transmission of mythological legends and ritualistic communication (Lu, 1998, p. 6): "Ritualistic communication, often accompanied by music and performance, transmitted and perpetuated Chinese cultural values characterized by an emphasis on morality, order, and hierarchy" (Lu, 1998, p. 6). The Chinese of this period used rhetoric to pass along information and explain the nature of life and its meaning.

They also used rhetoric to communicate with the spiritual world, in the form of ancestor worship. Lu (1998) explains that "It was their belief that death imbued the departed with more spiritual power than they possessed while alive. By consulting with deceased ancestors for advice and asking for blessings and protection, the living were able to keep the lines of communication open" (p. 49). People during this time period also worshipped a supernatural being called *shang di,* or High God, who was thought to have feelings and purpose and controlled political affairs (Lu, 1998).

Communication with ancestors took the form of divination or poetry. Divination involved "burning bones to produce crack lines to be read and interpreted" (Lu, 1998, p. 51). The interpreter of the crack lines and the speaker at the divination ceremony was known as the *zhu guan.* This person was the medium for the spirits and possessed "well-developed oral and written communication skills and a facility for interpreting signs" (Lu, 1998, p. 51). Poetry was another form of communication at ceremonies of divination and ancestor worship. These poems, some of which have been recorded, were "carefully crafted by highly educated diviners or religious seers" and illustrative of the aesthetic and moral consciousness of the Chinese people of this time period.

Persuasion also took place between officials and kings and between the rulers and the masses. Lu has identified this type of communication as political. Typically, the persuasive appeals that were used related to *tian ming,* or the "Mandate of Heaven." This form of rhetorical appeal was given as advice by the king's ministers and officials to the royalty. The officials would advise the king to "act virtuously toward his people, and perform properly at ceremonies of divination and ancestor worship" (Lu, 1998, p. 53). In one instance, a minister approached the king and warned him that king's luxurious lifestyle has offended Heaven and that the harvests would not be good until the king reformed his behaviors.

The next major time period in Chinese history is the Zhou dynasty, which lasted from the eleventh to sixth century B.C.E. Lu (1998) notes that an orderly society with an aristocratic rule class had been established by this time. Keep in mind that this time period is still prior to the time we discussed in the chapter about the Greeks. According to Lu, ancestor worship and divination were still practiced during this period, but that other forms of communication also took place.

In particular, the "Mandate of Heaven" was replaced by a human-based code of moral conduct:

> While still believing in the notion of Heavenly Mandate, they regarded the living king, referred to as tian zi (the Son of Heaven), rather than dead ancestors, as the ultimate rulers of human affairs. According to this view, the king would enact the Will of Heaven through his morally responsible actions. *De* (virtue) became the ultimate criterion for evaluating royal behavior, while *li* (rites) became important political and ideological means of control. (Lu, 1998, p. 55)

As a result, the type of rhetoric used became more moral and official, the poetry became more structured and refined, and formal speeches and official decrees became popular forms of political persuasion.

Lu (1998) notes that Chinese people were aware of the power of words and there arose an increasing demand for speeches, instead of oral poetry as the form of ritualistic and moral communication. Rulers gave speeches at public events that had emotional ethical, psychological and rational appeals. Famous speeches were also recorded for the first time. In fact, the book of Zhou Li (the Rites of Zhou) was developed to specify the rules and norms for political, official, and ritualistic speechmaking. As Lu has explained, "The essential purpose of Zhou Li was to regulate the thoughts and actions of the Zhou people by providing and enforcing certain prescribed rules of moral conduct and harmonious relations in social, official, and family life" (p. 59).

The final period of Chinese history we'll examine is that of the Spring-Autumn and Warring States Period, which lasted from the sixth century to the third century B.C.E. We are now discussing the era of Aristotle, Plato, and Isocrates of Greece. During this time period, the order that had characterized China started to unravel. The lower-middle class became more upwardly mobile, there were wars between the autonomous states of China, and the cultural values of the Zhou dynasty were in crisis (Lu, 1998). As a result, "Power struggles among the individual states and military expediency demanded skilled advisers and political consultants" (Lu, 1998, p. 6). Consequently, a more highly refined form of rhetoric was developed and used to communicate between political consultants and rulers. In addition, Chinese society was more open and free than it had been previously.

During this period persuasion characterized rhetorical practice in politics, education, and philosophy. First, in politics, the king's advisers used persuasion to get him to adopt particular policies. Second, in education, persuasion was used to teach students using a lecture and discussion method. Because it was thought that individuals could improve their social standing, students began to engage in systematic instruction to learn how to be effective in rhetoric and other disciplines. Third, in philosophy, persuasion was used to decide moral, political, and epistemological issues. At the time, there were various schools of philosophical thought, which engaged each other in debates, using a form of rhetoric.

Defining Rhetoric

Understanding some of the cultural uses of rhetoric in ancient China, we can now look more closely at the various types of rhetoric used in this culture. In attempting to define rhetoric in much of our discussion in this book, we have, for the most part, treated the term as if it had one meaning that didn't vary in usage or according to culture. In Chinese culture however, multiple terms describe various aspects of rhetoric. As Lu explains, "There is, in fact, no single unified signifier, equivalent to the term rhetoric, in Chinese texts. This does not mean, however, that rhetoric did not exist in ancient China. In fact, the ancient Chinese had a well-developed sense of the power and impact of language in their social, political, and individual lives" (1998, p. 3). Instead, a series of words were used to refer to terms related to rhetoric and its functions. We'll briefly discuss some of these terms and their meanings and uses. You'll note that some of these terms seem to overlap in their meaning with other terms. Without the proper context for these terms, it may be difficult to understand how they referred to specific, distinct activities. This discussion will give you an idea of the type of actions the Chinese thought rhetoric to perform. Table 9.2 summarizes the various definitions.

Table 9.2 Chinese Terminology

LITERARY/POPULAR MEANINGS				PHILOSOPHICAL/THEORETICAL MEANINGS	
Yan	**Ci**	**Jian**	**Shuo/shui**	**Ming**	**Bian**
Act of using oral language or speech; also, a particular speech or oration	Eloquent or elegant speech	Advisory speech to the king that was ethical in nature	Advisory speech to the king that was practical in nature; explanations, ideas, or thoughts	Naming correctly, symbol use	Argumentation, classification, or distinguishing

Yan   The word *yan* is used to refer to oral speech and language. In earlier periods of Chinese history, the word was added to poems so that they appeared more musical. The sound of the word was pleasing to its listeners. Later, during the Zhou dynasty, the word had a more formal meaning of "to speak or to use language" (Lu, 1998, p. 73). It could be used as both a noun and a verb. The word also took on increasing importance and was transformed to mean a talk or a speech, such as a political speech. This shift in meaning, according to Lu, parallels the shift in importance given to speaking, or rhetoric, in Chinese culture. Where it once it was purely aesthetic, speech later became an important political tool. Later, the word *yan* would refer to a threat to authority. In more modern times, yan would refer to the philosophical "field of moral and dialectical inquiry" (Lu, p. 77).

Ci   The next term related to rhetoric in Chinese is *ci*. Today, noted Lu, the word is the equivalent of rhetoric, but an historical analysis of this word's use provides us with additional insight about how the Chinese people have used rhetoric. Historically, *ci* referred to "eloquence and embellishment of written and spoken words, or as a mode of speech used for artistic effect" (Lu, 1998, p. 77). *Ci* has also been used negatively, to mean excessive speech, quibbling speech, or twisted speech (p. 78). This meaning of rhetoric is similar to how the term is often used today to refer to speech that is full of ornamentation, but lacks substance. Lu summarizes the meaning of *ci*: "In practical terms, *ci* is revealed through a fluency in reciting and improvising poems, in citing the classics, and in manipulating stylistic devices" (p. 78).

Jian   *Jian* is a word used to describe political speech that was used for gaining power or self-defense (Lu, 1998, p. 78). This type of rhetoric was used for the advising or persuading of kings by subordinates. Lu explains the nature of *jian* as follows:

> The activity of *jian* (advising, persuading) prescribed a dominant–subordinate relationship between the audience (the ruler) and the speaker. The determining factor for persuasion to take place was not the persuasive ability of the speaker, but rather the moral integrity of the ruler. In other words, if the ruler choose not to be persuaded, there was nothing but his own moral integrity requiring him to do otherwise, since sanctions could not be imposed. (p. 79)

Thus, the rhetor's skill was not a factor in whether he or she was successfully in using *jian*.

Shui/Shuo Our next two terms, *shui* and *shuo,* share the same character in the Chinese language. When pronounced as *shui* ("shwee"), the term was used synonymously with *jian.* Both were used to persuade the king about some type of political matter. But the two terms differed in several respects, according to Lu (1998). For instance, *shui* used the persuasive technique of listing the advantages and disadvantages of a particular action; *jian* relied primarily on doing what is morally correct. Shui relied on practical reasoning; *jian* on ethical appeals. *Shui* was used to provide the king with a practical plan to achieve some of goal. The users of *shui,* called *you shui,* often worked with several kings at one time and were not as committed to a single king as were the users of *jian,* called *jian yi da fu.* When pronounced as *shuo,* this character referred to "an idea, a thought, an expression, and an explanation" (Lu, 1998, p. 81).

Often found in ancient literary texts, the terms *yan, ci, jian,* and *shui/shuo* are still used today, retaining much of the same meanings we have discussed. The fact that these terms appear in literary texts—and not philosophical texts—indicates that they were not employed in a systematic, reflective, or contemplative sense. They were used instead to refer to everyday kinds of experiences. As the Chinese began to study rhetoric more systematically and philosophically, two additional terms were developed, *ming* and *bian.* These terms were used in philosophical texts to more fully theorize the use of rhetoric in Chinese culture.

Ming Often found in philosophical texts, the term *ming,* in social and epistemological contexts, referred to the correct naming of objects or people. When used to give titles to people, the term made clear the hierarchy that ordered the society. For Confucius, *ming* allowed the culture to operate properly. For other philosophers, such as Laozi, *ming* revealed the arbitrary and symbolic nature of society. Lu explains that "While Confucius recognized the power of ming in shaping human behavior and political structure, Laozi perceived the limitation of ming in preventing humans from seeing the totality of truth" (1998, p. 83). In fact, a philosophical school of thought, Mingjia, would emerge in China to debate the relationship between naming and understanding the nature of the universe. Later, *ming* would become a method of inquiry into issues of epistemology and ontology.

Bian The next term we'll discuss, *bian,* relates to argumentation. *Bian shi* were advisers to the king who helped to define and classify concepts and ideas. Their type of speech was called *bian.* Lu (1998) explains, "In a sense, bian was a rudimentary expression of a Chinese rational process of reasoning, although the ancient Chinese did not provide an explicit map of the thinking process" (p. 85). *Bian* would later refer to moral, rational, and artistic aspects of speech and argumentation as well. *Bian,* noted Lu, is still widely used in China to refer to argumentation, whereas *ming*'s usage has faded.

Major Theorists and Schools of Thought

With a better understanding of several key forms, or styles, of rhetoric and how they have been used in the Chinese culture, let's focus on two of the key theorists and their schools of thought.

Mingjia The School of Mingjia was founded by Deng Xi (546–501 B.C.E.) and Confucius (552–479 B.C.E.). These thinkers lived at approximately the same time as Plato and Aristotle. The primary interest of the Mingjia was "the function of language in political settings as well as in rational thinking" (Lu, 1998, p. 128). Some of the central ideas to come from the Minjia with respect to rhetoric include:

- *Adapting to one's audience.* According to Deng Xi, it was necessary for a rhetor to use three strategies when speaking to an audience: observing the situation, understanding different perspectives, and learning all the wisdom of the world (Lu, 1998, p. 133).

- *Metaphorical and analogical reasoning.* Another Minjian, Hui Shi, made great use of metaphors and analogies in reasoning. He saw these techniques as ways of learning.

- *Names and reality.* As we have suggested, the Mingjia school of philosophy was interested in the process of naming. They realized that names did not equal the real world they represented (Lu, 1998, p. 145). Like the general semanticists (see Chapter 5), the Mingjia saw inherent fallacies in naming.

Confucianism Founded by Confucius, the school of Confucianism provided a humanistic account of moral and political uses of rhetoric. The three main philosophers of this school include Confucius (551–479 B.C.E.), Mencius (390–305 B.C.E.) and Xunzi (298–238 B.C.E.). Confucianism was such a powerful philosophical perspective that it was institutionalized by emperor Han Wu (156–87 B.C.E.) and became an official philosophy and state ideology for China until the middle part of the nineteenth Century (Lu, 1998, p. 154). Some of the major rhetorical contributions of Confucianism include:

- *Correct naming.* Confucius believed that the improper use of naming resulted in social disorder. He sought to find the perfect name for each object, idea, or person. According to Lu (1998), the goal of rhetoric, for Confucius, was "to regulate the public order by ensuring that everyone knew his/her place and acted accordingly" (p. 161). Confucius used many definitions in his own rhetoric so that the naming process was clear.

- *Virtuous speaking.* Confucius believed that a virtuous person would be an eloquent speaker. He developed nine standards by which virtue could be judged, including modesty, honesty, and temperance. According to Lu (1998), Confucius "was primarily concerned with the speaker's moral character, which determines the intention and effect of a speech as opposed to its presentation and delivery" (p. 164). Mencius, too, believed a speaker's words revealed his or her morals.

- *Complete view of argumentation.* Lu notes that the Confucian philosopher Xunzi "was perhaps the first Chinese philosopher to offer a complete system of Chinese persuasion and argumentation" (1998, p. 191). He identified three uses for bian: to explain right from wrong, to define proper names, and to defend ritual and moral principles.

To find out more about Confucius, see Box 9.2, Biography of a Theorist.

BOX 9.2   Biography of a Theorist: Confucius

Born in 551 B.C.E., Confucius was a Chinese philosopher who influenced many facets of Chinese life and culture, including how it practiced rhetoric. His birth name was Kong, which was later changed to Confucius by Jesuit missionaries. Later in life he held a series of public positions, but his views at the time were not widely held or respected. Leaders who went to him for advice were frequently persuaded not to do so. Confucius was known to be outspoken on subjects and this may have alienated other government officials.

Largely self-taught, Confucius was highly regarded as a teacher of many subjects, including rhetoric and morality. His view of education was that it should be practical, combining reading and thinking with actual experience. Confucius encouraged people to live according to certain values. He taught that they should have compassion toward others.

After his death, Confucius's teachings became much more popular. His students recorded many of his lectures and their conversations in what is known as the *Confucian Analects*. Additionally, his teachings were codified into a form of religion that became the official religion of China for many years. Although no longer officially recognized, Confucian principles maintain a strong footing in Chinese and East Asian cultures.

Key Concepts in Chinese Rhetoric

Having learned about the cultural influences on Chinese rhetoric and some of the specific ways in which speech, rhetoric, and argumentation have been used in China, we can now begin to summarize some of the key concepts in Chinese rhetoric and give some contemporary examples. Keep in mind that at various times, Chinese philosophers and theorists have had very different conceptions of rhetoric, its use, and its power. Thus, the general observations discussed here are not meant to suggest that Chinese rhetoric is monolithic. Rather, like Western rhetorical theory, Chinese theory is diverse and evolutionary.

Persuasion   Like many of the other cultural theories of rhetoric we have discussed, Chinese theory sought to achieve persuasive effects. Chinese theorists looked at a variety of contexts for persuasive rhetoric, such as that between king and adviser, king and subjects, or diviner and dead ancestors. Their guidelines for how to be persuasive were varied, including both aesthetic and rule-based standards. Even those theorists who saw the negative or dangerous side of rhetoric recognized its persuasive force (Lu, 1998, p. 294).

Emphasis on Morality   Chinese theorists believed that only moral rhetoric had ability to persuade others. Likewise, only a moral person could persuade others (Lu, 1998). Since the beginning of recorded history, Chinese rhetors have been concerned with using rhetoric for moral purposes. You'll recall that the "Mandate of Heaven" was used to persuade kings to act morally. Additionally, notes Lu (1998), Confucius, Mencius, and Mozi emphasized "moral/ethical persuasion for the purpose of maintaining peace and social order at the cultural level, and moral perfection at the individual level" (p. 290).

Emphasis on Epistemology   Throughout the text, we have explored how rhetoric has been used as a way of knowing. Chinese rhetoric has also been used for this purpose. Although not all Chinese theorists have focused on the relationship between rhetoric and epistemology, many have. In particular, the Mingjia school of thought focused on the relationship between names and the external reality names represented. This school explicitly questioned ideas about epistemology.

Dialectics   Chinese culture, including and apart from rhetoric, focuses on dialectics, or the juxtapositioning of seeming opposites. This idea is probably best expressed in terms of yin and yang, which are the two primary forces in Chinese philosophy. Importantly, Chinese culture looks for interplay and interrelatedness between things, objects, and ideas. The unity between opposing ideas can also be found in Chinese rhetorical theory. Lu notes that the dialectical view of Chinese rhetoric differs from Western ideas of rhetoric as war or battle: "The activity of bian, accordingly, was not polarizing; nor did it consist of imposing one's view on others. Instead, bian was a process for connecting and transcending apparent differences and polarized positions" (p. 292) or, to put it another way, "The purpose of ming bian was to embrace the whole by balancing and reconciling apparent opposites" (p. 300). In short, the Chinese view of rhetoric offers a "careful consideration of the subtlety and intricacy of human interactions" (p. 300).

Rationality   Lu (1998) contends that despite the view that Chinese rhetoric lacks a rational/logical basis, this system of rhetoric does have elements of rationality. She explains that "metaphorical and analogical thinking, though not logical by Western standards of rationality, is, in fact, 'logical' according to its own rhetorical standards. It is also a highly effective means of persuasion" (p. 290).

Conclusion

We have looked at the historical uses of rhetoric in China. According to Lu, many of these same principles apply in Chinese rhetoric today. For example, "Although Confucianism, considered synonymous with traditional Chinese culture, has been severely criticized since the beginning of this century and is no longer a state ideology, its cultural influence, along with the influence of other schools of thought and individual thinkers, is still make its presence felt in Chinese thought and communication" (Lu, 1998, p. 303). Additionally, other historical aspects of Chinese rhetoric can be found in the country's rhetoric today.

A CASE STUDY OF NATIVE
AMERICAN RHETORIC

In the final section of this chapter, we'll examine rhetoric from the Native American culture. One of the most influential rhetorical theorists to study Native American rhetoric is Randall Lake. We'll examine his work regarding Native American protest rhetoric presented in a 1983 issue of the *Quarterly Journal of Speech*.

This glimpse of Native American rhetoric will help us to see yet another way that culture and rhetoric intersect. Lake examined the Red Power movement of the 1960s and 1970s, which sought to "regenerate traditional Indian religious beliefs and to restore the ancient ways of life" (Lake, 1983, p. 129). Notably, the Red Power movement was involved in a 1972 occupation of the Bureau of Native American Affairs (BIA) headquarters and the 1973 siege at Wounded Knee, South Dakota. Among the leaders of the movement were Vernon and Clyde Bellecourt, Leonard Peltier, Dennis Banks, and Russell Means. The American Indian Movement (AIM) is perhaps the most visible organization associated with the Red Power movement.

Lake argues that whites have mistakenly viewed the goals of Native American protest rhetoric and the Red Power movement. He explains that "the judgments of failure so often leveled against Native American protest rhetoric are problematic because they misanalyze this rhetoric's primary audience" (1983, p. 128). Put simply, whites expect Native American protest rhetoric to be aimed at them, but instead, according to Lake, "Most Red Power rhetoric is directed at movement members and other Indians for purposes of gathering the like-minded" (p. 128). In short, Native American protest rhetoric serves a ritualistic function in keeping with Native American culture. White expectations of the rhetoric's effectiveness are based on a faulty perception of the rhetoric's goal, according to Lake. Let's examine his ideas more closely.

The Red Power Movement

Lake explains that to understand Native American protest rhetoric, one must first understand the nature of the Red Power movement. As stated previously, the goal of the movement is to restore Native American religious beliefs and ancient ways of life. Instead of assimilating with white culture, Red Power advocates seek to return to traditional tribal values (Lake, 1983, p. 129). Related to this goal are several demands of the Red Power movement. Lake explains that movement leaders desired that a viable land base be returned in accordance with treaties. Economically and spiritually, restoration of Native American lands is necessary for the native people, claims Lake. Additionally, Red Power advocates sought recognition of Indian tribes, restoration of traditional tribal government forms, and that the BIA be abolished, returning its duties to the appropriate tribes.

Rhetorical Constraints

Lake explains (1983) that Native Americans do not view rhetoric, or persuasion, in the same way that whites do. We'll discuss some of those differences in more detail later. As Lake summarizes, "the Red Power movement's ideology contains assumptions about the conditions under which its members speak, and thereby restricts the process of persuasion" (p. 133). For now, recognize that the Red Power advocates faced a difficult choice: if they used white methods of persuasion, they might effectively argue their point to white audiences, but they would fail to realize their goal of restoring Native American culture.

Specifically, Lake identified two restrictions on how Native Americans use rhetoric. First, neither humans nor language is considered a primary agency of change in

Native American culture. In white culture—as we have discussed at great detail throughout this book—rhetoric is seen as a way of moving people to new beliefs or actions. For Native Americans, firsthand experience is the way knowledge is created; knowledge is not created through symbolic exchange, according to Lake. Thus, it is difficult to persuade Native Americans of an idea; they must experience the idea in order to be persuaded. Second, Native American culture emphasizes the spoken word over the written word. In fact, Native Americans have mistrust for written words that can be altered, manipulated, and changed from their original meaning. As a result, notes Lake, "communication [with whites] is jeopardized because whites have destroyed the sanctity of the word" (p. 135). Additionally, rhetoric directed toward whites is thought to be seen as dangerous because the Native American culture could be corrupted by the "lies" of white culture (Lake, 1983, p. 135).

Power through Rhetoric

Given the cultural view that humans and language cannot bring about change, Native American culture turns to *Power,* or supernatural force, to explain the processes of nature and life. Anything that exhibits Power, such as the winds, rocks, animals, and water, are thought to possess it. Personal experience establishes for the individual Native American his or her source of Power. Lake explains that "The hunting tribes historically depended upon individual acquisition of Power via the dream or vision quest. In both, Power, incarnated in some animal, bird, or other being, appears to the individual and performs certain actions or creates certain images which become the means by which it may be recalled later" (1983, p. 136). The planting tribes de-emphasized personal experience and relied upon tribal ceremonies to reveal Power. In either case, "once Power is encountered, a link with the supernatural has been established which may be drawn upon in the natural world, through ceremonial reenactment, for the purposes of protecting, healing, ensuring a successful hunt or harvest, and so on (Lake, 1983, p. 136).

Rhetoric is used not to address other individuals, but to address Power. "Through ritual, through the proper recitation of songs, prayers and dance," Power is called upon (Lake, 1983, p. 136). Further, "the proper ritual, correctly performed, invokes the auspices of the supernatural, which then performs as bidden" (p. 136). Ritual language, Lake further explains, gives humans power over their world: "Without ritual language, humans are greatly reduced in stature and their control of the independently existent world around them is greatly impaired" (p. 137). Additionally, the rhetorical rituals of Native American cultures that have been passed down from generation to generation make use of traditional languages.

Lake argues that the symbolic actions of the Red Power movement in the 1970s involved occupations of sacred grounds, such as Wounded Knee, South Dakota (see Figure 9.3). Although sit-ins and occupations are typical social movement strategies, these tactics become more symbolic when they are conducted as part of the native ritual of invoking Power. As Lake explains, "The actions described achieve their purpose simply by being; they are, thus, ends in themselves for those who acknowledge the ritual dimension of symbolic acts" (p. 140). If nothing else, the acts helped the Native Americans feel that they were returning to their traditional way of life. Yet for the whites—who thought they were the sole audience

© Bettmann/CORBIS

FIGURE 9.3   Native American Activists at Wounded Knee in 1973.

for the protests—the Native American actions seemed comical, unbelievable, and, ultimately, ineffective rhetorical statements.

Conclusion

Lake's account of Native American protest rhetoric provides us a glimpse at the rhetorical practices of yet another culture. From this example, you can see the vast difference between European rhetorical practices and those of Native Americans. To apply what you have read about Native American rhetoric, complete the Internet Activity, Analyzing the American Indian Movement (Box 9.3).

SUMMARIZING ALTERNATIVE
RHETORICAL THEORIES

As we have seen in this chapter, there are very different conceptualizations of rhetorical theory and practice depending on the culture in which it occurs. In this chapter, we have examined African, Chinese, and Native American approaches

---

BOX 9.3 Internet Activity: Analyzing the American Indian Movement

The American Indian Movement (AIM) played a key role in the 1973 Wounded Knee controversy. Log on to the group's website at http://www.aimovement.org/ and think about the questions that follow. Who is the audience for the website? Why do you think so? How does the website attempt to restore Native American culture?

How does it seek to influence the dominant culture's view of Native Americans? How does the site feature the spoken as well as the written word? How does the site's rhetoric appeal to power? Is the website effective? Which standard do you think is most applicable in answering this question?

Table 9.3 Summarizing Rhetorical Theory

	African	**Chinese**	**Native American**
Definition	Rhetoric restores harmony where there is disharmony.	Rhetoric is contextually based.	Rhetoric is performed as part of rituals to invoke supernatural forces.
Rhetorical Knowledge	Arises through the interaction with the higher being and through caller-respondent interaction	In some situations, knowledge is produced through rhetorical interaction.	Is revealed through experience; distinct from rhetoric.
Identity	Through rhetoric humans achieve shared harmony.	Humans and rhetoric participate in the oneness of the universe.	Human agents use the agency of rhetoric to gain power.
Judgment	Revealed through rhetorical practice	Revealed through rhetorical practice	Revealed through experience.

to rhetoric. Each form of rhetoric has different ways of defining rhetoric and conceptualizing its intersection with knowledge, identity, and judgment. Refer to Table 9.3 for a summary of these views as we review our discussion in this chapter.

Defining Rhetoric

From the African perspective, rhetoric exists to create harmony where there is disharmony. The diversity of Chinese approaches to rhetoric precludes a common definition of the activity. In Chinese culture, rhetoric is practiced in a variety of contexts and for a variety of purposes. Native American culture sees rhetoric as part of traditional rituals that invoke supernatural forces.

Rhetoric and Knowledge

Knowledge is created in African culture through the caller's interaction with the higher being as well as with the caller's interaction with the respondents. Thus, the production of knowledge is a collaborative activity involving a variety of actors who interact with each other through rhetoric. In Chinese culture, rhetoric is thought to create knowledge in much the same way as it did in ancient Greek or Roman cultures. In Native American cultures, knowledge exists apart from human activity but is revealed to humans through experiences.

Rhetoric and Identity

African cultures seek to create communal identities through the creation of harmony in the rhetorical event. By inviting the respondents to share the views of the caller, the speaker and audience forge a distinct identity and way of relating to each other. In Asian cultures, identity is thought to be holistic, integrated, and implicit. Native American cultures view humans as the agents who use the agency of rhetoric to gain the power of the supernatural. Humans are thought to be dependent on the supernatural to have personal effectiveness.

Rhetoric and Judgment

Both African and Chinese cultures see judgment as arising through the practice of rhetoric. For Africans, the sharing of harmony is thought to have an ethical dimension, since it is channeled from the higher being. For the Chinese, judgment is always conscious of differences in status and the dead are often called upon to communicate judgment and give their blessing. In Native American cultures, judgment is revealed through experience. Humans become ethical when they respond to supernatural forces that make themselves known through experience.

DISCUSSION QUESTIONS

1. What are some similarities between African, Chinese, and Native American rhetoric? How do you account for those similarities? What are some differences? To what do you attribute these differences?

2. Compare and contrast the approaches to rhetoric in this chapter with those of ancient Greece and Rome, which we studied in the second and third chapters.

3. Name a speaker from your experience who seems to have an Afrocentric style of speaking? Is this style effective for the speaker? Why or why not?

4. Identify similarities between how the Chinese used rhetoric in their history with how people from the United States have historically used rhetoric. Identify some differences.

5. Locate examples of Native American rhetoric and assess Lake's ideas. Who is the audience for the rhetoric you have found? What is the goal of the rhetoric? What rhetorical strategies are used by the Native American speakers?

GLOSSARY TERMS

culture   The complete way of life of a people. Often used to denote distinctions based on race, ethnicity, or gender.

Afrocentricity   A philosophical and critical school of thought that places African ideals, traditions, and customs at the center of its way of thinking.

styling   The conscious or unconscious manipulation of language or mannerisms by a speaker to influence favorably the audience.

Nommo   The power of words to move audiences; includes the sounds that words make.

PART V

Fragments of Rhetoric

10

Rhetoric, Media, and Technology

Learning Objectives

After reading this chapter, you should be able to:

1. Identify the influence of media on culture and rhetoric.
2. Describe a style of verbal communication that is effective in mediated cultures.
3. Describe the basic premises of semiotics.
4. Explain how visual images produce meaning in viewers.

We are constantly surrounded by media and images. From the moment we awaken until we turn out the lights, we are bombarded by the sounds and sights of television, radio, magazines, billboard advertising, corporate logos, and other forms of rhetoric. The advent of television, in particular, ushered in a new way of communicating in our culture. Rhetorical theorists contend that images are replacing words as the primary form of rhetoric in our culture today. These changes in how rhetoric is practiced have made it necessary to re-examine our theories of rhetoric, revise them when necessary, and develop new theories to better explain the dominance of media and images on how we think about what is true, what is real, and what is ethical.

Our central argument in this chapter is that media have had a strong influence on the way rhetoric is practiced and on the theories that have been developed to explain rhetoric. We'll begin by surveying a brief history of media. Then, after examining the work of two theorists, Walter Ong and Marshall McLuhan, to understand how they see media and rhetoric, we'll study Kathleen Hall Jamieson's view of how verbal rhetoric is used within mediated cultures. Finally, we'll look specifically at the rhetoric of images.

NEW FORMS OF COMMUNICATION MEDIA

Our emphasis in this text has been largely focused on verbal communication. That is, we have discussed theories and uses of language and other discursive forms of rhetoric. In this chapter, we focus primarily on nondiscursive media and their impact on rhetoric. In other words, we'll look at the ways that printing and electronic media have influenced rhetorical practice and theory. We'll begin our discussion by surveying the historical development of these media.

Oral Communication

The oral medium, which relies exclusively on vocalizations and body movements to express thought and which connects source and receiver through face-to-face communication, was first used by *Homo sapiens* some 4–5 million years ago (Chesebro & Bertelson, 1996). Early communication by humans probably was limited to crude gestures and oral sounds that signified events and relationships that were immediately present in the communication context. It has only been in the past four thousand to five thousand years that humans have used oral languages as we now know them, to communicate (Chesebro & Bertelson, 1996). Researchers contend that changes in the brain and vocal system allowed humans to begin using what we might call words. Oral communication takes advantage of the immediate presence of speaker and listener to make sense of what is being discussed. In fact, it is impossible to isolate one aspect of the communication situation—speaker, message, and receiver—apart from their relationship to the other components. It is important to keep in mind that 700 million people around the world still rely primarily on the oral medium of communication (Chesebro & Bertelson, 1996).

Writing and Printing

Humans were forever changed when they first put their ideas in written form on paper, a development that took place three thousand years after they developed language. The first alphabet probably consisted of simplified Egyptian hieroglyphics, using the phonetic component of the system. The first complete alphabet is thought to be that of the ancient Greeks, which first appeared in 1500 B.C.E., well before the days of Plato and Aristotle. With an alphabet, communicators could now write their ideas down without having to depend on their memory or various memory devices to express their thoughts. Still, widespread dissemination of written communication was impossible because of the work it took to manually copy texts. It was not until the invention of the movable-type printing press in the mid-1440s that writing became a dominant form of communication:

between 1450 and 1500, the number of books in print surged from several thousand to more than 9 million (Chesebro & Bertelson, 1996).

Radio and Television

Electronic media—in the form of the radio—first appeared at the late part of the nineteenth century. There are several claims to the first successful transmission of radio signals, but most accounts place their occurrence in the period between 1892 and 1895. Early uses of radio included monitoring ships at sea to facilitate rescue attempts, if necessary. The first commercial radio station is often listed as KDKA in Pittsburgh, which began broadcasting in 1920. Today, 99 percent of Americans listen to the radio. Most historians credit Philo Farnsworth with the first successful transmission of video images in 1927. NBC is often credited with opening the first television station in 1932. Only a few people owned televisions until about 1950, when it is estimated there were 1 million sets in American households. By 1953, there were 20 million sets in the United States. Like radio, television soon became widespread. Nearly everyone in the United States watches television today.

The effects of electronic media such as radio and television have been profound. Electronic media unite audience members in new ways, exposing them, over vast distances, to the same images, news events, and entertainment programming. Television, in particular, has made visual images a constant part of our culture. The rhetorical theorists we will discuss in this chapter focus primarily on the influence of electronic media, and the television in particular, on rhetoric.

The Internet

Although the Internet was created in the 1960s, it was not until the 1990s that its use became widespread in our culture. Today, just about every company, university, and large organization has an Internet hookup. Perhaps you have a personal website yourself, and like many of your peers, you are used to interacting with others through e-mail, chat rooms, or videoconferencing. The Internet has united the rhetor and audience in new ways. It is an interactive medium that can be controlled by either the rhetor or the audience member(s). Rhetorical theorists are just beginning to address the ways that the Internet is shaping rhetoric.

MARSHALL McLUHAN

One of the first theorists to study the effect of media on how we communicate was the Canadian philosopher Marshall McLuhan. He studied how media influence the thought processes of media consumers. Specifically, he saw media as extensions of the human nervous system that allow us to experience the world in new ways. Although his ideas have not enjoyed wide acceptance, he does provide several important ideas for our discussion in this chapter. You can read more about McLuhan in Box 10.1.

BOX 10.1   Biography of a Theorist: Marshall McLuhan

Marshall McLuhan was a Canadian philosopher made famous by the phrase, "The medium is the message." He was born in Edmonton, Canada, in 1911. He received academic degrees from the University of Manitoba and Cambridge University. He received a doctorate from Cambridge University in 1942. He taught at several schools, including the University of Wisconsin, the University of St. Louis, Assumption College, and the University of Toronto. It was at the University of St. Louis that he was a professor to Walter Ong, who would become an influential theorist in this own right. McLuhan was also the Chair of the Ford Foundation Seminar on Culture and Communication. He also worked in the Office of Education in the United States consulting on educational television.

McLuhan's works were very popular during his lifetime, among academics and nonacademics alike. In fact, McLuhan's popularity landed him a cameo appearance in Woody Allen's film *Annie Hall*. His appearances on television shows and interviews in print publications were always provocative, some devotees even calling them mystical. His main works include *The Gutenberg Galaxy*, published in 1962; *The Making of Typographic Man*, of same year; *Understanding Media*, published in 1964; and *The Medium is the Massage*, which appeared in 1967. These books often contain pictures and cartoons and adopt a casual rather than academic style. Despite the controversial nature of his ideas, McLuhan remains one of the most prominent early-media theorists.

The Medium is the Message

McLuhan is perhaps best known for stating, "the medium is the message" (1964, p. 23). He explained, "This is merely to say that the personal and social consequences of any medium—that is, of any extension of ourselves—result from the new scale that is introduced to our affairs by each extension of ourselves, or by any new technology" (p. 23). McLuhan is saying that the medium used to transmit a message will affect how audience members perceive that message. In other words, the meaning of the message is dependent on the medium used to convey that message.

Think for a moment about your experience with media. You may watch the news on the television and read about the same news event in a newspaper or magazine. The real-time visual images conveyed by television affect how you think about that story in ways that the print medium cannot express. The meaning you get from television news is distinctively different than that from print news. Likewise, the meaning of a song listened to on a music video is different from that of the same song when listened to on a CD or radio. The medium is indeed the message, in these situations.

Not only do different media create different meanings for audience members, they also reshape and restructure human experience, wrote McLuhan: "The medium, or process, of our time—electric technology—is reshaping and restructuring patterns of social interdependence and every aspect of our personal life" (1967). McLuhan elaborated on this statement:

The alphabet, for instance, is a technology that is absorbed by the very young child in a completely unconscious manner, by osmosis so to speak. Words and the meaning of words predispose the child to think and act automatically in certain ways. The alphabet and print technology fostered and encouraged a fragmenting process, a process of specialism and of detachment. Electric technology fosters and encourages unification and involvement. It is impossible to understand social and cultural changes without a knowledge of the workings of media. (McLuhan, 1967)

Consider for a moment a simple example that illustrates his point.

You may take notes on lined notebook paper, as do many students. Lined paper is a communication technology that forces you—unconsciously, probably—to write notes in single lines, horizontally across the paper. This communication technology makes it very difficult to take notes in other ways, vertically, for instance. If you take notes on a computer in a word processing program, it is even more difficult to escape the straight-across-the page-form of writing. Importantly, this way of writing influences how you think about the notes you take. It may also influence how you think about your social and cultural environment. In American culture, for instance, we view time, history, and other events as linear. Other cultures, though, are more circular in their orientation to their experience.

In very simple terms, McLuhan believed that how we think and how we perceive the world are dependent on the communication media we use. In fact, he hypothesized that electronic media would one day unite all of us in a "global village." Thus, the rhetoric of a culture reflects the media of that culture. We'll return again to rhetoric more specifically in the next section when we discuss the work of one of McLuhan's students, Walter Ong. For now, let's look a bit more closely at McLuhan's view of media.

Media Types

McLuhan (1964) distinguished between hot and cool media. He explained that a hot medium "extends one single sense in 'high definition'" (p. 36). That is, the hot media are filled with data and do not require much participation from those who use them. A photograph, for instance, is an example of a hot medium, since it provides the necessary information needed to make sense of it. When you look at a photograph, you aren't as involved as you would be with a line sketch or cartoon, for instance. A cool medium requires that the audience member fill in information; it provides "a meager amount of information" and requires a high level of audience participation. A telephone is an example of a cool medium. When you talk on the phone, you have to fill in a lot of information. You have to guess about what the other person is expressing, for instance. See Table 10.1 for a list of other communication media and their classification, according to McLuhan. As you think about hot and cool media, keep in mind that these are general distinctions and that there is a range of "hotness" and "coolness" within each category.

You'll note that television is an example of a cool medium on the list in Table 10.1. That's because a television image contains thousands of tiny pixels that we must assemble into a meaningful image. Film is continuous and does not require the audience to participate in creating the image. In today's world of digital and high-definition television, however, McLuhan's distinction may seem a bit dated.

Table 10.1 Media Types According to McLuhan and Innis

Media	Definition	Effect	Examples
Hot Media	High-definition media that provide a great deal of information and require little involvement.	Space-binding: Allow the rapid spread of information; create individual isolation.	Photograph Radio Movie Seminar Paper
Cool Media	Low-defintion media that require a great deal of audience interaction to fill in the missing information.	Time-binding: Require close interaction and involvement; preserve history and rituals.	Hieroglyphics Telephone Television Lecture Cartoon Stone

SOURCE: McLuhan, 1964; Innis, 1951.

McLuhan's distinction between media types is important because it sought to explain the different types of effects each medium has on its users. McLuhan's ideas as we have discussed them echo in some ways those of his former teacher, Harold Innis. McLuhan and Innis are called *media determinists* because of the role they believed technology and communication played in the development of thought within cultures. Carey (1989) summarizes Innis's view of the relationship between communication, culture, and thought thus: "Innis argued that changes in communication technology affected culture by altering the structure of interests (the things thought about) by changing the character of symbols (the things thought with), and by changing the nature of community (the arena in which thought developed)" (p. 160). Let's discuss this statement further by tying together McLuhan's concepts of hot and cool media with Innis's ideas of "time-binding" and "space-binding media."

Innis introduced the ideas of time-binding and space-binding media to explain the impact of media on cultures. Time-binding media reinforce ritual, history, and the shared space of their users. McLuhan's cool media are time-binding. Consider a stone tablet in which certain laws may have been written. The tablet would be heavy, so moving it around would be difficult. It would also have to be read, requiring a reader and audience participation. The laws written on the tablet would reinforce order, structure, and permanence. In short, communication via the medium of a stone tablet was "cool"—requiring audience participation—and it focused on preserving and reinforcing history.

Space-binding media are more readily disseminated and can lead to the rapid spread of ideas. Paper is an example of space-binding media. With paper, multiple individuals can simultaneously read what has been written and they can do so from multiple locations. They do not have to be present to each other; in fact, they can isolate themselves from others as they read what has been written. Innis attributes the development of space-binding media with the rapid spread of the Roman empire. To summarize, communication via the "hot" medium of paper allows ideas to quickly spread across space.

Let's consider two ways that college students have registered for their classes. When I was in college, we had to physically go to a room on campus to register. We reviewed printouts of classes that were open, filled out a paper registration form, and waited in line to find out if we were able to get into the courses we wanted. If the course was full, you had to repeat the procedure until your schedule was complete. The process could easily take the entire afternoon, but we viewed the process as a rite of passage and enjoyed sharing stories about our difficulties. Importantly, though, the university used the opportunity to communicate with us about a variety of issues and we were forced to interact with live people during the process.

Today many universities use online or telephone registration. Students can log in from anywhere, instantly check to see which courses are available, click a button or two to register for the course, and receive instant feedback concerning whether the registration was successful. University officials have little ability to interact with the students, and the students do not interact with each other.

Although paper, as we have said, is a hot medium, it is not as hot as the Internet. Consequently, the paper method of class registration is time-binding. It requires that people be in physical contact with each other and allows for a great deal of communication to take place. Online registration is space-binding and does not allow for interaction or the passing on of rituals. There are many faculty at my school who attribute the ease of online registration with other attributes, such as high absentee rates in class and high rates of students who fail to complete a course. Innis and McLuhan provided us with a way to think about the effect of media such as those discussed here.

RHETORIC, CONSCIOUSNESS, AND CULTURE

McLuhan's student, Walter Ong, was a scholar who has written a great deal about the impact of a communication medium on its users and their culture. Like McLuhan's, a central argument in Ong's work is that each medium creates different ways of thinking, feeling, and states of awareness. That is, a medium alters the consciousness of its users. Ong, however, gives more attention to the specific type of communication used by the members of the different cultures. That is, he addressed in specific ways how rhetoric is practiced by people who are accustomed to using particular media.

Ong (1982) identifies three major types of media in the world's history: oral, written, and electronic. Ong contends that for a given culture, one form of communication will be dominant. Electronic media, specifically, television, dominate U.S. culture today.

Orality

According to Ong, the first type of culture is *orality,* which is based on oral communication: speaking and gesturing. It is a culture untouched by writing. There is no trace, no record, and no way of looking up what someone said or meant.

The speaker and audience must share together the moment of rhetoric, and once that moment has passed it can never be recaptured.

Ong (1982) claims that orality creates a certain kind of consciousness. He explains that people who communicate only via the oral medium must develop memory aids to help them recall complex thoughts. You probably learned some of these aids as you developed the ability to write. For example, the phrase, "i before e, except after c," helps you spell words such as "receive." Oral communicators are also less likely to use abstract thought and refer to larger categories of objects. For example, a hammer is only a hammer, it is not a "tool." Oral communicators usually refer only to the specific object that is present in time and space. Oral communication is also redundant; speakers constantly repeat themselves so that the audience understands their message. Finally, oral communicators have a close relationship to their audiences. In fact, oral communicators know their audiences, share certain characteristics with their listeners, and identify with them.

Literacy

Once communicators used written language, Ong says, their consciousness was forever altered. In literate cultures, the sender and the receiver of messages may be separated, and the context in which the message was initially created may not be readily apparent to the receiver of the message. As a result, the receiver cannot immediately question the sender of the message. Printed words are arranged in a linear fashion, providing for a different type of cognitive processing than in oral cultures. Written communication allowed the formation of such concepts as logic. The use of clichés, an important memory device used in oral cultures, is now a sign of shallow thought and expression. Thanks to writing, abstract thought is possible, and ideas can be grouped into categories, allowing for subordination of ideas. We can now understand the concept of a "tool" as referring to a set of objects including hammers, saws, and chisels. As you can see, using alphabets and printing presses creates a very different orientation to the world.

In literate societies, rhetors use evidence to support their claims, create logical relationships between their ideas, and call upon the audience's emotions. In the Chapter 2, we discussed Aristotle's theory of rhetoric, which describes, in detail, how rhetors create their messages. It is important to note that the society to which Aristotle belonged was only just beginning to use writing, but it did not yet have access to printing presses.

Electronic Media

Today, literacy, or the medium of writing, still exerts its influence on our consciousness. That is, we still tend to think in ways that resemble those of ancient, literate peoples. We cling to our traditional ideas about rhetoric, which includes evidence, reasoning, and organized thoughts. Yet, our consciousness more often reflects that of characsitics of the electronic media to which we are exposed. In our country, the medium of television dominates how we communicate and see the world. Throughout the world, however, only 3 percent of the world's people rely on electronic communication to the extent that we do in the United States (Chesebro & Bertelsen, 1996).

Just as spoken and written media changed the consciousness of the world's citizens, so too have electronic media. Electronic media reunite the sender and receiver, but in a way that is different from that in oral cultures. Ong (1982) explains that the electronic media create a *sense* of participation for receivers, but those listeners are still physically separated from the source. The receivers resemble the audiences of ancient times but are more numerous and more diverse in composition. Listeners have a great deal of control over the communication situation. We can easily change the television station when we want to watch something else, for instance. Information is decontextualized—it exists without history and background—and visual images are commonplace. Our written communication often looks less like writing and more like the electronic media that it imitates.

Electronic media also allow us to vicariously experience the events we see on television or the Internet. We have "real" experiences that aren't real. We experience the joys and sadness of those individuals who fill our media. This is true of real-life individuals as well as fictional characters. While watching the news, we may see a story about someone who has been victimized by crime. We feel empathy toward the individual and may be able to put ourselves in that person's position. We may also feel empathy toward a character on our favorite soap opera. In either case, electronic media allow us the sense that we are experiencing real events, when in fact we are not.

Walter Ong's ideas about rhetoric, media, and culture have influenced a great number of contemporary theorists. Following his death in 2003, a website was created to pay tribute to him. You can access the site at http://www.rememberingwalterong.com/. It contains a great number of tributes, pictures, and other information about Ong.

ELECTRONIC ELOQUENCE

The widespread use of the television has created a different environment for rhetors wishing to communicate with audiences. Whereas rhetors used to appear in person to large crowds of people, today rhetors are more likely to chat with us while we are seated in our living rooms, family rooms, bedrooms, or even bathrooms. As a result, the style of language used by rhetors has changed. Today, rhetors communicate with a more intimate style, one more characteristic of the personal, informal, and intimate medium of television (Figure 10.1). This rhetorical style, which Kathleen Jamieson (1988) has called **electronic eloquence,** has, according to Jamieson, five characteristics: it is personalized, self-disclosive, conversational, synoptic, and visually dramatic.

Jamieson (1988) notes that the intimate style of today resembles a style of oratory traditionally used by females. She explains that men use language as an instrument to accomplish goals, whereas women see it is a means of establishing relationships by expressing internal states. Language used in this manner is primed

FIGURE 10.1   The introduction of the television to the homes of America greatly changed rhetorical theory and practice. The intimate environment created by this medium meant that rhetors had to use electronic eloquence if they were to be effective.

to establish emotional connections with audience members. When communicating to audience members in the privacy of their living rooms, establishing relationships takes precedence over verbal sparring. Let's look more closely at the ways rhetors can develop an intimate discourse with their audiences.

Personalization

Building intimacy with an audience is accomplished by using an individual to embody, or represent, the ideas of the rhetor's message. When rhetors tell stories of individual courage, for instance, they are personalizing the values of courage and bravery. They also create a relationship with the audience because the audience sees the rhetor as caring about the their individual needs and values. John Kerry, 2004 Democratic presidential candidate, used personalization in a December 14, 2003 speech in Cedar Rapids, Iowa:

> I met Myrtle Walck in Council Bluffs. Myrtle's worked all her life, but at
> 82-years-old she's not finished giving to her country. Myrtle volunteers at a
> local school each week, teaching kids how to read. And what has her country

given her? A $400 monthly Social Security check that just barely covers her two daily prescriptions. I believe Myrtle Walck deserves someone on her side fighting for her.

I met Bob Anderson in Waterloo. Bob's a part of this so-called "jobless recovery" President Bush now brags about—he was laid off about ten months ago from Iowa Concrete. Now Bob's wife was just diagnosed with a chronic illness and their health insurance has run out. I believe Bob Anderson deserves someone on his side fighting for him.

And I met Virginia Noble in Des Moines. Virginia owns a sandwich shop right near my headquarters, called Beggar's Banquet. Virginia wants to provide her 11 employees with health insurance, but with prices skyrocketing and premiums rising every day, she just can't afford it no matter how much she tries. I believe Virginia Noble deserves someone on her side fighting for her.

Audience members may have felt empathy for these individuals' situations and transfer those feelings to Kerry and his fight to change laws that will affect them.

Self-Disclosure

Another way that rhetors achieve intimacy with their audience is through self-disclosure. Through self-disclosure, we (the audience) learn about the rhetor's personal convictions and the experiences that shaped them. We come to know and like the person speaking to us. Self-disclosure in this sense refers to the personal, as opposed to professional, experiences of the rhetor. In other words, self-disclosure does not refer to the accomplishments or résumé of the rhetor. As Jamieson explains, "Self-disclosure is not meant to be trumpeted to an assembled throng but spoken softly to intimates" (p. 182).

The use of self-disclosure by a speaker, notes Jamieson (1988), helps to create an intimate bond with the audience. She points out that despite the unpopularity of many of President Reagan's policies, most of his opponents liked the president as a person. She attributes this to his use of self-disclosure. Talking about one's personal experiences also provide dramatic narratives that not only entertain but serve as proof for a rhetor's claims. Howard Dean, 2004 Democratic presidential candidate, used self-disclosure frequently when discussing his profession, medicine, and his plan to create a better health care policy in the United States. At one campaign stop, he said:

> I am a physician, and until I became Governor of Vermont in 1991, I shared a medical practice in Burlington with my wife. In our office, we have not only treated the physical pains and illnesses of children and their parents, but helped them work out everything from complicated insurance forms, to covering their bills, to affording their medications.

Dean, in this excerpt from his speech, does not promote or describe his policy, instead he offers his experience as a way for audience members to bond with him and come to the belief that he is knowledgeable and compassionate about health care.

Conversational Tone

In addition to self-disclosure, rhetors also use a conversational style of speaking to forge an intimate relationship with an audience. This style of speaking refers both to how the words in the speech are used as well as the way those words are presented to the audience.

Conversational language is, first and foremost, informal. For instance, conversational speakers often use contractions, informal transitions such as "Well" and "Now," and incomplete sentences. They use a casual vocabulary as well as simple, not compound or complex, sentences. Finally, conversational rhetors know how to promote dialogue: they allow the audience to take part in the conversation. In short, a conversational style of delivery gives the impression that the rhetor is "plainspoken."

A conversational style also helps to convey stories to the audience. Narratives, or storytelling, create an identity for the audience, involve the audience, and bond the audience to the rhetor, notes Jamieson (1988). Accordingly, President Reagan, understood "the importance of invoking sentiments in the audience through use of vivid detail and delivered conviction" (Jamieson, 1988, p. 137).

Carol Mosley Braun, Democratic candidate for president in 2004, effectively used the conversational style in her presidential campaign announcement speech:

> Just last week, my little 9-year-old niece Claire called me into her room to show me her social studies book. Turning to the pages on which all of our Presidents were pictured, she looked at me and complained: But Auntie Carol, all the Presidents are boys! I want Claire, and your daughters and sons to know that in America, everyone has a chance to serve and contribute. I believe that America is ready to take the next great step in the direction of her most noble ideals of service and merit and equality.
>
> This campaign is our way of fighting to give Claire and every American girl or boy not only the opportunity to become President of this great country, but the freedom to decide to lead a quality private life if they choose to do so. There is no human power greater than a made-up mind, and we have decided not to let them take away our liberty, our opportunity, our hope for a better future.

In her speech, Braun told a story that was designed to help the audience see the purpose in helping Braun get elected. She created an identity for them and for herself by her use of a specific example.

Verbal Distillation

Today, rhetors do not use language to convey complex notions; instead they rely on short snippets of words to communicate their ideas. As Jamieson (1988) explains, "A talent for digesting a speech into a memorable phrase is a characteristic of eloquent persons. In our age of television where political speakers are more likely to be heard in news clips than in any other environment, the value of this talent is magnified" (p. 90). Another term, *synecdoche,* is often used to describe this style of speaking. Synecdoche is the *representation* of large amounts of information by using a short, memorable part of that body of information. Let's look more closely at this figure of speech.

Jamieson (1988) explains that a mark of eloquence today is the ability to represent an issue in a clear, concise, and dramatic statement. In fact, we make judgments about rhetors based on how skillfully they create short, memorable phrases. Jamieson identifies several functions that synecdoche fulfills for rhetors today.

First, synechdocic phrases *are more likely to be aired on news broadcasts.* As the time devoted to the words of rhetors continues to decrease on newscasts and in newspapers, succinctly stating a point is the best way to assure that the rhetor receives coverage. Jamieson points out that a short, concise, dramatic statement "is more likely to be seen and heard on broadcast news" than statements that are long and complex. In fact, a synoptic phrase often becomes the next morning's headline. In the advertising realm, spot ads are continuing to decrease in length as well. Again, it becomes important for the rhetor to be able to say in a short statement what he or she wants the audience to remember.

Second, besides speaking in a way that reflects the needs of the news media, short phrases *reinforce the communal bond between audience members and the rhetor.* The phrase, "life, liberty, and the pursuit of happiness," makes certain guarantees about the equality of opportunity that we have. "Innocent until proven guilty," assumes that our legal system has the burden to prove the guilt of suspected criminals. Nike's "Just Do It" is another example of an effective slogan. These phrases do more than bring us together; they become the "truths" upon which future discourse is based, explains Jamieson (1988).

Third, synecdochic phrases also *become the "capsule" by which the audience stores the rhetorical event.* The phrase is remembered long after the moment has passed. In fact, Jamieson (1988) claims that a phrase can stand for an entire construction of reality. The O. J. Simpson trial, for example, will always be remembered by the phrase, "If it doesn't fit, you must acquit," which referred to the inability of the prosecution to link a piece of evidence—a glove—to Simpson.

Visual Dramatization

Electronic eloquence is most effective when it combines words and images. Jamieson (1988) explains that words, combined with images, can create memorable vignettes for audiences. The synergy that occurs when language is combined with images creates a lasting, visual impression on audiences. Jamieson concludes that President Reagan was one rhetor who effectively used visual dramatization. She notes the effects of this rhetorical technique: "By dramatizing and digesting, Reagan shows and tells in the visual bits televisions crave. By evoking common visual experiences and reducing complex issues to dramatic narratives, Reagan uses the oral medium, speech, particularly speech on radio, to simulate our experience of an audiovisual medium, television" (1988, p. 119).

Today's rhetors often surround themselves and their words with visual props that are captured on video or photographs (Jamieson, 1988). President Reagan, notes Jamieson, staged his first inaugural on the west side of the U.S. Capitol.

BOX 10.2   Internet Activity

Read one of the president's speeches, located at www.whitehouse.gov. In particular, you may wish to find one that was delivered to a television audience, such as the State of the Union Address. Determine the degree to which the president used electronic eloquence. How does the president self-disclose? How does he use visual dramatization? How is the speech conversational? Are there any slogans used in the speech? Evaluate the overall effectiveness of the speech.

This was the first time in history that this side of the Capitol had been used for this purpose. The advantage for Reagan was that television cameras could show the monuments of former presidents whose names Reagan evoked in his address. For instance, Reagan recalled the image of President Washington: "Directly in front of me, the monument to a monumental man, George Washington, founder of our country. A man of humility who came to greatness reluctantly" (qtd. in Jamieson, 1988, p. 120). Reagan used the visual prop of the Washington monument, which stood amid the crowd of spectators to reinforce his point. You'll also note that Reagan used a conversational tone in this passage, which lacks complete units of thought.

Also, according to Jamieson, visual dramatization helps to evoke a common visual experience shared by the rhetor and audience. Jamieson elaborates: "When visual images can communicate meaning instantaneously to individuals of different languages and faiths around the world, the function of words changes. In such a world, words contextualize pictures and specify desirable or practical courses of ensuing action" (1988, p. 126). Reagan, for example, was able to remind audiences of images that they had seen and remembered. By evoking these popular and commonly viewed images, he was able to harness the power of the image in his verbal rhetoric.

Jamieson's ideas about electronic eloquence help us to envision a rhetorical theory that is common, and effective, in today's world. Complete the Internet Activity for this chapter (Box 10.2) to gain a better understanding of electronic eloquence and to see how it can be used to assess contemporary rhetoric.

SEMIOTICS

Although Jamieson's ideas are influenced primarily by the mediated culture of television, her theory focuses on verbal rhetoric. In this section, we'll turn our attention to understanding how images and visual symbols function rhetorically. In doing so, we'll begin by surveying the field of **semiotics,** which is often traced to the work of the Swiss linguist Ferdinand de Saussure and the American philosopher Charles Sanders Peirce. Primarily, semiotics is concerned with how signs have meaning. Peirce's theory of semiotics is very similar to that of Ogden and Richards that we discussed in Chapter 5. Saussure took a slightly different approach to meaning. His theory focuses more on signs and their relationships to other signs; Peirce and Ogden and Richards focused more on how individuals determine meaning for a sign. For our purposes in this chapter, we'll look more closely at some of Peirce's ideas and the ways that semiotics has been extended to focus on visual symbols in today's mediated culture.

Types of Meaning

Peirce helps us understand how signs take on certain meanings. He identified three types of signs: iconic, indexical, and symbolic. **Iconic signs** closely signify that which they represent. The meaning for these signs is determined by its relationship to that which it represents. A photograph is a good example of an iconic sign because it is clearly similar to what is being represented. The words "boom," "splat," and "drip" are examples of words that sound like what they mean.

Indexical signs get their meaning because of the association they have with another object. Peirce says that you might think of an index finger pointing at another object to remember the concept of indexical meaning. In other words, you when you see one sign, you immediately think of another related sign. Smoke, as a sign of fire, is an example of indexical meaning, or a temperature and headache are signs of influenza.

The third type of meaning, symbolic meaning, is much more ambiguous and makes language and other signs confusing and rich with meaning at the same time. Symbolic meaning is based on convention, or agreement, about what they mean. For instance, we define a "chair" as something that you sit on; a "table" is something with legs and a flat surface. There is no logical reason why we use these signs to refer to these objects. We could have just as easily used the word "table" to refer to the object we sit on and "table" to refer to the flat surface with legs. Numbers are also symbolic as are some visual signs, such as a stop sign. There is no relationship between a stop sign and its meaning. Peirce argues that because these words have an arbitrary relationship with what they mean, there are many possibilities for their meanings.

Paradigms and Syntagms

Another aspect of semiotics that is useful for our study of rhetoric in mediated cultures is the way that signs are classified and analyzed. Saussure identified two ways that signs are classified, as paradigms and syntagms. A **paradigm** is "a set of signs from which the one to be used is chosen" (Fiske, 1990, p. 56). The alphabet is a paradigm of codes; numbers, on the other hand, belong to a different paradigm. On a larger level, all the words in a particular language belong to a paradigm. There are also subdivisions of this paradigm, such as nouns, verbs, adverbs, and so on. Likewise, you might think of the paradigms of road signs, clothing articles, or colors. When we choose to communicate with someone, we choose a sign from one or more of these paradigms. A doctor, for instance, uses words from a medical paradigm; an attorney uses words from the legal paradigm. If you are having an informal discussion with a friend, you would probably wouldn't use words from either the legal or medical paradigm. To use rhetoric effectively, the rhetor must choose the signs from the appropriate paradigm.

Fiske explains that our choice of signs to use within a particular situation is also important: "the meaning of the unit we choose is determined largely by the meanings of the units we did not" (p. 58). That is, the signs we use have specific and unique meanings. When we choose to use a word, we are implying that the other words that are available are not as useful as the word we chose. Berger (1998) takes this idea a step further by saying that opposite terms that are excluded from rhetoric can also be meaningful. According to Berger's line of thinking, an advertisement for an engagement ring that depicts a man and woman, for instance, might suggest that marriage is for heterosexuals. Homosexuals, then, are excluded from marriage.

Signs are classified into paradigms—the categories of available signs—as well as **syntagms,** which are meaningful combinations of signs (Fiske, 1990). We combine letters to form the syntagm that is a word, and we combine words to the form the syntagm that is a sentence. We also combine camera shots to form the syntagm that is a film, and we combine plot developments and dialogue to form the syntagm that is a novel.

It is important to note that syntagms are governed by rules or conventions. I can't order the letters "a–g–j–o" and form anything that is meaningful within the paradigm of English vocabulary. Likewise, I can't meaningfully structure a sentence with the order of words "cat–fast–the–ran."

Codes

Although the meanings of iconic and indexical signs are often apparent, we must understand how symbolic signs come to have meaning. To make sense of symbols, we use **codes.** Fiske (1990) explained that codes are "the systems into which signs are organized" (p. 64). That is, a code refers to the paradigms of a symbol system as well as to the syntagms of that system, the way that symbols can be combined. English language, for example, is a code that helps us determine what words mean as well as how they may be combined with other words to form meaningful sentences. Let's consider how Americans typically celebrate New Year's Eve. A variety of signs form part of the paradigm of available signs for this event, including the song "Auld Lang Syne," counting from 10 to 1, and wishing someone "Happy New Year." Typically, we count from 10 to 1 at midnight, then wish someone Happy New Year and then sing "Auld Lang Syne." If we were to count from 1 to 10 at 9:35 P.M. in the middle of July and then sing "Happy Birthday," we couldn't use the New Year's Eve code to make sense of the situation. Codes, then, have a paradigmatic dimension and a syntagmatic dimension; that is, there is a set of signs available in a given situation and way to combine those signs.

A number of theorists have discussed codes, including Umberto Eco, who offered a comprehensive system for discussing them. Eco's focus is on the role culture plays in creating codes. Thus, he defined a code as "a system of rules given by culture" (Eco, 1968, pp. 130, 134). If you think about the culture of a particular group of people, it is full of rules for determining what things mean. Think about some of the symbols of the United States, such as its flag, the Statue of Liberty, or the White House. We have been taught the meaning of these symbols, we have been taught the relationships between them, and we associate them with our culture and its heritage.

We live life switching between various codes to determine the meaning of the signs we encounter. Language codes permit us to understand that the word "cat" means a "four legged mammal." Scientific codes allow us to make sense of chemical symbols, such as H_2O and CO_2. Insignia codes help us to understand flags, uniforms, and shop signs. Etiquette codes help us to function in various social and interpersonal settings. Fashion codes enable us to understand the meaning of the clothing we wear. Ritual codes allow us to make sense of weddings, funerals, and graduations. Our lives are full of codes. In fact, one theorist has identified more than a hundred types of codes. We learn codes in school, at home, and through popular culture.

When words mean different things to different people or when a word can have several meanings, codes do not help us make sense of signs we encounter. This lack of coherence, which Berger (1998) calls code confusion, results in a struggle to determine meaning. He identifies several causes. Meanings may change for signs so that it is no longer apparent what they mean. Likewise, signs may be ambiguous; a sign may have several meanings, or several signs may mean the same thing. In any case, codes may be difficult to decipher. Contemporary rhetorical theorists are interested in learning how audience members assign meaning to particular signs. We'll examine these theorists in much greater detail in Chapters 11 and 12.

VISUAL IMAGES AND RHETORIC

As we have seen, semiotics provides a broad and useful way to understand how visual rhetoric prompts meaning for audiences. In this section, we'll study some additional theories of how visual images impart meaning.

Roland Barthes

The French semiologist Roland Barthes provides a way to understand the meaning of images. An influential French theorist, he was one of the first to study visual images. (You can read more about Barthes in Box 10.3). His analysis focused on advertisements. He identified three types of messages contained in the visual imagery of advertisements (Table 10.2). The first type of message is the *linguistic* message, which results from the words used in the image. These words can have both *denotative* and *connotative* meaning. That is, they can refer to something specific or they can conjure cultural images for the viewer. Barthes used an example of an advertisement for pasta that featured the brand name "Panzani." This word, he explained, functiond denotatively to refer to the brand of the pasta advertised, but the word also conjured images of Italy, or, in Barthes terminology, "Italianicity." That is, the connotation is that the pasta is authentically Italian.

Barthes also identified two additional types of messages in visual images. The second and third messages stem from the iconic nature of images. Barthes distinguishes

BOX 10.3   Biography of a Theorist: Roland Barthes

Roland Barthes was a French social and literary critic who specialized in semiotics. Barthes was born in Cherbough, France, in 1915. He studied at the Sorbonne and received degrees in classical literature and grammar and philology. Bouts with tuberculosis prevented him from obtaining his doctoral degree. Nevertheless, he taught at numerous schools in France and was chair of literary semiology at College de France when he died in 1980 in a car accident.

Throughout his work, Barthes analyzed the meanings of texts, such as films, shows, newspapers, and exhibitions. He sought to explore the ways that symbols contain meaning. In particular he was interested in the structure of signs and how they convey meaning. In academic terms, Barthes was a structuralist. His primary works include *Mythologies* (1957), *S/Z* (1970), and *Image, Music, Text* (1977). He also wrote numerous articles that have been compiled into readers.

Table 10.2 Barthes's Three Levels of Meaning

Meaning	Variation	Definition
Linguistic	Denotative	Literal meaning for the words contained in an image.
	Connotative	What is implied by the words in the image.
Coded Iconic		Deliberate and obvious story told by the images.
Noncoded Iconic		Nondiscursive and emotional meaning that arises from the totality of an image.

between the two iconic messages in several ways. He calls one a *coded,* or denotative, message and the other a *noncoded,* or connotative, message. The distinction between the second and third messages isn't always distinct, however. Let's examine a bit more the second and third messages of Barthes's theory.

The coded iconic message is the story that is told by the images that make up the advertisement. This message can be easily understood because the images have a clear relationship to that which they represent. That is, they are coded in a particular way to create a certain kind of meaning. Barthes says that they have denotative value because their meaning is more or less obvious. He explains that the second meaning "forces itself upon me" and that it is intentional (1977, p. 54). Further, the symbols that create the second message and their meanings are "taken from a kind of common, general lexicon of symbols" (1977, p. 54).

Yet Barthes also believes that a third type of message is evident. He calls the third message the *noncoded iconic.* This message concerns the completeness of the advertisement as an image and cannot be easily described or put into words. As he explains, "I am still held by the image. I read, I receive (and probably even first and foremost) a third meaning—evident, erratic, obstinate. I do not know what its signified is, at least I am unable to give it a name, but I can see clearly the traits. . ." (1977, p. 53). The third meaning, which he calls the *obtuse* meaning, "appears to extend outside culture, knowledge, information" (1977, p. 55). The third meaning

---

BOX 10.4   Critical Insights: Analyzing Advertisements

Examine the Web page in Figure 10.2. We can use Barthes's theory of the three messages of visual images to analyze the page. The page explains and promotes President Bush's plan to reform the social security system. Linguistically, the page contains arguments in favor of allowing individuals to invest a portion of their social security taxes in private investment accounts. Denotatively, Bush lays out the arguments for his plan. The masthead for the page contains the phrase "Strengthening Social Security." Connotatively, this phrase associates strength with Bush's plan, calling on a range of emotional and logical beliefs his audience may hold true.

We can also see the coded iconic message in the Web page. President Bush is pictured embracing an elderly woman. Also shown are pictures of an elderly man and two women, one of whom appears to be African American. The stately columns of a federal building are shown and the seal of the United States is superimposed on the background of the masthead. The page also bears the seal of the White House and contains

links to a variety of pages and topics. These coded iconic messages are designed to convey the power of the presidency, and they are used to argue that Bush's social security plan will be beneficial for all elderly people, including those who are nonwhite. Bush is clearly shown to be friendly toward the elderly, implying that he would not harm their financial security.

Finally, we are left with the noncoded iconic message. Barthes observed that a third message escapes language. So, as you look at the Web page, consider its effect on your emotions and feelings. Visit the White House site at http://www.whitehouse.gov and view this page and similar pages. Do the pages—in their entirety—make you feel optimistic? Hopeful? Do they confirm your beliefs that Bush is an effective president? Why do these pages cause you think and feel as you do? As you struggle with these questions and consider your feelings about the page, keep in mind what we have discussed about Barthes's theory.

---

is emotional, contributes to the other meanings, and cannot be adequately expressed with language. To better understand Barthes's theory, look at the Critical Insights feature for this chapter in Box 10.4.

Paul Messaris

Drawing on the theory of Charles S. Peirce, Paul Messaris (1997) explained that visual signs obtain meaning in one of three ways: iconic, indexical, or symbolic. *Iconic* signs, which resemble that which they represent, are the most common. Photographs or drawings are examples of iconic signs. *Indexical* signs involve a cause–effect relationship, and we understand what they mean because of this relationship. When we see smoke, we think there is a fire nearby. *Symbolic* signs are arbitrary. That is, there is no obvious relationship to what they mean, so we must learn their meaning. A flag is an example of a visual sign that has arbitrary meaning. We have simply decided that the stars and stripes of the U.S. flag, for example, represent the United States. Based on Peirce's distinctions, Messaris (1997) identifies three functions served by visual signs: image as representation of reality, image as proof, and image as argumentative claim.

Messaris (1997) argues that one function of images is to represent reality. Images are able to represent reality because of their iconic properties. Images, such as photographs and drawings, resemble what they mean. Consider that

FIGURE 10.2   White House Social Security Web Page.

photography is an interpretive enterprise that does not accurately capture the "reality" of a situation. Messaris acknowledges this, but contends that the link is close enough for us to perceive the image as being a representation of something "real." Messaris explains, "Nevertheless, all of these kinds of pictures are capable of capturing and conveying to our eyes the distinctive features that our brains need in order to be able to figure out what we are looking at" (1997, p. 3). Messaris (1997) identifies two ways images represent reality: first, they attract attention to the persuader's message and, second, they elicit an emotional response from the audience. As we discuss Messaris's theory, we'll refer to the photograph of Hillary Clinton campaigning for the U.S. Senate in Figure 10.3.

Messaris (1997) argues that persuaders must get the attention of the audience if they are to be successful. The use of celebrities who look into the camera and talk directly to us about a particular product is an example of the attention-getting function of images. This technique works because we like to look at people who look at us. Images attract attention in several ways, contends Messaris (1997): violating reality, using a metaphor, playing on a visual parody, using direct eye gaze, or employing sexual imagery. The photograph of Clinton prominently features the former First Lady, attracting a viewer's attention. Additionally, viewers are drawn to the image because of the close-ups of the people she is meeting.

Iconic images also elicit an emotional response from their viewers. Political campaign advertisements that feature an upward-looking camera shot are examples of emotion-eliciting ads because the camera encourages a reverent attitude

FIGURE 10.3   Picture of Hillary Clinton campaigning.

toward the candidate. Messaris (1997) identifies four ways that visual images elicit emotion: camera angle, look of superiority, identification, and sexual appearances. The smiling image of Clinton communicates a great deal of emotion as does the energy that exudes from her supporters. Viewers may feel an emotional connection to Clinton because of how the image has been composed.

Images also point to or suggest that something has happened (Messaris, 1997). In this sense, they serve as "proof" for a persuasive statement or of what has happened at a particular time and place. Footprints in the snow, for example, are proof that someone recently walked through an area. A photograph shows a rendering of a particular time and place and "testifies" about what has happened (Messaris, 1997, p. 130). Keep in mind, however, that pictures can be deceptive. Through the use of editing techniques, camera angles, and other technical elements, photographs and other images can be altered. We trust what we see though. Examine again the photograph in Figure 10.3. The smiling people eager to meet Clinton suggests that she is popular and worthy of election. Surveying the ethnicities and sexes of those pictured "proves," in some ways, the widespread appeal of Clinton.

Finally, notes Messaris, images function symbolically as words for persuaders. Messaris (1997) contends that images can say things that words cannot. They do so because of the meanings that our culture has associated with particular images. We tend to equate particular images with particular meanings because we have learned the code that unlocks their message. Thus, images "show us the unspoken" (Messaris, 1997, p. 221). Images are sometimes used instead of words when the content of the message is inappropriate to express with words. Since images are ambiguous, they can be useful for persuaders in stating controversial claims. An advertisement that relates a product to a lavish lifestyle symbolically suggest that the products is necessary for a lavish lifestyle. Referring to Figure 10.3, you see an image of a successful politician. In some ways, this image reinforces the view that politicians are attractive, charismatic, and eager to meet people. The photograph reinforces the standards we use to judge political candidates in this culture.

VISUAL ARGUMENTS

Messaris's claim that visual images can make arguments is somewhat controversial. Many theorists continue to view argument as essentially grounded in language. On the other hand, David S. Birdsell and Leo Groarke (1996) has provided strong support for the position that images can function as arguments . First, he argues that although images can be "arbitrary, vague, and ambiguous," so too are words. That is, the subjective nature of images should not disqualify them from serving as arguments. You can probably think of many verbal arguments whose meaning was uncertain or unclear. Birdsell claims that images are no more or less clear than verbal statements: "We merely observe that both [verbal statements and visual images] can be ambiguous or cogent and that both can convey claims and arguments" (1996).

Second, Birdsell explains that images should be considered as part of the context to which they belong. In this way, they are similar to words, which must also be viewed in context. Images express arguments when they are viewed in relationship to other images. Watching a film, for instance, is really watching a series of images projected on a screen. You can understand a single frame in the film by seeing its relationship to other frames. Additionally, the verbal captions—the linguistic message of Barthes's theory—provide a way to determine the meaning of an image. Birdsell also explains that visual culture can be useful in helping us determine the meaning of an image. We use cultural knowledge that we have to make sense of verbal images and decode their arguments.

Third, the ways visual images represent that which they signify can serve as an argument. If an image does not adequately represent an object, another image can be used to challenge the accuracy of the first image. For instance, a political campaign advertisement can be used to unfairly characterize an opponent. To challenge this unfair portrayal, the attacked candidate can create an advertisement containing images that effectively counter it. Birdsell (1996) summarizes this question of meaningful representation: "The point is not that the preferred alternative is or is not 'genuinely' more accurate, but that through the application of visual techniques rather than verbal narrative, the question of resemblance has entered directly into the argument."

Finally, Birdsell (1996) argues that the theory of argumentation must be broadened beyond that of verbal arguments: "Without this expansion, argumentation theory has no way of dealing with a great many visual ploys that play a significant role in our argumentative lives." In sum, Birdsell sees the need to reconsider the distinction between argumentation and persuasion when visual images are involved. Even an emotional appeal, for instance, can be reduced to an argumentative statement: "We argue a person into a state of feeling." Birdsell provides a way for us to think about the visual nature of arguments and their possibility.

RHETORICAL FEATURES OF HYPERTEXT

We have discussed in this chapter the effect of television on rhetoric and various theories that can be used to explain visual images, ranging from photographs to advertisements. In the final part of this chapter, we'll turn our attention to hypertext, the technology that makes the Internet possible. A hypertext is a digital document that contains links to other documents, images, websites, or information. When you click a link on a Web page, you are using hypertext, a central feature of which is that the user chooses his or her path through the document. Hypertext thereby disrupts traditional ways of creating and using rhetoric. Keep in mind that hypertext documents do not need to be hosted on the Internet. You could, for instance, create a set of linked documents on your computer that only you would read and access. Hypertext is, in some ways, a combination of the hot and cool media McLuhan discussed. Hypertext is cool—requiring interaction—but it is also hot, when combined with video. Hypertext is very much a space-binding medium, allowing users rapid access to highly individualized information. Holtz (1999) has identified four central characteristics of hypertext rhetoric: it is nonlinear, two-dimensional, interactive, and it makes use of multimedia. Let's explore these characteristics further.

Hypertext Characteristics

A traditional rhetorical text is linear, created and often used in a beginning-to-end manner. Think of this textbook. It is designed to be read from the first page to the last page. You might skip around or use the index to find specific information, but as the author, my intent is for you to read it word-for-word in its entirety. A television program, radio broadcast, or magazine is created and used in the same way. These are linear media.

Hypertext creates the possibility for *nonlinear* rhetorical texts. Consider your experience with the Internet. You enter sites from other sites, skip around a bit within the site, and then exit the site following a link provided by the site's author. We rarely use hypertexts in a linear manner.

Holtz (1999) further explains that hypertext is often referred to as *two-dimensional*. Unlike a book, television, or newspaper, hypertext cannot be picked up, carried, or set down. Hypertext occupies only a two-dimensional space. Because of its nonlinear nature, users must scroll through pages and pages of information if it is not adequately indexed. A user would spend far less time flipping through a novel and looking at its key features. Of course, its two-dimensional nature makes it easier to search and, potentially, easier to navigate. Interestingly, hypertext creators are searching for ways to make their content appear more like the three-dimensional forms with which we are most familiar. For instance, there are online magazines that have pages that appear to "turn" upon the user's command. Additionally, Tablet PCs allow users to write on the computer screen as if it were paper.

A third characteristic of hypertext is its *interactivity*. As we mentioned previously, users can choose which links to follow, video to watch, or forms to fill out. The creator of the site must design it so that users can quickly and efficiently find what they desire. In fact, sites that have more interactive features—such as polls, flashing messages, or customized content—are usually more effective than sites that simply offer information. Hypertext also allows users to interact with each other. The latest trend on the Web is blogging, which allows ordinary individuals to disseminate messages to others while at the same time facilitating the interactions of those who read the messages. Really Simple Syndicate (RSS) technology further enhances access to blog entries and news.

Finally, Holtz (1999) notes that hypertext makes use of *multimedia*. In addition to text and images, hypertext rhetoric incorporates sound, animation, and video. You have probably experienced the multimedia nature of websites, and perhaps you have already used textbooks with multimedia components, such as video and sound. As technology makes it easier to interact with electronic documents, you'll likely see an increase in the ways that multimedia is used.

Rhetorical Techniques

With these characteristics in mind, let's examine some ways that rhetors can create effective hypertext:

- Holtz (1999) explains that when compared to print, the *length* of a hypertext message should be 50 percent shorter. The rationale is that it takes longer to read a message on a computer screen. Brevity also allows users to determine the text's central message in a clear, concise manner.

- Hypertext should also be scannable, according to Holtz (1999). Scannable text allows users to find exactly what they are looking for without having to read the page word-for-word. Using lists and short sentences and limiting the variety of fonts and styles are ways to create scannable text.

- Rhetors should also structure the document systematically, so that the relationships between pages are clear and deliberate. The user should also be able to find their way to key information quickly.

The medium of hypertext continues to evolve, and the rhetorical principles that guide its creation are becoming increasingly the subject of research and discussion.

SUMMARIZING RHETORICAL THEORY

In this chapter, we have studied the ways that rhetoric and rhetorical theory have responded to the media that permeate our culture. We have surveyed several approaches to understanding the influence of media and how to decode the images and verbal messages of today's electronic media. In this section, we'll summarize our discussion by returning to the key issues related to rhetoric that we have examined in this text.

Defining Rhetoric

The theorists reviewed in this chapter have broadened the definition of rhetoric to include visual images as well as words. Also, they recognize that the media that transmit visual images—film, television, radio, the Internet—are viable sources for rhetorical messages. In fact, contrary to those we covered in previous chapters who were also interested in modern forms of rhetoric, the focus of these theorists is almost exclusively on the rhetoric of media. Their definitions will be useful as we continue our study in the remaining chapters.

Rhetoric and Knowledge

Knowledge for theorists of media rhetoric is related both to the medium used to transmit a message and to the culture in which the message exists. McLuhan and Ong are the strongest proponents of this view. For McLuhan, you'll remember, the medium is the message. He is saying that the meaning of the message—the knowledge it creates—is related to the medium used by the rhetor. Thus, there will be different truths that result from different media. The truth told by television is different, according to McLuhan, than that revealed through the print medium. For Ong, entire cultures will view truth in different ways, depending on the media they use. People who communicate in oral cultures have a different sense of what is true than those who can store and recall information using literate or electronic forms of communication.

Epistemologically, an important aspect of the work of media rhetoric theorists is that they recognize that appearances can be deceiving, verifying anew the age-old wisdom that truth may not be as it appears. In particular, Barthes and Messaris make the distinction between representation and signification. That is, visual images are not necessarily the most accurate way of representing an object, but they do suggest a meaning for that object based on how it is represented. In fact, the notion of "accuracy" may not be that meaningful in an age dominated by media. All we have to go by are the images—visual or mental—of rhetoric. Thus, truth is seen to be highly contingent on the form that rhetoric takes. We'll take up this issue in greater detail in Chapter 12, but here we have seen how the seeds for this way of thinking were planted.

Rhetoric and Identity

Like our ideas of what's true, the theorists of media rhetoric challenge our ideas about what it means to be human. That is, there is an ontological dimension to the study of rhetoric and media. In this sense, McLuhan, perhaps, makes the strongest argument when he claims that a medium is an extension of our senses. That is, human experience and our conception of what it means to be "real" is directly linked to the media we use to experience the world. We are different beings when we use different media. Ong's work, too, has an ontological dimension. He believes that human consciousness is linked to the type of media culture in which one lives. That is, our very way of thinking and feeling is linked to the dominant media of our culture.

Rhetoric and Judgment

The theorists we have discussed do not directly address issues of ethics and morality. Instead, they present us with a framework that will see used in future chapters to make moral and ethical claims about rhetoric. In particular, the cultural studies theorists we will study in Chapter 12 use semiotics to critique the mediated cultures in which we live.

DISCUSSION QUESTIONS

1. What media do you use each day? How do those media affect your perception of the world, yourself, and others? Do these media affect you in ways that you may not notice?

2. To what degree do you think rhetors use electronic eloquence? How effective do you think it is? Can you think of examples of effective rhetors today who do not use electronic eloquence?

3. Choose an advertisement in a magazine. What are some of the signs used in this ad? To what paradigm do they belong? Are there any members of the paradigm that are missing from the ad? What is the significance of their absence?

4. Choose another advertisement. What is the linguistic message of the ad? What is the coded iconic message? Do the two agree? How does the ad get the attention of the audience? How does it prove arguments to the audience? Are there any premises in the ad that aren't explicitly stated but that are implied for the audience?

5. How effective do you think visual images are in expressing arguments? Do you believe there is a clear distinction between argumentation and persuasion? (You may have to refer to our previous discussion of argument for this question.)

GLOSSARY TERMS

electronic eloquence   A style of rhetoric that is personalized, self-disclosive, conversational, synoptic, and visually dramatic.
semiotics   The study of signs and their meaning.
iconic sign   A sign that resembles what it means.
indexical sign   A sign that points to or is directly linked to what it means.
paradigm   A set of signs that are unified by a common purpose.
syntagm   Rules that govern how signs are arranged.
code   A set of rules used to determine the meaning of symbols.
symbol   A sign that gets it meaning in a purely arbitrary or subjective way.

11

Postmodern Approaches to Rhetoric

Learning Objectives

After reading this chapter, you should be able to:

1. Describe some of the key differences between modernism and postmodernism.

2. Describe how postmodern theorists see the creation of knowledge.

3. Deconstruct texts to understand the range of differences between symbols and their referents.

4. Outline the various ways of thinking about identity from the postmodern perspective.

5. Describe hyperreality and locate examples of hyperreality in our culture.

6. Identify and describe instances of localized politics and their effect on power struggles.

If you do a Google search for the word "postmodern," you'll likely discover a great variety of Web pages. You'll find references for postmodern thought, postmodern culture, and even postmodern Bible study. You can find references about postmodern architecture, art, and music. Indeed, postmodernism is a philosophical school of thought that has influenced virtually every part of our culture, from MTV to advertising to rhetorical theory.

The postmodern movement has also had a significant impact on how rhetorical theorists have conceived of rhetorical practice. In particular, postmodernists have explored the link between and symbols and what they mean. The implications of their investigation influences the most fundamental questions about knowledge, identity, and ethics. In fact, postmodern theorists have as their central focus the very touchstones to which we have referred throughout this entire book. In this chapter, we will survey the central ideas of some of the key postmodernists and how these theories relate to our study of rhetoric.

WHAT IS POSTMODERNISM?

Before describing postmodernism, let's briefly discuss modernism, the historical era to which postmodernism has responded. Since the industrial revolution of the early 1900s, U.S. culture and that of other Western, industrialized nations have been characterized as **modern.** Modernization is "a term denoting those processes of individualization, secularization, industrialization, cultural differentiation, commodification, urbanization, bureaucratization, and rationalization which together have constituted the modern world" (Best & Kellner, 1991, p. 3). Lucaites and Condit (1999) add, "In the modern worldview, the universe is a relatively simple, stable, and highly ordered place, describable in and reducible to absolute formulas that hold across contexts" (p. 11). For academic researchers and theorists, social discord, according to Lucaites and Condit, is cured by "greater research, less passion, more rationality, and more education" (p. 11). Put simply, the use of supposedly objective research methods were thought to provide adequate explanations for social life and offer solutions to problems humans faced during the modern era.

Despite this effort to rationally and objectively describe, explain, and predict human behavior, humans in the modern world have continued to experience alienation because of industrialization and associated problems. According to Best and Kellner (1991), modernity "produced untold suffering and misery for its victims, ranging from the peasantry, proletariat, and artisans oppressed by capitalist industrialization to the exclusion of women from the public sphere, to the genocide of imperialist colonization" (p. 3).

Partially in reaction to the difficulties endured by some in the modern world and partially because of new forms of technology, communication, and media, a **"postmodern** social formation" has developed. That is to say, we are experiencing new ways of relating to others and our world, and these new experiences are very different from those of the modern period.

Let's consider a brief example to illustrate some of these differences. A modern organization, such as a business, may have relied on a top-down management style in which the top leaders of the organization controlled the information flow within the organization and made decisions that were very autocratic, relying on the leaders' knowledge and expertise. A postmodern organization, thanks to new forms of communication—such as the Web, e-mail, chat, or videoconferencing—may be characterized by communication that flows in all directions—upward, downward, and horizontal. Because more people can share more information, leaders realize that the more input they can gather to make a decision, the better the decision will be. Thus, they encourage "quality circles," which bring together a diverse group of workers, managers, and executives who meet regularly to offer suggestions about how the organization can be run. Additionally, given the Internet, many members of the organization may work virtually, never stepping foot in the actual building that houses the organization. You can see that the differences in management style between modern and postmodern organizations are related to several factors, such as technology, potentially more democratic ways of thinking, and diverse ways of viewing knowledge. With this distinction in mind, let's delve further into the topic of postmodernism.

Best and Kellner (1991) explain that "postmodern theory provides a critique of representation and the modern belief that theory mirrors reality, taking instead 'perspectivist' and 'relativist' positions that theories at best provide partial perspectives of their objects, and that all cognitive representations of the world are historically and linguistically mediated" (p. 4). In other words, postmodern theory acknowledges that all theories are human constructions and may not provide objective statements about human nature. Theories, it is believed by postmodernists, are highly subjective and influenced by the biases of the theorist.

Additionally, Best and Kellner explain that "postmodern theory also rejects modern assumptions of social coherence and notions of causality in favour of multiplicity, plurality, fragmentation, and indeterminacy" (p. 4). They are saying that postmodern theorists reject simple cause-effect relationships in viewing communication. Postmodernists are also leery of generalizing to larger populations of human subjects. Much social science research, for instance, generalizes from a sample to a larger population. A survey looks at only a small number of a population and surmises that what is true of the sample—if the sample is chosen correctly—is true of the population. Postmodernists are skeptical of such claims.

Lucaites and Condit summarize the various views of postmodernism, explaining that it, "prefers interpretation over scientific study because it operates with the assumption that all knowledge is subjective and/or intersubjective, morally culpable, and local. In the postmodern worldview, the universe is a rapidly changing, highly complex entity" (Lucaites & Condit, 1999, p. 11). In essence, they believe that multiple truths exist in the world and that trying to identify a single, prevailing truth is difficult, if not impossible. For another way of thinking about this, one of the most noted postmodernists, Jean-Francois Lyotard, defined postmodernism as "incredulity towards metanarratives" (1984, p. xxiv). What he is saying is that postmodernism views with skepticism those definitive statements about that nature of knowledge, truth, ontology, or ethics. For Lyotard, grand theorizing is replaced in the postmodern era by localized knowledge and understanding.

THE POSTMODERN AND RHETORIC

Our previous discussion in this book has readied us for our study of rhetoric's relationship to the postmodern. In Chapter 7, we examined the link between rhetoric, power, and ideology. In doing so, we relied on several implicit postmodern assumptions about the nature of knowledge, ontology, and ethics.

In Chapters 8 and 9, we looked at alternatives to Western rhetorical theory posed by women, African, Native American, and Chinese rhetors. Although cultural views of rhetoric are not themselves postmodern, the fact that researchers are attempting to uncover and bring to light these practices in the face of the dominant view of Western rhetoric has, in some ways, been prompted by postmodern sensibilities. For women, the link to postmodernism is much more direct; many feminist theories of rhetoric are in fact based on a postmodern view of the world, or at least on a view of the world that rejects modern ideas. Lucaites and Condit (1999) comment on Campbell's article concerning the paradox of the women's liberation movement you read about in Chapter 8: "[Campbell] argued that classical rhetorical theories failed to provide an appropriate or useful guide for the type of rhetoric that shaped women's liberation" (p. 12).

In the previous chapter, we focused on technology and electronic media and how our world and sensibilities have been shaped by these forces. You will now read about theories that continue this thread of thought and meet a group of theorists who have, at least in some ways, responded to the postmodern challenge.

The intersection of postmodernism and rhetoric occurred in 1972, according to some scholars, when the *Quarterly Journal of Speech* published an article by Forbes Hill that prompted a great deal of discussion within the rhetorical community. According to Lucaites and Condit (1999) Hill's rhetorical analysis of a speech by Richard Nixon attempted to objectively describe and explain his rhetoric. Hill (1972) outlined specific boundaries for rhetorical criticism, claiming that other analyses of Nixon's speech were inappropriate. In fact, Hill claimed that analyses by other critics were neither "objective" nor "systematic" (p. 385). Using strict Aristotelian standards, Hill believed, critics could not make judgments about the truthfulness of a rhetor or the cultural impact of a rhetor's speech.

Hill's analysis was met by discussion from other rhetorical experts, who claimed that objectivity was next to impossible and that rhetorical critics should embrace their biases and perspective in their analyses. Of course, developing a suitable replacement for a narrow, Aristotelian reading of rhetorical texts has been difficult in the years since Hill's article. In fact, identifying acceptable standards and goals for rhetorical criticism is the central problem we'll face in this chapter. Lucaites and Condit (1999b) note that "Rejecting the rigid modernist spirit of positivism and scientism in rhetorical studies proved to be relatively easy. Determining specifically what ought to replace it has been a much more difficult problem, and trying to solve that problem has been an issue that the discipline has visited over and again" (p. 12) since the 1972 Hill article. In this chapter, we'll discuss some of the key issues that rhetorical theorists have used as they attempt to understand rhetoric from a postmodern perspective. Specifically, we'll examine knowledge, meaning, identity, reality, and politics.

KNOWLEDGE

We have addressed epistemology—the study of knowledge—throughout this text. The French philosopher Michel Foucault links epistemology, rhetoric, and power in his theory. He claims that the content and form of rhetoric and who is allowed to be a rhetor are all products of a particular set of rules that exist in

---

BOX 11.1 Biography of a Theorist: Michel Foucault

Michel Foucault was born in Poitiers, France, on October 15, 1926. Receiving a distinguished education, Foucault earned degrees in philosophy, psychology, and psychopathology. In 1950, Foucault joined the Communist Party—as did many intellectuals of the time—but he left the party in 1953. For the next several years, Foucault taught at the University of Uppsala in Sweden, at the University of Warsaw, and at the University of Hamburg. He returned to France in 1960 as the head of the Philosophy Department at the University of Clermont-Ferrard. He would later teach at the University of Paris-VIII at Vincennes and at the prestigious College de France. Foucault chose for himself the title "Professor of the History of Systems of Thought." This title reflected the general theme of his writing: uncovering the conditions by which rhetoric produces subjects of study. Foucault died in 1984.

Foucault published his first major work in 1960, *Madness and Civilization,* which was his doctoral dissertation. Foucault wrote *The Order of Things* in 1966 and *The Archeology of Knowledge* in 1969. He published *Discipline and Punish: The Origin of the Prison* in 1975, following his involvement with a prisoner-rights activist group. *The History of Sexuality: Volume 1* was published in 1976, and the second and third volumes of this work were published in 1984. Foucault's work encompasses a wide range of issues, topics, and disciplines. We'll focus here on his most direct contribution to the study of rhetoric and its relationship to knowledge and power, our central themes in this chapter.

---

a culture. Thus, the knowledge produced through rhetoric in a culture is subject to a set of conditions that permits some kinds of knowledge while disallowing other kinds of knowledge. To learn more about Foucault, read Box 11.1 Biography of a Theorist. We'll now study Foucault's theory in greater detail.

Discursive Formations

Foucault sought to discover fundamental unifying historical themes. Traditional views of history focused too much on causal relationships, disparities, and continuity in and between historical events. Instead of focusing on the causes of an historical event, for instance, Foucault is more interested in locating similarities between various time periods. Although Foucault studies what seem to be historical ideas, he did not wish to be called an historian of ideas. Instead, he preferred the title "Professor of the History of Systems of Thought." This title is instructive, because it alerts us to the fact that Foucault was interested in identifying how ways of thinking have come to exist throughout history. In other words, his work was a descriptive study of discourse and how knowledge is created through language. Foucault preferred the term "discourse" to "rhetoric," but the two can be thought of as synonyms for our purposes.

Foucault uncovered a series of what he called discursive formations, or **epistemes. A discursive formation** is the consistent pattern of discursive use that creates knowledge, or truth, for a culture. A discursive formation is determined and governed by a set of rules, a discursive practice, that determines exactly what discourse can be uttered. Foucault explains:

In a society such as our own we all know the rules of exclusion. The most obvious and familiar of these concerns what is prohibited. We know perfectly

Table 11.1 Foucault's Discursive Formations

Discursive Formation	Role of Human	Knowledge Produced
Resemblance	Nonexistent; humans existed as any other natural creature. They sought to determine what objects resembled.	Natural order of things understood
Representation	Determine what words represent	Science
Modernity	Determine influence of words on our perception of the world.	Knowledge is produced by a series of linguistically structured relationships.

well that we are not free to say just anything, that we cannot simply speak of anything, when we like or where we like; not just anyone, finally, may speak of just anything . . . these prohibitions interrelate, reinforce and complement each other, forming a complex web, continually subject to modification. (1972, p. 216)

You're probably aware of such rules that exist at your school. Although student input may be welcome on many matters, you cannot probably attend the president's cabinet meetings and say what you want without being invited to do so. Additionally, it would be difficult for you, a student, to change the curriculum or the courses that you are taking. It's not always easy for faculty to influence curricular or administrative decisions because of the rules and practices that exist at your school. Your school, then, is subject to a particular kind of discursive formation that regulates what may be said and who may say it.

Foucault, though, was interested in the larger picture; he looked to history to determine what sets of rules governed a particular historical era. Table 11.1 displays Foucault's distinction between historical discursive formations. He believed that the structure governing a discursive formation is so fundamental that only one can be controlling for a culture at any particular period in time. The sixteenth century, or what Foucault (1970) called the Renaissance, was based on *resemblance*. Language, during this period, did not play a key role in how people thought or perceived their world. Instead, the focus was on objects and what those objects resembled. The sky, for instance, resembled heaven and was believed to have a close association with it. Humans were not concerned so much during this period with discovering knowledge as they were with discovering what objects resembled.

The seventeenth and eighteenth century, the Classical Age, was characterized by *representation,* according to Foucault. Here, for the first time, according to Foucault, humans sought to use language as a way of representing or symbolizing ideas or objects. For the first time, Foucault explains, humans played a key role in how they perceived the world and their place in the world. Humans stopped seeking resemblances between objects and began asking questions about what words meant. Humans began to use science to understand their world. So, during the discursive formation of representation, humans became active players in the quest for scientific knowledge.

Table 11.2 Discursive Practices, Rules, Roles, and Power

Term	Definition	Example
Discursive practices	Discourse that is true because it meets certain rules and expectations.	Methods of diagnosing illness
Rules	Determine what is appropriate in a culture	It is appropriate for doctors—using medical techniques—to diagnose illness.
Objects	What can be discussed	Ilness
Rhetors	Whose discourse is privileged	Doctors
Sites	Locations from which privileged discourse emerges	Hospitals, clinics, or research labs
Structure	Format or structure of acceptable discourse	Medical journals
Roles	How people are related to language	We play roles such as that of patient or doctor.
Power	Set of relations that exist in discourse	Doctors have a superior position to patients, but patients have legal power to sue doctors.

The late eighteenth, nineteenth and twentieth centuries are called *modernity*. Humans began to question the accuracy of language and its lack of intrinsic meaning. We saw the late stages of this discussion in Chapter 5, when we looked at the work of Ogden and Richards, for instance. Instead of necessarily looking to understand objects in the world, humans focused on language and the inherent difficulties present in language to describe the world.

Each of these discursive formations is characterized by rules governing what can be spoken about, who can speak on that object, and how that person or institution may speak about the object. Ultimately, each discursive formation yielded a particular kind of knowledge. As we continue to explore discursive formations, keep in mind their link to knowledge.

Formation of Discursive Formations

Discursive formations arise through four elements, according to Foss and Gill (1987). Those elements are discursive practices, rules, roles and power. Keep in mind that knowledge is the product of the interaction of these elements. Let's survey these four elements (see Table 11.2).

Discursive Practices Foss and Gill (1987) explain that discursive practices refer to the "discourse that, because it follows particular rules or has passed the appropriate tests, is understood to be true in a culture" (p. 387). A physician's diagnosis, for instance, might be considered a discursive practice because physicians have generally been afforded the privilege to speak about what is true concerning medicine, in our culture. In a different culture, for instance, a spiritual leader might be the one who can diagnose illness. A physician's words might be seen as false, or misleading.

Foss and Gill (1987) note that discourse, for Foucault, is not limited to words and sentences. Discourse may include architecture, use of space, institutional practices, or social relations (p. 387).

Rules   Rules govern discursive practices: "The rules are not likely to be conscious and often cannot be articulated without great difficulty, but they determine the possibilities for the content and form of discourse" (Foss & Gill, 1987, p. 388). It may be difficult for you to understand why in some cultures, physicians are able to diagnose medical diseases while in other cultures they are not permitted to make such diagnosis. In this case, the history and beliefs of the culture have led to rules that govern its discursive practices. There are four main types of rules, according to Foucault:

- Rules concerning what may be talked about.
- Rules concerning who may do the talking.
- Rules concerning the sites from which discourse may originate.
- Rules concerning how decisions are made about the truthfulness of discourse.

First, Foucault explains that the object of discourse emerges from a complex set of relationships, that what is spoken about in a culture is often that which is abnormal or different. Additionally, members of the culture seek to classify or label what is abnormal. Foucault uses the example of mental illness. He says that during the nineteenth century individuals who exhibited "abnormal" characteristics were first identified and labeled by the family. During other periods, the courts, church, or medical community fulfilled this role. Additionally, privileged rhetors may nominate objects of discourse. In our culture, large media companies may choose topics for the public to discuss. For instance, the latest clothing becomes fashionable—it becomes an object for discourse—because of how it is featured in the media.

A second rule concerns who may do the speaking in a culture. Not all rhetors are equal in terms of their ability to communicate within the rules of the discursive formation. In Foucault's study, doctors, pastors, and family members have all been seen as having the authority to communicate about mental illness. In today's culture, high-level politicians—such as the president of the United States—are often seen as having more ability to use discourse than others. However, our society is also highly specialized, which means that a large number of individuals who are narrowly trained in a particular field may communicate about a particular topic, as long as it falls within their area of expertise.

Third, Foucault says that rules exist concerning the sites from which discourse occurs. Discourse about the need to go to war with Iraq that originated from President Bush was thought by many to be more truthful and believable than that which came from his political opponents and antiwar activists. Even after reports emerged that said Iraq had no weapons of mass destruction, President Bush continued to have the support of at least half of the American public.

Finally, Foucault suggests that the structure and appearance of some forms of discourse make it more believable than others. In particular, he is interested in how the language of science gives some statements credibility in the age of modernism.

For instance, an article published in a medical journal is thought to be more believable than an opinion piece on the same subject written by a layperson. Foucault specifically addresses the structure, ordering, and language of the statement. In other words, a medical journal article sounds like other medical journal articles and has credibility because it does.

Roles   Next, Foucault is interested in the "roles played by rhetors in a discursive formation" (Foss & Gill, 1987, pp. 388–389). Foucault understands that since the beginning of time, humans have played a different role in the creation of knowledge. Only since the beginning of modernity—in the late eighteenth century—did humans play an active role in creating discourse. When humans came to the realization of linguistic reflexivity—which we discussed in Chapter 5—they realized they had the power over language. Rhetors realized there were not natural relationships—as they previously sought to establish—only arbitrary ones that they could control. Humans, then, created the episteme of modernity and thus, the knowledge that it produced.

Power   Finally, Foucault is interested in how power contributes to the creation of a discursive formation. Despite his belief that discursive formations controlled who could speak and what they could speak about, Foucault theorized that power was more complex than it might seem. Even those who used discourse on the margins of the discursive formation had power. Foss and Gill define Foucault's view of power thus: "He defines power as the overall system, process, or network of force relations spread through the entire discursive formation" (1987, p. 389). It's important to keep in mind the word "network" as we look more closely at Foucault's ideas about power. As we do so, we'll discuss how the Internet exemplifies his conceptions of power. Foucault advanced several ideas, among them: "Power is not something that is acquired, seized, or shared." (Foucault, 1978, p. 94). Power is omnipresent and everyone is involved in power relationships at all times. If you consider the Internet, you know that anyone with access to the Web can create and disseminate content to the entire world. All users have the power to get their message out to other users. Despite the fact that large media companies control much of the Web, rhetors do not necessarily have to gain power in a formal way to be influential. Such is Foucault's view of power.

Foucault theorized that power relations were not always apparent. Individuals who have power didn't always know the ways that they could exercise their power. Likewise, Internet users may not know exactly what kind of power they possess. It may be apparent that large media companies have power, but by visiting certain sites, ordinary users can also exercise power. They can also post information in various ways that have the potential of attracting large audiences.

Foucault also wrote that there existed any number of local centers of power. That is, in a culture there is no single center from which power is exercised. Instead, there are a number of local centers that are locally powerful. No one organization or individual controls the Internet, for instance. However, there are certain sites that are more powerful and influential than others. These sites would be considered local centers of power.

BOX 11.2   Internet Activity: How Open is the Internet?

The Internet holds the promise of being open for all to use. We can discuss matters with others, post whatever we want on Web pages, and question what we see posted by others. At the same time, legal liability and the commercial nature of the Internet make it necessary to impose guidelines from time to time. Read the guidelines posted for Yahoo! at http://docs.yahoo.com/info/guidelines/community.html. These guidelines are for use of certain Yahoo! functions such as chat or groups. Thinking about Foucault's idea of the discursive formation, evaluate Yahoo!'s guidelines. What can be talked about? What cannot be talked about? What form must the communication take? That is, what are the rules of decorum on the Web site? Why do you think these limitations are in place? What do you think is the result of these guidelines (and others like them), in terms of how knowledge is created and transmitted online?

Foucault also argues that power relations are always changing. As you might know from your use of the Internet, it, too, is always changing. New sites emerge that become popular, and formerly popular sites are replaced by new sites.

Finally, and perhaps most important, Foucault argues that "Discourse transmits and produces power; it reinforces it, but also undermines and exposes it, renders it fragile and makes possible to thwart it" (Foucault, 1978, p. 101). Power is a product of discourse, consequently. In a similar way, the Internet exists only as discourse but provides the basis for the creation of power relations in society.

Power and knowledge are not distinct, rather they are reliant on each other and reinforce each other: "Indeed, it is in discourse that power and knowledge are joined together" (Foucault, 1978, p. 100). In sum, the knowledge of a particular culture at a particular point in time is dependent on the discursive formation and set of power relations that exist within the culture. Having surveyed Foucault's theory of discursive formations, complete the Internet Activity, found in Box 11.2 to put his ideas to practice.

Application

Foss and Gill (1987) use Foucault's theory of discursive formations to study the type of knowledge created by the discursive practices, rules, roles, and power present at Disneyland. Let's examine some specific ways that rhetoric is used at Disneyland to create knowledge.

The design elements of the park, the visitor's role, and the image of the employees are three types of discursive practices present at Disneyland. In terms of design elements, the park is structured to make it easy for people to get around. The various shops appear to be working together, since you can access one shop from another. The lines at the rides are structured to appear shorter than they are. In terms of the visitors, Foss and Gill (1987) explain that nothing is required of them. People who go to Disneyland sit and absorb the rides and events. Employees are clean and homogenous. Name tags don't feature last names, for instance, and men are not allowed to wear facial hair.

The rules of the park encourage the view that it is clean. Foss and Gill (1987) note that the currency used in Disneyland is colorful, clean, and fun. Only certain types of music are played in the park and punk rock is not among the accepted types of music. By using plastic, the park is able to create objects that appear to be better than the real thing.

Rhetors—park workers and visitors—fulfill a particular role: "one that is clean, sexless, polite, passive, follows orders, and does not initiate action or assert individ- uality" (Foss & Gill, 1987, p. 396). In addition, "Employees exemplify these traits, the design elements of the park give voice to these traits, and the visitor is expected to express them as well" (p. 396).

Likewise, power is ever present and surrounds everything in the park. From the happy music, to the way the queues are structured that make the lines appear shorter, to the cleanliness of the park, visitors don't question what is asked of them or the feelings they are supposed to have. Foss and Gill (1987) summarize the use of power in the park: "The power embodied in the system dictates acceptance of and preference for the inauthentic over the genuine" (Foss & Gill, 1987, p. 397).

The interaction of discursive practices, rules, roles, and power create a particu- lar type of knowledge at Disneyland. Ultimately, Disneyland "succeeds in making people accept as normal what they generally would not, enjoy what they gener- ally would not, repress aspects of themselves that they generally would not, and not question what they generally would" (Foss & Gill, 1987, p. 397). In particular, "the discursive practices embody rules and power relations that promote whole- some, sterile, and predictable behavior and that produce rhetors who fill passive, clean, unquestioning roles" (p. 397).

MEANING

A second significant concern of postmodern theorists is the meaning of signs. In previous chapters, meaning was more or less stable. That is, theorists believed that users of symbols had a basic level of understanding about the meaning of those symbols. When I write the word, "dog," for instance, you will likely think of a four-legged animal with a tail that many people have for pets. You'll recall that our discussion in Chapter 5 focused on linguistic relativity, exploring some of the ways that symbols come to have different meanings for people and yet there is still basic agreement that rhetoric can be used effectively despite these differences. In this chapter, we look at some of the extreme ideas about meaning. One of the leading poststructuralists is the French philosopher, Jacques Derrida. His theories about meaning and deconstruction virtually preclude the assumption that symbol users can ever agree upon meaning. In addition, rhetorical texts are open to multiple readings and interpretations and are never really restricted to a single meaning.

Difference

At the heart of Derrida's theory is the idea that signs—words or other symbols— only have meaning because of other signs. That is, signs don't mean anything by themselves; they have no essence or essential meaning. Instead, the meaning for a sign exists within a network of other signs and meanings. We only know what a red light on a stop light means because of its relationship to the green and yellow lights. By itself, a red light means nothing. If you think "stop" when you see a red light, it's because of your previous association between red lights and traffic laws. Likewise, the word "cat" only means something because of its relationship to a dog, hamster, or other animal.

Because the meanings of words lie in the differences between them and in the differences between them and the things they name, Derrida suggested that all language is constituted by **differance,** a word he has coined that puns on two French words meaning "to differ" and "to defer." That is, words are the deferred presences of the things they "mean," and their meaning is grounded in difference (Murfin, 1994, p. 285) As Chesebro (1995) explains, "As a critical concept, differance is a metaphor for a semiological method for determining the degree of variation or difference between a sign and what it signifies in terms of time and space. In other words, differance is designed to allow the critic to identify the temporal and spatial differences between a word and a thing" (p. 181).

According to Chesebro (1995), "a sign will always differ from what it signifies along two dimensions, temporization and spacing" (p. 182). Temporization refers to the time difference between a sign and its referent, whereas spacing refers to the placement of a sign among other signs to which it relates.

In terms of temporization, a sign takes the place of the present. When you tell a friend about a concert you went to over the weekend, the signs you use substitute for the concert. That is, you create in the present discussion with your friend a past event. As Derrida explained, "When the present cannot be presented, we signify, we go through the detour of the sign" (1982, p. 9). When you explain the concert with symbols, you can never do so perfectly. There is always some kind of gap between the signs you use and the actual experience of the concert. Thus, you cannot accurately or adequately use signs to refer to object, because there is always a time lag present in your description.

The second way that a sign differs in meaning from its referent is spacing. According to Chesebro, "Spacing also distinguishes a sign from what it signifies, for a sign exists within a 'chain' or sentence structure of other signs. These other signs within a 'chain' or sentence structure define the context for a sign, thereby attributing characteristics to a sign that do not exist for the sign's referent spatially" (1995, p. 182). Because we have to use the rules of grammar when we use signs, we alter their meanings in ways that we cannot avoid.

Deconstruction

Our discussion of differance, or the gap between a sign and what it means, leads to the idea of **deconstruction,** which is the critical methodology Derrida developed. "Deconstruction, as conceived by Derrida, is a method of interpretation of a text that focuses upon the logical consistency among the premises expressed or implied with a text and assesses the relationship that is claimed to exist between the text as sign and what it signifies" (Chesebro, 1995, p. 183). That is, deconstruction is a method for locating how a group of signs inherently contradicts itself because of its lack of essential meaning.

Chesebro outlines four dimensions to deconstruction:

- "First, deconstruction focuses upon the historical and anthropological identity of each sign within a text" (Chesebro, 1995, p. 183). That is, the critic attempts to understand the variety of meanings that exist for signs and how those signs have become meaningful.

- "Second, a deconstructive analysis examines the logical relations among the various signs within a text" (Chesebro, 1995, p. 183). The critic must show what relationships exist between signs.

- "Third, specific attention is devoted to inconsistencies contained within a text, especially to implied premises within the text that contradict each other and thereby undermine the thesis of the text" (Chesebro, 1995, p. 184). Because signs have multiple and contradictory meanings, it is quite likely that signs contained in a text will have contradictory meanings.

- "Fourth, the critic examines the relations among signs within the text; what they are said to signify in reality; and how others can perceive these sign-signified relationships, with particular attention given to whether or not the sign-signified relationship conveyed within a text is shared by different kinds of external audiences" (Chesebro, 1995, p. 184).

Let's consider how deconstruction might be used to see how an advertisement subverts its own message. See Box 11.3, Critical Insights.

IDENTITY/THE SELF

A third significant focus of postmodern theorists is the nature of human identity and being. They note that what it means to be human has varied over time. We have discussed some of these orientations toward ontology at the end of each chapter of this book. You should be able to see how conceptions of human identity, or ontology, have varied across time and cultures. The ancient Greeks and Romans, for instance, saw themselves in a subordinate relationship to their gods and nature. In the Middle Ages and the Renaissance, human identity was dictated first by the church and then by science. Through the scientific insights of Bacon, Locke, and others, humans came to see themselves as thinking, rational creatures who could reason and use science to better understand themselves and their world. Postmodern theorists recognized this subjectivity and point out that the human subject is constantly shifting because we use language to define who we are. If language is constantly shifting, then so too are the ways we define ourselves. Let's briefly examine some of the key ways of thinking about the human subject in the postmodern age.

Derrida

Derrida extended the idea of differance (see earlier discussion) to thinking about human identity. According to Biesecker (1989), "Derrida deconstructs the subject by showing us how the identity of any subject, what I earlier called the core of the

---

BOX 11.3   Critical Insights: Deconstructing Best Buy's Advertising

A recent advertisement for Best Buy depicts a woman in a bikini reclining in what seems to be an ocean of compact discs, DVDs, and Playstation games. She has these products wedged between her toes, and she is partially buried by them. She also has a pleasurable look on her face and a slight smile. The ad reads, "Thousands of possibilities. Get yours." Using Chesebro's description of deconstruction, let's deconstruct this advertisement.

First, we can examine the various signs in the advertisement and what they mean. One prominent sign is the Best Buy logo, a yellow "price tag" that contains the words "Best Buy." The logo is clearly a symbol for the store and its brand. The CDs, DVDs, and Playstation games are shown to extend to the horizon, and the clouds and blue sky prompt the reader to think of the ocean. The slogan, "Thousands of possibilities. Get yours," refers to the wide selection of electronics contained in Best Buy stores and available for purchase online. The woman, with her cool blue bikini and flower in her hair is the image of grace and comfort; things we would expect to find on a tropical vacation.

Next, Derrida and Chesebro would have us consider the logical relationships among the signs. Clearly the Best Buy name and logo are thought to relate to comfort, enjoyment, and a wide range of electronics products. The "Thousands of possibilities" slogan relates to what can be purchased at Best Buy, products that extend as far as the eye can see. The woman's

relationship with Best Buy is thought to be comfortable and enjoyable for her.

Third, deconstruction looks to the inconsistencies in these relationships that undermine the text. By claiming to offer thousands of possibilities and by substituting their products for the ocean, Best Buy is actually reducing the range of possibilities it offers; nature offers millions of colors and possibilities. Best Buy's "nature" can in no way compare with the real thing. Additionally, the woman, while apparently comfortable resting on the jewel cases and with jewel cases stuffed between her toes is, in actuality, probably very uncomfortable. Again, nature would be far more comforting to the woman than Best Buy's meager representation of nature. In two basic ways, then, Best Buy's ad undercuts its claim: that its product line is as big as nature's and that its products lead to comfort and enjoyment.

Finally, we are to address the effect of the text on various kinds of external audiences. Though the Best Buy advertisement might be effective for some audiences, this deconstruction has pointed to ways that the advertisement might be read differently by different audiences. Environmentalists, for instance, would probably scoff at the idea that Best Buy is trying to pass itself as natural. Likewise, fans of independent films and music would likely be unconvinced that Best Buy offers them enough possibilities to satisfy their tastes. By deconstructing this Best Buy advertisement, we can gain better understanding of Derrida's theory of difference and his method of deconstruction.

---

human being, like the value of any element in any system is structured by differance. This forces us to think of subjectivity not as an essence but as an effect of the subject's place in an economy of differences" (p. 124). That is, human subjects, like symbols, are products of differance. We differentiate ourselves from each other in much the same way as a red light is differentiated from a green light. Like the traffic signals, we obtain meaning only by the differences between us and others. In fact, Biesecker notes, "Against an irreducible humanist essence of subjectivity, Derrida advances a subjectivity which, structured by differance and thus always differing from itself, is forever in process, indefinite, controvertible" (Biesecker, 1989, p. 125). Human identity is not set. We constantly shift our conceptions of who we are based on the rhetoric we use and the rhetoric to which we are exposed.

Foucault

Foucault also extended his analysis of knowledge and power and looked at how humans constitute themselves. In particular, his historical view of knowledge and power led him to conclude that humans are products of certain historical periods. Humans today are thought to have power over language and meaning, but Foucault noted that this idea is only temporary and that our conception of being a human will again change.

He identified language practices as emerging that would control how humans communicate and think of themselves. In particular, Foucault was interested in how disciplinary practices created certain kinds of beings. Thus, he concluded, humans will become the products of discursive practices instead of controlling discursive practices themselves. He has even gone as far to say that the "author is dead," indicating that the producer of rhetoric is less significant than the rhetoric itself or how it is used in a society. You might think of a play in which actors play roles assigned to them by the script. It is not uncommon on Broadway for under-studies—substitute actors—to appear onstage from time to time in place of a lead actor or actress. Despite the change in actors, the show is essentially the same. The same lines are delivered, the same motivations are present, and the same story is told. Foucault believed a similar situation to exist in our postmodern world.

Deleuze and Guattari

The postmodern theorists Deleuze and Guattari take a slightly different approach to defining human identity. Best and Kellner note that "Unlike Foucault, Deleuze and Guattari's work is less a critique of knowledge and rationality than of capitalist society; consequently, their analyses rely on traditional Marxist categories more than Foucault's" (1991, p. 77). However, they do not consider themselves to be Marxists; they reject the methodology of Marxism in favor of postmodern ideas of difference, perspectives, and fragmentation (Best & Kellner, 1991, pp. 77–78).

Deleuze and Guattari believe that we are beings that desire in ways that are consistent with capitalist society. In other words, our identities are tied up in what we desire—and what we desire is dictated in large part by advertising and consumerism. "Deleuze and Guattari focus on the colonization of desire by various modern discourses and institutions" (Best & Kellner, 1991, p. 78). Thus, the human subject is a product of capitalist society and its goal of producing subjects to purchase goods and services: "Hence everything is production: *production of productions,* of actions and of passions; *productions of recording processes,* of distributions and of co-ordinates that serve as points of reference; *productions of consumptions,* of sensual pleasures, of anxieties and of pain" (Deleuze & Guattari, 1983, p. 4).

Consider again the Best Buy ad we just discussed to better understand the ideas of Deleuze and Guattari. We might say that Best Buy is attempting to manufacture desire. The reclining sexual pose of the woman and the slogan—"Get Yours"—create an appetite for the goods Best Buy advertises. Fulfilling this appetite by purchasing Best Buy's products, then, is analogous to having sex. In turn, sensual desire is shown to be fulfilled through the purchase of consumer goods. For Deleuze and Guattari, capitalist culture has coopted sex for the purpose of selling consumer goods. Thus, the identity of an individual in a postmodern culture is based not on real physical or emotional needs, but on perceived needs fulfilled through consumption of consumer goods.

In sum, Best and Kellner explain that "All three theorists [Foucault, Deleuze, and Guattari] reject the modernist notion of a unified, rational, and expressive subject and attempt to make possible the emergence of new types of decentred subjects, liberated from what they see to be the terror of fixed and unified identities, and free to become dispersed and multiple, reconstituted as new types of subjectivities and bodies" (1991, p. 78).

Judith Butler

Judith Butler has further explored the concept of identity by examining sex and gender. Butler argues that the categories of male-female and masculine-feminine are linguistic creations that have no essential qualities. In much the same way that we have been discussing, Butler argued that the term masculine gets its meaning only in relationship to a concept thought of as feminine. Because of differance, it is impossible to have any kind of real, or essential, category for either. Let's begin to discuss Butler's ideas by exploring her observations about the feminist movement.

Butler explains that feminism has to be *about* something. That is, it has to have a subject for its political agenda: "For the most part, feminist theory has assumed that there is some existing identity, understood through the category of women, who not only initiates feminist interests and goals within discourse, but constitutes the subject for whom political representation is pursued" (Butler, 1999, p. 3). In addition, "For feminist theory, the development of a language that fully or adequately represents women has seemed necessary to foster the political visibility of women" (Butler, 1999, p. 4). As a result, we attempt to create categories, such as "men" and "women" and then force people into those categories whether the categories are accurate or not.

The category of "woman," Butler argues, was constructed by and for men and the patriarchal system of power that exists today. Consequently, "the feminist subject turns out to be discursively constituted by the very political system that is supposed to facilitate its emancipation" (Butler, 1999, p. 4). Butler believes that to adequately reform the patriarchal system, a new conceptualization of woman is necessary: "It is not enough to inquire into how women might become more fully represented in language and politics. Feminist critique ought to also understand how the category of 'women,' the subject of feminism, is produced and restrained by the very structures of power through which emancipation is sought" (Butler, 1999, p. 5).

Butler also argues that there is a "political problem that feminism encounters in the assumption that the term women denotes a common identity. Rather than a stable signifier that commands the assent of those whom it purports to describe and represent, women, even in the plural, has become a troublesome term, a site of contest, a cause for anxiety" (Butler, 1999, p. 6). That is, the meaning of "woman" and "feminine" is not consistent from person to person, culture to culture, or time to time. Gender, Butler explains, "is not always constituted coherently or consistently in different historical contexts" (1999, p. 6). In fact, gender "intersects with racial, class, ethnic, sexual and regional modalities of discursively constituted identities" (p. 6).

As a result, Butler conceives of gender and sex as not being tied to any particular, essential qualities. For feminism, this move makes sense: "Perhaps, paradoxically, 'representation' will be shown to make sense for feminism only when the subject of 'women' is nowhere presumed" (Butler, 1999, p. 9). She elaborates on this point: "When the constructed status of gender is theorized as radically independent of sex, gender itself becomes a free-floating artifice, with the consequence that man and masculine might just as easily signify a female body as a male one, and woman and feminine a male body as easily as a female one" (Butler, 1999, p. 10).

It is common to consider sex apart from gender. That is, men can be feminine and women can be masculine. For Butler, however, sex is just as culturally inscribed as gender. "Gender is not to culture as sex is to nature; gender is also the discursive/cultural means by which 'sexed nature' or 'a natural sex' is produced and established as 'prediscursive,' prior to culture, a politically neutral surface *on which* culture acts," she explains (1999, p. 11).

What is significant for Butler is how sex and gender are performed from time to time by men and women. That is, gender is performative; it constitutes the "identity it is purported to be" (Butler, 1999, p. 33). Butler explains that gender is "always a doing, though not a doing by a subject who might be said to preexist the deed" (1999, p. 33). Gender does not exist apart from its performance by people. To put it simply, your sex and gender are not essential parts of your being or identity. Instead, they are performances we enact.

REALITY

We have so far discussed the postmodern view of knowledge, meaning, and identity. In this section, we turn to the concept of reality. One postmodern theorist, Jean Baudrillard, has developed a theory that explains how the postmodern world is organized around objects and signs and what the implications of such a world are for its citizens. Baudrillard is one of the most famous of the postmodern theorists, and his ideas have had far-reaching impact on several disciplines, including rhetoric. Best and Kellner (1991) note, "Baudrillard has developed the most striking and extreme theory of postmodernity yet produced and has been highly influential in cultural theory and discussions of contemporary media, art, and society" (p. 111). Let's begin to explore the concept of hyperreality by looking at what Baudrillard has to say about signs and objects.

Living in the World of Signs and Objects

Baudrillard's theory attempts to describe "the ways that subjects relate to, use, dominate—or are dominated by—the system of objects and signs which constitute our everyday life" (Best & Kellner, 1991, p. 113). He points out that the postmodern period has been marked by a concern for the production of signs and objects that have particular meanings for those who consume them. Baudrillard draws a distinction between use-value and exchange-value for signs. Use-value is based on the objective needs of a person. For instance, we all have the need to eat, drink, have shelter, and so forth. Products that fulfill these needs are said to have use-value. On the other hand, in a consumer society, products and services also have an exchange-value, which is a subjective value for a sign based on a culture's understanding of what that sign means. For instance, a pair of tennis shoes has a use-value—to keep one's feet warm and protected from the elements—but a pair of tennis shoes also has exchange-value—a pair of Nike basketball shoes endorsed by a major athlete and selling for $200 per pair. A $20 pair of nonbrand tennis shoes accomplishes the same function as the more expensive pair, but it clearly doesn't have the same exchange-value in a culture. For instance, people are not killed for their $20 pair of nonbrand tennis shoes. Today's consumer society, said Baudrillard, is concerned with generating exchange-value for its signs and objects. For this reason, Nike signed celebrated basketball player LeBron James to a large contract to capitalize on his exchange-value in promoting its tennis shoes.

Hyperreality

The problem, for Baudrillard, is that consumers organize their experience around the exchange-value of signs. What results is a world built on simulations of the real, instead of the real itself. As Best and Kellner explain, "Baudrillard claims that in the postmodern world the boundary between image or simulation and reality implodes, and with it the very experience and ground of 'the real' disappears" (p. 119). Baudrillard calls this phenomenon **hyperreality,** which Best and Kellner explicate as the "blurring of distinctions between the real and the unreal in which the prefix 'hyper' signifies more real than real whereby the real is produced according to a model" (Best & Kellner, 1991, p. 119). The numerous makeover shows on television—*Extreme Makeover, Dr. 90210,* and *The Swan,* for instance—show that with medical help, people can create new realities for themselves. Of course, these realities are only skin deep and do not relate in any way to the essence of the individual who had the makeover.

In essence, the simulations of the real become real for us. We react to the Nike tennis shoes as if they could magically transform the user into a star basketball player. To take this concept to another level, consider Best and Kellner's words:

> The hyperreal for Baudrillard is a condition whereby models replace the real, as exemplified in such phenomena as the ideal home in women's or lifestyle magazines, ideal sex as portrayed in sex manuals or relationship books, ideal computer skills as set forth in computer manuals, and so on. In these cases, the model becomes a determinant of the real, and the boundary between hyperreality and everyday life is erased." (Best & Kellner, 1991, pp. 119–120)

Thus, when you think that you "need" a certain item of clothing in order to look fashionable or that you "need" to drive a particular kind of car in order to feel "sexy," you have fallen victim to hyperreality. Baudrillard would encourage you not to confuse use-value with exchange-value. Sexy sports cars and designer clothing that carry certain weight in a society are examples of exchange-value. Let's consider a more profound example.

Hyperreality and Celebration, Florida

Perhaps nothing reflects Baudrillard's ideas about hyperreality more than the town of Celebration, Florida. Constructed in 1994, nearly eight hundred people live in the town, which was founded by the Walt Disney Company. The website for Celebration, Florida, explains the concept of the town: "Take the best ideas from the most successful towns of yesterday and the technology of the new millennium, and synthesize them into a close-knit community that meets the needs of today's families. The founders of Celebration started down a path of research, study, discovery, and enlightenment that resulted in one of the most innovative communities of the 20th century."

The result is a carefully planned community in which houses have front porches, the downtown has an old-fashioned ice cream shop, and fiber optic cable unites the town's residents. Additionally, events in the Town Center are held regularly to bring the community's residents together. Perhaps most striking are the "leaf falls" and "snowfalls" that occur in the community. The leaf falls occur on two evenings in October at 6, 7, 8, and 9 p.m. The snowfalls occur on several evenings in November and December at 6, 7, 8, and 9 P.M. The snowalls last for ten minutes at a time and are accompanied by festive music and entertainment. Keep in mind that this town is located in central Florida where snow does not regularly fall. However, manufactured snow—that is, simulated snow—is used to bring realism—Baudrillard might say, hyperrealism—to Celebration's holiday events. In fact, much of the community is created based on idealized perceptions we have of a simpler life of long ago. These are hyperreal conceptions that may or may not bear any relationship to a reality that once was. You can learn more about the town by visiting its website at http://www.celebrationfl.com/.

Implosion

The founders of Celebration, Florida, hope to use technology to restore the human spirit and encourage the socialization of its citizens. Baudrillard is concerned that hyperreality will have the opposite effect. He applies the concept of implosion, the collapsing of boundaries between what is real and unreal, to the collapse of the social system of a culture. We can understand what he means by the collapsing of boundaries by considering the example of television news. We generally think that the news tells us what we need to know about the world and that it reflects "real" events. During the summer of 2004, television news instead spent a great deal of time on events manufactured by the entertainment industry. In particular, the series finale of *Friends* gained a great deal of "news" coverage, dominating the morning and evening news shows for the weeks leading up to the final episode. Baudrillard takes this a step further to argue that even the "news" that we consider to be "real" is also manufactured to be hyperreal.

The collapsing of boundaries between what is real and unreal is cause for alarm for Baudrillard, and he uses the term implosion to identify this danger. Baudrillard notes that "the humans of the age of affluence are surrounded not so much by other human beings, as they were in all previous ages, but by **objects** [emphasis original]" (1998, p. 25). We talk not of real events, feelings, emotions, and so forth, but of those that are manufactured for us. For example, explains Baudrillard, "We live by object time: by this I mean that we live at the pace of objects, live to the rhythm of their ceaseless succession" (1998, p. 25). As an example, consider the back-to-school shopping tradition of many Americans. While buying new clothes for growing youth each year might be a necessity, the tradition continues for those of us who are out of school and have stopped growing rapidly, yet we are conditioned to think that each fall should bring a new wardrobe and we continue marking time to the objects in our lives. Baudrillard believed that the realm of the social, including human relationships with other humans, is in danger of becoming lost in our obsession with signs, objects, and exchange-value.

POLITICS

A key topic of importance for postmodern theorists is determining what, if any, standards may be used to make decisions about ethics and morality. From our previous discussion in this chapter, it should be clear that postmodern theorists are concerned with questioning totalizing statements or grand theories about how the world operates. Foucault's examination of how particular rules govern what can be said and how it may be said in particular historical periods and Derrida's discussion of differance and deconstruction lead us to a view of the world in which ethical standards are highly relative and contextual. Foucault, Derrida, and the other theorists we have discussed seek to delegitimize claims to truth, seeking instead to explicate how a variety of truths can come to exist. As we discuss this point further, we'll again turn to Lyotard.

Lyotard focuses on the games that people play with language to legitimate particular values or ideas. Particularly, he focuses on science and how the rules that dictate what is true and false in science permeate other aspects of society. In science, for instance, the standards of universality and certainty dictate what is true and false, and thus we seek these standards in other aspects of our existence. Lyotard attempts to take apart those rules and show that how we make decisions is based on a series of language games that are governed by particular rules and methods of speaking. He attempts to replace the universal, taken-for-granted rules with ones that are "local, modest, provisional, and centered on the rhetorical effects of discourse" (Best & Kellner, 1991, p. 162).

For Lyotard, the larger picture of how language games help us determine what is true and false centers on politics. Politics—in the broadest sense—has been influenced by the language games of science. Best and Kellner (1991) explain Lyotard's approach to politics thus:

> Political struggle for Lyotard is a matter of discursive intervention within language, contesting rules, forms, principles and positions, while offering new rules, criteria, forms of life, and perspectives. The struggle takes place within a given language game (such as politics, philosophy, and art), and perhaps between these language games. Yet Lyotard insists that there is no overarching language game, no privileged discourse, no general theory of justice within which struggles between different language games could be adjudicated. (p. 163)

Thus, for Lyotard, the postmodern opens opportunities to rethink how we talk about justice and other similar values. He encourages us to think critically about the language games that are used to make ethical decisions.

This approach to knowledge and politics is evident in some recent scholarly work about sexual harassment. In 1992, the *Journal of Applied Communication Research* published the stories, or narratives, of women in academia who had experienced sexual harassment. The goal was to use the actual, lived experiences of women to inform "both theoretical and practical efforts to understand the discursive construction and perpetuation of sexual harassment" (Wood, 1992, p. 350). Thus, the journal's editors sought to localize and contextualize knowledge about sexual harassment so that the language games that dictate how sexual harassment is understood in society might be reexamined.

Wood (1992) argues that sexual harassment can not be properly understood by looking at universal statements about its meaning: "Whatever else it may be, sexual harassment is a range of personal experiences, each of which is embedded in particular historical, social, and institutional contexts. Given this, efforts to unravel its genesis, dynamics, and meanings should be informed by close attention to actual experiences of harassers and victims as well as to conditions that surround and influence their behavior" (p. 356). By publishing the stories of women who experienced sexual harassment, the journal sought to create local theories of sexual harassment that were more valid than previous theories. Wood explains that, "From individuals' accounts of sexual harassment scholars can inductively derive powerful conceptual frameworks consonant with the lived experiences of those involved. In turn, this enhances the likelihood that resulting knowledge will be theoretically sound and pragmatically useful" (1992, p. 356).

By examining a number of detailed, first-person narratives from victims of sexual harassment, scholars can identify a "number of legitimate truths" rather than a single truth. By situating the knowledge about sexual harassment in these truths, Wood hopes scholars can better describe, predict, and explain sexual harassment, and, consequently, formulate more effective intervention strategies. For instance, traditional ways of handling sexual harassment were shown to be ineffective after reading the accounts of its victims. By avoiding generalizations about sexual harassment and focusing instead on the individualized—localized—stories of women involved, readers were thought to gain a more realistic understanding of sexual harassment.

RETHINKING RHETORIC
IN THE POSTMODERN AGE

A long-standing belief of rhetorical theorists is that rhetoric is created in response to a situation by a speaker who makes deliberate and creative choices about the rhetoric. As Biesecker (1989) explained, "In all cases, however, critics still take as their founding presumption a causal relation between the constituent elements comprising the event as a whole. Either speaker or situation is posited as logically and temporally prior, or the other is taken as origin." Biesecker uses the insights of postmodernism, specifically of Derrida, to question the degree to which rhetoric is produced by either a situation or speaker. Instead of focusing on the production aspects of rhetoric—as was previously the focus—Biesecker suggests that rhetorical theorists instead focus on reception elements of rhetoric.

Earlier in this chapter, we discussed the idea that the human subject, from a postmodern perspective, is thought to lack an essence, but is instead constituted and reconstituted in numerous ways. Recall, for example, Butler's discussion of gender. Rhetoric, according to Biesecker, plays a fundamental role in how humans think about themselves. Her attention in thinking about rhetorical theory is on how rhetoric is received by human subjects as they consider themselves as subjects. She explains,

> Simply put, the deconstruction of the subject opens up possibilities for the field of Rhetoric by enabling us to read the rhetorical situation as an event structured not by a logic of influence but by a logic of articulation. If the subject is shifting and unstable (constituted in and by the play of difference), then the rhetorical event may be seen as an incident that produces and reproduces the identities of the subjects and constructs and reconstructs linkages between them. (Biesecker, 1989, p. 129)

She explains further,

> From within the thematic of difference we would see the rhetorical situation neither as an event that merely induces audiences to act one way or another nor as an incident that, in representing the interests of a particular collectivity, merely wrestles the probable within the realm of the actualizable. Rather, we would see the rhetorical situation as an event that makes possible the production of identities and social relations. (Biesecker, 1989, p. 126)

SUMMARIZING POSTMODERN APPROACHES TO RHETORIC

Our examination of postmodernism and rhetoric has touched on all of the key concepts we have explored throughout this book. We'll briefly review here the highlights of our discussion.

Defining Rhetoric

The theorists we have encountered in this chapter do not deal directly with rhetoric in the way we saw earlier theorists do and in fact many prefer the term "discourse" to that of "rhetoric." At the same time, however, their focus is unmistakably on symbols and the impact of symbols on knowledge, meaning, identity formation, ethics, and reality.

Rhetoric and Knowledge

Postmodernists maintain that knowledge, truth, and reality are constantly shifting concepts because of the gaps in meaning between symbols and their referents. Postmodern theorists are skeptical of narratives that seek to establish a definitive, objective truth. As Wood explains, "Within postmodernist thinking, situated knowledge emerges as the key term, one that would be oxymoronic in prior world views. According to postmodernity, all knowledge, all experience is necessarily situated and, thus, can be interpreted only in light of its unique historical location" (Wood, 1992, p. 357).

Rhetoric and Identity

Likewise, our conception of what it means to be human is constantly shifting because the categories we use to create and establish identities are constantly shifting. There is no essence to our identity. Foucault adds that discourse and disciplinary practices create certain kinds of beings, while Deleuze and Guattari focus on capitalism's production of beings that have particular kinds of desire. Butler maintains that even our understanding of sex and gender is linguistically mediated and controlled by hegemonic forces.

Rhetoric and Judgment

Fundamentally, postmodernism questions the standards that are used to make judgments. In the place of global theorizing about universal ethical standards, postmodernists prefer localized ethics and politics. Our discussion of Lyotard makes this point most clearly.

DISCUSSION QUESTIONS

1. What are some examples of postmodern influences on the art, architecture, music, or literature with which you are familiar?

2. Consider a debate that is occurring in our culture. You might consider abortion, doctor-assisted suicide, affirmative action, or economic policy. Who is entitled to speak about this issue? What are some of the rules that govern what is said and how it is said? What is the widely accepted knowledge about this issue?

3. Deconstruct a recent political speech. Visit our president's website or access the site for a political candidate, senator, U.S. representative, or other political figure. Follow the four-step method of deconstruction presented here. What are some of the different meanings for the text suggested by your deconstruction?

4. Which view of identity is closest to how you understand yourself? Do you consider your identity in ways that are different than what is suggested here?

5. Locate another example of hyperreality (other than Celebration, Florida). How is the replica made to seem real? What is the effect on audiences?

6. To what degree do you accept that knowledge and truth are situated in specific circumstances and that they are subject to change? What rules do we follow in a world where the rules constantly change?

GLOSSARY TERMS

modern   A time period governed by rationality, grand narratives, and industrialization.

postmodern   A time period marked by skepticism for grand narratives, objectivity, and universal truth.

episteme   A set of discursive practices, roles, rules, and power systems that create knowledge in a culture. See *discursive formation*.

discursive formation   A set of discursive practices, roles, rules, and power systems that create knowledge in a culture. See *episteme*.

differance   A term coined by Jacques Derrida to point to the difference between a symbol and its referent.

deconstruction   A critical method developed by Derrida to show how texts subvert themselves.

hyperreality   A state of being in which the replica of an object is thought to be more real than the object it replicates.

12

Cultural Rhetorical Studies

Learning Objectives

After reading this chapter, you should be able to:

1. Define the key elements of cultural studies.
2. Show how cultural studies and rhetorical studies are related.
3. Discuss key terms related to cultural studies.
4. Identify ways the cultural studies and rhetorical studies complement each other.

No matter how busy we are, most of us make time to watch at least one television show each week. My favorite is Donald Trump's *The Apprentice*. Without fail, I watch it to see what kind of tasks the groups have to accomplish and who gets fired. The theorists we'll discuss in this chapter are interested in popular rhetorical texts, such as television shows, movies, and advertising. They are also interested in political and historical rhetorical texts as well. Although *The Apprentice* is an interesting way to observe communication practices, I also recognize that the show is a vehicle through which Trump can promote his image and that of his companies. The show is situated in a culture that appreciates wealth, and that gives particular meanings to shows like *The Apprentice*. I cannot help but be influenced by the messages from the show that wealth and hard work are positive values. The cultural studies theorists we'll discuss in this chapter appreciate the range of messages contained in popular rhetorical texts, and they explore those messages to learn what the members of a culture take from these texts.

This chapter explores one possible direction for the future of rhetorical theory: its alignment with the discipline of cultural studies. By "cultural" we are not referring to a specific culture based on ethnicity, race, or sex. Instead, we will be looking at culture in the broadest possible sense: as the complete way of life for a group of people. Specifically, we'll examine the contemporary culture of industrialized nations such as the United States or Great Britain. We'll begin by briefly reviewing the past five chapters in our study of rhetorical theory, then we will define the field of cultural studies and examine several of its key ideas. Finally, we'll look at how cultural studies and rhetorical studies intersect and how they contribute to our understanding of the way texts function in modern industrialized culture.

REVIEWING RHETORICAL THEORY

In Chapters 5 and 6, we discussed the linguistic turn in rhetorical theory by looking at the link between symbols and meaning and how symbols create realities for their users. We specifically examined Scott's idea that rhetoric is epistemic; that is, rhetoric *creates* knowledge and is not used to simply *transmit* knowledge.

Chapter 7 examined the ideological turn in rhetorical theory. We addressed concepts of ideology, hegemony, and power. We specifically examined the idea of critical rhetoric and the shift in emphasis from theory to the goal of empowerment. Chapters 8 and 9 addressed the rhetoric and rhetorical theory of women, Africans, Chinese, and Native Americans. We saw in these chapters that rhetoric is related to culture, cultural practices, and empowerment.

In Chapter 10, we looked at media and its impact on rhetorical theory. We discussed the discipline of semiotics and McLuhan's theory of how rhetoric is shaped by the media it uses. Chapter 11 examined postmodernism's influence on rhetoric.

To summarize, there are four trends evident in the past seven chapters of our study. First, our study of rhetorical theory has, since the beginning of the twentieth century, focused on language, or discourse, and its power to create realities and social relationships. You'll recall that the linguistic turn we first discussed in Chapter 5 has been a prominent feature of much of our recent study.

Second, the attention of rhetorical scholars is increasingly more critical and less theoretical—in other words, scholars interested in rhetoric are doing less theorizing and more rhetorical criticism. In fact, Kurt Wilson (2003) found that in recent publications of rhetoric-related articles in journals, the overwhelming majority was focused on criticism, not theory. This change reflects two shifts in thinking. First, rhetorical theorists are using more of an inductive approach in developing theory. That is, instead of developing theory and showing how it can be used to describe and interpret specific rhetorical practices, critics are looking first at the rhetorical practices to surmise what general principles arise from those practices. Second, rhetorical theorists are exploring in greater detail the implications of rhetorical practice rather than how rhetoric can be effectively produced.

Earlier in our study, we were interested in how rhetors could effectively create messages for audiences. Now we are more interested in the implications of the messages they create for culture.

Third, the study of rhetoric is becoming increasingly ideological. Since our discussion in Chapter 7, we have focused on how rhetoric and rhetorical theory are used to manage power relationships in a culture. We have discussed ideas about how rhetoric creates certain ways of thinking and relating. We have also seen how women and people from other cultures have used rhetoric and theorized about it.

Finally, the look and appearance of rhetoric has changed. Where rhetorical practice once consisted of public speeches made by men for political purposes, rhetoric is now practiced by anyone in nearly every setting and using a variety of media. We are just as likely to view architecture as rhetoric as we are a speech by the president of the United States.

Rhetorical theorists are trying to account for these changes in their theories and critical practices. At the same time, a new discipline—cultural studies—has emerged that also has as its focus a careful analysis of culture, ideology, and communication. We will now turn our attention to how rhetoric and cultural studies overlap and how each discipline may learn from the other. The relationship between rhetoric and cultural studies is too close to ignore, and we can gain much insight about both disciplines from this discussion. We'll begin our study by briefly discussing the key aspects of cultural studies.

WHAT IS CULTURAL STUDIES?

Many students of **cultural studies** trace the discipline to two books published in the 1950s, Richard Hoggart's *The Uses of Literacy* and Raymond Williams's *Culture and Society*. Each of these writers took up the task of exploring how cultures were created not just by "elite" works of literature and art but also by the more popular cultural texts to which everyone is exposed. Hall (1996) notes that there was also a political agenda to these works. The authors sought to examine how culture could be made more democratic and free of ideological constraints. As members of the English Department at the University of Birmingham in England, Hoggart and Williams attracted similarly minded colleagues and formed the Centre for Contemporary Cultural Studies in 1964. Stuart Hall, whom we will study later in this chapter, was an influential chair of the department for ten years. You can read more about Hall in the Biography of a Theorist feature for this chapter (Box 12.1).

Fiske (1996) offers a succinct definition of cultural studies as the exploration of "the generation and circulation of meanings in industrial societies" (p. 115). Culture, as viewed by cultural studies critics is a "way of living within an industrial society that encompasses the meanings of that social experience" (Fiske, 1996, p. 115). Beyond this brief definition, though, the complexities and range of cultural studies are difficult to pin down. Sparks (1996) notes, "It is extremely difficult to define 'Cultural Studies' with any degree of precision. It is not possible to draw a sharp line and say that on one side of it we can find the proper province of

---

BOX 12.1   Biography of a Theorist: Stuart Hall

Stuart Hall was born in Kingston, Jamaica, on February 3, 1932. He attended Jamaica College before moving to England to attend Oxford University as a recipient of a Rhodes Scholarship. In the 1950s, Hall became the editor or two radical journals, *The New Reasoner* and the *New Left Review*, which opposed British imperialism. Hall taught secondary school before teaching at Chelsea College and the Centre for Contemporary Cultural Studies at the University of Birmingham.

Hall was appointed as a professor at the Open University in 1979, where he retired from in 1997. He currently sits on the Runnymede Trust's commission on the future of multiethnic Britain.

Hall's works include *What is Black in Popular Culture?* (1992), *Cultural Identity and Diaspora* (1994), *Questions of Cultural Identity* (1996), *Stuart Hall: Critical Dialogues in Cultural Studies* (1996), *Cultural Representations and Signifying Practices* (1997) and *Visual Cultural* (1999).

---

cultural studies. Neither is it possible to point to a unified theory or methodology which are characteristic to it or of it" (p. 14). Instead, cultural studies critics use a variety of theories, methods, and ideas from disciplines such as literary criticism, sociology, history, media studies, and others. Although there are some universities that have specific programs or departments in cultural studies, typically the discipline is taught in a particular course or series of courses.

As Fiske's definition implies, cultural studies takes up the definition of culture advanced by Williams, that culture is a "whole way of life." Sparks (1996) explains how this view informed the critical practice of cultural studies: "culture arose from a whole way of life and was a means by which those within that pre-given structure gave meaning to their experiences" (p. 16). Essentially, cultural studies is interested in signification, or how signs come to have meaning within a culture. This perspective assumes that meaning is not something fixed or permanent. Instead, meanings are varied, temporary, and based on personal experiences—a view that has much in common with postmodernism. Two people might watch the same television show, for instance, and come to different meanings about what the show and its characters mean. These different meanings are based on the experiences of those viewers and the context in which the show takes place. Cultural studies critics do not focus specifically on a communication text as the variable in their study. Instead, they look to all variables involved in how culture is created and maintained: the process by which texts are created, the situations of receivers, the dominant political ideology at the time, the previous meanings that have existed, and the competing meanings for a text.

As we have suggested, cultural studies is ideological in its orientation and has been influenced by Marxism (see Chapter 7). Storey notes that "All the basic assumptions of cultural studies are Marxist" (1996, p. 3). Specifically, cultural studies is interested in how meanings in a culture are related to the social structure and history of the culture (Storey, 1996) Additionally, cultural studies, like Marxism, assumes that inequalities exist along gender, ethnic, generational, and class lines (Storey, 1996). Culture is seen as a way of dividing groups and as a site of struggle between those groups over the meanings that exist within a culture.

However, cultural studies critics do not see ideology in quite the same way as did Marx. It's also worth pointing out that cultural studies does not trace its history or way of thinking to the theorists we discussed in Chapter 7—Habermas, in particular—that have influenced rhetorical theorists.

The goal of cultural studies is to show the political aspects of culture. Cultural theorists think of politics in a broad sense, illustrating how particular cultural practices and texts privilege one set of values or beliefs within a culture. In essence, cultural studies seeks to theorize about politics in a very broad sense. Cultural studies tries to theorize about what kinds of political actions can be taken within a given cultural and communication structure. As Grossberg (1997) explains, cultural studies

> is not about interpreting or judging texts or people, but about describing how people's everyday lives are articulated by and with culture, how they are empowered and disempowered by the particular structures and forces that organize their lives, always in contradictory ways, and how their everyday lives are themselves articulated to and by the trajectories of economic and political power. (p. 4)

Nelson (1996) offers a sixteen-point "manifesto" of cultural studies beliefs and practices. We won't discuss each of the sixteen points here, just briefly summarize some of the most instructive:

1. Cultural studies involves more than a "close reading" of nonliterary cultural texts. Instead, cultural studies has a history and literature that must be considered when one performs a "cultural studies" critique.

2. Cultural studies does not necessarily have to concern itself with artifacts of popular culture.

3. Cultural studies may make use of semiotics—which we studied in Chapter 10—but it is not synonymous with semiotics. Cultural studies instead is concerned with cultural context and the politics of signification, a process we will discuss later in this chapter.

4. Cultural studies is concerned with the production, reception, and uses of cultural texts, not necessarily their internal characteristics.

5. Cultural studies considers the relationships between texts, objects, and cultural forces. The focus is not on a text in isolation from culture, but rather on a text's operation within a cultural structure.

6. Cultural studies does not provide a "fixed, repeatable methodology" that can be used over and over again on cultural phenomena.

7. Cultural studies criticism suggests future courses of action for members of a culture.

8. Academic disciplines that teach cultural studies must take seriously the politics of disciplinarity. It is not enough to simply rename a class or department "cultural studies" without a commitment to how the unique cross-disciplinary nature of cultural studies fits within the university framework.

Having surveyed some of the key tenets of cultural studies, we can now turn to a discussion of how it is related to rhetorical studies.

RELATIONSHIP BETWEEN CULTURAL STUDIES AND RHETORICAL STUDIES

Rosteck (1999) notes that cultural studies and rhetoric share much in common:

> Cultural studies and rhetorical studies seem to share in much that is taken to be important these days: both aiming to reveal the relationship between expressive forms and social order; both existing with the field of discursive practices; both sharing an interest in how ideas are caused to materialize in texts; both concerned with how these structures are actually effective at the point of 'consumption'; and both interesting in grasping such textual practices as forms of power and performance. (p. 2)

To further explore these ideas, we'll examine the similarities and differences between cultural studies andrhetorical studies before addressing how the two disciplines may already be merging in critical practice. For a summary of the similarities and differences between the two disciplines, see Table 12.1.

Similarities

Rosteck (1999) notes that the two disciplines have much in common. First of all, in terms of culture, both rhetoric and cultural studies seeks to understand how meanings are created within cultural frameworks. Practitioners of either discipline are interested in questions related to how power in a culture is managed through communication texts such as movies, television shows, or advertising, for example.

Second, both rhetoric and cultural studies entail critical practice. Throughout this book, we have examined rhetorical criticism, which is the application of rhetorical theory to rhetorical practice to make a judgment about rhetoric. Cultural studies shares this same type of critical tool. Thus, the critical processes used by each discipline are similar.

Finally, despite the differences between the two disciplines in terms of theory and method, the end result of each is the same. Rosteck argues that both rhetorical studies and cultural studies "concern themselves chiefly and finally with the ultimate and complete disclosure of the artifact or practice being studied rather than dogmatically attempting to separate their work into its 'cultural' and 'rhetorical' components" (p. 7).

Differences

Several key differences between the two disciplines exist, however. First, rhetorical critics tend to examine a cultural text apart from context in which it occurs. For rhetorical critics, the rhetoric, or artifact, is of primary consideration. A rhetorical critic may study the symbolism of a movie, for instance, to learn the meaning of

Table 12.1 Comparisons between Rhetorical Studies and Cultural Studies

Similarities	Differences
1. Both seek to understand how meaning is created and power managed within a cultural context.	1. Rhetorical studies focuses primarily on texts; cultural studies focuses on context as well.
2. Both share a critical methodology.	2. Rhetorical studies has traditionally taken a neutral position toward the artifact; cultural studies takes a political position toward it.
3. Both pursue a similar outcome: complete and ultimate disclosure of an artifact.	3. Rhetorical studies has traditionally focused on legitimate social institutions, whereas cultural studies has emphasized alternative institutions that resist the establishment.

the movie. A cultural studies critic, on the other hand, would look at the movie's symbolism, but also the time in which it appeared, the competing cultural forces at the time, and the cultural position of the company that created a film.

Second, historically, rhetorical studies has assumed a more neutral position regarding criticism, whereas cultural studies has always been political in its analysis of cultural texts. Although rhetorical studies, especially the idea of critical rhetorical studies, is moving toward a partisan reading of cultural texts, there is historical precedent that calls for a more neutral understanding of rhetoric.

Finally, the objects of study for rhetoric and cultural studies has, at least in the past, been different. Rosteck explains, "Rhetoric traditionally has been concerned with how a struggle for power happens through legitimate social institutions, whereas cultural studies assumes that political empowerment occurs outside legitimate social institutions and in resistance to those institutions" (Rosteck, p. 7). That is, rhetorical critics are more likely to study famous speeches by powerful rhetors, and cultural critics are more apt to study artifacts such the online blog of an environmentalist.

Merging Cultural Studies and Rhetorical Studies

As we have seen, though, not all rhetorical theorists and critics hold fast to the distinctions we have previously identified. That is, many examine the context of rhetoric as well as the rhetoric itself; many do not believe a critic should be neutral about the artifacts they study; and many do accept that political change happens outside of legitimate social institutions. In fact, much evidence suggests that rhetorical studies and cultural studies are, in many ways, merging or overlapping.

Rhetorical critics are today quite likely to examine the kinds of texts looked at by cultural studies critics. Gronbeck (1999) has noted that cultural studies and rhetoric have much more in common with each other than either does with the social science researchers with whom they may coexist in academic departments. Likewise, rhetorical critics have much more in common with cultural studies critics than they do with rhetorical theorists.

Despite the apparent movement toward each other, some critics are concerned that one or the other discipline may lose its identity if the two would become one. Rosteck proposes a title that suggests a melding of the two without risking such a loss: "Cultural rhetorical studies."

The title for this chapter reflects Rosteck's nomenclature. Assuming, at least, that our study of rhetorical theory can be informed by understanding cultural studies, let's look at some of the basic principles of cultural studies.

REPRESENTATION AND SIGNIFICATION: THE BASIS OF CULTURAL STUDIES

Central to cultural studies is the investigation of how members of industrial societies create meaning. Typically, media are a primary way that individuals learn about the possible meanings for symbols, people, or objects. Stuart Hall, one of the most influential cultural theorists, has explained that previous views of meaning focused on how communicators present, or represent, a person, object, or idea that already has meaning. He points out that from this perspective, critics often look for a gap between what is true and what is presented (see Jhally, 1997). Previously, critics assumed that there is an "accurate" way of depicting something in the media. Media critics working from this perspective might make the argument that a television show portrays a minority person inaccurately or incorrectly. For Hall, this view—that you can accurately portray an idea through media—is outdated and inaccurate.

Representation

Instead, Hall offered the idea of **representation,** which is one of the main theoretical orientations of cultural studies. Initially, Hall questions whether events have one essential, fixed, or true meaning against which they can be measured for distortion. Meaning can always be contested, he suggests. In fact, Hall asserts that there is never anything "fixed" in the first place to re-present. There are never "true" meanings. Instead, meaning depends on how ideas, objects, or people are represented. Meaning doesn't exist until the idea has been represented. Meaning is part of the event and doesn't exist outside the event. Meaning certainly doesn't exist prior to the event's depiction in the media. Also, Hall explains, it doesn't exist after the event. Instead, meaning is part of the event itself. Meaning is constitutive of the event. "Reality," he asserts, "does not exist outside the event" (see Jhally, 1997). Meaning exists *within* the event.

An example will help to clarify this point. One of the key events of the Iraq War was the capture and rescue of Jessica Lynch. Lynch, along with several of her fellow soldiers, was captured by Iraqi troops in the early days of the Iraq war. Although several of the Americans died, Lynch survived and was held in an Iraqi hospital until she was rescued by American troops ten days later—a rescue that was captured by the military on video. Following her rescue, Lynch was portrayed as a hero in the media who fought valiantly against the Iraqis until her gun ran out of ammunition. She became the symbol for American resolve, courage, and bravery. Lynch received a hero's welcome upon returning to the United States. A made-for-TV movie was quickly created, and a book was written about her ordeal. Although her fellow captives were subsequently released, none gained the iconic status of Lynch.

Lynch-as-hero was only one interpretation of the events surrounding her capture and rescue. In the days following her rescue, new details emerged that created a different meaning. Lynch's gun was allegedly jammed, which indicated that she had never fired a round at the Iraqis. Additionally, Iraqi troops had reportedly abandoned the hospital where the "valiant" rescue took place. People struggled to define the meaning of Lynch and her rescue. For some, her rescue—and her status as a hero—represented what was right with the war. For others, the seemingly contrived nature of Lynch's story represented all that was wrong with the Bush Administration's spinning of the war and its rationale. It's important to note, from a cultural studies perspective, that prior to her capture and rescue, Lynch was just one of thousands of American soldiers in Iraq. Today, as the war and Lynch have faded from our memories, the nature of what she stands has faded as well. But in the few months surrounding her ordeal, Lynch took on a meaning that was larger–than life. Lynch—a quiet, unassuming soldier from West Virginia—had assumed political, cultural, and strategic importance. Lynch's culture assigned her meanings that were both consistent and at odds with the culture's feelings toward the war. Lynch's image wasn't represented in the media, it was created by and through the media's depictions of her.

Culture, thus, becomes a primary element in a discussion of meaning. Culture, according to Hall, is "the way we make sense of, give meaning, to the world" (see Jhally, 1997). We all don't make sense of things the same way, but we do share some concepts with other people and this sharing allows us to make sense of the world. Meaning arises because of the "shared conceptual maps" that we share with others in our culture. Culture, then, plays a central role in representation, or how we make meaning of events. Hall says that cultural studies begins with understanding the shared conceptual maps that people within a culture have. Conceptual maps help us to classify objects, ideas, and people in our world. We classify a hammer, saw, and chisel as part of the category of objects called "tools," for instance. Hall says that humans have an innate ability to classify. He is interested in how we have learned to classify ideas in particular ways. To become a cultured subject, he explains, we have to learn how to classify things in the same way as the others in our culture. In fact, says Hall, "culture is a system of representation." That is, culture is the process by which we learn how to classify ideas, objects, or people. Meaning also allows us to think about things that are not physically present to us. These meanings, thus, are not mirror images of real objects.

Hall says that we use language, or communication, to exchange cultural maps with others. He claims that "Language externalizes the meanings that we are making of the world" (see Jhally, 1997) and it "closes the circle" of representation. The only thing that exists is meaning: "Nothing meaningful exists outside of discourse" (see Jhally, 1997). You need discourse, the frameworks of understanding or interpretation, to make sense of things. Hall uses the example of a soccer ball. A soccer ball is a tangible object that you can feel, touch, bounce, and kick, yet the ball's meaning is incomplete without knowledge of its context: the rules of the game. If you were unfamiliar with those rules, you wouldn't have access to the full range of meanings for the soccer ball. Without the context of soccer, the soccer ball would not seem that much different from a volleyball or basketball. The soccer ball becomes more meaningful when you know the discourse of which it is a part. Hall and other cultural studies theorists are interested in how things become meaningful. They ask, "What is the context(s) through which meaning takes place?" To answer this question, they turn to signification.

Signification

Signification is the study of the production of meaning. We shouldn't assume that meaning is fixed or set in any way. There is a kind of symbolic work or practice that goes on to give meaning to things. **Signifying practices** are practices involved in the production of meaning" (see Jhally, 1997). Media are widely used systems of signifying. Talking with other people is another way in which signifying practices occur. Often, however, a medium such as computer technology takes the place of face-to-face communication and becomes very widespread. Questions of power arise in this discussion. Hall says we should ask "who has the power to circulate which meanings to whom?" (see Jhally, 1997). To answer this question, one must consider the economic system in which message producers exist. It is difficult today to separate news organizations, for example, from their business of producing profit.

It is important to look not only at what is communicated but also at what is *absent* from communication. What is left out or what is not said may be an important way of creating meaning. Hall says that what we expect to find is contrasted with what we find in the image. Indeed, "Absence means something; signifies something as much as presence" (see Jhally, 1997). Every image we see is read against what is not there. As you determine what something means, you cannot ignore what is missing from the the defining situation.

An advertisement for the FirstHealth health plan promotes the idea that its members will be covered for medical emergencies wherever they go. A woman is holding a young girl, and the two are pictured in what looks like a hotel room. Presumably, the girl is the woman's daughter, they are on vacation, the girl is sick, and they may not know if she can obtain medical care. Although these premises are not explicitly stated, we assign this meaning based on the context of the ad and what we know about the symbols contained in it. Hall encourages us to look for what is missing from an image as well as what is contained in the image. What may be missing from this ad is the girls' father. We see only a woman, who we presume to be her mother. Without usually giving it much thought, we might make several assumptions based on the lack of the father. Maybe the father is calling the hospital. Of course, there might be no father in the girl's life and she is being raised by a single mother. However, we might be most likely to think that taking care of sick children is a mother's duty and not that of the father. Since this is a prevalent attitude in our culture, it may be the meaning that a viewer of this ad would be most likely to construct because of the father's absence. Thus, images, discourse, and other rhetorical texts have meaning because of what is included in the text, but also because of what is not included.

The process of signification also carries with it the idea of an identity claim. Hall explains that we "project ourselves into the image" (see Jhally, 1997). Most advertising works, for instance, by identifying with the people in the advertisement. If there were no identification between the viewer and the advertisement, the ad would not be successful. Hall explains that "Advertising tries to construct a position of identification for the viewer in relation to what is depicted in the image" (see Jhally, 1997). He says we should ask what the viewer gets out of the advertisement. We only get something out of the image if we position ourselves somehow in regard to it. Hall says we are implicated in how we look at an image. It is not that the image has a meaning, but instead the image has a range of meanings; our position in relation to the image determines the meaning we give to it. There is a range of potential meanings, and we choose one depending on how we position ourselves toward the image.

If you again consider the advertisement for FirstHealth, you can consider how you project yourself into the advertisement. That is, you can consider how you identify with the claim of the advertisement. If you have good health insurance, don't travel much, or don't have children, the ad may not present a compelling call to you to be read in a particular way. However, if you have children and fear the lack of good health coverage, the ad certainly calls upon a range of emotions, including fear, compassion, and comfort. In particular, the ad positions mothers to accept the idea that FirstHealth provides superior coverage to the reader's own health care plan. If you identify with the woman pictured in the ad, you may be inclined to accept this claim as true.

Meaning relies on interpretation, explains Hall. Images have no fixed meanings but potentially a wide range of meanings. Semiotics, for instance, tries to determine meaning through scientific study. Hall says that semiotics attempts to prove what an image means, but this is impossible, because meaning always is contextual. We assign meaning based on our particular context and with how we position ourselves toward the image. Cultural studies does not believe that the critic can escape the circle of representation and say that something means something else once and for all. The meaning of an image constantly changes.

Additionally, meaning is contested in culture. There is a struggle between powerful groups to determine what things mean. Hall is quick to say that things don't mean a "thousand" different things. The meaning can never be fixed completely, but we do tend to privilege one meaning at a particular moment in time. Power, or ideology, tries to "absolutely" fix the meaning of images through language (see Jhally, 1997), but "because the fixing of meaning cannot be guaranteed, it can be unfixed—it can 'loosen and fray'" (see Jhally, 1997). Hall rejects the postmodern playfulness that we discussed in the previous chapter. He believes that there are temporary meanings but that they can be changed. Powerful forces want to make meaning seem fixed. Power attempts to "naturalize" meaning. Power in signification is designed to close meaning and make other meanings seem impossible.

Although there are a variety of ways of explaining the absence of a man in the advertisement, most likely we accept the meaning that nurturing children and caring for them when they are sick is a mother's responsibility. Although FirstHealth might not have meant to reinforce this idea, the ad is situated in a culture where this is a dominant view. Thus, the culture's assumptions shape how we read the advertisement.

The discussion in this section has focused on representation and signifying practices. Understanding these concepts opens the door to understanding additional concepts and ideas involved with cultural studies. In the next several sections, we'll focus on additional aspects of cultural studies and then look at some examples of how cultural studies and rhetorical studies can be used to analyze rhetorical practices.

IDENTITY, ETHNICITY, CLASS, AND GENDER

We learn who we are by how we are represented, or constituted, in a culture. Recall our discussion about how cultural texts encourage identification on the part of the audience member. If I look at advertisements for expensive cars, elegant homes, and designer clothing, these advertisements encourage me to identify with the people pictured in the ads. In so doing, I construct an identity for myself based on these images. My feelings of who I am are deeply influenced by how I identify with images or symbols in my culture.

On a more profound level, Hall and other cultural theorists, believe that ideas of identity are linked to ethnicity, class, and gender as well. We ascribe meaning to the members of a group of people based on the representatives we have seen featured in our culture. Stuart Hall, who is black, constructs a meaning for his ethnicity based on how it has been created in his culture, Great Britain. When I say that I am a white male who lives in Minnesota, my understanding of what those terms mean—of who I feel I am—depends on the meaning those terms have in my culture. If I care to see a media representation of who I am, I can listen to Garrison Keillor's National Public Radio show, *Prairie Home Companion.* On that show, Keillor portrays midwesterners. For Hall, the question is not whether those portrayals are accurate or not but that they are influential in how I think about myself and how others think about me. You can listen to excerpts of *Prairie Home Companion* at http://prairiehome.publicradio.org.

Hall and other cultural theorists argue that race, ethnicity, class, and gender are all politically, historically, and socially constructed terms. That is, what it means to be black or white or male or female or rich or poor is created through our political and historical experiences. Julien and Mercer (1996) notes that "black" is a "politically and culturally constructed category" that is not fixed by nature but by "historical formations of hegemony" (p. 454). While the concept of ethnicity can not and should not be replaced, Hall encourages us to think about identity and ethnicity in a new way. He invites us to realize that "we all speak from a particular place, out of a particular history, out of particular experience, a particular culture, without being contained by that position" (1996, p. 447).

This leads to a discussion of stereotypes. Stereotyping involves circulating a limited range of definitions about what people can do, be, or become. However, culture behaves and acts based on stereotypes. If we think that black men are violent criminals because that is how they have been stereotyped, explains Hall, we will act toward black men as if this stereotype were true. Stereotyped images produce knowledge about the world. According to Hall, cultural studies seeks to increase the diversity of images and show new possibilities for stereotypes.

ARTICULATION

Another concept that emerges from our discussion of representation is **articulation.** Articulation is often used in a way that seems synonymous with representation, but articulation is a more complex notion. One meaning of with which you may be familiar is "the act of speaking clearly." Another meaning, though, is a "joining together." The second meaning is closest to what Hall means by articulation, but he is also aware of the first meaning as well: "An articulation is thus the form of connection that can make a unity of two different elements, under certain conditions. It is a linkage which is not necessary, determined, absolute and essential for all time" (1986, p. 53). An articulation, then, is a type of representation. As Storey (1996) explains "cultural texts and practices are not inscribed with meaning, guaranteed once and for all by the intentions of production; meaning is always the result of an act of 'articulation' because meaning has to be expressed, but it is always expressed within a specific context, a specific historical moment, within a specific discourse(s)" (p. 4). Hall puts it a different way: "The 'unity' that matters is a linkage between that articulated discourse and the social forces with which it can, under certain historical conditions, but need not necessarily, be connected" (Hall, 1986, p. 53).

To illustrate the concept of articulation, Hall uses the example of religion. He explains that religion has no necessary connection to politics. Religion may exist in a culture without being tied to the dominant political structure or ideology. In fact, the founders of the United States declared that the religion and government should be separated. However, "in one historical-social formation after another, religion has been bound up in particular ways, wired up very directly, as the cultural and ideological underpinning of a particular structure of power" (Hall, 1986, p. 53). That is to say, religion has been articulated with politics and ideology. Hall noted that if a person would move into a culture in which religion has been articulated with the political structure, "it would be idiotic to think that you could easily detach religion from its historical embeddedness and simply put it in another place" (1986, p. 54). That is, once two ideas have been articulated, it is difficult to separate them in people's minds.

In his State of the Union speech of January 28, 2003, President Bush clearly articulated Iraqi president Saddam Hussein with the Al-Quaeda terrorists who are

allegedly responsible for the 2001 attacks on New York and Washington, D.C.
Bush stated:

> And this Congress and the America people must recognize another threat.
> Evidence from intelligence sources, secret communications, and statements
> by people now in custody reveal that Saddam Hussein aids and protects
> terrorists, including members of al Qaeda. Secretly, and without fingerprints,
> he could provide one of his hidden weapons to terrorists, or help them
> develop their own."

Bush's articulation of Hussein and the terrorists would serve as one of the key justifications for going to war. Despite evidence to the contrary, this link would continue to persuade Americans that war with Iraq was justified. Usually articulation
functions more implicitly, but this example serves to illustrate how articulation
may be a persuasive and conscious attempt to join two ideas.

Despite the persuasiveness of Bush's link between Hussein and terrorism,
articulations can be realigned, or rearticulated. Remember that there is no necessary or intrinsic linkage between ideas that have been articulated. However, the
articulation must be disrupted in some way for a new articulation to occur.
Returning again to the example of religion, we find that, according to Hall, in a
culture in which religion has been articulated to politics, a political movement
must confront this connection: "No political movement in that society can
become popular without negotiating the religious terrain" (Hall, 1986, p. 54).
Because the culture has been "'languaged' by the discourse of popular religion,"
the culture has come to a certain kind of consciousness that links religion and
politics (Hall, 1986, p. 54). Hall explains that the producers of texts articulate their
interests to other interests. However, audience members, too, articulate the meanings they have for texts with their own interests. Producers of texts desire that
audiences will articulate the meanings for the text in the same was as they
intended. For an example of how articulation is historical and implicit, read the
Critical Insights box for this chapter (Box 12.2), which also provides an example
of how articulations can be refigured.

AUDIENCE RESPONSE

Our preceding discussion indicates that meaning does not exist in the actual texts
of culture, but rather in how audience members respond to those texts based on
their position within a cultural context. The concepts of representation and signification clearly indicate that multiple meanings are possible for texts; articulation
reveals how power is used to shape meaning. Our discussion of these concepts can
be further explored by looking at the role of the audience in determining meaning. Cultural critics place great emphasis on understanding the audience members
who serve as active creators of meaning for cultural texts.

Encoding/Decoding

In a traditional model of communication, we say that the source encodes a message for a receiver, who then decodes the message to understand the meaning

---

Box 12.2   Critical Insights: Articulation and College Drinking

For another example of how articulation theory can explain widely held beliefs in a culture, let's consider how the consumption of alcohol has been articulated with "the college experience." Many college students, when asked why they consume alcoholic beverages, reply that because they're in college, it's natural for them to do so. Dr. Henry Wechsler from the Harvard School of Public Health identifies several ways that drinking alcohol has been articulated with college life:

Colleges, since the beginning of our country, have been associated with alcohol. Thomas Jefferson complained that when he was President of the University of Virginia about student drinking. So this has been a problem that has been with us for a long time. What has happened is that over the years it's increased. Women, for example, now drink more on college campuses than they ever did before and this equality of the sexes has

added to the drinking environment. Why is it there? It's there in college rituals. It's there in alumni's fond recollections of awful times that they had when they were in college (Blake 2005).

Weschler believes that students have articulated alcohol consumption with college life. As a result, college students may believe that other college students are consuming just as much alcohol and for the same reasons. Experts contend that the amount of alcohol consumed by college students is actually much less than a typical student may think. This approach to curbing alcohol consumption is known as social norming. Its proponents try to de-articulate drinking and college life to show that there is no natural connection between the two. By looking at how alcohol has historically been associated with college life, the social norming approach offers hope for those interested in reducing alcohol consumption on college campuses.

---

intended by the sender. It's important to note that from the traditional perspective, there are correct and incorrect meanings. If the receiver doesn't decode the text correctly, we say that there has been a "miscommunication" and usually the sender and receiver try to clear up the misunderstanding so that the receiver arrives at the same meaning as the sender. Cultural studies takes a different perspective, as you probably realize by now (see Figure 12.1).

In the cultural studies view, the sender encodes the text in a particular way, but the receiver may decode the text in any number of ways. The receiver's previous experiences with the topic, knowledge, attitudes, or position in society (as a woman, black, etc.) determine how the text is decoded. Thus, there is not one correct meaning, but multiple meanings contingent on many cultural factors. Fiske explains the importance of this concept: "Hall's influential essay 'Encoding/Decoding' is often seen as a turning point in British cultural studies, for it introduces the idea that television programs do not have a single meaning but are relatively open texts, capable of being read in different ways by different people" (1996, p. 121).

The encoding process is a rich source of analysis for cultural critics. Institutions that have an interest in maintaining the dominant ideology in the culture often create texts. For instance, the magazine *Maxim* relies on advertisers, who in turn rely on consumers to purchase consumer goods. Thus, *Maxim* may be likely to encode texts in a way that supports their interests—the magazine will glorify and promote consumerism, for instance. Likewise, the sources of texts—the publishers of *Maxim,* for example—rely on other cultural texts to give meaning to their message. In other words, sources *articulate* the meaning of their text to

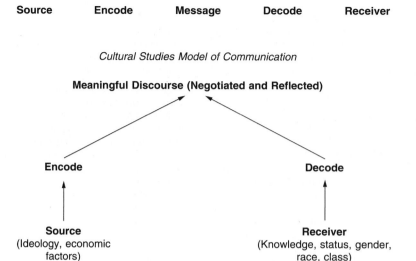

Traditional Model of Communication

Source   **Encode**   **Message**   **Decode**   **Receiver**

Cultural Studies Model of Communication

Meaningful Discourse (Negotiated and Reflected)

Encode   **Decode**

Source   **Receiver**
(Ideology, economic   (Knowledge, status, gender,
factors)   race, class)

FIGURE 12.1   These two models of communication depict traditional and cultural studies ways of defining how meaning is reached through communication.

other texts and meanings. Audience members, when they decode texts, rely on their experiences with other texts to make sense of the text's meaning.

Not all audience members approach a text from the same position, or perspective. Viewers of the hit television show *Extreme Makeover: Home Edition* no doubt watch the show for a variety of reasons. The show features a design-and-construction crew who totally remodel a house for a family that has been through a difficult experience, such as a death, disability, or military action. In fact, the show does well with many demographic groups. Some probably watch the show to see its host, Ty Pennington, one of *People* magazine's fifty "sexiest bachelors." Some viewers are attracted to the emotional story told in the home-remodeling series. Others are probably interested in the design and construction decisions made in the show. Given that audience members approach texts from various positions, cultural critics tend to say that meaning is *negotiated* between the audience member and the text. Fiske (1996) explains that "Use of the word negotiation is significant, for it implies both that there is a conflict of interests that needs to be reconciled in some way and that the process of reading television is one in which the reader is an active maker of meanings from the text, not a passive recipient of already constructed ones" (p. 121). Thus, as you watch a television show, read an advertisement, or listen to music, you are determining what meaning you should take from the text. You don't sit and passively soak up the information presented. Instead, you determine what is true or false in the text, you consider how

Table 12.2 Subject Positions

Subject Position	Definition	Example
Preferred	A reading of the text that accepts the dominant ideology.	*Maxim* magazine portrays consumerism in a way that its readers embrace. Readers desire to purchase items advertised in the magazine and pursue its suggested lifestyle.
Negotiated	A neutral reading of the text.	Readers believe that *Maxim* is a humorous magazine that is not to be taken seriously.
Oppositional	A reading that opposes the dominant ideological message present in the text.	Feminists may believe that *Maxim* promotes the objectification of women and leads to discrimination and violence against women.

much you identify with what is communicated, and you decide whether the text "rings true" to you.

Subject Positions

Since texts can be "read" in different ways, audience members are said to take different subject positions toward texts (see Table 12.2). A **subject position** is "a stance, role, or perspective one takes in relationship to a text so as to read or engage the text" (Brummett & Bowers, 1999, p. 118). That is, a text positions its readers or viewers to look at it in a particular way. This textbook, for instance, calls for you to read it as a student of rhetoric who is probably enrolled in a college course in rhetoric. Cultural theorists identify three types of subject positions: preferred, negotiated, and oppositional.

A *preferred subject position,* or a preferred reading, is "produced by a viewer situated to agree with and accept the dominant ideology and the subjectivity it produces" (Fiske, 1996, p. 121). The preferred position, which is often taken for granted, is not questioned by audience members. Cultural theorists note that the significance of the preferred subject position is that audience members subject themselves to the hegemony of the dominant ideology. In addition to the compelling story line and dramatic construction footage, the television show *Extreme Makeover: Home Edition* prominently features the products of Sears throughout each episode. The readers are positioned in such a way that Sears seems to be a valuable partner in the home remodeling and is heroic for its donation of tools and products. For Sears, this is the preferred subject position for the show's viewers and the reason it spends so much money advertising its products on the show. Sears and ABC, the network that produces the series, want viewers to associate the show with helping others. Thus, they position viewers in a way that supports this view.

A *negotiated subject position* is one in which the audience member does not accept the ideological message of the text but does not form a position contrary

---

BOX 12.3   Internet Activity: Considering Subject Positions

Log on to the website for your favorite television show. You can usually find its website by going to the homepage for the network on which it airs. In particular, you might want to examine how advertisements or product promotions appear on the page. Do any pop-up or banner advertisements relate to the show and its content? How are fans involved in the page? Are there oppositional views of the show that are countered? How? Overall, how does the website position its viewers toward the show?

---

to that message either. Often, there is some way that the audience member is able to "decode" the text in a way that suits his or her interests and subject position. Brummett and Bowers (1996), for instance, observe that comedy, particularly farce and satire, call upon this subject position. The viewer knows not to take the text seriously because it is comedic, but he or she also does not openly reject the text. Perhaps the extreme nature of *Extreme Makeover: Home Edition* has viewers that do not readily associate the show with commercialism and product placement. Instead, viewers watch it to see what the construction crews and designers will attempt next. For instance, the show has featured makeovers that include two-level home gyms and elevators in the home. Viewers might watch the show for its own sake, fully aware that it is a vehicle for product promotion.

On the other hand, viewers who resist the dominant ideological message of the text take an *oppositional subject position*. In fact, the text reinforces the audience member's opposition to its meaning and often motivates a response. Someone may watch *Extreme Makeover: Home Edition,* for instance, and observe that the show is simply exploiting the hardships faced by a family to sell products for Sears. Thus, ABC and Sears are seen as capitalistic opportunists instead of philanthropic companies. Oppositional subject positions are often carried from one text to another. That is, people form oppositional subject positions in one situation and then use those experiences to "decode" other texts they encounter. A viewer who takes an oppositional subject position toward *Extreme Makeover: Home Edition* may have developed attitudes about product placement and exploitation from other shows, for instance. To learn more about the show and its use of product placement, check out the show's website at http://abc.go.com/primetime/ xtremehome/. The Internet Activity for this chapter has you consider various subject positions you might take toward a media text. Take a moment to complete the exercise, found in Box 12.3.

TEXTUALITY

A key distinction between cultural studies and rhetorical studies is textuality. We might say that cultural studies is contextual, whereas rhetorical studies is textual in its orientation. That is, rhetorical theorists and critics are interested in rather discrete rhetorical texts—a speech, advertisement, or film—and how the symbolic nature of that text becomes meaningful for an audience. Rhetorical theorists and critics focus their attention on the symbols that are contained within the text and the relationships that exist between the various symbols.

> Cultural studies seeks to keep in equilibrium the different moments of cultural production—material production, symbolic production, textual production, and the "production in use" of consumption. To narrow one's focus to one moment only, and think this will adequately account for the others, is to think and act (to borrow a phrase from the good old days of certainty) "ideologically." (Storey, 1996, p. 2)

Nelson describes this orientation more succinctly: "Cultural studies typically maintains that meaning is the product of social, cultural, and political interaction" (Nelson, 1999, p. 214). That is, cultural studies is not interested solely in the text but in how the text interacts with its cultural, social, political, and historical environment.

Additionally, cultural studies is interested not only in the production of texts but also in how they are circulated within a culture. Johnson notes, "But the ultimate object of cultural studies is not, in my view, the text, but the social life of subjective forms at each moment of their circulation, including their textual embodiments" (1996, p. 97). Johnson summarizes the contextual orientation of cultural studies thus: "All of this points to what is usually called 'context.' Context determines the meaning, transformations or salience of a particular subjective form as much as the form itself. Context includes the cultural features described above, but also the contexts of immediate situations (e.g. the domestic context of the household) and the larger historical context or conjecture" (Johnson, 1996, p. 102).

USING BOTH RHETORICAL
AND CULTURAL STUDIES

At the beginning of this chapter, we suggested that our study of rhetoric may benefit from understanding the discipline of cultural studies. A case study illustrates to what extent the two perspectives can coexist and how the work of cultural studies can be used to inform rhetorical analyses. Blair and Michel (1999) have examined the Astronaut's Memorial at the Kennedy Space Center Visitors Center from rhetorical and cultural studies perspectives. Initially, the critics tried to use a rhetorical approach alone to analyze the memorial but found the explanation suggested by a rhetorical analysis to be inadequate, so they used a cultural studies analysis to complete their analysis. Let's discuss their study to learn how the rhetorical and cultural studies critical frameworks can both be useful in understanding cultural texts.

The Astronaut's Memorial (see Figure 12.2), located in Florida at the Kennedy Space Center, features a prominent Space Mirror, which contains the names of astronauts killed during their missions. The mirror is composed of a 42.5-by-50-feet polished black granite wall. The wall sits on a turntable and visitors access the

FIGURE 12.2　The Space Mirror Memorial uses a variety of rhetorical techniques that operate within a context influenced by cultural meanings.

 memorial by way of a wide, ascending ramp. Large mirrors, which are programed by computer to follow the sun, shine light through the names. Opposite the mirror is a dedication plaque and benches so that visitors may contemplate the memorial and the lives that have been lost in space travel. To learn more about the memorial, access the website at http://www.nasa.gov/missions/shuttle/107_mirror.html.

As you read about Blair and Michel's analysis of the memorial, refer to Table 12.3, which lays out the various observations the critics made from each perspective. Blair and Michel (1999) initially took a rhetorical perspective to the the memorial:

> Commemorative monuments traditionally have done rhetorical work similar to a eulogy. They mark death, declare particular relationships between the commemorated and the living, offer a space in which a community may gather to acknowledge its loss and reaffirm its sense of collectivity, and suggest or even advocate a future for the community that is somehow linked to the lives or events commemorated. (pp. 34–35).

The Astronaut's Memorial, Blair and Michel explain, performs the commemorative function effectively, announcing the deaths in a eulogistic manner: "Whether one reads these gestures as marking the separation of the astronauts from the living by death, as enacting a symbolic elevation of their stature, or both, s/he remains linked to them by the mirror plane and by his/her entry onto the

**Table 12.3 Rhetorical and Cultural Approaches
to the Astronaut's Memorial**

	Object of Study	Meanings	Judgment
Rhetorical Approach	Symbolism of the memorial, including mirror, plaque, and names	Names appear to be suspended in the sky forever. Memorial reads like a eulogy, praising the astronauts.	The Astronaut's Memorial is a fitting and effective tribute.
Cultural Studies Approach	Visitor attributes, including their clothing and comments while observing the memorial.	The Astronaut's Memorial is similar to Disneyland, and they both promote similar ways of thinking.	The Astronaut's Memorial is ineffective. It does not position its viewers in a way that they contemplate the memorial's full impact.
Combined Approach	Symbolism of the memorial as well as visitor attributes.	The symbolism of the memorial positions visitors in the same way as an amusement park.	The memorial was created in a way that should have made it effective, but the context undermined the memorial's design.

platform of the Memorial" (p. 35). The design of the memorial and its use of mirrors, makes it seem that the astronaut's names are suspended in space, forever to remain there.

The memorial also encourages the viewer to think about space travel. In particular, the memorial links the astronaut's deaths to the never-ending question to explore space. Even if the viewer does not agree that the risk of space travel is worth the rewards, the memorial makes it seem that astronauts believed this to be true and died in accord with their own values and beliefs (Blair & Michel, 1999). In fact, the memorial invites contemplation about the future of space travel, making it consistent with other commemorative memorials in the United States.

Rhetorically, at least, Blair and Michel conclude that the memorial is appropriate to the situation and "legible" to the viewers: "Our rhetorical reading suggests that the Astronaut's Memorial draws from its generic predecessors in offering a culturally legible and appropriate commemoration, that it is symbolically rich and interesting, and that it bids for the kind of experience that appears to make contemporary commemoration 'work' for its audiences" (p. 46).

While judging the memorial to be a success, Blair and Michel realize that the audiences to the memorial "did not appear to share our reaction to the Space Mirror" (p. 46). Visitors either ignored the memorial altogether, or they wondered aloud what the structure was and, upon figuring it out, paused for a moment before moving other to other attractions at the space center. Only the space center employees reacted to the memorial as one would predict, pausing to give reflection and commemoration to the lives that were lost. Other visitors—regardless of age, sex, race, or class—did not share this sense of quiet reflection.

Blair and Michel began to take notice of the large numbers of Disney hats, t-shirts, and other items at the Kennedy Space Center. Located only forty-five minutes from Disney World, it appeared that many visitors to the memorial had previously visited the Disney theme park. Blair and Michel then decided to add a cultural studies aspect to the analysis and investigated how Disney World created a context for experiencing the amusement park.

After a trip to Disney World, Blair and Michel observed that much of the same "syntax" of the Disney park was evident at the space center. That is, the parking lots, exhibitions, and roving costumed characters had much in common between the two attractions. The differences, note Blair and Michel, were minor. In essence, the Kennedy Space Center "demands very little from the visitor in terms of altering the position already constructed for him/her by" Walt Disney World (Blair & Michel, 1999, p. 62). Thus, when confronted with the memorial, visitors are unable to respond in the way it suggests: "After days of exposure to texts that essentially ask the visitors not to think, or that at least excuse them of the responsibility, they are confronted suddenly and unexpectedly with a text that is readable, but not without effort" (Blair & Michel, 1999, p. 64). The memorial also asks for contemplation and commemoration, which is "an alien, perhaps even unwelcome, interloper in the theme park perimeter" (p. 64).

Blair and Michel (1999) explain that the distinction between cultural studies and rhetorical studies was not as clear in the paper as it might have been presented here: "It is not an easy task to identify the moments at which our perspective shifted from rhetoric to cultural studies, because those moments blurred together and never seemed marked by a border crossing" (p. 67). They began to ask questions of the Astronaut's Memorial that rhetorical critics typically would not ask.

First, the two critics began to try to closely understand the audience's response to the memorial. Rhetorical critics, Blair and Michel contend, often view audience in "perfunctory or assumptive ways" (1999, p. 68). By watching the audience response to the memorial, the two critics were able to dramatically change the final evaluation they offered of the memorial. They assert that "Because we paid even just a little attention to an audience's reactions and its peculiar characteristics—neither very difficult in this case to detect—we believe we were better able to account for the rhetorical failure of a discourse that we believed ought to have been a success" (p. 68). Second, Blair and Michel believe, as do many rhetorical critics, that rhetorical texts are discrete, have clear borders and distinctions, and that they are what they appear to be. In this case, the Astronaut's Memorial was, in practice, not a memorial, but a "anomalous landmark in a vacation dreamscape" (p. 69).

Blair and Michel (1999) conclude that "Reading a text through the lens of a rhetorical theory—rhetorical criticism's usual tendency—is not wrong, but it is only *a* way of reading" (p. 70). Their study of the Astronaut's Memorial offers an excellent illustration of how critical methodology can include both rhetorical studies and cultural studies dimensions.

SUMMARIZING THOUGHTS

We have discussed the relationship between cultural studies and rhetorical studies in this chapter. In many ways, the two disciplines are interested in similar kinds of phenomena and they can both be used to make judgments about the function of texts in a culture. Let's summarize here the main orientations of cultural studies.

DEFINING RHETORIC

We have said that rhetorical studies is more textual and cultural studies more contextual. Thus, cultural studies does not seek to define rhetoric in the ways that we have seen it defined in previous chapters. Rather, cultural studies looks to understand how texts—in the broadest sense—obtain meanings in a culture.

Knowledge

In many ways, cultural studies is a response to postmodernism in that it sees knowledge as somewhat fixed and not as something that continually escapes representation. Cultural studies theorists look at the processes of signification and representation and to how ideology fixes the meaning of text at a particular moment. Thus, knowledge is created when people share meanings. The "truth" may be fleeting, though.

Identity

Cultural studies theorists argue that we seek to determine our identity based on how we are positioned toward specific texts and by how we are represented in a culture. Our understanding of our own ethnicity, class, and gender is influenced by the meanings a culture has for these concepts.

Judgment

Cultural studies has promoted the interests of those who are marginalized by the dominant culture and has looked to ways of intervening on behalf of these groups. Based on the principles of Marxism, cultural studies is interested in ideology, power and hegemony. Specifically cultural studies looks at how cultures create meanings for texts based on the power relationships that exist as part of the cultural context.

DISCUSSION QUESTIONS

1. What are some additional similarities and differences between cultural studies rhetorical studies that aren't discussed in the chapter?

2. How might cultural studies be used to explain popular "reality" television shows?

3. Choose a popular issue or event currently covered in the media. What are the meanings associated with that event? How did those meanings come to exist? What are some competing meanings for the event?

4. Examine an advertisement from a magazine. What are some of the ideas that are articulated in the advertisement? What is the implication of these articulations?

5. Watch several popular television shows. In these shows, how are gender, race, and class represented? What is significant about these representations? Do the shows offer stereotyped views of people from different races or classes? How might those stereotypes be overturned?

6. Find another advertisement from a magazine. Describe the encoding process for the advertisement. What are some possible ways the advertisement might be decoded? What is the preferred subject position for the advertisement? What is an oppositional subject position? From what position do you read the advertisement?

GLOSSARY

cultural studies   A discipline that is concerned with the production, circulation, and reception of meanings in industrialized societies.

representation   The meaning for a symbol as created through interaction.

signification   The study of the process of meaning.

signifying practices   The ways that symbols obtain meaning.

subjection position   A way of reading a text from a particular perspective.

articulation   The joining together of two ideas that do not necessarily have any kind of natural connection.

Appendix

Timeline of Rhetorical Theory

Period	Date	Theorist	Chap.	Historical Events
	551 B.C.E.	Confucius	9	
Greek Republic	490–390 B.C.E.	Sophists (Gorgias, Protagoras, Hippias)	2	Greek City-States
	392 B.C.E.	Isocrates	2	
	387 B.C.E.	Plato	2	
	350 B.C.E.	Aristotle	2	
Roman Republic	106–43 B.C.E.	Cicero	2	
	100 B.C.E.	*Rhetorica ad herennium*		
	35–100	Quintilian	2	
Roman Empire	213–273	St. Augustine	3	
Second Sophistic		Longinus	3	
Middle Ages	1135	*Rationes dictandi*	3	
	1200	Preaching texts	3	
Renaissance	1515–1572	Peter Ramus	3	Printing Press Christopher Columbus
	1600–1630	Francis Bacon	4	
	1637	Rene Descartes	4	
	1690	John Locke	4	
Enlightenment	1759–1783	Hugh Blair	3	
	1762	Thomas Sheridan	4	
	1776	George Campbell	4	American Revolution
	1828	Richard Whately	4	
Contemporary	1918–1979	I. A. Richards	5	Radio
Theory	1920s–1930s	George Herbert Mead	5	
	1930–1940	Alfred Korzybski	5	Television
	1953	Richard Weaver	5	
	1958	Stephen Toulmin	4	
	1958	Chaim Perelman	4	
	1931–1990	Kenneth Burke	6	
	1951–1967	Susanne K. Langer	5	
	1964–1967	Marshall McLuhan	10	
	1970s	Jurgen Habermas	7	
Postmodernism	1970s	Michel Foucault	11	
	1970s	Jacques Derrida	11	
	1990s	Stuart Hall	12	Internet

References

Ackerman, B. A. (1993). Crediting the voters: A new beginning for campaign finance. *American Prospect,* pp. 71–80.

Aristotle. (1991). *On rhetoric.* (G. A. Kennedy, Trans.). Oxford: Oxford University Press.

Asante, M. K. (1987). *The Afrocentric idea.* Philadelphia: Temple University Press.

Asen, R. , & Brouwer, D. C. (2001). Introduction: Reconfigurations of the public sphere. In R. Asen and D. C. Brouwer (Eds.), *Counterpublics and the state* (pp. 1–34). Albany: State University of New York Press.

Aune, J. A. (1994). *Rhetoric and Marxism.* Boulder, CO: Westview Press.

Barilli, R. (1989). *Rhetoric.* Minneapolis: University of Minnesota Press.

Barthes, R. (1977). *Image, music, text.* New York: Hill and Wang.

Baudrillard, J. (1998). *The consumer society: Myths and structures.* Thousand Oaks, CA: Sage.

Baumgardner, J., & Richards, A. (2003). *Manifesta: Young women, feminism, and the future.* New York: Farrar, Straus, and Giroux.

Benson, T. W. (1998). Editor's preface. In X. Lu, *Rhetoric in ancient China, Fifth to Third Century, B.C.E.: A comparison with ancient Greek rhetoric* (pp. ix–x). Columbia, SC: University of South Carolina Press, 1998.

Benzie, W. (1994). Thomas Sheridan. In M. G. Moran (Ed.), *Eighteenth-Century British and American Rhetorics and Rhetoricians: Critical Studies and Sources* (pp. 197–206). Westport, CT: Greenwood Press.

Berger, A. A. (1998). *Media analysis techniques.* (2nd ed.). Thousand Oaks, CA: Sage.

Best, S., & Kellner, D. (1991). *Postmodern theory: Critical interrogations.* New York: Guilford Press.

Biesecker, B. (1989). Rethinking the rhetorical situation from within the thematic of différance," *Philosophy and Rhetoric, 22,* 110–130.

Birdsell, David S., and Groarke, Leo. (1996). Toward a theory of visual argument. *Argumentation and Advocacy, 33,* 1–10.

Bitzer, L. (1963). Editor's introduction. In L. Bitzer (Ed.), *The Philosophy of Rhetoric* (pp. ix–x). Carbondale: Southern Illinois University Press.

Bitzer, L. F. (1959). Aristotle's enthymeme revisited. *Quarterly Journal of Speech, 45,* 399–408.

Blair, C., & Michel, N. (1999). Commemorating in the theme park zone: Reading the Astronauts Memorial. In T. Rosteck (Ed.), *At the Intersection: Cultural Studies and Rhetorical Studies* (pp. 29–83). New York: Guilford Press.

Blair, H. (1965). *Lectures on rhetoric and belles lettres.* (H. F. Harding, Ed.). Carbondale: Southern Illinois University Press.

Blake, J. (2005). About health: College binge drinking. Retrieved February 10, 2005, from http://www.abouthealth.com/ahtv_related_material.cfm?Transcript_ID=36

Bormann, E. (1972). Fantasy and rhetorical vision: The rhetorical criticism of social reality. *Quarterly Journal of Speech, 58,* 396–407.

Brock, B. L., Scott, R. L., & Chesebro, J. W. (1990). *Methods of rhetorical criticism: A twentieth-century perspective.* Detroit, MI: Wayne State University Press.

Brockriede, W. & Ehninger, D. (1960). Toulmin on argument: An interpretation and application. *Quarterly Journal of Speech, 46,* 44–53.

Brown, B. K. (1994). John Walker. In M. G. Moran (Ed.), *Eighteenth-Century British and American Rhetorics and Rhetoricians: Critical Studies and Sources* (pp. 230–233). Westport, CT: Greenwood Press.

Brownstein, O. L. (1965). Plato's Phaedrus: Dialectic as the genuine art of speaking. *Quarterly Journal of Speech, 51,* 392–98.

Brummett, B. (1984). Burkean comedy and tragedy, illustrated in reactions to the arrest of John DeLorean. *Central States Speech Journal, 35,* 217–227.

Brummett, B. (1994). *Rhetoric in popular culture.* New York: St. Martin's Press.

Brummett, B., & Bowers, D. L. (1999). Subject positions as a site of rhetorical struggle: Representing African Americans.

In T. Rosteck (Ed.), *At the Intersection: Cultural Studies and Rhetorical Studies* (pp. 117–136). New York: Guilford Press.

Bryant, D. C. (1953). Rhetoric: Its functions and its scope. *Quarterly Journal of Speech, 39,* 401–424.

Bryant, D. C. (1974). Rhetoric: Its functions and its scope rediviva. In W. R. Fisher (Ed.), *Rhetoric: A tradition in transition* (pp. 231–246). East Lansing: Michigan State University Press.

Burke, K. (1966). *Language as symbolic action: Essays on life, literature, and method.* Berkeley: University of California Press.

Burke, K. (1968). Dramatism. In D. L. Sills (Ed.), *International Encyclopedia of the Social Sciences* (pp. vii, 445–452). New York: Macmillan.

Burke, K. (1969a). *A grammar of motives.* Berkeley: University of California Press.

Burke, K. (1969b). *A rhetoric of motives.* Berkeley: University of California Press.

Burke, K. (1970). *The rhetoric of religion: Studies in logology.* Berkeley: University of California Press.

Burke, K. (1972). *Dramatism and development.* Worcester, MA: Clark University Press.

Burke, K. (1973). *The philosophy of literary form: Studies in symbolic action.* (Rev. ed.). Berkeley: University of California Press.

Burke, K. (1984). *Attitudes toward history.* (Rev. ed.). Berkeley: University of California Press.

Butler, J. (1999). *Gender trouble: Feminism and the subversion of identity.* New York: Routledge.

Calhoun, C. (1992). Introduction: Habermas and the public sphere. In C. Calhoun (Ed.), *Habermas and the public sphere* (pp. 1–50). Cambridge, MA: MIT Press.

Campbell, K. K. (1973). The rhetoric of women's liberation: An oxymoron. *Quarterly Journal of Speech, 59,* 74–86.

Campbell, K. K. (1989). *Man cannot speak for her: A critical study of early feminist rhetoric.* New York: Greenwood Press.

Carey, J. W. (1988). *Communication as culture: Essays on media and society.* Boston: Unwin Hyman.

Carlson, A. C. (1986). Gandhi and the comic frame: *"Ad bellum purificandum."* *Quarterly Journal of Speech, 72*, 446–455.

Carlson, A. C., & Hocking, J. E. (1988). Strategies of redemption at the Vietnam Veterans Memorial. *Western Journal of Speech Communication, 52*, 203–251.

Cathcart, R. S. (1993). Instruments of his own making: Burke and media. In J. W. Chesebro (Ed.), *Extensions of the Burkeian system* (pp. 287–308). Tuscaloosa: University of Alabama Press.

Cheney, G. (1983). The rhetoric of identification and the study of organizational communication. *Quarterly Journal of Speech, 69*, 143–158.

Chesebro, J. W. (1995). Kenneth Burke and Jacques Derrida. In B. L. Brock, (Ed.), *Kenneth Burke and contemporary European thought: Rhetoric in transition* (pp. 166–206). Tuscaloosa, AL: University of Alabama Press.

Chesebro, J. W. (1999). Multiculturalism and the Burkean system: Limitations and extensions. In B. L. Brock (Ed.), *Kenneth Burke and the twenty-first century* (pp. 167–188). Albany: State University of New York Press.

Chesebro, J., & Bertelsen, D. (1996). *Analyzing media: Communication technologies as symbolic and cognitive systems.* New York: Guilford.

Cicero, M. T. (1942). *De oratore* (H. Rackham, Trans.). Cambridge, MA: Harvard University Press.

Cloud, D. L. (1994). The materiality of discourse as oxymoron: A challenge to critical rhetoric. *Western Journal of Communication, 58*, 141–163.

Condit, C. M. (1995). Kenneth Burke and linguistic reflexivity: Reflections on the scene of the philosophy of communication in the twentieth century. In B. L. Brock (Ed.), *Kenneth Burke and contemporary European thought* (pp. 207–262). Tuscaloosa: University of Alabama Press.

Condit, C. M. (1997). In praise of eloquence diversity: Gender and rhetoric as public persuasion. *Women's Studies in Communication, 20*, 91–116.

Conley, T. M. (1990). *Rhetoric in the European tradition.* New York: Longman.

Cosslett, T. (1994). *Women writing childbirth: Modern discourses on childbirth.* New York: Manchester University Press.

Daly, M. (1973). *Beyond God the Father: Toward a philosophy of women's liberation.* Boston: Beacon Press.

Daly, M. (1978). *Gyn/Ecology: The metaethics of radical feminism.* Boston: Beacon Press.

Daly, M. (1984). *Pure lust: Elemental feminist philosophy.* Boston: Beacon Press.

Daly, M. (1992). *Outercourse: The be-dazzling voyage.* San Francisco: Harper.

Davis, F. (1991). *Moving the mountain: The women's movement in America since 1960.* New York : Simon and Schuster.

Deleuze, G., & Guattari, F. (1983). *Anti-oedipus: Capitalism and schizophrenia.* Minneapolis: University of Minnesota Press.

Dow, B. J., & Tonn, M. B. (1993). With Mari Boor Tonn. Feminine style and political judgment in the rhetoric of Ann Richards. *Quarterly Journal of Speech, 79*, 286–302.

Dow, B. J. (1995). Feminism, difference(s), and rhetorical studies. *Communication Studies, 46*, 106–117.

Duncan, H. D. (1962). *Communication and the social order.* New York: Bedminster Press.

Ehninger, D. (1950). George Campbell and the revolution in inventional theory. *Southern Speech Journal, 9*, 271–276.

Ehninger, D. (1963). Editor's introduction. In D. Ehninger (Ed.), *Elements of Rhetoric* (pp. ix–xxxii). Carbondale: Southern Illinois University Press.

Ehninger, D. (1955). Campbell, Blair, and Whately: Old friends in new light. *Western Speech, 19*, 263–269.

Ehninger, D. (1975). A synoptic view of systems of Western rhetoric. *Quarterly Journal of Speech, 61*, 448–453.

Enos, R. L. (1995). *Roman rhetoric: Revolution and the Greek influence.* Prospect Heights, IL: Waveland Press.

Farrell, T. B. (1990). From the Parthenon to the bassinet: Death and rebirth along the epistemic trail. *Quarterly Journal of Speech, 76*, 78–84.

Ferreira-Buckley, L. (1994). Hugh Blair. In M. G. Moran (Ed.), *Eighteenth-Century*

British and American Rhetorics and Rhetoricians: Critical Studies and Sources (pp. 21–33). Westport, CT: Greenwood Press.

Fisher, W. R. (1987). *Human communication as narration: Toward a philosophy of reason, value, and action.* Columbia: University of South Carolina Press.

Fiske, J. (1989). *Understanding popular culture.* Boston: Unwin Hyman.

Fiske, J. (1990). *Introduction to communication studies.* London: Routledge.

Fiske, J. (1996). British cultural studies and television. In J. Storey (Ed.), *What is cultural studies? A reader* (pp. 115–146). London: Hodder Headline Group.

Forgacs, D. (1988). *An Antonio Gramsci reader.* New York: Schocken.

Foss, K. A., & Foss, S. K. (Eds). (1991). *Women speak: The eloquence of women's lives.* Prospect Heights, IL: Waveland Press.

Foss, K. A., Foss, S. K., & Griffin, C. (1999). *Feminist rhetorical theories.* Thousand Oaks, CA: Sage.

Foss, S. K. (1996). *Rhetorical criticism: Exploration and practice.* (2nd Ed.). Prospect Heights, IL: Waveland Press.

Foss, S. K., Griffin, C. L., & Foss, K. A. (1997). Transforming rhetoric through feminist reconstruction: A response to the gender diversity perspective. *Women's Studies in Communication, 20,* 117–135.

Foss, S. K., & Foss, K. A. (1994). *Inviting transformation: Presentational speaking for a changing world.* Prospect Heights: Waveland.

Foss, S. K., & Gill, A. (1987). Michel Foucault's theory of rhetoric as epistemic. *Western Journal of Speech Communication, 51,* 384–401.

Foss, S. K., & Griffin, C. L. (1995). Beyond persuasion: A proposal for an invitational rhetoric. *Communication Monographs, 62,* 2–18.

Foss, S. K., Foss, K. A., & Trapp, R. (1991). *Contemporary perspectives on rhetoric.* (2nd ed.). Prospect Heights, IL: Waveland.

Foucault, M. (1970). *The order of things: An archeology of the human sciences.* New York: Vintage.

Foucault, M. (1972). *The archeology of knowledge.* New York: Pantheon.

Foucault, M. (1978). *The history of sexuality: Volume I. An introduction.* New York: Vintage.

Freeley, A. J. (1993). *Argumentation and debate.* Belmont, CA: Wadsworth.

Garrett, M. M. (1993). Classical Chinese conceptions of argumentation and persuasion. *Argumentation & Advocacy, 29,* 105–115.

Gearhart, S. M. (1979). The womanizing of rhetoric. *Women's Studies International Quarterly, 2,* 195–201.

Golden, J. L., & Corbett, E. P. J. (1968). *The rhetoric of Blair, Campbell, and Whately.* New York: Holt, Rinehart, and Winston.

Golden, J. L., Berquist, G. F., & Coleman, W. E. (1976). *The rhetoric of Western thought.* Dubuque, IA: Kendall/Hunt Pub. Co.

Gronbeck, B. E. (1999). The triumph of social science: *The Silent Language* as master text in American cultural studies. In T. Rosteck (Ed.), *At the Intersection: Cultural Studies and Rhetorical Studies* (pp. 266–291). New York: Guilford Press.

Grossberg, L. (1997). *Bringing it all back home: Essays on cultural studies.* Durham, NC: Duke University Press.

Gusfield, J. R. (1989). Introduction. In J. R. Gusfield (Ed.), *Kenneth Burke: On Symbols and Society* (pp. 1–53). Chicago: University of Chicago Press.

Habermas, J. (1970). *Toward a rational society.* Boston: Beacon Press.

Habermas, J. (1973). *Theory and practice.* Boston: Beacon Press.

Habermas, J. (1975). *Legitimation crisis.* Boston: Beacon Press.

Habermas, J. (1979). *Communication and the evolution of society.* Boston: Beacon Press.

Hall, S. (1986). On postmodernism and articulation: An interview with Stuart Hall. *Journal of Communication Inquiry, 10,* 45–60.

Hall, S. (1996). Cultural studies: Two paradigms. In J. Storey, J. (Ed.), *What is cultural studies? A reader* (pp. 31–48). London: Hodder Headline Group.

Harding, H. F. (1965). Editor's introduction. In H. F. Harding, *Lectures on Rhetoric and Belles Lettres* (pp. vii–xxxv). Carbondale: Southern Illinois University Press.

Hauser, G. (1998). Civil society and the principle of the public sphere. *Philosophy and Rhetoric, 31,* 19–40.

Heath, R. L. (1986). *Realism and relativism: A perspective on Kenneth Burke.* Macon, GA: Mercer University Press.

Hill, F. (1972). Conventional wisdom—traditional form—the president's message of November 3, 1969. *Quarterly Journal of Speech, 58,* 373–386.

Hollihan, T. A., & Baaske, K. T. (1994). *Arguments and arguing: The products and processes of human decision making.* New York: St. Martin's Press.

Holtz, S. (1999). *Writing for the wired world: The communicator's guide to effective online content.* San Francisco: IABC.

Howell, W. S. (1961). *Logic and rhetoric in England, 1500–1700.* New York: Russell and Russell.

Innis, H. (1951). *The bias of communication.* Toronto: Toronto University Press.

Jamieson, K. H. (1988). *Eloquence in an electronic age: The transformation of political speechmaking.* New York: Oxford University Press.

Japp, P. (1999). "Can this marriage be saved?": Reclaiming Burke for feminist scholarship. In B. L. Brock (Ed.), *Kenneth Burke and the twenty-first century* (pp. 113–130). Albany: State University of New York Press.

Jarratt, S. C. (1991). *Rereading the sophists: Classical rhetoric refigured.* Carbondale: Southern Illinois University Press.

Jhally, S. (Producer). (1997). *Representation and the media.* (Videorecording). Available from Media Education Foundation, Northampton, MA.

Johannesen, R. L., Strickland, R., & Eubanks, R. T. (1970). *Language is sermonic: Richard M. Weaver on the nature of rhetoric.* Baton Rouge: Louisiana State University Press.

Johnson, R. (1996). What is cultural studies anyway? In J. Storey (Ed.), *What is cultural studies? A reader* (pp. 75–114). London: Hodder Headline Group.

Julien, I., & Mercer, K. (1996). De margin and de centre. In D. Morley & K. Chen (Eds.), *Stuart Hall: Critical dialogues in cultural studies* (pp. 450–464). London: Routledge.

Kennedy, G. (1963). *The art of persuasion in Greece.* Princeton, NJ: Princeton University Press.

Klumpp, J. F. (1999). Burkean social hierarchy and the ironic investment of Martin Luther King. In B. L. Brock (Ed.), *Kenneth Burke and the twenty-first century* (pp. 201–241). Albany: State University of New York Press.

Knowles-Borishade, A. F. (1991). Paradigm for classical African orature: Instrument for a scientific revolution? *Journal of Black Studies, 21,* 488–500.

Korzybski, A. (1958/1933). *Science and sanity: An introduction to non-Aristotelian systems and general semantics.* Clinton, MA: Colonial Press.

Kramarae, C. (1981). *Women and men speaking: Frameworks for analysis.* Rowley: Newbury House.

Lake, R. (1983). Enacting Red Power: The consummatory function in Native American protest rhetoric. *Quarterly Journal of Speech, 69,* 127–142.

Langer, S. K. (1942). *Philosophy in a new key.* Cambridge, MA: Harvard University Press.

Linden-Ward, B., & Green, C. H. (1993). *American women in the 1960s: Changing the future.* New York: Maxwell Macmillan International.

Littlejohn, S. (1996). *Theories of human communication.* (5th ed.) Belmont, CA: Wadsworth.

Lu, X. (1998). *Rhetoric in ancient China fifth to third century B.C.E.: A comparison with classical Greek rhetoric.* Columbia: University of South Carolina Press.

Lucaites, J. L., & Condit, C. M. (1999a). Epilogue: Contributions from rhetorical theory. In J. L. Lucaites, C. M. Condit, & S. Caudell (Eds.), *Contemporary rhetorical theory* (pp. 609–614). New York: Guilford Press.

Lucaites, J. L., & Condit, C. M. (1999b). Introduction. In Lucaites, J. L., Condit, C. M. & Caudell, S. (Eds.), *Contemporary Rhetorical Theory* (pp. 19–24). New York: Guilford Press.

Lucaites, J. L., Condit, C. M., & Caudill, S. (1999). Part 1: What can a rhetoric be? In J. L. Lucaites, C.M. Condit, & S. Caudell, S. (Eds.), *Contemporary Rhetorical Theory* (pp. 19–24). New York: Guilford Press.

Lyotard, J. F. (1979). *The postmodern condition: A report on knowledge*. Minneapolis: University of Minnesota Press.

Lyotard, J. F. (1984). *The postmodern condition: A report on knowledge*. Minneapolis: University of Minnesota Press.

Marx, K., & Engels, F. (1955). *The communist manifesto*. Arlington Heights, IL: Harlan Davidson.

McBurney, J. H., O'Neill, J. M., & Mills, G. E. (1951). *Argumentation and debate: Techniques of a free society*. New York: Macmillan.

McCarthy, T. A. (1978). *The critical theory of Jürgen Habermas*. Cambridge, MA: MIT Press.

McCarthy, T. A. (1992). Practical discourse: On the relation of morality to politics. In C. Calhoun (Ed.), *Habermas and the public sphere* (pp. 51–72). Cambridge, MA: MIT Press.

McGee, M. C. (1980). The "ideograph": A link between rhetoric and ideology. *Quarterly Journal of Speech, 66,* 1–16.

McGee, M. C. (1990). Text, context, and the fragmentation of contemporary culture. *Western Journal of Speech Communication, 54,* 274–289.

McKerrow, R. (1989). Critical rhetoric: Theory and praxis. *Communication Monographs, 56,* 91–111.

McKerrow, R. (1991). Critical rhetoric in a postmodern world. *Quarterly Journal of Speech, 77,* 75–78.

McLuhan, M. (1964). *Understanding media: The extensions of man*. New York: Signet.

McLuhan, M. (1967). *The medium is the massage*. New York: Signet.

Mead, G. H. (1934). *Mind, self, and society: From the standpoint of a social behaviorist*. Chicago: University of Chicago Press.

Messaris, P. (1997). *Visual persuasion: The role of images in advertising*. Thousand Oaks: Sage.

Murfin, R. C. (1994). Deconstruction and Hamlet. In Susanne L. Wofford (Ed.), *Hamlet* (pp. 283–293). New York: St. Martin's Press.

Murphy, J. J. (1960). St. Augustine and the debate about Christian rhetoric. *Quarterly Journal of Speech, 46,* 400–410.

Nelson, C. (1996). Always already cultural studies: Academic conferences and a manifesto. In J. Storey (Ed.), *What is cultural studies? A reader* (pp. 273–286). London: Hodder Headline Group.

Nichols, M. H. (1963). *Rhetoric and criticism*. Baton Rouge, LA: Louisiana State University Press.

O'Donnell, J. J. (1985). *Augustine*. Boston: Twayne Publishers.

Ogden, C. K., & Richards, I. A. (1928). *The meaning of meaning*. New York: Harcourt, Brace.

Ong, W. J. (1982). *Orality and literacy: The technologizing of the word*. London: Methuen.

Ono, K. A., & Buescher, D. T. (2001). Deciphering Pocahontas: Unpacking the commodification of a Native American woman. *Critical Studies in Media Communication, 18,* 23–43.

Perelman, C. (1982). *The realm of rhetoric*. Notre Dame, IN: University of Notre Dame Press.

Perelman, L. (2004). The Medieval art of letter writing: Rhetoric as institutional expression. In C. Bazerman & J. Paradis (Eds.), *Textual Dynamics of the Professions: Historical and Contemporary Studies of Writing in Professional Communities*. WAC Clearinghouse Landmark Publications in Writing Studies: http://wac.colostate.edu/aw/books/bazerman_dynamics/. Originally published in print, 1991, by University of Wisconsin Press, Madison, Wisconsin.

Plato. (1952). *Gorgias*. (W. C. Hembold, Trans.). New York: Macmillan.

Potter, D. (1965). Foreword. In H. F. Harding (Ed.), *Lectures on Rhetoric and Belles Lettres* (pp. v–vi). Carbondale: Southern Illinois University Press.

Quintilian. (1920). *Intitutio oratoria.* (H. E. Butler, Trans.). Cambridge, MA: Harvard University Press.

Ray, J. W. (1978). Perelman's universal audience. *Quarterly Journal of Speech, 64,* 361–375.

Reeve, C. (1996). *Keynote address.* Democratic National Convention, Chicago, IL.

Rhetorica ad Herennium. (1954). (H. Caplan, Trans.). Cambridge, MA: Harvard University Press.

Richards, I. A. (1936). *The philosophy of rhetoric.* New York: Oxford University Press.

Rosteck, T. (1999). Introduction: Approaching the intersection: Issues of identity, politics, and critical practice. In T. Rosteck (Ed.), *At the Intersection: Cultural Studies and Rhetorical Studies* (pp. 1–24). New York: Guilford Press.

Rueckert, W. H. (1993). A field guide to Kenneth Burke—1990. In J. W. Chesebro (Ed.), *Extensions of the Burkean system* (pp. 3–41). Tuscaloosa: University of Alabama Press.

Scott, R. L. (1967). On viewing rhetoric as epistemic. *Central States Speech Journal, 18,* 9–17.

Scott, L. (1975). A synoptic view of systems of Western rhetoric. *Quarterly Journal of Speech, 61,* pp. 439–447.

Sheridan, T. (1968). *A course of lectures on elocution.* New York: Benjamin Blom.

Shuter, R. (2000). The cultures of rhetoric. In A. Gonzalez & D. Tanno (Eds.), *Rhetoric in Intercultural Contexts* (pp. 11–17). Thousand Oaks, CA: Sage.

Sparks, C. (1996). The evolution of cultural studies. . . In J. Storey, J. (Ed.), *What is cultural studies? A reader* (pp. 14–30)). London: Hodder Headline Group.

Spitzack, C., & Carter, K. (1987). Women in communication studies: A typology for revision. *Quarterly Journal of Speech, 73,* 401–423.

St. Augustine. (1958). *On Christian doctrine.* (D. W. Robertson, Jr., Trans.). New York: Liberal Arts Press.

Tonn, M., Endress, V., & Diamond, J. (1993). Hunting and heritage on trial: A dramatistic debate over tragedy, tradition, and territory. *Quarterly Journal of Speech, 79,* 165–81.

Toulmin, S. (1958). *Uses of argument.* New York: Cambridge University Press.

Toulmin, S. (1969). *The uses of argument.* Cambridge: Cambridge University Press.

Twichell, D. Y. (1955). Susan B. Anthony. In M. K. Nichols (Ed.), *A history and criticism of American public address* (Vol. 3., pp. 97–132). New York: Longman, Green.

Wander, P. (1984), The Third Persona: An ideological turn in rhetorical theory. *Central States Speech Journal, 35,* 197–216.

Warnick, B. (1993). *The sixth canon: Belletristic rhetorical theory and its French antecedents.* Columbia: University of South Carolina Press.

Weaver, R. M. (1953). *The ethics of rhetoric.* Chicago: Henry Regnery.

Weaver, R. M. (1970). *Language is sermonic.* Baton Rouge: Louisiana State University Press.

Whately, R. (1963). *Elements of rhetoric.* (D. Ehninger, Ed.). Carbondale: Southern Illinois University Press.

Williams, R. (1977). *Marxism and literature.* Oxford: Oxford University Press.

Wilson, K. (2003). Where theory and practice meet: The quickening of rhetorical criticism. Paper presented at the 2003 National Communication Association Convention, Miami Beach, FL.

Wood, J. T. (1992). Telling our stories: Narratives as a basis for theorizing sexual harassment. *Journal of Applied Communication Research, 4,* 349–363.

Ziegelmueller, G. W., & Kay, J. (1997). *Argumentation: Inquiry and advocacy.* Boston: Allyn and Bacon.

Index

Demonstrative rhetoric, 34
Demonstrative speeches, 40
Demosthenes, 32, 33
Deng Xi, 243
Denotative message, 272
De Oratore (Cicero), 41, 42
Derrida, Jacques, 291–294
Devil term, 136
Dialectic, 41, 132–134, 135
Dialectics, 245
Dialectique (Ramus), 71
Diamond, John N., 152, 153, 160
Diction, 62
Differance, 292
Dionysius, 61
Discourse, 15
Discursive formations, 285–290
Discursive practices, 287–288
Discursive rhetoric, 128–130
Disneyland, 290–291
Disney World, 326
Disputed facts, 44
Distinction, 51–52
Dow, Bonnie J., 213–215
Doxastic, 192
Dr. 90210, 298
Dramatism, 143–168
  action, 149
  Burke, Kenneth, 144–159
  comic redemption, 158–160
  guilt, 147, 148, 155, 160
  hierarchy, 148
  identification, 150–152
  motion, 149
  narrative, 160–163
  negative symbols, 147–148
  pentad, 152–155
  perfection, 148–149
  ratio, 153–154
  redemption from guilt, 155–160
  symbolic convergence theory, 163–166
  symbols, 146–148
  tragic redemption, 155–158
"drip," 269
Duncan, Hugh, 158

Earth/Share advertisement, 94
Eastern theory. *See* Non-Western
  rhetorical theories
Ebonics, 235
Eco, Umberto, 270
Ehninger, Douglas
  argumentation, 99–102, 105–106
  authoritative arguments, 105
  grammatical period, 19
  motivational arguments, 106
  Whately, Richard, 96–97
Electronic eloquence, 263–268
  conversational tone, 266
  personalization, 264–265
  self-disclosure, 265
  verbal distillation, 266–267
  visual dramatization, 267–268
Electronic media, 257, 262–263
Elements of Elocution (Walker), 81

Elements of Logic (Whately), 98
Elements of Rhetoric (Whately), 83, 98
Elocutionary movement, 83
Elocutionism, 21
Eloquence, 78–79
Emphasis, 82
Empowerment, 214
Encoding, 319–321
Endress, Valerie A., 152, 153, 160
Engels, Frederick, 173, 177–178
Enlightenment, 158
Enthymeme, 46–47
Epideictic speeches, 40
Epilogos, 49
Episteme, 285
Epistemic, 137–139
Epistemologists, 72, 87–90
Epistemology, 23, 245, 284
Equal Rights Amendment (ERA), 201
Essay on Human Understanding,
  An (Locke), 88
Essentialism, 214
etc., 123, 124
Ethics, 24, 135–136
  argument, 135–136
  rhetoric as epistemic, 139
  ultimate terms, 137
Ethnicity, 316
Ethos, 45
Etiquette codes, 271
Eunoia, 45
Exchange-value, 298
Exercises. *See* Internet exercises
Extemporaneous style, 67
Extensional devices, 123–125
Extreme Makeover: Home Edition, 298,
  320–322

Fact-finding committee, 134
Fantasy, 163
Fantasy sharing, 163–164
Fantasy theme, 164
Fantasy type, 164
Farnsworth, Philo, 257
Farrell, Thomas, 7
Fashion codes, 271
Fatalistic scapegoats, 156
Federal welfare system, 154
Feelings, 129–130
Feminine Mystique, The (Friedan), 200
Feminine style, 203, 213–215
Feminism, 198, 296, 297. *See also* Gendered
  rhetorical theories
Fidelity, 162–163
Figurative language, 77–78
Figures of diction, 52
Figures of thought, 52
Film, 173
FirstHealth, 314–316
First order of knowledge, 134
First persona, 174
First-wave feminism, 198–200
Fisher, Walter, 161–163
Fiske, John, 270, 307, 319–321
Five canons of rhetoric, 43–53

arrangement, 47–49
delivery, 52–53
invention, 43–47
memory, 53
style, 49–52
Fixing women's images, 221–222
Flag, 273
Flexibility (vocal delivery), 53
Footprints in the snow, 275
Foreground, 220–222
Foss, Karen, 197, 203, 207–208
Foss, Sonja, 197, 203, 207–208, 212,
  287–291
Foucault, Michel, 284–290, 295
Foundations of the Theory of Signs
  (Morris), 125
Frame of mind, 230
Freedom, 137
Friedan, Betty, 200
Friends, 159, 299

Gearhart, Sally Miller, 203, 210–212
Gender, 197, 296, 297
Gender diversity perspective, 203, 204,
  215–220
Gendered rhetorical theories, 196–225
  background, 222–223
  definitions, 197–198
  feminine style, 213–215
  foreground, 220–222
  frameworks, 202–204
  gender diversity perspective, 215–220
  inclusion, 202–203
  invitational rhetoric, 212–213
  private rhetoric of women, 207–208
  public rhetoric of women, 204–207
  reconceptualizing, 204
  theories, summarized, 203
  womanization of rhetoric, 210–212
  women's liberation movement,
    208–210
  women's rights movements, 198–201
Generalized other, 125
General semantics, 121–125
Gesture, 53, 82
Gill, Ann, 287–291
Glamour, 221
God term, 136
Golden age of rhetoric, 39
Gorgias (Plato), 36, 39, 42, 55
Graceful sentence, 77
Grammatical period, 19
Gramsci, Antonio, 174, 181–182
Grandeur, 75
Grand style, 49
Greenspan, Alan, 77
Griffin, Cindy, 197, 203, 212
Grimké, Angelina, 206
Grimké, Sarah, 199
Groarke, Leo, 276
Group consciousness raising, 209
Group fantasy sharing, 164
Guattari, Felix, 295–296
Guilt, 147, 148, 155, 160
Gusfield, Joseph, 4

Credits